PIRANDELLO'S
LOVE LETTERS TO
MARTA ABBA

Pirandello's

LOVE LETTERS TO

Marta Abba

EDITED AND TRANSLATED BY

Benito Ortolani

PRINCETON UNIVERSITY PRESS

PRINCETON, NEW JERSEY

Copyright © 1994 by Princeton University Press
Published by Princeton University Press, 41 William Street,
Princeton, New Jersey 08540
In the United Kingdom: Princeton University Press, Chichester, West Sussex

Library of Congress Cataloging-in-Publication Data
Pirandello, Luigi, 1867–1936.
Pirandello's love letters to Marta Abba / edited and
translated by Benito Ortolani.
p.   cm.
English translation of 164 letters written originally in
Italian by L. Pirandello which are now in the
Library, Princeton University. Cf. Editor's remarks.
Includes index.
ISBN 0–691–03499–0
1. Pirandello, Luigi, 1867–1936—Correspondence.
2. Abba, Marta—Correspondence.
3. Authors, Italian—20th century—Correspondence.
4. Princeton University. Library.
I. Ortolani, Benito.   II. Title.
PQ4835.I7Z482   1994
852'.912—dc20   93–38617 CIP   [B]

This volume contains a selection of 164 letters from the complete edition of 552,
which Princeton University Press will publish in cooperation with
Mondadori, in the original Italian, in 1995.

All letters and illustrations, donated by Marta Abba, are from the
Luigi Pirandello and Marta Abba papers. Department of Rare Books
and Special Collections. Princeton University Library.

This book has been composed in Adobe Garamond

Princeton University Press books are printed on acid-free paper
and meet the guidelines for permanence and durability of the
Committee on Production Guidelines for Book Longevity
of the Council on Library Resources

Printed in the United States of America

1   3   5   7   9   10   8   6   4   2

CONTENTS

a Marta
il suo
Nanni

Parigi 30. XII. 1930.

INTRODUCTION

THE NATURE of Pirandello's relationship with Marta Abba has been a subject of curiosity and controversy since the world-famous aging writer met the beautiful young actress for the first time in 1925. Sixty years later, an octogenarian Marta, referring to the love letters still locked in the vault of a bank in Milan, told me several times, "The truth is all there, clear and simple; nothing needs to be added."

At the end of several years of editing the thousands of pages so neatly handwritten by the Sicilian playwright, I must acknowledge that Marta was right. The reader will find Pirandello's secret emotions and the sad reality of his love story fully revealed in the letters selected and published here for the first time in English translation.

For decades Marta was hesitant about making these important documents available to the public. She seemed unable to make up her mind— torn between her desire to disclose to the world an intimate, still-unknown Pirandello and her reluctance to lift discreetly the veil cloaking a treasured love secret that most readers would probably misunderstand and some even defile with mockery. In 1984, at the age of eighty-four, the actress finally resolved to proceed with publication. Through Peter Putnam, her American friend Mildred Andrews Putnam's son, who as a child in Cleveland was bounced on her knee and who later tried for years to convince her to publish the much-talked-about correspondence, she was put in contact with Princeton University. Princeton was pleased to accept the coveted gift, guaranteeing its preservation and publication both in the original Italian and in the present English version.

Marta confided to me many times that she had finally come to her decision because she felt it was her duty "to make known how much Pirandello suffered." She explained that for her it was most important to disclose the extent of his existential anguish—so far hardly suspected by anyone. In fact, the letters most dramatically reveal a Pirandello "horribly alone" for the better part of the last ten years of his life, prostrated with long periods of deep depression and cruel despair, drowning in an ocean of intimate pain and "going mad from it." His martyrdom ended only in the bosom of death, so often desired and so often entertained as a voluntary way out of his unbearable torment.

At Peter Putnam's suggestion, I went to Italy and met Marta for the first time in the resort village of San Pellegrino Terme on September 7, 1985. By nature suspicious, she needed to be sure that I was an editor/translator suitable for the task, one she could entrust with the care of this "sacred" part of her life. She screened me carefully with respect to my deep feelings about the Maestro, and I plainly told her what I had always thought: that Pirandello is a poet of human suffering, and that to understand and appreciate him there is no other way but to learn to hear the agony echoing from within his dramatic voice, a voice that is in essence an excruciating scream of pain. Marta's mistrust quickly melted away. She said to me with great ingenuousness that the Maestro was overwhelmed by his own sensibility, consumed by an intense longing for love, integrity, and trust, but that he lived, on the contrary, with the constant feeling of being "betrayed at all levels." I was moved by this revelation of Pirandello's most intimate confidante and, later, developing her insight, I proposed to her an interpretation of the Pirandellian oeuvre as flowing from a keen obsession with tragic betrayal. The writer, in his "abyss of sadness without end," suffered immensely because he felt betrayed by the people closest to him and whom he loved most; betrayed professionally by his "friends" and "collaborators"; betrayed by the disastrous political-administrative situation of his country under fascism; and finally, betrayed also at the cosmic-universal level by a hostile and cruel "fate" that seemed almost to enjoy its little game, encouraging man to dream the most beautiful dreams, only to delude him afterward with a mocking smirk, indifferent to the immense pain inflicted.

Against the backdrop of this dark tragedy of betrayal suddenly loomed his love for Marta, a love that soon became the sole source of light for his spirit, the inspiration of his art, and consequently the only reason for keeping on with his involuntary, tormented, and aimless journey on earth. This love absorbed and consumed the last years of his "most useless existence" with a total and obsessive intensity of which his biographers until now have had hardly a clue.

The gamut of guesses about the real nature of Pirandello's love for Marta has swung from a purely platonic, literarily elaborated romantic involvement to ironic assumptions of a long-lasting, trite sexual affair. The letters definitely exclude this last hypothesis. Yet it is enough merely to glance at the entry Love contained in the Subject Index of the present volume to conclude without a doubt that Pirandello's feelings for the actress were not comparable to a father's affection for his daughter, nor can they be characterized as a merely literary infatuation. The letters explicitly reveal the forcefulness of his feelings and the demands made on Marta for a reciprocal correspondence of a much different quality than she was ready to provide. Pirandello, in fact, writes as one who loves in toto. Until his very last days he insistently begged his beloved accurately to describe everything about herself so that he would be able to follow her in every moment of her life, to "see her" as a living fantasy, in every posture—including the most intimate—and he pressed the issue to the point of provoking indignant replies from an offended Marta. He never ceased imploring her to offer even a small token of reciprocation—as rejected lovers often demand on the brink of despair. Only a rapturous adoration can explain the obsession of counting the days and hours required by the mail service to deliver her letters, morbidly awaited and cried out for. The longing for a tender word or a special lover's sign never abandoned him—although bitter experience had made very clear to him that all he could realistically expect was news related to business and sparse routine expressions of respectful devotion.

"Hostile fate" determined that Pirandello would meet the greatest love of his life far too late, and amid moral and legal circumstances that would render a joyous conclusion unthinkable. They first met in Rome at the Odescalchi Theater, where the playwright was forming a company with the intent of giving to Italy an artistic theater of the highest level. The actress, originally from Milan, not yet twenty-five and at the beginning of her career, was engaged to debut in the leading role in Massimo Bontempelli's *Our Goddess.* Pirandello was fifty-eight years old and in the throes of a painful family situation, because his wife's illness had already progressed beyond any serious hope for recovery and made her permanent confinement in a mental clinic unavoidable. Divorce at this time in Italy was nonexistent. His children were older than Marta. An authentic, old-fashioned Sicilian gentleman, honorable and faithful to traditions, Pirandello tried to control the intense feelings that threatened to overwhelm him. He was also very conscious of his international fame and felt the eyes of the world focused on him. Imminent old age obsessed him.

In a scene from his last autobiographically inspired play, *When One Is Somebody,* Pirandello presents a very famous elderly poet who is being castigated by the young and beautiful Veroccia. She bitterly recalls a previous time when, consumed by love, she offered everything he wished: "Everything—and you know it—you didn't want it, you coward . . . you didn't have the courage to take me, to take the life that I wanted to give

you—you who were suffering because you had none." It is the end of the
second act, and the poet, left alone, begins speaking with infinite tenderness to Veroccia as if she were still there: "You were ready for everything,
and now you berate me for the wrongs I didn't do to you . . . you're still
not aware of the restraint in me . . . the humiliation of old age . . . and the
shame inside, the shame then, as of an obscenity, because I felt, behind
that old appearance, a heart still young and warm." The drama probably
mirrors a real event in Pirandello's life. It certainly reflects the writer's
desperate feeling of an immense pain for the irreparably lost last chance to
grab life when it offered itself—a feeling that permeates a number of the
most moving letters in this epistolary. The fire of yearning for the realization of his unattainable great love was destined to burn unsatiated to the
end, leaving the desolate lover in an agonizing limbo into which he seems
to have fallen after a mysterious, traumatic episode. Pirandello probably
refers to it in a letter of August 20, 1926, as to an event well known to
Marta—an "atrocious night spent in Como." Three years later, abandoned by Marta in Berlin, the playwright attributes his misery to "a feeling that is no longer there" in the heart of his beloved, thus implying that
the feeling had been there previously. The secret hope, however remote,
that things might still change and that the feeling might rekindle itself is
never relinquished until his death.

In the course of her lifetime the actress showed little or no inclination
for amorous adventures. Under Pirandello's tutelage she reinforced her
negative attitude toward matters of the flesh. An engagement at a very
young age was arranged by her family but did not survive Marta's overwhelming priority—to succeed in a major way in show business. After
Pirandello's death, her 1938 marriage to the wealthy socialite Severance A.
Millikin resembled the glow and the vicissitudes of a Hollywood melo-
drama, with a glamorous honeymoon among the riches and the power for
which she had always strived. The harsh reality of an impossible union in
the milieu of Cleveland's conservative high society led to a bitter separation after long years of fighting. Later on, at the rare times she touched on
the topic of her marital experience, she would rapidly dismiss the subject
with gestures of loathing. A divorce was granted in 1952, based, at least
partly—if we give any credence to the local gossip—on Marta's persistent
refusal to live the conjugal life. Ever since her youth the actress was extraordinarily reserved in her relationship to the opposite sex. In the years
of her development as an actress everybody knew that she was "very busy"
with Pirandello, which might also have served her well as a convenient
shield from unwanted male attentions. No record is available of any affair

or romantic involvement. She was very attached to her family and totally dedicated to art, pledging all her energies in the relentless struggle to survive and succeed in the junglelike world of Italian theater. Raised as a Catholic and sincerely attached to her faith, she couldn't reconcile Pirandello's aspirations for their relationship with her religious and moral convictions. She was therefore duty bound to disallow the realization of any expectations on his part that might trespass the limits of the paternal affection of a teacher and a guide.

Marta was at his side during the three years in which Pirandello's company toured throughout Italy and abroad (1925–1928). After the troupe's breakup, she spent approximately six months in Berlin—living most of the time with her sister Cele in a room next to Pirandello's and always keeping the necessary distance. During that period she was Pirandello's shadow and adviser, sustaining him with affection and pragmatism while he struggled with dreams of boundless riches, fits of rage at a "gang of enemies," grand plans to radically reform the Italian theater, and the childish expectation that Mussolini would solve, like magic, all of its problems with one act of authoritarian intervention. She comforted him during bitter family feuds and his never-ending legal entanglements with agents and lawyers.

After her traumatic departure from Berlin in 1929, Marta's role as confidante continued from afar. His desperate cries of love, however, and the even more desperate requests for an answer to his agonizing doubt about her sentiments were systematically and coldly neglected by the actress as "useless chatter" that merited no response. Marta never abandoned her habit of addressing the Maestro formally, using the respectful Italian pronoun "lei," which excludes intimacy and familiarity with the person to whom it is directed. "For me he was like a god," she confessed to me with a tone that left no doubt as to her sincerity.

The reading of the letters does exclude not only the hypothesis of a trivial sexual relationship, but also that of a senile infatuation in a platonic literary romance. In the daily messages we are confronted with a man whose blood has long reached the boiling point, whose tears are real and abundant, whose capacity for torment seems almost unlimited. There is the mad grabbing for every thin thread of hope; the unbearable frustration resulting from the long distances away from Marta and the subsequent loneliness; and even the palpable temptation closing in on him to reach into a drawer containing an implement of death and turn it on himself. But there is also relief. We read of his unbridled joy over every fulfillment of his beloved's desires and the generous offering of his time, his creative energies, and his moral and economic support in the effort to make Marta a happy, admired, and envied woman.

The final curtain of this extraordinary drama of an impossible love is drawn on a semihappy ending. Pirandello is ecstatic at seeing realized his ambitious dream of making Marta a "star" of international fame. This new, most exalted glory of his beloved is construed into a supreme moment of almost divine radiance during which Pirandello feels he is finally able to tiptoe out of this life and abandon this earth, which had lately seemed to him too small, remote, extraneous—leaving behind the torments of loneliness, the bitterness over his now-ruined plans to reform the Italian theater, the recurring financial worries, and the wretchedness of a peripatetic existence without any permanent mooring.

Emerging from this scenario of unrequited love we perceive, rendered with vivid immediacy, the stark contours of a personality central to the arts and culture of our century at some of his most distinctive moments. We experience with Pirandello the triumphs of recognition (nomination to the Italian Academy, conferring of the Nobel Prize, his many dramatic successes across the stages of the world, honors conferred by many prestigious international cultural institutions); his satisfaction in gaining access to the highest levels of power (personal rapport with Mussolini and with the most prominent exponents of fascism in Italy and nazism in Germany); his relations with the most influential figures of his time in the most varied fields of endeavor (science, finance, show business: Einstein, the Rothschilds, Chaplin); and also his defeats (the Berlin fiasco of *Tonight We Improvise*).

Numerous letters are devoted to the problems encountered by Marta in her daily battle to assert herself with her company in the jungle of the Italian theater, struggling against a hostile monopoly of owners/managers who controlled the use of every important theater in Italy for profit alone, without any interest in the artistic level of the performances. Other letters depict Pirandello's frustrations in his lifelong fight against that hated "gang of enemies," who had been the main cause of the demise of his Teatro d'Arte and now were trying to make the continuation of his work through Marta Abba's company impossible. Pirandello appears as a very poor businessman, often exploited and cheated by dishonest or incompetent agents, frequently ensnared in lawsuits that compelled him to maladroitly swindle himself amidst a hallucinatory, Kafkaesque judiciary system.

The letters—written during a decade of fascism's rising and undisputed power in Italy—reveal a Pirandello lacking a solid conviction in his political orientation. His feelings toward Mussolini are imbued at times with faith and even enthusiasm, at other times with disillusion and contempt. Pirandello, impelled by the conviction that only an act of "lofty" rule could put an end to the arrogance of those who were sacrificing art to the boorish thirst for profit, turns suddenly full of hope and support for the dictator when Mussolini seems to be personally ready to realize the dream of a state-funded artistic theater. We listen to the Maestro applaud colonialism in Ethiopia, parroting the bombastic speech of Fascist propaganda, but we also hear him hurling bitter criticism against the dictator and his corrupt government when the appalled playwright sees the state-allocated funds—originally promised by Mussolini to establish a noncommercial national theater under Pirandello's artistic direction—actually wind up in the pockets of the usual unworthy profiteers.

Although they do not shed any substantial new light on Pirandello's literary-theatrical opinions and theory, the letters reveal interesting aspects of his process of artistic creation, confided to the beloved while in the flowery throes of an irresistible inspiration, or in a laborious search for plots and solutions to scenes and plays still in outline form. They contain, also, sharp echoes of the heated controversy then surrounding the talking cinema. This novelty initially disconcerted the playwright, producing in him a sense of "horror" that quickly abated as he accepted sound film as an "art form" that would develop unlimited possibilities for the future and create new artworks of great beauty and originality. He became enthusiastic about the idea of creating films as sequences of beautiful images illustrating famous musical compositions—out of which project he hoped himself to harvest immense profits. The letters offer candid descriptions of the symptoms of his illnesses, their frequency and seriousness, and his deep mistrust of medicine and physicians; they also show Pirandello's extraordinary capacity to concentrate on his creative work and on a neverending series of negotiations with managers, editors, agents, directors, translators—while in the midst of much spiritual turmoil and physical pain.

The intimate Pirandello of these letters does not discuss the fundamental questions of human existence: the mystery of its origin, the disturbing question of why we live, or the relativistic and atheistic philosophy that goes under the label of "Pirandellism." He does, however, confess an envy of Marta's faith in God and on more than one occasion implore his beloved to pray to that God for him. He also frequently appeals to indisputable principles of justice, upholding rigorous standards of public and private morality, always struggling for their triumph and implicitly affirming the universal truth and value of an objective ethic. We meet in the letters a Maestro who teaches his disciple Marta never to compromise the dictates of her conscience, never to give up her lifelong pursuit of the highest moral and artistic standards.

Pirandello often appears angry at envious and malicious enemies, especially in his own country, against whom he does not spare harsh words. His repeated attempts to relocate permanently—first to Berlin and then to Paris—can be explained as a reflection of his resentment against a native country that did not recognize him as he would have liked. Marta, when deciding the final destination of the letters, believed she was faithfully interpreting Pirandello's will by choosing a library in the United States, perhaps urged by the recurring echo of one of the writer's exhortations that she had heard and read many times: "Away, away, out, out of Italy!"

The style of the correspondence, which flows monotone for long paragraphs in order clearly to communicate news and practical instructions, changes suddenly when Pirandello shifts into inspirational passages—often followed by swift returns to the perfunctory language of plain business. In his masterful use of the rethoric of persuasion, Pirandello implores, praises, remembers, argues, and appeals to Marta's sense of responsibility—sometimes construing convoluted sentences just as his characters do in his plays; that is, using the same dubious consistency of logic that leaves the mind unconvinced but moves the heart because of its underlying, heartbreaking despair. Brief touches of almost childlike self-justification—when Pirandello catches himself in the uncontrollable act of breaking the thousands of promises to his beloved not to perturb her mind anymore with his heart-wrenching laments—alternate with powerful descriptions of his unhappy existence, without purpose or hope after Marta abandoned him. Adjectives abound—two or three often synonymous qualifiers for one substantive are not unusual. Inversions in the sentence order—with the object at its beginning—as well as repetitions of the same word, two, three times for the purpose of emphasis, are common. When Pirandello allows his fantasy to elaborate on idyllic dreams and fervent longings and amorous enlightenment, his ornate language and similes might well remind us of the great classic lovers, from Petrarch singing his rapture for Laura's beauty to Abélard affectionately instructing his beloved Héloïse. Some passages of the letters, written in moments of profound inspiration, do reveal in their spontaneity and immediacy the master of Italian narrative at his best. In general, however, the reader must be forewarned that these letters were not written as a literary work, were not edited or corrected for publication by the author, and therefore contain many repetitions, run-on sentences, tedious borrowing from slogans of Fascist propaganda, and pathetic exaggerations.

This correspondence rewards its reader with the unique experience of living in intimacy with a profound poet of human pain, along the arc of the last ten years of his life—in moments when he was not trying to communicate through dramatic characters conceived in his imagination and set loose in a fictional world. This is a Pirandello without the mask of art, nakedly exposing his own tragedy of perennial, meaningless suffering—an immensely sad, authentic confession, directly reflecting, therefore, the great writer's helpless weakness and hopeless loss of his own self.

The present publication was made possible by a grant from the Mildred Andrews Fund—of which Mrs. Andrews' son, Peter Putnam, was the founder and generous administrator until his death—and through the assistance of the Library of Princeton University and of Princeton University Press. Grateful acknowledgment is due to the many people, especially at Brooklyn College, who assisted me in the preparation of the Italian edition, which serves as foundation for this partial English translation. Special thanks are also due to Elio Providenti and my brother Oddone Ortolani, who reviewed the lengthy Italian manuscript; to Andrea and Pierluigi Pirandello, to Maria Luisa and Alessandro D'Amico, who provided me with important suggestions and information; to Robert Karpen, who patiently revised my first draft of the English translation, and to Glenn Loney and David Garfield, who read the manuscript and made valuable suggestions; to my daughter Laura-Lee Griffith Carrasquel, who spent countless hours at the computer; and above all to my wife, Maria, who generously comforted and sustained me with patient love through the endless postponements, complex legal vicissitudes, and mishaps that almost turned the making of this publication into a true-to-life Pirandellian scenario.

EDITOR'S REMARKS

1. The 164 letters contained in this book were selected from the collection donated by Marta Abba in November 1986 to the Library of Princeton University. The complete collection consists of 552 handwritten letters of Luigi Pirandello, addressed to Marta Abba, and a few more addressed to Marta's younger sister, Cele, and to her parents, Pompeo and Giuseppina Abba. The announcement given to the press at the time of the donation, that the letters numbered 560, was because that sum included letters not addressed to Marta, plus a very few additional envelopes that on later inspection proved not to contain letters to Marta. The almost complete collection in the original Italian is scheduled to be published by Princeton University Press—and by Mondadori in Milan in two volumes of the collection *I Meridiani*—approximately one year after the present English translation. The original handwritten letters are all available for research purposes at the Princeton University Library, Special Collections.

2. Importance of contents and literary relevance were the main criteria in the selection. I tried to avoid the tedious chronicle of lesser business transactions and the ennui of endless repetitions in Pirandello's protestations of love and self-pity—which remain available for the specialist to study in the Italian edition.

3. Every letter carries a six-digit number, which shows the date on which it was written. The first two digits indicate the year, the following two indicate the month, and the last two the day. For example, the letter 260805 was written on 5 August 1926.

4. The requirement of respecting Marta's wish—that the English language remain as close as possible to the original Italian—made my effort to translate this important but uneven body of literature very arduous. As already remarked in the introduction, Pirandello writes effortlessly, spontaneously, with many repetitions, using very long sentences and still adding to them thoughts, as they come, often with a copula. He doesn't shy

away from topical idioms and from repeating, almost *ad litteram,* occasional slogans of Fascist propaganda—without the usual stylistic consistency that characterizes material meant for publication. Marta did not want me to introduce choices that, at first, might sound as "better English" but that would, in the total rhythm of the translation, give a less than genuine impression of the main original characteristics of the letters—their immediacy and truthfulness.

5. Marta Abba requested that the work of introduction and comment be minimal. She wanted to give the Maestro a chance to speak directly to the readers just as he had spoken to her—without the filter of an interpreter or the distraction of learned literary exegesis. Introductions and footnotes are therefore kept brief; only essential information and the most necessary references for a correct reading of the text are provided, without literary analysis, scholarly quotations, or lists of bibliographic references. It will be the task of specialists in future years to research the many problems these letters leave unsolved and discuss their literary value and their position in the history of the epistolary genre. It would be, for example, very important to establish the degree of objectivity in the picture drawn by Pirandello about himself to his beloved and about his relationship to his children. Again, in some cases it appears very difficult to reconcile the author's description of an absolute, paralyzing despair with the experience of people who lived very close to him, with the content of other correspondence addressed on the very same day to his children or to friends, and with the extraordinary activity of the writer at the time. The process of literary and historical interpretation—even before the publication of the texts—has already begun, with a book by Pietro Frassica, *A Marta Abba per non morire: Sull'epistolario inedito tra Pirandello e la sua Attrice* (Milan: Mursia, 1991), and will no doubt continue.

6. Judgments expressed by Pirandello about people and institutions are not discussed in the commentary. These are often impulsive, momentary reactions to events, confided on the spot to his beloved. An overwhelming passion for art and for Marta led the writer to express certain obnoxious characterizations of family members or personalities of the political and theatrical world. In a number of cases, Pirandello later did correct, explicitly or implicitly, hasty pronouncements that are, therefore, to be considered the result of his passionate temper.

7. Pirandello's original handwritten letters show almost no corrections, and the Italian is almost flawless. When Pirandello introduces foreign

words or the names of non-Italian people, he does misspell quite often. In the present translation, such errors are corrected in the text and only rarely reported in the footnotes. Only the correct form is used in the indexes.

8. I was not at liberty to use in my commentary the letters written by Marta to Pirandello. A copy of them was sent to me by Peter Putnam, but Marta requested the copy back, and I returned it personally during a trip to Milan. The essential elements of Marta's writings can be reconstructed from Pirandello's letters themselves—with the caveat that the loving Maestro sees in those plain letters, almost totally dedicated to business and news about her company, nonexisting literary merits. Moreover, some of Marta's most important letters, written at the time of Pirandello's greatest distress after her departure from Berlin in 1929, were destroyed by Pirandello, who reluctantly obeyed Marta's precise instructions. At this time I am aware that a publication of Marta's surviving letters is being prepared in Italy.

9. Hundreds of names are mentioned in Pirandello's letters, many of which are obviously unknown to most readers. In most cases a brief footnote provides essential information when a name appears for the first time. The same information is repeated in the Name Index at the end of this volume. The rule is not applied to names obviously known to everyone, such as Shakespeare or Dante.

10. The Subject Index and the brief title of each letter in the Contents provide further points of reference to the wealth of information contained in the correspondence.

CHRONOLOGY

·⟨⟨⟩⟩·
·

{ 1924 }

While performing in Milan with the Talli Company Marta Abba scores a remarkable success with her interpretation of Chekhov's *Seagull*.[1] Pirandello is impressed by a review written by critic Marco Praga on that occasion and decides to hire the actress as leading lady of his Compagnia del Teatro d'Arte di Roma—then in the process of being formed. Marta Abba (born in Milan on June 25, 1900) is still unknown, at the very beginning of her professional acting career.

Pirandello's better-known plays, such as *Sei personaggi in cerca d'autore*, *Enrico IV*, *Così è (se vi pare)*, and *La vita che ti diedi*, are performed in Paris, Berlin, Vienna, Warsaw, Athens, and London, and also in Japan and Brazil. Over the last two decades Luigi Pirandello (born in Agrigento, Sicily, on June 28, 1867) has been universally recognized as one of the leading European authors of narrative and drama.

Pirandello writes the novel *Uno, nessuno, e centomila*, which is published in installments during the following two years in *Fiera Letteraria*, and then in one volume by Bemporad in Milan.

MAY 22. The Niccodemi Company presents the world premiere of Pirandello's *Ciascuno a suo modo* at the Teatro dei Filodrammatici in Milan.

SEPTEMBER 19. In an open letter to Mussolini published in *L'Impero* Pirandello applies for membership in the Fascist party.

SEPTEMBER 30. Pirandello's one-act play *Sagra del Signore della nave* is published in *Convegno*.

OCTOBER 6. The Teatro d'Arte di Roma is legally incorporated under Pirandello's leadership. This event marks the beginning of Pirandello's triennium as artistic director / manager, during which he will travel with his company to a great number of Italian and foreign cities.

---

[1] Only some of the facts mentioned in the chronology are directly referred to in the letters. All of them, I hope, will help in providing a frame of reference for a better understanding of the letters themselves.

{ 1925 }

FEBRUARY 7. First letter written by Pirandello to Marta Abba.

LATE FEBRUARY. Pirandello and Marta meet for the first time in Rome. On February 25 Marta signs the contract as leading actress of the Teatro d'Arte. The love for Marta marks the beginning of a new phase in Pirandello's life, which lasts until his death. Marta begins to inspire and become the main interpreter of Pirandello's works.

APRIL 2. At the Teatro Odescalchi in Rome the inauguration of the Teatro d'Arte takes place in the presence of Mussolini with the premiere of Pirandello's *Sagra del Signore della nave.*

APRIL 22. Marta Abba triumphantly debuts in Rome in the premiere of *Nostra Dea* by Massimo Bontempelli.

JUNE 15–JULY 15. Pirandello's company performs *Sei personaggi in cerca d'autore, Enrico IV, Vestire gli ignudi, Così è (se vi pare),* and *Il piacere dell'onestà* in London, Paris, and Geneva.

BETWEEN OCTOBER 1 AND 6. This is the probable date of the "atrocious night" in Como, which had catastrophic repercussions on the love relationship between Pirandello and Marta.

OCTOBER 12–NOVEMBER 7. Pirandello's company performs in Basel, Berlin, Frankfurt am Main, Cologne, Düsseldorf, Kassel, Dresden, Leipzig, Halle, Magdeburg, Hannover, Hamburg, Bremen, and Münster, with the same repertory.

NOVEMBER 12–JULY 30, 1926. Pirandello's company performs in twenty-two Italian cities. Pirandello accompanies the actors during the tours in Italy and abroad and is therefore always close to Marta. The actress is confirmed as the company's leading lady and more and more recognized as the main interpreter of Pirandello's theater. Fifty different shows are produced during the three years of the company's existence, and Marta plays the lead in thirty-six of them.

{ 1926 }

During this year Pirandello writes nine letters to Marta.
   Several of Pirandello's plays are performed in Italy and abroad.
   Pirandello's novel *Uno, nessuno, e centomila* is published by Bemporad.

AUGUST 5–25. Pirandello writes frequently to Marta during the short summer break. Back in Rome, Pirandello discovers he is on the brink of bankruptcy, accuses his son-in-law and his daughter of being responsible for his financial troubles, and wants to sell the brand-new *villino* in the Via Panvinio. Pirandello revises *Diana e la Tuda* and completes *L'amica delle mogli*. He negotiates with the governor of Rome for the lease of the Teatro Argentina and has a temporary reconciliation with the theatrical impresario Paolino Giordani in order to present with him to the Duce a common project for the institution of a state-subsidized national theater.

NOVEMBER 20. At the Schauspielhaus in Zürich the world premiere of Pirandello's *Diana e la Tuda* takes place (in the German translation by Hans Feist). It is the first play inspired by Marta and dedicated to her.

DECEMBER 5. Pirandello publishes in the *Fiera Letteraria* the project for the state theater, prepared together with Giordani.

DECEMBER 14–22. Pirandello's company performs *Sei personaggi, Così è (se vi pare)*, and *Vestire gli ignudi* in Prague, Vienna, and Budapest.

{ 1927 }

Pirandello and Marta are together practically the whole year long. There is no record of letters written to Marta during this year.

JANUARY 14. At the Teatro Eden in Milan the Italian premiere of Pirandello's *Diana e la Tuda* takes place, interpreted by Marta.

MARCH. Pirandello's company changes its name and becomes the Compagnia del Teatro Argentina.

APRIL 28. At the Teatro Argentina in Rome the world premiere of Pirandello's *L'amica delle mogli*, the second play inspired by Marta, takes place. Pirandello's work and Marta's interpretation receive excellent reviews and are cheered by the audiences.

MAY 27. At the Teatro Eden in Milan the Almirante-Rissone-Tòfano Company presents Pirandello's one-act play *Bellavita*. The play is adapted from Pirandello's short story *L'ombra del rimorso*.

JUNE 15–SEPTEMBER 15. Pirandello's company performs in Argentina, Uruguay, and Brazil. The repertory is mostly made up of Pirandello's plays interpreted by Marta.

Pirandello writes a number of short stories, and Bemporad publishes a revised edition of his novel *L'Esclusa.*

{ 1928 }

During this year Pirandello writes thirteen letters to Marta.

MARCH 24. At the Teatro Argentina in Rome Pirandello's *La nuova colonia* premieres, with Marta Abba and Lamberto Picasso in the leading roles. It is the last important production of Pirandello's company, which is close to folding because of financial difficulties.

JULY 4–17. Pirandello writes almost daily from Nettuno, a resort on the seashore near Rome, to Marta, who is vacationing in Salsomaggiore, a fashionable spa resort near Milan. Pirandello decides to leave Italy because of the distressing political situation, the financial failure of his company, and the loss of the hope of transforming it into a state-supported national theater. The Maestro deals with German and American agents, trying to approach the international world of cinema and find there the financing for his dream of a new artistic theater company independent of state funds. The first written declarations of his great love for Marta take place.

AUGUST 15. In Viareggio, the final performance of Pirandello's company takes place.

AUGUST 16–SEPTEMBER 20. Pirandello and Marta spend their summer vacations on the Tyrrhenian coast. Marta leaves Viareggio for Milan on September 19, and Pirandello leaves for Rome on the twentieth.

SEPTEMBER 21–26. Pirandello writes almost daily from Rome to Marta, who lives in her father's house at Via Caiazzo 52 in Milan. There are preparations for the trip to Germany and hopes of great business deals in America.

SEPTEMBER 28. Pirandello arrives in Milan, where he spends several days with Marta until their departure for Berlin. During his visits in Milan Pirandello stays at the Hotel Corso Splendid.

OCTOBER 9. The probable date of Pirandello's and Marta's departure for Berlin, where Marta stays until March 13, 1929. Pirandello's addresses in Berlin are 9, Hitzingstrasse, and then Hotel Herkuleshaus, 13, Friedrich-Wilhelmstrasse. Pirandello and Marta live in adjacent rooms, and Marta is very often accompanied by her sister Cele.

New volumes of Pirandello's works are published by Bemporad (*Liolà, La giara, Il viaggio, Candelora*).

In Berlin Pirandello writes, in collaboration with Adolf Lanz, a film scenario for *Sei personaggi*, published in 1929 by Reinmar Hobbing—but the film is never realized.

{ 1929 }

During this year Pirandello writes ninety letters to Marta.

MARCH 13. Marta abandons Berlin because none of Pirandello's promises have materialized and returns to Milan, where she spends a couple of months trying to reenter the Italian theatrical world. Pirandello writes almost daily letters—full of despair because of her departure.

MARCH 22. In Berlin Pirandello receives a telegram from Mussolini announcing his nomination to the Accademia d'Italia.

APRIL 12. Pirandello goes to London to see the very first examples of "talking films" and is horrified by them.

MAY 9. Marta goes to Terme di Miradolo (Pavia) for a couple of weeks of rest.

JUNE 1–16. Pirandello takes a short trip to Italy for the first meeting of the Accademia d'Italia in Rome. On June 2 he sees Marta briefly in Milan, and again he visits her from the eleventh to the fifteenth. He is back in Berlin on the sixteenth.

JULY 4–15. Pirandello travels from Berlin to Paris, where he meets Marta. He is back in Berlin on the sixteenth.

JULY 9. At the Royal Theatre in Huddersfield, England, the world premiere of Pirandello's "myth" *Lazzaro* takes place, in the translation by C. K. Scott Moncrieff.

AUGUST 3–SEPTEMBER 13. Pirandello, in Italy for the summer vacation, is preparing with Marta the first season of her new Compagnia Marta Abba, of which she is the artistic director/manager. On his return to Berlin he sues his German translator Hans Feist, now transformed into a bitter enemy. This feud will have serious consequences in the near future.

MID-SEPTEMBER. Marta goes to the Grand Hotel of Salice Terme (Voghera) for ten days of rest/treatment, and by the end of the month is again in Milan. There she spends very tiring weeks trying to put together her new company and ensure bookings for her tour. Pirandello's letters are full of advice and encouragement for the difficult enterprise.

EARLY OCTOBER. At last the villino in the Via Onofrio Panvinio is sold for nine hundred thousand lire, providing a period of relaxation in Pirandello's never-ending financial worries.

OCTOBER 18–NOVEMBER 17. Pirandello is in Milan to advise Marta on the repertory of the new company she is recruiting among young actors. For the upcoming first season Marta chooses a repertory of plays mostly by Pirandello, among which are the new *Lazzaro* and *Il grillo del focolare*, an adaptation by S. Strekowsky and C. V. Ludovici of Dickens's *The Cricket on the Hearth*.

LATE OCTOBER. Pirandello travels to Rome for the inauguration of the Accademia d'Italia. On October 30 he is back in Milan with Marta, on his way to Vienna, where he arrives on November 2 and negotiates for a European tour of Marta's company, which never takes place. On the sixth he leaves Vienna for Berlin.

NOVEMBER 4. At the Teatro di Torino in Turin the Almirante-Rissone-Tòfano Company presents Pirandello's *O di uno o di nessuno*.

MID-NOVEMBER. Pirandello leaves Berlin to settle his finances in Rome after the sale of the villino in the Via Panvinio. He travels afterward to Turin, where he assists Marta in the production of *Lazzaro*, in which Marta interprets the role of Sara.

DECEMBER 7. In Turin at the Teatro di Torino the Italian premiere of *Lazzaro* takes place. Right after the failure in Turin, Pirandello travels to Milan to help out in the production of the same work at the Teatro Olimpia in Milan, with Maria Melato in the role of Sara. The end of the year finds Marta and Pirandello distressed because of the failure of *Lazzaro* and the financial losses of the new company.

{ 1930 }

During this year Pirandello writes 113 letters to Marta, addressed to the many cities where she is performing.

Marta is completely absorbed by the fatiguing tour of her company to a great number of Italian cities. At the beginning Pirandello accompanies her from town to town, but soon his despair over his unrequited love drives him to the brink of suicide. At the end of February he flees to Berlin, where he remains until the beginning of June.

JANUARY 25. At the Neues Schauspielhaus in Königsberg the world premiere of *Questa sera si recita a soggetto (Heute abend wird aus dem Stegreif gespielt)* takes place in the German translation by Harry Kahn.

FEBRUARY 18. At the Teatro dei Filodrammatici in Milan the world premiere of Pirandello's *Come tu mi vuoi* takes place, with Marta in the leading role.

FEBRUARY 27. A desperate Pirandello returns to Berlin, where he again stays at the Hotel Herkuleshaus.

MARCH 4–6. Pirandello travels to Königsberg to be present at a performance of his *Questa sera si recita a soggetto*, which is having an extraordinary success in that provincial city.

MARCH 12–18. Pirandello is in Paris to be present at the premiere of *La vie que je t'ai donnée (La vita che ti diedi)* on March 13 at the Petite Scène.

MARCH 19. Pirandello is back in Berlin. He is working on the rewriting of the comedy *Coquette* by Ann Preston Bridges and George Abbot for the use of Marta's company.

EARLY APRIL. In Berlin Pirandello conceives his first idea for *Quando si è qualcuno.*

APRIL 14. In Turin at the Teatro di Torino the Italian premiere of *Questa sera si recita a soggetto* takes place, performed by a company under the artistic direction of Guido Salvini.

MAY 31. In Berlin at the Lessing-Theater the disastrous premiere of *Questa sera si recita a soggetto* takes place, directed by Gustav Hartung. A wave of anti-Pirandellism in the German press reveals signs of a rising fierce xenophobic nationalism in the unstable political situation. Pirandello feels betrayed and distressed and decides to flee from Berlin forever.

JUNE 13. This is the probable date of Pirandello's departure from Berlin, to which he will come back only for short visits. Pirandello travels to Italy to appear in person at the Appellate Court in Rome, and then he stays near Marta for five weeks.

JULY 23. Pirandello arrives in Paris to meet the American impresario Lee Shubert, who buys on the spot the U.S. rights for four Pirandello's plays.

AUGUST 3–6. Pirandello travels from Paris to Berlin and back.

AUGUST 12. Pirandello arrives in London to discuss with Charles B.

Cochran a contract for Great Britain similar to the one he has just signed with Lee Shubert for the U.S.

Second half of August–October. Pirandello is back in Italy, visits Marta in Milan and his children in Positano (Naples), and then spends a longer time working near Marta. The trip to the U.S., previously planned for the end of September, is put off because of the severe economic depression in America.

October 9. Pirandello is in Rome for the election of new members of the Accademia d'Italia, while Marta is performing with her company in Venice.

During October the film *La canzone dell'amore*, freely adapted from Pirandello's short story *In silenzio* and directed by Gennaro Righelli for the Cines of Rome, is distributed in Italy. It is the first Italian talking film to appear on the market, and it has success also in the French and German versions, which are distributed in the following year.

December 5. Pirandello returns to Paris, where he stays for a few days at the Hôtel Vendôme, but soon establishes his residence in an apartment on the first floor at 5, Avenue Victor Emmanuel III. He begins a tireless activity to make Paris the center of his international contacts with the world of the movies.

December 12. At the Teatro Manzoni in Milan the Compagnia Marta Abba presents for the first time in Italy Heinrich Mann's play *Madame Legros*. Marta's repertory for this theater season includes Maugham's *Penelope*, Molnár's *La buona fata*, P. A. Antoine's *La nostra compagna (L'Ennemie)*, Tolstoi's *Anna Karenina*, and the ever popular *Il grillo del focolare* (The cricket on the hearth). Marta is very tired and very preoccupied with serious financial problems.

At the end of the year the Shubert production of Pirandello's *As You Desire Me (Come tu mi vuoi)* has a great success in Philadelphia on its way to Broadway.

Mondadori, who is now the publisher of Pirandello's work instead of Bemporad, publishes *Questa sera si recita a soggetto* and *Come tu mi vuoi*.

{ 1931 }

During this year Pirandello writes 126 letters to Marta, who is touring major Italian cities with her company: in January she performs in Turin,

Alessandria, Bergamo, Cremona, Como; in February in Genoa and Florence; in mid-March in Rome; from the beginning of April through the end of May in Naples. Most of Pirandello's letters are written from Paris.

JANUARY 28. At the Maxine Elliott Theatre in New York the Broadway premiere of Pirandello's *As You Desire Me (Come tu mi vuoi)* has great success. The play runs for 142 performances.

FEBRUARY 21. The rights for the filming of *As You Desire Me* are sold by Shubert to Metro-Goldwyn-Mayer for the then enormous amount of $40,000. Pirandello is now sure that his dream of great riches will soon become a reality.

MARCH 19–14. Pirandello meets Shubert again in Paris. The impresario acquires the U.S. rights for Pirandello's *La nuova colonia* and proposes an American tour for a company selected and managed by Marta with a repertory of Pirandello's plays.

In the first two weeks of June Marta is in Milan with her parents in the new residence at Via Aurelio Saffi 26.

JUNE 14–JULY 16. Marta is in Paris with Pirandello. Marta is shopping for furniture for her rooms in her father's new apartment.

AUGUST 1. Pirandello moves to an apartment on the top floor of Rue La Pérouse 37, near the Étoile in the center of Paris.

AUGUST 20. Pirandello leaves Paris to visit Marta, who is ill in Genoa.

LATE AUGUST. Pirandello and Marta travel first to Milan and then to the mountain village of Caspoggio (Sondrio) for a period of vacation.

MID-SEPTEMBER. Pirandello returns to Paris for a short visit on the way to Portugal.

SEPTEMBER 17–28. Pirandello leaves for Portugal to participate in the Fifth International Congress of Critics. There he is publicly honored and made the object of enthusiastic affection by the Portuguese audiences.

SEPTEMBER 20. At the National Theater of Lisbon Pirandello's play *Sogno (ma forse no)* is performed in the Portuguese translation by Caetano de Abrau Beirão.

LATE SEPTEMBER. Pirandello is back in Paris.

OCTOBER 9. Pirandello sends to Marta—who was still recuperating from her sickness—a proposal to perform in French at the Saint-Georges in Paris the role of "the virtuous signora Perella" in Pirandello's *L'uomo, la bestia e la virtù*. Marta accepts and leaves almost immediately for Paris to start rehearsals without delay.

DECEMBER 3. At the Accademia d'Italia Pirandello gives a controversial lecture in honor of the Sicilian writer Giovanni Verga, in which he attacks Gabriele D'Annunzio. The lecture is published the following day in the Roman newspaper *Tevere*.

Pirandello prepares a new edition of his novel *I vecchi e i giovani* for the publisher Mondadori. He also publishes two short stories (*Uno di più* and *Il soffio*) and the first act of *Giganti della montagna*.

{ 1932 }

During this year Pirandello writes seventy-one letters to Marta, most of them from Paris—except those from Rome and from Castiglioncello during the summer.

JANUARY 17. Marta leaves Paris at the end of her contract for the performances of Pirandello's *L'uomo, la bestia e la virtù*.

FEBRUARY 2 OR 3. In Rome at the Palazzo Venezia Marta is received in audience by Mussolini and remains disillusioned. Her interview, however, prepares the way for Pirandello's long audience the following month.

MID-FEBRUARY. Pirandello, who had been suffering from a relapse into his major depression after Marta's departure from Paris, has a heart attack.

MARCH 13. A long colloquy with Mussolini marks for Pirandello the beginning of a period of enthusiastic work in cooperation with the Fascist government for the establishment of a state-subsidized national theater. Pirandello resides now in Rome with his son Stefano at Via Piemonte 117.

EARLY APRIL. Marta goes to Rapallo for a couple of weeks' rest and then returns to Milan. In April Marta buys a summer home, the Villino Mezzaluna in Lido di Camaiore, a beach resort near Viareggio on the Tyrrhenian coast.

LATE APRIL. Pirandello participates in the International Theatre Congress in Rome, during which his play *Pensaci, Giacomino!* is presented with great success. He has an encounter with Max Reinhardt.

APRIL 29–MAY 3. Pirandello leaves Rome to visit Marta in Viareggio and Lido di Camaiore, and then returns to Paris on May 3.

MAY 13 OR 14. Marta, accompanied by her mother, joins Pirandello in France and helps him out in closing his Parisian apartment. Pirandello thus officially terminates his self-imposed exile and makes his son Stefano's apartment in Rome, Via Piemonte 117, his temporary official residence. Toward the end of May, before coming back to Italy, Pirandello completes *La favola del figlio cambiato*.

LATE MAY. Pirandello is back in Rome. In collaboration with his son Stefano he completes the scenario *Giuoca, Pietro!* which is later published in *Scenario* (January 1933) and used for *Acciaio*, a film directed by Walter Ruttmann and produced by Cines.

JUNE 25. Pirandello is Marta's guest at the Villino Mezzaluna in Lido di Camaiore until the end of July, then goes to Castiglioncello, where he remains through October with his son Stefano and his family at the Villino Conti.

MID-SEPTEMBER. In Castiglioncello Pirandello completes *Trovarsi*.

FIRST WEEK OF OCTOBER. In Castiglioncello Pirandello completes *Quando si è qualcuno*.

SECOND WEEK OF OCTOBER. Pirandello goes back to Rome and then goes on to Naples to assist Marta in the production of *Trovarsi*.

NOVEMBER 4. Pirandello is present at the premiere of *Trovarsi* in Naples. Marta is on her tour with a repertory of Italian plays, including, besides Pirandello's novelties, *La vedova scaltra* by Goldoni, *La corsa dietro l'ombra* by Enrico Roma, *La sedicesima notte* by Curio Mortari, and *La cacciata dal Paradiso* by Goffredo Ginocchio. Marta's company performs in major Sicilian cities, such as Palermo and Trapani in November, and Catania and Messina in December.

NOVEMBER 7. Pirandello is present at the Parisian opening of *Come tu mi vuoi*. In Paris Pirandello is honored with extraordinary recognitions and festivities.

DECEMBER 4. A depressed and sickly Mussolini receives Pirandello at the Palazzo Venezia and makes it clear that because of the menacing international circumstances Pirandello's project for a national theater has to wait.

During this year the publisher Mondadori reprints a number of volumes of Pirandello's work which had been previously published by Bemporad.

{ 1933 }

Only thirteen letters written by Pirandello to Marta during this year are preserved.

At the beginning of January Marta is in Cagliari, Sardinia, with her company. At her return Pirandello goes to the harbor of Civitavecchia to meet her and remains near her during her performances in Rome.

FEBRUARY 8. Probable date of Marta's departure from Rome for Turin, where she performs with her company until the beginning of March. She then performs in Genoa, and on February 21 she is back in Milan to perform at the Teatro Manzoni.

FEBRUARY 23–MARCH 8. Pirandello travels to Paris in a vain attempt finally to get rid of his agent Saul Colin.

MARCH 11. Pirandello is in Rome for the Premio Mussolini, and then reaches Marta in Milan.

BEGINNING OF MAY. Marta is in Venice, where she performs at the Teatro Goldoni; in mid-May she travels to Trieste.

MAY 15–16. In Bologna Pirandello participates in the Writers' Congress.

JUNE. Marta is in Rome, where she stars in the film *Il caso Haller*, directed by Alessandro Blasetti and produced by Cines.

JULY–MID-AUGUST. Pirandello is in Castiglioncello, where he works on *Giganti della montagna* and helps Marta organize the new Compagnia Stabile San Remo Marta Abba. The repertory of that company will include *Quando si è qualcuno* by Pirandello, *Il caso del dottor Hirn* by Rino Alessi, *L'Olimpo* by Umberto Fracchia, *Il Maestro* by Luigi Antonelli, directed by Pirandello, *Il marito che cerco* by Salvator Gotta and Sergio Pugliese, and *Un mese in campagna* (A month in the country) by Ivan Turgenev.

AUGUST 17. Pirandello sails for South America.

SEPTEMBER 20. In Buenos Aires at the Teatro Odeon Pirandello is present at the world premiere of *Cuando se es alguien (Quando si è qualcuno)* in the Spanish version by Homero Guglielmini.

SEPTEMBER 26. Pirandello lectures on Ariosto and Cervantes at the Teatro Solis in Montevideo.

OCTOBER–NOVEMBER. Pirandello is in San Remo with Marta for the preparation of the Italian premiere of *Quando si è qualcuno*, which takes place on November 7 at the Teatro del Casino Municipale di San Remo.

FALL. Pirandello takes up residence in the villino located at Via Bosio 15, Rome, where he will reside until his death.

During this year Mondadori publishes new editions and reprints of a number of Pirandello's works, including *Quando si è qualcuno*. Ricordi publishes *La favola del figlio cambiato*.

{ 1934 }

During this year Pirandello writes twenty-one letters to Marta, most of them from Rome.

JANUARY 13. At the Landestheater of Braunschweig in Germany the world premiere of Pirandello's *La favola del figlio cambiato (Die Legende vom vertauschten Sohn)* takes place, translated by Hans Redlich, with music by G. F. Malipiero.

FEBRUARY–MARCH. Pirandello informs Marta that he is going through financial difficulties, while Marta is facing problems with the administration of the Compagnia Stabile San Remo Marta Abba, which has been losing substantial amounts of money during the season. During the second half of March Marta performs in Venice and Turin.

MARCH 24. At the Teatro Reale dell'Opera in Rome, the Italian premiere of *La favola del figlio cambiato* takes place. Mussolini, who is present at the opening, does not like the opera and forbids further performances.

MAY 2. In Milan at the Teatro Manzoni Pirandello is present at the performance of *Six Characters in Search of an Author* directed by Max Reinhardt. At the beginning of May Marta performs in Verona, at the Teatro Nuovo.

MAY 9–END OF MAY. Pirandello is with Marta, who is performing in Milan. At the beginning of June Pirandello must go back to Rome for the preparations for the Volta Congress, of which he is the president.

MAY 12. In Turin Pirandello gives a lecture, "Teatro nuovo e teatro vecchio," which is published in the newspaper *La Stampa* of Turin, May 13.

JUNE 9. After fulfilling the terms of her contract with her company

Marta arrives in Rome for the filming of *Teresa Confalonieri* directed by Guido Brignone.

July–August. In Castiglioncello Pirandello works at *Non si sa come*.

August 23. Marta is at the Lido di Venezia for the premiere of the film *Teresa Confalonieri*, which receives the prize of the Festival Internazionale Cinematografico. Pirandello is not in Venice to share the glory of his beloved because he is in the middle of a fervent moment of creativity in the peaceful atmosphere of Castiglioncello.

October 8–14. In Rome Pirandello presides over the Fourth Congress of the Volta Foundation on the theme "The Dramatic Theater." On the occasion of that international congress Gabriele D'Annunzio's *La figlia di Iorio*, directed by Pirandello and interpreted by Marta Abba and the actor Ruggero Ruggeri, is performed at the Teatro Argentina.

Early November. The news of the awarding of the Nobel Prize to Pirandello is announced. Marta goes to Salsomaggiore for a few weeks of treatment/rest. Pirandello publishes the second act of *I giganti della montagna* in the journal *Quadrante*.

Second half of November. Pirandello is honored with great festivities in Paris and London.

December 10. In Stockholm the king of Sweden awards the Nobel Prize for Literature to Pirandello.

December 19. At the National Theater of Prague Pirandello is present at the world premiere of *Non si sa come* in the Czech translation by V. Jirina.

During this year Mondadori continues the publication of further volumes of Pirandello's works. The newspaper *Corriere della sera* of Milan publishes four short stories by Pirandello ("I piedi sull'erba," "Di sera un geranio," "Un'idea," "C'è qualcuno che ride").

{ 1935 }

During this year Pirandello writes forty-three letters to Marta, mostly from Rome.

Early January. Pirandello goes to Paris with Marta and her mother.

January 27. Marta leaves from Paris for London to study English and prepare herself for a career in the international theater and film world.

Early February. At the Teatro San Carlo in Naples the opening of an opera with music by Giuseppe Mulè and libretto by Arturo Rossato takes place, drawn from Pirandello's play *Liolà*. Pirandello travels to Milan and then to Rome, where the hope for the establishment of a state theater is once more revived.

February 18. Pirandello has an audience with Mussolini, who seems greatly interested in realizing immediately Pirandello's plan for a state-subsidized theater. Pirandello begins a period of feverish work to prepare with Bottai and other key Fascist personalities the realization of the project. In the meantime, as a result of the Nobel Prize, Pirandello's plays are performed all over the world.

Late March. Pirandello spends a week in London to visit Marta and attend to business. On the way back he visits Paris and is in Rome on April 7.

April 24. Great festivities take place in Pirandello's honor at Palazzo Ruspoli in Rome.

April 26. Pirandello inaugurates the cycle of Conferenze internazionali d'alta cultura at the Palazzo Vecchio in Florence with a talk on an introduction to the Italian theater.

May–October. Marta returns to Italy from England and works at finding her place again in the Italian theater. In July she is in Venice for the Festival di Venezia, where she interprets the role of Portia in Shakespeare's *The Merchant of Venice*, directed by Max Reinhardt. During August and September Marta is again in Milan, and in October she goes to Salsomaggiore for a vacation, after which the preparations for her next roles with the company of Guido Salvini begin.

July 20. Pirandello arrives in New York aboard the Italian liner *Conte di Savoia*. He stays in New York for about two and a half months, without reaching any concrete results, after endless discussions and negotiations. Pirandello's support of the Italian aggression in Ethiopia and the international tension are powerful obstacles to any successful business transaction.

October 13. Pirandello arrives in Naples aboard the *Conte di Savoia*, where he suffers a violent heart attack right before disembarking. On the fifteenth another, even more violent heart attack follows. During the rest of October Pirandello is convalescing in Rome, while Marta is now the leading actress of the Compagnia dei Grandi Spettacoli d'Arte directed by

Guido Salvini. She is busy with the preparations for her interpretation of the role of Saint Joan in Shaw's play and for her role in the troublesome play *Simma* by Pastonchi.

October 29. Pirandello gives a short speech at the opening of the theater season of the Teatro Argentina in the presence of Mussolini. Pirandello is seen more and more, in the eyes of everybody, as a deeply respected living symbol of the Italian theater—at the same time everybody is aware of the precarious state of his health.

Late October–December 5. Marta is in Rome.

December 13. In Rome, at the Teatro Argentina, the Italian premiere of *Non si sa come*, performed by Ruggero Ruggeri, takes place. It has great success with an audience that wants to pay homage to the author, now definitely old and in poor health. Pirandello's relationship to Marta becomes more and more fatherly, while the thought of impending death appears more often in the letters.

During this year Mondadori publishes *Non si sa come* and reprints several volumes of Pirandello's work.

At this time Pirandello writes at least a great part of his *Informazioni sul mio involontario soggiorno sulla terra*, published after his death in *Corriere della sera* (March 30, 1937), in *Meridiano di Roma* (May 2, 1937), and in *Almanacco letterario Bompiani* 1938 (Milan, 1939).

The film *Ma non è una cosa seria*, adapted from the comedy by Pirandello, is realized by director Mario Camerini for Colombo-Film of Rome, with Vittorio De Sica and Elisa Cegani.

{ 1936 }

During this year Pirandello writes fifty-two letters to Marta, almost all of them from Rome.

First weeks of January. The "elitist" project of the state theater is temporarily set aside by the Fascist government, which is now concentrating its resources on the planning and construction of Cinecittà—with the purpose of producing propaganda movies for the masses. After many contradictory hesitations by the author about the timing of the publication, Marta's memoirs are eventually published, under the title *Note*, in three installments of *Italia letteraria*.

January 11. Pirandello's *Sogno, ma forse no* is broadcast by the Italian national radio network EIAR—a "first" in the history of Italian radio drama.

JANUARY 21. Pirandello is in Turin for the opening of his son Stefano's play *Un padre ci vuole*, performed by the Tòfano-Maltagliati-Cervi Company at the Teatro Alfieri.

LATE JANUARY–MID-FEBRUARY. Pirandello is in Milan, where he remains until Marta opens at the Teatro Lirico as leading lady of the Compagnia dei Grandi Spettacoli d'Arte directed by G. Salvini, in Shaw's play *Saint Joan*.

MID-FEBRUARY. Marta falls ill and the company cannot continue the planned tour.

LATE FEBRUARY. The tour of the Compagnia dei Grandi Spettacoli is resumed in Turin. Marta performs with that company at the Teatro Corso in Bologna, Teatro Verdi in Florence, and Teatro Argentina in Rome.

MARCH 14. Marta arrives in Rome with the Compagnia dei Grandi Spettacoli.

LATE MARCH–BEGINNING OF APRIL. There are feverish negotiations with the American impresario Gilbert Miller, who offers Marta the leading role in a Broadway-bound comedy, *Tovarich*. In the meantime the actress continues her tour in Leghorn, La Spezia, Genoa, Padoa, and Venice.

LATE APRIL. Marta is again in Milan, preparing for her meeting with Gilbert Miller. Pirandello, suffering from high blood pressure, declines an invitation to go to South America, where great festivities in his honor had been widely publicized by the press.

MAY 7. Marta is in Rome, meets with Gilbert Miller, and signs the contract that will take her to her "dream-come-true" success on Broadway.

MAY 23. Marta leaves for London to start rehearsals for *Tovarich*. Pirandello, who had been with Marta during her last few days in Milan, now goes to Anticoli Corrado, a picturesque village in the province of Rome, as a guest of his son Fausto and spends his time painting. Pirandello is depressed and as though numbed by Marta's departure.

MID-JUNE. Pirandello is a guest of Marta's parents in Marta's villino at Lido di Camaiore.

June 23. Pirandello is present at the Roman premiere of his son Stefano's play, *Un padre ci vuole.*

Late June–early July. Pirandello is again in Anticoli Corrado.

July 15–18. Pirandello is in Venice, where he attends the performances of Goldoni's plays *Il ventaglio* and *Le baruffe chiozzote*, directed by Renato Simoni. He is back in Rome for a few days, then again in Anticoli Corrado with his son Fausto and his family.

July 28. Marta's first performance in English takes place. Marta continues her successful performances in the tryouts of the play *Tovarich* in the suburbs of London until mid-August.

Second half of August. Marta is back in Italy for some rest with her family before leaving for the United States.

September 17. Marta arrives in New York on the *Conte di Savoia.*

Late September. Pirandello is in Berlin for the International Congress of Authors and Publishers. There are promises of a revival of Pirandello's theater in Germany with the favor of the new Nazi regime.

Late September–first week in October. Success of *Tovarich* in Philadelphia and Baltimore.

October 15. Success in New York of the opening of *Tovarich* at the Plymouth Theatre. Marta receives excellent reviews on her Broadway debut.

October. Pirandello's daughter Lietta returns with her two daughters from Chile to live in Rome. She occupies the apartment where her brother Stefano and his family used to live, right underneath Pirandello's apartment in the villino in the Via Bosio 15. Pirandello is upset because of his daughter's separation from her husband and the new burden imposed upon his already strained financial situation.

End of October. In Paris the Comédie-Française presents Pirandello's *Così è (se vi pare).*

First days of December. In the studios of Cinecittà (Rome) Pirandello becomes fatally ill while attending the filming of *Il fu Mattia Pascal,* drawn from his novel with the same title. The film is directed by Pierre Chenal for Ala-Colosseum, with dialogues by Pirandello and music by Jacques Ibert.

December 10. Pirandello dies of pneumonia in his home at Via Bosio 15 in Rome. Marta announces the demise of the Maestro from the stage of the Plymouth Theatre on Broadway.

During this year Pirandello publishes six short stories in the *Corriere della sera*, and Mondadori reprints a number of volumes of his work. Gennaro Righelli directs the film *Pensaci, Giacomino!* adapted by Guglielmo Giannini for the screen from Pirandello's comedy.

After Pirandello's death Marta completes her theatrical commitments with Gilbert Miller in the United States. In 1937 she receives the award of the American Dramatic League, and on January 28, 1938, she marries the wealthy heir Severance A. Millikin. She takes up residence in Cleveland, Ohio, and abandons the stage under pressure from her husband. The glamorous but unhappy marriage ends in divorce in 1953. Marta returns to Italy, where she makes a few appearances on the stage with a short-lived company she forms with the actor Piero Cornabuci. She lives in Milan, Lugano (Switzerland), Monaco (where she takes up residence), and on the Lake of Geneva. In 1986 she travels, although bound to a wheelchair, to New York and is honored at Princeton University on the occasion of her donation of the Pirandello letters to that university's library. She dies in Milan on June 24, 1988, one day before her eighty-eighth birthday.

PIRANDELLO'S
LOVE LETTERS TO
MARTA ABBA

The Short Note
of 1925

·⟨⟨⟩⟩·

THE CORRESPONDENCE begins with a brief note dated February 7, 1925. It was addressed to the Teatro Chiabrera in Savona, where Marta Abba was performing with the Talli Company. Pirandello's few words accompany the script of the play *Nostra Dea* and a short introductory letter by its author, Massimo Bontempelli.[1]

Pirandello's note was written a couple of weeks before the first meeting with the actress on the stage of the Teatro Odescalchi. That fateful moment was described by Marta on several occasions: "I arrived in Rome accompanied by my mother. It was my first trip to a company with which I would later perform on tour. On the stage I saw a few people in the half-darkness, and one of them bent with age, with silver hair and a short white beard. I entered the stage and somebody said: it's Marta Abba. Pirandello then sprang from his armchair and came toward me with his marvelous vitality: he certainly did not look old! He shook my hand again and again and told me: 'Welcome, signorina; we are happy you arrived.'"[2]

The expectations of Bontempelli and Pirandello were fulfilled. Marta's debut in the role of Dea on April 22 was a hit with the critics and the public. Bontempelli wrote in a letter of May 1, 1925, to Marta's father: "A great part of the success is due to the extraordinary art of signorina Marta, who is a miracle of intelligence and fascination." *Nostra Dea* was the only play that continued in the repertory during the three years of the existence of Pirandello's company.[3] Virgilio Marchi, the architect who was

[1] Massimo Bontempelli (1878–1960)—poet, critic, playwright, teacher, and faithful friend of Pirandello until the end—was one of the founders of the Teatro d'Arte di Roma, October 6, 1924. Bontempelli's letter is preserved in the library of Princeton University.

[2] Translated from Elio Providenti, "Marta Abba: Una vita per il teatro," *Scena Illustrata*, 122/3 (1987), p. 37. A similar description is found in Marta Abba, "La mia vita di attrice," *Il Dramma*, no. 237 (July 1, 1936), p. 5.

[3] Pirandello's company existed as the Compagnia del Teatro d'Arte di Roma until March 1927, then was renamed Compagnia del Teatro Argentina until August 1928, when it was officially dissolved in Viareggio. See Alessandro D'Amico and Alessandro Tinterri, *Pirandello capocomico* (Palermo: Sellerio, 1987), for the history of this period, and especially pp. 97–111 about the production of *Nostra Dea*.

responsible for the renovation of the Teatro Odescalchi, writes: "Marta Abba had been hailed as a new dawn. The truth is that the star would in a short time dominate the mind of the Maestro and change everything. *Nostra Dea* was the debut. A great success. The actress seemed especially right for the rapidly changing moods of the protagonist. There was a fire, an instinct and a fickleness, a suffering that fitted her immediately for the intimate world of Pirandello's characters."[4]

Here follows the text of Pirandello's note.

[4] Ibid., p. 413.

{ 250207 }

Dear Miss Abba,

Please learn *Nostra Dea*'s leading role with love and be assured that your performance will be backed by a *prestigious* staging, which will make easier all the changes from one *costume* to the *next*.[1]

I rely very much on your care in its interpretation. In the meantime I send you cordial regards,

Luigi Pirandello

[1] The play *Nostra Dea* requires of the leading lady a great number of costume and character changes.

Letters of 1926
from Rome

T HE NINE LETTERS of 1926 cover the brief period of August 5–25, during the summer vacation of Pirandello's company. Marta spent that time at her father's house, Via Caiazzo 52 in Milan, and Pirandello at his new home at Via Onofrio Panvinio 11 in Rome.

During the one-and-a-half years between the first note of 1925 and these letters, Marta lived very close to the Maestro, extremely busy with the feverish work of the company. After the first Italian season, which closed with a performance of Pirandello's *Enrico IV* at the Teatro Argentina in Rome (June 12, 1925), the company immediately began to make preparations for a tour abroad, with London (Oxford Theatre, June 15–28) and Paris (Théâtre Edouard VII, July 1–15) as principal stops. The season started again on September 19 in Milan. The company toured to Como, Basel, Berlin, Frankfurt a.M., Bonn, Cologne, Düsseldorf, Kassel, Leipzig, Halle, Magdeburg, Hannover, Hamburg, and Bremen. The tour abroad ended with a performance in Münster (November 7). After a few days of rest, on November 12, the tour began again in Modena and continued until July 30, 1926, touching more than twenty cities in northern and central Italy, including Rome, Milan, Florence, and Bologna.

The main subjects of this first small group of letters are a domestic quarrel that shakes Pirandello's family and upsets his relationship with his beloved daughter Lietta and her husband, Manuel Aguirre; the process of revision of the play *Diana e la Tuda*, and the completion of *L'Amica delle mogli*; the negotiations for the use of the Teatro Argentina in Rome and the efforts of the journalist Telesio Interlandi for a reconciliation between Pirandello and the theatrical impresario Paolo Giordani, with the purpose of strengthening the case for a state-funded dramatic theater in Italy at the Argentina.

In the first letter written on his return to Rome after so much traveling, Pirandello describes his shock at the discovery that his personal finances—entrusted to the care of his son-in-law Manuel Aguirre—appeared to be in danger of imminent collapse. The playwright interpreted some of his son-in-law's actions as dishonest maneuvers at the expense of his other two sons. He remained so dismayed by what he felt to be an unbelievable betrayal of his complete trust, that he was never able to reestablish any relationship with his son-in-law, and only in time could he warm up again, in a limited way, to his once-favorite daughter. Pirandello's grandchild Maria Luisa Aguirre D'Amico (daughter of Manuel and Lietta) has proposed an interpretation of her father's behavior according to which the allegedly dishonest disappearance of large amounts of Pirandello's money was the result of the many requests for payments made by the playwright himself—to take care of large bills for the construction of the new home in Rome and to cover with substantial amounts of his own money the great losses of his company.[1]

Pirandello had begun to discuss in public the project for a state theater as early as 1924. It was now his dream to transform his own company—already successful in Italy and abroad in pioneering an artistic, noncommercial repertory—into a state-subsidized institution. This national company, under Pirandello's artistic direction, was planned to include the best artists available in the country and to present an Italian repertory in three major theaters, to be placed by the government at its disposal (Teatro Argentina in Rome, Teatro Manzoni in Milan, and Teatro di Torino in Turin). Pirandello, enthusiastic about this project, calls it "impressive, totally worthy of the Italian capital city renewed by fascism." In order to make a stronger case in its favor with the government, the Maestro even seems inclined to negotiate a reconciliation with his powerful archenemy Paolino Giordani.

In the short vacation period between the theatrical seasons Pirandello also worked at two plays inspired by his love for the actress: he rewrote parts of *Diana e la Tuda* and finished *L'amica delle mogli*. The letters show the importance of Marta as Pirandello's muse, confidante, and consultant.

[1] See note 2 of letter 260805.

{ 260805 }

To Marta Abba
Milan
Via Cajazzo, 52

Rome, August 5, 1926
Via Onofrio Panvinio

Dear Marta,

At last I can give you some news about what is being prepared for the next theater season. First of all, however, I have to tell you that I did not write before because my home, on the day after my arrival,[1] unfortunately became a stage for savage quarrels between my sons and my son-in-law.[2]

... You can imagine how I feel. In a few days I got more run down than in ten years. But I still have so much strength in me that I can recover at once, as soon as this stormy moment is over.[3] Today at five the lawyer will finish verifying how things are, and we'll decide on a settlement and everyone's *modus vivendi*.[4]

... Thanks to the faculty that I possess in the highest degree, not to pay attention to all the miseries of life, I was able—even during these stormy days—to read over again *Diana e la Tuda* and rewrite the whole second half of the third act more dramatically and, I believe, by now in a perfectly smooth way. I have been waiting until now for your reaction, counting on the promise you made me, to read the work again with a rested mind. I am still waiting, full of anxiety. And I am waiting for your news. Please give my regards to your parents and to Cele, and you, dear Marta, have my cordial greetings.

Luigi Pirandello

[1] Pirandello arrived in Rome probably on July 31, following the last performance of the company in Tuscany on July 30. The family quarrel happened probably on August 1.

[2] Pirandello's sons Stefano and Fausto quarrelled with their brother-in-law Manuel, who since 1924 had been entrusted with the administration of Pirandello's affairs. A version of the painful family "tempest"—which is not acceptable to all of Pirandello's grandchildren—was given by Manuel's daughter Maria Luisa Aguirre D'Amico in her book *Vivere con Pirandello* (Milan: Mondadori, 1989), pp. 134–37: "It appears that, as soon as Luigi returned from one of his frequent trips with his company, Stefano and Fausto— who watched Lietta living in great luxury while Manuel often delayed the payment of their checks—began a fight with their brother-in-law." According to her explanation of the events, the accusations of fraud and embezzlement were the result of a hasty and angry interpretation—by Pirandello and his sons—of Manuel's legitimate efforts not only to pay for Pirandello's new home and for the debts incurred by Pirandello's company, but also to recoup for himself a considerable amount of money promised to him by Pirandello as Lietta's dowry. "Manuel is accused, and no time is given him to answer. Lietta and

Manuel are asked to get out of the house. Pirandello later said: 'I threw them out,' or 'they fled away'" (p. 135). Maria Luisa Aguirre D'Amico also mentions the existence of a type-written statement by Manuel that allegedly proves the honesty of her father's behavior, but at the same time shows his "incredible lack of *savoir faire*"—an inflexibility probably partly responsible for the serious quarrel.

[3] Pirandello's violent reaction to money problems can be better understood in the context of the consequences of his father's bankruptcy in 1903—a disaster that had a tragic influence on the mental condition of the author's wife, Antonietta. Moreover, only one year before the present letter was written, the playwright had been in serious danger of personal bankruptcy because the government had delayed the payment of a large amount of money he had personally advanced to his theater company on the assumption that official promises of state subsidies would be kept on time. Pirandello's desperate appeals to high Fascist functionaries who were responsible for the payment, and a telegram to Mussolini imploring a personal intervention to save his family from financial ruin, are published in Alberto Cesare Alberti, *Il teatro nel tempo del Fascismo. Pirandello e Bragaglia* (Rome: Bulzoni, 1974), pp. 161–63.

[4] In a following passage here omitted, Pirandello talks about negotiations with the governor of Rome to obtain the Teatro Argentina for his project of a state-funded national theater. It is in this context that he calls his plan "impressive, totally worthy of the Italian capital city renewed by fascism."

{ 260817 }

To Marta Abba
Milan
52, Via Cajazzo   Rome, 17. VIII. 1926
    Dear Marta,
    I received in this very moment your refreshing letter written in the early morning of the 16th, and I breathe "the still biting air of the night" entering from the little balcony of your dining room—with so much open space in front of it. And I see you as you look in the morning, a bit chilly as you write to me. Yes, the cocks are supposed to crow early in the morning. Oftentimes I hear them crowing even during the night. And I never heard them so many times as during these nights in which I cannot sleep anymore!
    I am really in the most lamentable condition of spirit!—But I do not want to talk about me.
    How good you were! Getting up at six in the morning, you! And back to study! Your digging deep into the role of "Ellida" is perfect.[1] In her longing for freedom there is certainly a longing for love. You have got it

[1] The role of Ellida Wangler, the protagonist of Ibsen's *The Lady from the Sea*, which Marta interpreted for Pirandello's company from 1926 to 1928.

right. The husband is old, the sea is immense and always restless; the wave turns into itself, breaks out rumbling and then sucks itself again into a whirlpool, to start over once more turning into itself, without pause. I never understood the sea so well; I, who possess in my soul so many of its swirling waves, always new! And I feel as you do, about this poor Ellida. Make her sound like the breaking of the surf.

I am happy that *my* "Fulvia Gelli"[2] also begins to become *yours*, if you tell me that you like her more and more. Also there, I believe, there is room to go deeper. And I am sure that nobody will ever be able to get more completely inside her than you do.

Now, in order not to lose my mind (and believe me, dear Marta, I am really at the point of going mad!),[3] I plunged myself into *L'amica delle mogli*. I finished the second act. I won't tell you anything. You'll read it! I hope that in a few days also the third act, which I already started, will be finished. I will bring you in Genoa a second comedy to put together with the first. It is really written that salvation, in moments of the worst tempest, must come from work, to which I desperately cling.

Work, work . . .

Everything will pass. Also this tempest will pass. There is no need to find a buyer soon for the villino.[4] By the way, there are already two prospective buyers. But even if I do not find any, I already have a way to meet all my financial obligations. A lot of money is coming from abroad: Livingston[5] has announced the receipt of two thousand dollars from New York, which today is worth more than sixty thousand lire; and I have more than thirty with me; and Bemporad will have soon three more volumes ready: the novel *Uno nessuno e centomila* and the two volumes of the one-act plays, already corrected. During this year (and we are still far from the end of the year) I have already earned more than half a million.[6] All gone! Do you know that this daughter of mine was spending between twenty and twenty-five thousand lire every month?

Work, work . . .

[2] The role of Fulvia Gelli, the protagonist of Pirandello's *Come prima, meglio di prima*, was interpreted by Marta beginning October 17, 1926 (premiere at the Teatro Garibaldi in Padua).

[3] Pirandello refers here and a few lines lower to the family "tempest" of which he writes in letter 260805 (see also my notes to that letter and my introduction to the letters of 1926).

[4] Pirandello refers to his recently built home in the Via Onofrio Panvinio in Rome.

[5] Arthur Livingston, who translated a few plays by Pirandello into English.

[6] Although it is difficult to establish an exact correspondence of the value in today's dollars, there is no doubt that an annual income of half a million lire was substantial and should have allowed Pirandello to live comfortably without financial worries.

You'll see how *L'amica delle mogli* will turn out. I hope that this tempest will not prevent me from completing the third act. It would be a real pity. Because I do not know what other work is waiting for me, as you, dear Marta, remind me! But you will see me with all my strength undiminished.

. . . Yesterday, Monday, the contract for the Teatro Argentina was signed: it will be ours. This is of capital importance. I'll explain it to you later. The contract between me, Paradossi and Liberati[7] will be later discussed and signed in Genoa. I'll have you close to me and I'll have your advice, so precious to me. What are you doing? You don't tell anything about yourself. "God sings" is all right, but you are also Marta and I would like to know so many things! Enough! Regards to your parents, greetings to Cele, and always remember your Maestro.

Luigi Pirandello

[7] Giuseppe Paradossi and Franco Liberati had at the time a contract with the city of Rome for the use of the Teatro Argentina.

{ 260820 }

To Marta Abba
Milan
52, Via Cajazzo   Rome, 20 (evening). VIII. 1926
   Dear Marta,

I'm not getting any news from you nor any answer to my letters. What should I think? My mind is filled with the wildest suppositions; and in the meantime my work on *L'amica delle mogli*—which was flowing free and full of pure inspiration and getting near to completion—for the last three days has suddenly choked up and stopped.[1]

I think that your silence might have been caused by Feist's[2] visit to Milan. Did you see him? Did he tell you about the tempest in the middle of which he saw me? If so, however, I assume that you would have hurried to write to me, because the condition in which Feist saw me was much more serious than what I let you guess from my letters.

It is no better now, for sure.

[1] This is the first mention of Marta's important influence on the creative process of the Maestro. In the following letters of August 21 and 24, Pirandello first relates that he has started to write again, and then announces that he has finished the play, attributing the merit of it to Marta's desired letter, which in the meantime has arrived.

[2] Hans Feist, the translator into German of several works by Pirandello.

I can't wait for the next eight days to pass! I don't know how many of my things I'll be able to settle before leaving. I found a way to take care of all the payments now due. Eighty thousand lire are still left to pay before the end of the year; but I calculate at more than 160 thousand lire the income that is still outstanding. I can therefore relax. For the sale of the villino I am dealing with a certain Mr. Carlo Capo, who wants to pay me 950 thousand lire, 250 thousand at the time of closing and the rest, plus interest, over five years. I don't know whether I'll accept these terms— just to get rid of it. This villino is such a nuisance to me. If the guarantee of payment in installments is good, maybe I'll accept. But what shall I do with the money? For that matter, what should I do with my life, if I don't have anybody to whom I can give it? To me, life is of no use. I don't ask for any more beyond the time I need to finish the works that are left for me to write; because I feel it as an imperative obligation of my conscience, that I *must* write them. Without this, who knows where I would be by now—since that horrible night spent in Como![3]

But it is completely useless for me to write such things to you. And not even I know why I'm doing it. Please, forgive me! It is the moment I am going through!

Time is running out, and you must be all busy with the many things that are still to be taken care of, with the dressmaker, with the milliner: you do not find therefore a moment to write to your old Maestro—who maybe still deserves to be pitied if he laments the passing of something good that now is no longer there: your letters, so airy, so intelligent and full of life, in a moment of so many difficulties and so much sadness as the present one. They were the only air I could breathe! All the rest, suffocation!

. . . Best regards to your parents, warmest greetings to dear Cele and to you. Don't forget me! Cordially,

Luigi Pirandello

[3] Nothing is known about this "horrible night," here mentioned as something very familiar to Marta. We do not know the date, but it seems probable that it happened during the first of the two visits of the Compagnia di Pirandello to Como (October 1–6, 1925) rather than during the second one (May 11–21, 1926). Pirandello speaks of this night as of an event of catastrophic proportions in regard to his relation with Marta. As I already wrote in the Introduction, it is possible that an approximate description of the event is given by Pirandello himself in the final part of the second act of *Quando si è qualcuno*, when Veroccia throws in the old poet's face the memory of the traumatic moment in which she had offered herself totally to him and received a rational rejection. Something similar might have happened that night in Como, destroying Pirandello's hopes and plans of uniting his life totally to Marta's and precipitating the depression that caused him to

think many times about suicide. He was prevented from killing himself—at least if we believe his words—by an "imperative obligation" to continue writing imposed on him by his "conscience." The theme of "art as savior" as the only reason to keep living is constantly repeated in Pirandello. See, for instance, the *Epistolario familiare giovanile (1886– 1898)*, edited by Elio Providenti (Florence: Le Monier, 1986), pp. 40, 41, 51, or the end of letter CCIX 49 (1), in *Lettere da Bonn, 1889–1891*, Introduction and Notes by Elio Providenti (Rome: Bulzoni, 1984), p. 126. Hints at ending his own life are relatively frequent in the letters to Marta: see the entry Suicide in the Subject Index.

{ 260821 }

To Marta Abba
Milan
52, Via Cajazzo   Rome, 21 (evening). VIII. 1926
  My dear Marta,
  At last your letter—so clever and "volatile"—arrived today. With just a few strokes you made me see everything: you climbing a flight of stairs, with the perfect description of Bull;[1] you trying on a pink robe in front of the mirror; then asking me, with a pen in your hand: "What should I tell you?"; and quick you go out again, this time not really feeling like it, to try on your dress at Mrs. Palmer's,[2] with cordial and *trilling* greetings.
  As far as speed is concerned, your letter could hardly be quicker. That's why I called it *volatile*. I was a little disappointed when, reaching the point where you described yourself in the act of writing to me, you came up with the question: "What should I tell you about?" as if you really had nothing to tell me. But, right after that, I did remember that you really did tell me many things; that is, you had made me see many things as you went about your activities; and therefore my "thank you" is due, and I say so, with all my heart.
  I had not guessed wrong, when I wrote in yesterday's gloomy letter, that the reason for your delay in answering could have been Feist's visit in Milan. Dinner in your home, then a drive in the car with him. You did not tell me whether he spoke about me and about what he had seen and heard at my house.[3] I imagine that you must have asked something about

---

[1] Bull was Marta's dog; it appears in the letters also as Bullino.
[2] Marta Palmer, Marta's dressmaker.
[3] Dr. Feist had been an involuntary witness of the family quarrel described in letter 260805. Pirandello appears still extremely upset because of that "tempest" and confesses several lines later that it was spoiling his sleep and compelling him to write in order not to go mad.

me, at least whether he had seen me in Rome. But in the "volatile" letter you do not mention it; you get away with only one exclamation. "What a bore!" And Doctor Feist is disposed of.

Skipping away, you close the letter, letting me know that "you are rather happy!"

I do thank you again for sharing—with the exuberant whimsy that gallops through the whole letter—this happiness of yours (although I don't know where it comes from). It was the breath of fresh air I badly needed. I got back to the third act of *L'amica delle mogli* and I hope that tomorrow the play—one more play—will be finished. You see that, although in the middle of so much tempest *and with my soul prostrated,* I kept my promise. And believe me, I kept it only because I had made this promise to you. My keeping it is owing to the lack of sleep; so many nights I cannot sleep at all. *And I have been writing* in order not to go mad.

I hope at least some of your happiness is due to this—the new play was born from you and for you. And so it is really yours. Do you remember the first time we spoke about it together? And now, a few days later, it is finished.

Writing, oftentimes, is also a way of staying together with somebody.

My letters take a few days to reach you because I only get out of the house late in the evening, and not every night—just when I have a letter to mail to you. It is my excuse for my nightly walk to Porta Pia. There is a mailbox on the square in front of Porta Pia: I mail the letter and come right back. Only once Bontempelli did come to see me, after the duel.[4] Maybe after finishing the play I'll write a short story for the *Corriere della Sera,* since Ojetti[5] wrote to me again asking for one.

But now only seven days remain to get through: only seven days.[6]

Send me your news, less "volatile" please. Regards to your parents, warm greetings to Cele. Cordially from your Maestro,

Luigi Pirandello

---

[4] Pirandello refers to the duel between Massimo Bontempelli and the poet Giuseppe Ungaretti, on August 9 of that year, which took place in the garden of Pirandello's villino in Via Onofrio Panvinio.

[5] The writer Ugo Ojetti, then managing editor of the *Corriere della Sera* of Milan.

[6] On August 29 Pirandello and Marta were going to meet again in Genoa.

Letters of 1928
from Rome and Nettuno

DURING the two years since the last letter of August 25, 1926, Marta had been living very close to the Maestro. She had helped him with his intensive work at the helm of the company, sharing at his side the many struggles and the high hopes for the realization of the grand dream of transforming Pirandello's company into an all-star, state-subsidized national theater. The company's achievements since 1925 had merited national and international recognition and demonstrated the artistic feasibility of the enterprise: in almost four years of prodigious creativity as artistic director, Pirandello had presented fifty productions—some of which still rank in the history of the European theater as among the best of the period—in all major Italian cities, and also in Germany, Czechoslovakia, Austria, Hungary, Argentina, Uruguay, and Brazil. The collapse of official support and the consequent demise of the company, made unavoidable by its financial nonviability, had caused profound bitterness in the Maestro. He could never forgive those "enemies" who had made impossible the success of his noncommercial venture because they had systematically denied the use of major theaters in critical locations—thus undermining the company's very existence. No wonder that in these letters Pirandello uses violent expressions against this "gang of enemies," together with bitter criticism of the Italian situation under fascism. At this point, Pirandello felt compelled to flee from his country and look abroad for the success that was denied him at home. A new plan was taking shape in his mind and determining his new course of action: he and Marta were to tap the resources of countries that promised much larger financial rewards than Italy, become very rich abroad through the cinema, and eventually return to Italy surrounded with international fame and loaded with enough cash to allow him to independently finance a new noncommercial, truly artistic company centered on Marta Abba.

Pirandello's anguish and anger at the failure of the dream of a national theater was made even more difficult to bear by the continuing painful family situation. Pirandello had always been a family man, very attached to his children. Lietta, the daughter who, before Marta entered his life, had occupied a very special place in his heart, especially during the painful years of his wife's mental illness, was still in Chile, far away with her husband, and the relationship had not really warmed since the family quarrel of 1926.[1] Moreover Pirandello deeply resented the opposition of his family to his involvement with Marta, to whom he would tell his pain with expressions typical of a wounded paternal love—that he had no more family upon this earth.

The letters of 1928 are divided into two groups. The first consists of eight letters written during the short summer vacation of the company (June 29–July 15). The second consists of five letters written during the separation necessary to prepare the trip to Germany (second half of August to September 28).

The letters of the first group are addressed to the Grand Hôtel des Termes in Salsomaggiore, where Marta was vacationing; Pirandello writes—with the exception of the first letter sent from Rome—from the summer resort of Nettuno, Pensione Neptunia, Via di Anzio 39. The letters of the second group were all sent from Rome, Via Onofrio Panvinio 11, and addressed to Milan, Via Cajazzo 52.

The principal subjects treated in these letters are the negotiations with representatives of moving-picture companies; Italy as a "dunghill" from which it was necessary to go far away; the new dream of great riches and complete financial independence; advice to Marta's father on the occasion of a challenge to a duel; and the function of Pirandello as "physician" of Marta's soul.

Pirandello is in the middle of feverish negotiations with agencies and representatives of German and American film producers, with the pur-

---

[1] The correspondence of the years 1922–23 between father and daughter, published in part by Pirandello's granddaughter Maria Luisa Aguirre D'Amico in the already mentioned *Vivere con Pirandello*, gives an insight into the extraordinary importance for Pirandello of his love for Lietta during the unhappy years of Antonietta's illness before meeting Marta. Lietta's departure for Chile in 1922 after her marriage to Manuel had deeply wounded Pirandello, who uses in his letters such expressions as "I am longing, I am immensely longing to see you, to hug you hard, as hard as possible to me, to kiss you on your little head, to listen to your saying . . . *papy, papy* . . . I feel like there is nobody left anymore, there is nothing left anymore" (p. 107); "You must absolutely come back as soon as possible, if you don't want me to die of this anguish that cannot be relieved" (p. 107); and, desperate because of lack of news, he also writes: "Anxiety keeps me in a constant frenzy, like a madman, and I don't know what I should do" (p. 114). Such expressions, as well as those previously written to his future wife, Antonietta, during their engagement, should be taken into consideration when interpreting similar extreme expressions in Pirandello's correspondence with Marta—who replaced, in the function of confidante, Lietta, who earlier had replaced Antonietta.

pose of selling scenarios for silent movies he had himself drawn from his short stories, novels, and plays. Such negotiations are tied together with those to sell a "secret" creation of his fantasy; that is, the use of the newly discovered sound film as a visual illustration of musical masterpieces.

Pirandello reveals himself as increasingly disgusted and offended by what is happening in Italy; his great hope of an intervention by Mussolini to decide through an authoritarian fiat the foundation of a national theater in Italy has by now vanished; it has been replaced by the dismayed realization that the systematic inefficiency of the Fascist government was in reality tactics well planned by Mussolini himself to prevent anyone from reaching a position of success and therefore of power in Italy. This "revelation" of the deepest cause of the failure of his hopes for the transformation of his company into the impressive national theater disgusts Pirandello to such an extent that he decides to leave behind the Italian "dunghill" and to look for a new life abroad, not excluding the possibility of never returning to Italy.

A certain Mr. Zopegni had offended in public Marta's honor with a "lie"—probably related to Pirandello's much-talked-about infatuation for her—and Marta's father had punched him in public. Mr. Zopegni had challenged Mr. Abba to a duel. Pirandello is generous with advice and at the same time tries to calm Marta, who was evidently very upset about the whole thing. The duel never took place.

Letter 280713—a testimony of Pirandello's esteem for Marta as a person strictly bound in her conscience to religious and moral values—is of special importance for a definition of Pirandello's relationship to the actress. Pirandello believes that such "scruples" are damaging Marta's physical and spiritual health and offers to act as "physician" to heal all her diseases himself. Letter 280712 finally presents a first lifting of the veil that has so far covered the tumultuous love of the Maestro for the young actress.

{ 280705 }

Miss Marta Abba
Grand Hôtel des Termes
Salsomaggiore   Nettuno, 5. VII. 1928

My dear Marta,

I am writing from Nettuno, where I found a beautiful room here in the Albergo Neptunia, with a window overlooking the magnificent villa of the Borghese princes—the one surrounded by the famous pine grove. A wide terrace faces the sea, with Porto d'Anzio on the right, and the ancient Castello d'Astura far away to the left on the horizon. Everything is peaceful here. The silence in the pine grove is eroded by the steady chirping of the cicadas and embroidered with the merry sound of the birds. And over there, the wideness of the sea sparkles in the sunshine.

I did not have enough room in Stefano's small apartment. I'm not complaining; on the contrary, I am very happy. They'll be less crowded, and I'll be more comfortable. By the way, I don't really have to stay in Nettuno. I'll see how it works out with my writing here all day long. If it works out well, I'll stay, even though I have to go to Rome every other day. Otherwise I'll leave tomorrow morning and go and stay at the villino.[1]

. . . I'd love to have my paints here with me. Looking at the pine grove I am overcome with an immense longing to paint. I wish I could make you at least a sketch of this scene. The gray skeletons of two huge cypresses loom over the other dark green, sun-drenched trees. One is a little bent, very sad-looking; the other, on the contrary, is straight and powerful. It gives me great pain to look at it among so many living fellow trees; all dried up and without a single leaf, but still completely whole in the texture of the twigs and branches that outlined its crown on the once vigorous trunk. I am sure that if I had brushes, palette, and colors I could well express this pain; and you, some time later, looking at this tree, dead but still standing among the ones that are smaller but still alive, you would think. . . .[2] But away with gloomy thoughts! If you could only hear this shrill, insistent chirping of the cicadas! Maybe, by this time, they have started to chirp in the trees of the park in front of your hotel. It's a dear voice of the summer, though, this chirping of the cicadas.

Last night I sat out on the terrace until two A.M., just watching the moon on the sea. And I was thinking that it is a standing joke to say that nowadays people do not care about the moon anymore, since every city street has plenty of moons in rows. Yes, many; but one street lamp lights a twenty-yard circle; with this moon, on the other hand, while I was watching it this night on the sea, Marta could see it from her window over the trees of the park in Salsomaggiore. And I could picture you at the window of your little room. . . . But you, certainly, at two A.M. of this night, must have been asleep in your bed.

I can't wait to receive your news. How are you doing, how is your rest treatment working out, how are you spending these long, hot days? Your

[1] His new home on Via Onofrio Panvinio in Rome.
[2] Pirandello hints at how Marta will remember him after his death.

father wrote to me, transcribing the letter the challenging seconds sent to him, and asking my opinion about the one Prof. Geraci dictated to him to send in answer.[3] I replied immediately, approving that answer; and so the business will be finished and we'll not need to talk about it any longer.

I am petrified to be left alone with myself. All the beasts of my cage wake up to tear me to pieces. And I do not know how to placate them. What an anguish to watch life with this feeling I have, that I am deprived of it. I press against my bosom, as tight as I can, a consoling Image.[4]

Regards to your mother and Cele. I remain always cordially yours,

Luigi Pirandello

[3] The letter of July 6, 1928, which is not translated in this volume, is largely devoted to details of this painful issue.

[4] A photograph of Marta.

{ 280708 }

Miss Marta Abba
Grand Hôtel des Termes
Salsomaggiore   Nettuno, 8. VII. 1928

Dear Marta,

Yesterday I was in bed for the whole day with a high fever and an upset stomach. I probably caught a cold in my stomach. But it's nothing serious. No doubt I'll be completely over it by tomorrow, and I'll go back to Rome. I can't wait for these days of exile to be over. I don't get any rest and I can hardly even breathe anymore. If only I could work! I cannot. I have been without food for two days; and this heat, my weakness, and the flies. . . .

Enough. I don't want to bother you, dear Marta, by talking about myself. I read in the *Corriere* that His Excellency Bottai[1] has summoned for tomorrow the theater company managers, producers, critics, et al., to discuss the crisis of the theater. Tomorrow I'll be in Rome and I'll see what it's all about, and I'll report to you immediately.

It is, however, useless, for the time being, to hope that any serious decision might be taken. There will be the usual empty words. If the government really wants to do something for the theaters, it shouldn't consult anybody. It has consulted so many people so many times, and it

[1] Giuseppe Bottai was one of the founders of the Fascist party in 1919. In 1924, he became undersecretary, then minister of corporations, governor of Rome, and in 1936 minister of education.

has never done anything. If it keeps on consulting people who will never be able to agree with each other, because their interests are opposite, it is a sign that it intends to put up a show of concern for the theater, but after all that it will still do nothing—and who knows for how long!

. . . We must definitely go away from Italy for some time, and come back only when we will not be dependent on anyone for anything; that is, *da padroni.*[2] Here you see nothing but everybody tearing each other to pieces, in public and privately, with the purpose of making it impossible for anybody to actually achieve something that everyone is shamelessly fighting for. Politics pervades everything. Slander, calumny, and intrigue are the weapons everybody is using. Life in Italy has become stifling.

Out! out! far! far away!

How are you doing, Marta? The fact that your cough has not yet disappeared worries me; but it will clear up, I'm sure, by the end of your treatment. Don't worry about anything, and relax; know that everything will be all right as soon as we are free from the nightmare of the company,[3] in the new life that is opening before us.

Regards to your mother and to Cele. My best greetings to you. Cordially,

Luigi Pirandello

[2] Literally "like masters." Pirandello often repeats this expression, which summarizes his dream of independence from the monopoly of the "gang of enemies" and from the maddening Fascist bureaucracy. Pirandello sees only one possible way to realize in Italy his dream of an independent artistic theater; that is, to leave Italy and make a great deal of money in the film world abroad.

[3] By this time, Pirandello's acting company had turned into a nightmare because of the fiascos of the last months, the continuous opposition of its enemies, and the serious financial losses. The nightmare was to end in Viareggio only a few weeks after this letter, with the last performance on August 1.

{ 280712 }

Miss Marta Abba
Grand Hôtel des Termes
Salsomaggiore Nettuno, Thursday 12. VII. 1928[1]

My dear Marta,

. . . You tell me about the wonders of a film you went to see. Yes, dear Marta, wonderful things indeed can be done with the movies. I have been convinced of it for quite a while and, you'll see, I'll succeed in doing

[1] Pirandello dated this letter by mistake Thursday 11. The date stamped on the envelope

exactly that—things that will astonish everybody—if I only set my mind
to it. I have extraordinary ideas. And I cannot wait to wind up things
here[2] in order to carry them out and go away from this country of ours
where things happen that are never mentioned aloud—such that I cannot
narrate by letter but which I'll tell you about in person in Genoa. I spoke
at length about them with Interlandi,[3] from whom I received the information; and more and more I got confirmed in the idea of leaving my
country—convinced as I am that for someone like me it is no longer
possible to live in Italy. I'll return, if I ever return, when I will no longer
need anybody. In the meantime you should immediately get your pass-
port renewed.

. . . I was able to work very little at *Lazzaro* because of the intestinal
pain I mentioned to you before, which has continued through today. I
came and went to and from Rome on this, that, or the other errand, and
time has gone by more in reading than in writing. As far as writing is
concerned, I wrote to you, every day. I was so happy to see your previous
letters signed "Marta"—the last one, that of today, was on the contrary
signed "Marta Abba" and was cold, icy cold.

Please do not interpret this remark as a reproach. If you only could
realize how much good your letters do me and how I have blessed them
all! I wish I knew music to express, without being understood by anyone,
not even by you, all this tumult of life that swells my soul and my heart.
Nobody will ever know it, dear Marta, even if my heart should explode
because of it.[4] Enough. This exile will be over soon.[5] Best greetings to
your mother and to Cele, and please accept the most cordial greetings of
your

Luigi Pirandello

---

by the Nettuno post office is July 13. As he often did, Pirandello probably wrote the letter
during the night of the twelfth and mailed it on the following morning, Friday, July 13.

[2] Pirandello probably means the conclusion of pending business before leaving for Germany.

[3] The journalist Telesio Interlandi was the managing editor of the Roman newspaper *Il
Tevere*.

[4] Pirandello appears to be always afraid to write about his tumultuous love for Marta,
who used to dismiss such declarations as "useless chatter." The frequent hints at the torment of his heart are kept mostly behind a veil of shame and reservation and only rarely
explode into explicit words of passionate love. See in the Subject Index the entry Love.

[5] With the word "exile" Pirandello here means his separation from Marta, which was to
end in a few days.

{ 280713 }

Miss Marta Abba
Grand Hôtel des Termes
Salsomaggiore   Nettuno, Friday 13. VII. 1928

My dear Marta,

Here I have your letter, the first one to reach me here directly. It is long, beautiful, very beautiful, with that extremely effective description of a scene from the film, showing me that girl lost in the fog of a big city like London or Berlin with such expressive power that I had the feeling I was watching it on the screen with you. And then you say it is not true that with a little work and concentration you could become a writer! You are a born writer. But you are also ALL,[1] Marta mia. And believe me, all you are suffering—your tiredness, your aches, all the pains that seem to be coming from the body but are not, pains of which no physician will ever find the cause—have on the contrary their root in this: that they are Life, all the Life that is in you, all the possibilities of being that are in you and live in you, without your even realizing it. They wear you out, distress you, depress you, exasperate you, continuously and vehemently taking your spirit by storm, or trying to forcibly remove the blocks of your conscience—perhaps too narrow and bourgeois—inside which you keep yourself bottled up. Meanwhile your will remains inert and does not rise up either to defend your body from these violent winds of the spirit which so many times I see flashing through your astonished and engrossed eyes, or to persuade your conscience to release those brakes and satisfy the bursting demands of both your spirit and your flesh. I could be a great physician for you, my Marta. But it would be necessary that you be entrusted to my care alone.

Please do not think that I have neglected to give long, steady, and increasingly productive thoughts to the scenario of *Six Characters*.[2] I have it by now almost all completed in my mind. As soon as we'll be together,

[1] The word TUTTO, here translated as ALL and printed in capital letters, is written by Pirandello in letters double the size of the rest of the words. The same is true of other words a few paragraphs later, here printed in capital letters.

[2] This scenario of *Six Characters in Search of an Author* is published in F. Cállari, *Pirandello e il cinema* (Venice: Marsilio, 1991). The actual filming of *Six Characters* was never carried out, notwithstanding great efforts and great hopes on the part of Pirandello and the sincere interest of many companies, including UFA, Luce, Terrafilm, Paramount, and other individual producers. See the Name Index, under *Six Characters . . .* , Ferreira, Megole, Kahn, etc.

in Genoa, I'll explain it to you for your approval and, who knows, maybe also your collaboration, because I want this work to be in everything and for everything OURS, born from THE TWO OF US, one thing only and OURS. You'll see how many ideas I have thought about, and how well it will come out; and everything will be clear, extraordinarily powerful on the levels of fantasy and drama!

Ferreira and Megole[3] have not yet written; but in a letter from Fausto that arrived yesterday from Paris the business deal was described as concluded;[4] and it is certain that they themselves have told him. Maybe they are again in Berlin also for the other deal: the one about Beethoven, which would open a completely new field to cinematography, as visual expression, no longer of the word, but of music: melography. Marta, that is the way to our fortune.

The project of the newspaper?[5] Yes, I saw Interlandi every time I went to Rome and I spoke with him for more than two hours each time. He is ready to start the newspaper at the drop of my hat. But I do not have any confidence, now less than ever, because of all I know, because of all he himself told me and that I cannot write in a letter, but that I will communicate in person: incredible things, dear Marta, that have increased my horror toward my country and my firm belief that, at least for the time being, for me, life is no longer possible here. We must stay in Germany for one year at least, as I wrote you yesterday, and put together a great fortune. Then we'll come back rich, and independent of everyone, but da padroni.[6]

This is the next-to-last letter that I am writing to you.[7] Today is the 13th. I hope to receive tomorrow another answer from you with the indication of the time when you're arriving in Genoa on the 16th. I'll come to get you at the train station, and I'll make reservations at the hotel. I cannot believe it myself, that this exile is almost at its end.[8]

Regards to your mother and Cele, and all my most cordial greetings to you.

Your Luigi Pirandello

[3] Owners of a Paris-based company interested in producing the film of *Six Characters*.

[4] Pirandello's son Fausto was living in Paris.

[5] The project seems to have later evolved into the publication of *Lunario siciliano*, a journal that started in Rome in 1929. About the extreme characteristics of Sicilianism and Fascist purity of this publication, see Frassica, *A Marta Abba per non morire*, pp. 80–81, and the introductory essay by Leonardo Sciascia, "Del dormire con un solo occhio," to the *Opere, 1932–1946, di Vitaliano Brancati* (Milan: Bompiani, 1987), pp. x–xi.

[6] See footnote 2 to letter 280708.

[7] In reality this was the last letter of this group.

[8] The exile of the separation from Marta.

{ 280922 }

To Marta Abba
52, Via Cajazzo
Milan

Rome, 22. IX. 1928
Via Onofrio Panvinio 11

My dear Marta,

Yesterday evening Interlandi came to my house for supper and stayed until after midnight. He told me about the confusion in everyone's mind, because of the uncertainty of each individual's situation. By now the tactics are clear.[1] As soon as somebody gives a sign of achieving a preeminent position in any field—however diligently he might watch out and defend himself, being careful, with an eye on everything, ready to avoid traps and to foil plots—things start to happen in such a way that he himself will start to feel uncomfortable at any move he makes, at any step he takes, and he is thus obliged—being deprived of any support—to get back in line. For someone else, disparagements, vague accusations, or even open polemics immediately begin—starting, stopping, and starting all over again. For a third person, who already boasts of being sure of his influence and of having an acknowledged and recognized power, there is suddenly a flat denial, a definite setback that knocks him down into a most embarrassing position, and so on. The purpose of this all is to make sure that nobody gets his head up. Around Him, a level of heads reaching only to his knee, and not an inch higher. This way everything remains forcibly low and confused, and there is really nothing left but mediocrity and confusion.

We talked about Bisi,[2] at the helm of the Ente Nazionale per la Cinematografia. He seemed very favorably disposed toward me. But I found out that Bisi, so soon after his promotion, is no longer sure of his job. It looks as if he will be fired, and it is not known who will take his place. It's a continuous doing and undoing, putting in and putting out. A feeling of debilitating and distressing instability is growing in everyone.

After chatting for three hours, I felt more and more discouraged, as if I could not even breathe anymore.

---

[1] Pirandello talks here evidently of Mussolini and of his tactics to make impossible the rise of any rival power in Italy. This letter explains one of the main reasons why Pirandello decided to leave his country and reside in Berlin; that is, Italy's stifling atmosphere under Mussolini's dictatorship.

[2] Tommaso Bisi had been recently promoted from the position of undersecretary for national economy to director of the Ente Nazionale per la Cinematografia.

Yes, dear Marta, we must definitely go away, to breathe, to work, and regain a sense of our own personality. I can't wait!

I'm waiting for an answer to the telegrams I sent yesterday. In the meantime I'm getting ready to leave; and I'm lining up all the work I want to do. You'll see how much there is, and how many things we'll accomplish!

What did you find new in Milan? How are you spending these days of delay?

I'm waiting with an anxiety you can imagine for your news—hopefully today, maybe tomorrow.

Bemporad sent me a big bunch of galleys to proofread.

I'll see you again in a few days, dear Marta. Best greetings to your family. Cordially and affectionately yours,

Luigi Pirandello

{ 280925 }

To Marta Abba
52, Via Cajazzo
Milan

Rome, 25. IX. 1928
Via Onofrio Panvinio 11

My dear Marta,

Here it is, Via Cajazzo 52—not 56! Can you believe that I tore up the envelope of the first letter I wrote you, where I had written 52, because it did not look right to me? It did not look right because the 2 looked like it was borrowed from the 22 of Via Torino (and as if it could not belong just as well to the 50 of Via Cajazzo).[1] Therefore Via Torino 22 and Via Cajazzo 56 sounded right and I thought it was correct. So see where my hearing led me, my great driver of automobiles! It seems auspicious that you are learning how to drive. Soon in America you'll be driving not an ordinary Ford, but a supercar of a supermake on the superhighways of Hollywood; you, superstar Marta, queen of all the

---

[1] The address Via Torino 22 was the Chincaglieria Abba, the store of Marta's father, where a variety of articles were sold, such as perfumes, toys, umbrellas, luggage, leather goods, pearls, jewelry, glassware, and objects of art. Via Cajazzo 52 was Mr. Abba's home address, located on the then outskirts of Milan. Pirandello explains here how he made a mistake in writing the number of Marta's home, to which error he will attribute—in the letter 280926, here not translated—the possible loss of a few of his letters.

screens of the world! The telegram from Treuberg is most promising.[2] We have reason to expect that the big door will open for you![3] and also for me—the door of business. We'll make big money,[4] and then you'll go back—da padrona—to the theater. As far as I am concerned, after fulfilling my mission, I'll get out of your way, and my spirit will go on living in you, my dear Marta, if you choose to keep on giving me life in your memory![5]

Let's not talk about sad things! I just finished shaving, and I looked at myself in the mirror. I should never look at the mirror, I should only see myself for how I am and how I feel—in the power of my brain, the vigor of my soul, and the prodigious force of my nerves.

... We'll wait a few more days for news from Treuberg from New York. We'll go for sure to someplace or other, very soon; and therefore you are right to get ready in a hurry for the departure. We won't remain in Italy beyond October 8. Feist wrote to me that he is already in Berlin to prepare for our arrival. He is happy about our decision. He says it would be good to stay for the first few days at the Adlon because it is the headquarters of the whole motion-picture industry for both Germany and the world. But I hear it is very expensive.

... I have already booked the wagon-lit for the evening of the 27th, and therefore I'll be in Milan on the 28th at 8:30 A.M. As soon as you get up, call me at the Corso Hotel and tell me what I should do; I'm dying to see you again. I keep on working, and in the meantime I am getting ready for a long absence, and perhaps I may never return—although I know that Mr. Blanc is working at getting me together with Mussolini before my departure from Milan for Germany (in which case, maybe, I would have to run quickly to Rome for this audience, but I do not believe it will happen)[6] and notwithstanding the fact that Lucio d'Ambra[7] came yesterday to assure me that I'll be appointed senator in January and he was ready to bet a lot of money on it.[8] If it is true, the appointment will reach me in Germany or in America. But forget it! ... Away, away, away, from this dunghill! Air! air! air!

Best regards to your family. With warm affection, yours,

Luigi Pirandello

---

[2] Bubi Treuberg was in New York and was taking care of some business for Pirandello in the United States.

[3] The door to American show business.

[4] In a letter of his youth, in 1886, Pirandello had written: "From now on I'll follow no other inspiration but this one: making money" (see Elio Providenti, *Mnemosine: Archeologie pirandelliane* [Catania: Giuseppe Maimone, 1990], p. 39). In a true sense Pirandello

retained, as long as he lived, the same naïveté—always dreaming about making big money fast!

[5] Eight years later this prediction became partly true when Pirandello, after making possible Marta's debut on Broadway in 1936, "got out of her way" by dying alone in Rome—while his dream of making Marta famous in America was becoming a reality. Pirandello outlines here again his plan for the few years he thought were left for him to live: he will conquer the world of the German and American cinema, become super-rich, and at the same time open the door for Marta to reach international celebrity status as a movie star. All of the above with the purpose of getting back to Italy, loaded with glory and money, and devoting himself to "art theater" da padrone; that is, with no need of depending on the "dunghill" of Italian politics and on the financial omnipotence of the theatrical monopoly. The escape to Germany is considered an important step in the realization of the plan.

[6] The colloquy with the Duce before the departure for Germany never took place. It is, however, certain that Mussolini was not pleased with the voluntary exile of the famous playwright.

[7] Author of novels, plays, and criticism.

[8] Pirandello was never appointed to the Italian senate.

Letters of 1929 and 1930
from Berlin, Rome, and Milan

TWO TRAUMATIC EVENTS in Pirandello's life define the fifteen months covered by this large group of letters: the shock of Marta's departure from Berlin on March 13, 1929, and the dismay at the tumultuous fiasco of *Tonight We Improvise* on May 31, 1930—which precipitated Pirandello's decision to abandon Berlin a few days later on June 12.

Marta had been with the Maestro in the German metropolis for five months. They had arrived in Berlin together, probably on October 10, 1928, with great hopes of rapidly establishing a new career in the German silent-film industry and, through Germany, also in the French and American film world. They lived in two rooms, one adjacent to the other (Marta had with her most of the time her sister Cele). They were seen always together, in expensive restaurants, theaters, and fashionable night clubs. Negotiations with film companies were pursued relentlessly and appeared to promise good results. However, after five months, neither a contract for the purchase of a scenario by Pirandello nor an acting engagement for Marta had been signed. Meanwhile the pressure of the Abba family on Marta was steadily growing. Her parents were concerned that the long absence from the Italian stage would result in a serious loss of precious time for Marta's career in Italy. They were also afraid that Pirandello's promises of international stardom and enormous riches would never come true. Marta's family had maintained an ambivalent, and sometimes definitely contrary, attitude toward her relationship with the Maestro, which, at least from the outside, looked much more intimate than it really was, thus causing plenty of gossip and tasteless jokes in theatrical circles and in the tabloids. Marta had grown impatient and tired of waiting. A very active woman, full of initiative and down-to-earth common sense, and above all an authentic actress determined to succeed, she wanted to be on the stage. In Berlin she felt condemned to inertia and thoroughly isolated because she did not speak the language. By now the flame of love for the Maestro had cooled off, and his continually, obses-

sive attentions were probably no longer really welcome to her. Marta's
decision to leave and face the Italian theater world alone found Pirandello
completely unprepared. For the last five years he had been literally living
inside his dream of Marta's love. With an increasing passion that was
idealizing and almost deifying its object, he had built for himself an idyllic refuge, away from the desolation of his unhappiness, far from his existential pessimism and his habitual inward loneliness and pain. Because of
this love he had grown more and more alienated from his family, increasingly depending on Marta for everything. At this point, it would have
been absurd for him even to entertain the thought that the feelings of his
beloved for him could be of a different nature from his own for her or that
time had changed them. Marta's departure struck him like a bolt of lightning. His letters narrate a story of an almost constant despair following
that ill-fated moment; the ensuing depression leads him to the brink of
suicide, from which only Marta's compassionate visit saves him. He
counts Marta's letters, the time each one of them took to reach him. He
continually reproaches her for not writing enough and invariably declares his dejection, thus showing an obsessive condition at the limit of,
or already beyond the bounds of, sanity. At this point Pirandello repeats
several times that he is already dead, because his only life was Marta, and
now, without Marta, he is no longer alive. The trips to Paris and to Italy,
during which he briefly meets his beloved, do not heal; rather they worsen
a condition of despair that is expressed in the letters, with various degrees
of intensity, during this entire period.

Against the background of this anguish, Pirandello escapes into a restless creative activity. He certainly does not look "already dead!" The playwright completes *O di uno o di nessuno*, works at *Come tu mi vuoi*, develops the vast structure of *I giganti della montagna*, and outlines the first
ideas for *Quando si è qualcuno*. Admitted to the Accademia d'Italia, he
receives the first intimations of his candidacy for the Nobel Prize. The
negotiations he had been nurturing since his arrival in Berlin now start to
give the first concrete results. A trip to London gives him the opportunity
to experience sound film for the first time, but the new invention produces such a horrible impression in him that it suggests the idea of utiliz-
ing those grotesque sounds to produce the effect of deformed human
voices. He therefore comes out publicly against the spoken film, but only
for a short time. A while later, however, before leaving Berlin, he is already a fervent convert, a defender of sound film as a possible new means
of valid artistic expression. Toward the end of the Berlin period the first
contract with an American company is signed. Paramount promises a

large amount of money and paid trips to New York and Hollywood. This victory is celebrated by an enthusiastic Pirandello as the first step toward the fabulous riches that will allow him to return to Italy independently wealthy, da padrone. The trips to Paris and to Italy and the short visits to Marta, however, make him more and more aware that Marta will never give him the warm, exclusive, and total love that he so desperately needs. He finds Marta incredibly busy with the formation of her new company and the planning of a courageous tour of Italian cities. Marta is overtired and tense in the continuous struggle against a theater world that remains basically hostile to her and her enterprise. She has other things on her mind, and Pirandello's lovesick lamentations cannot but appear to her as "useless words," completely out of place. Pirandello is afflicted by a swollen cheek and a dangerous case of pleurisy, troubles that certainly do not help to heal his deep depression. In addition, never-ending legal complications and never-absent anger at incapable or dishonest agents as usual mar his daily life.

An unexpected, disastrous blow, which causes Pirandello to leave Berlin for good, hits him when *Tonight We Improvise* opens at the Lessing-Theater. Pirandello had set his highest hopes on the great success of this play in Berlin. In his plans, it was to mean the beginning of a long series of performances of his plays in major theaters all over Germany. At the time he was seriously considering settling down for good in Berlin, where he hoped also to establish his permanent base for his international film deals. In Germany he expected to get much larger profits from the royalties for his works than he had ever received in Italy. He was finally starting to feel recognized and highly esteemed. In order to ensure a smash hit he had taken care of every detail for the production of *Tonight We Improvise*: the trial runs out of town (which had an enormous success in Königsberg), the choice of a famous director and of the best available actors, the choice of the Lessing-Theater, and the details that would give the event an atmosphere of special importance, announced with the greatest expectation by the press. Pirandello was not aware that dark clouds of hostility had been gathering for some time because of rising extreme nationalism, the hatred against him drummed up by a group allegedly organized by his former translator, Hans Feist, the special circumstance of the failure of Max Reinhardt's latest play, the perception that Pirandello had ridiculed the revered German director in the new play, and, finally, because of the unpopularity of the director he had chosen and his inadequate staging. A well-organized group in the audience came prepared with whistles to disrupt the performance of the opening night, and an almost unanimous, violently negative series of reviews of the play and of Pirandello in all major newspapers made the play a resounding fiasco.

Pirandello could not take the defeat. Once again he felt persecuted, unwanted, offended, as he had felt in Italy. Once again he fled. Berlin, on the brink of becoming his chosen second home, suddenly became an intolerable nest of enemies. After fifteen months of residence in the German capital, the writer took the definitive decision to leave forever. Meanwhile the socioeconomic crisis that was to bring the Nazi party to power was raging and destroying the chances of success of Pirandello's many German hopes.

{ 290314 }

To Marta Abba
Via Cajazzo 52
Milan (Italy)   Berlin, 14. III. 1929
                                                          Hotel Herkuleshaus
                                                    Friedrich-Wilhelmstr. 10

My dear Marta,

You are still traveling, and I still follow you with my thoughts as I've been doing since the first moment the train departed.[1] How I was feeling—you can imagine. I don't know how you could assume that I would go for supper to the Aida.[2] Supper? How, with this lump of anguish that locks my throat? Do you believe that I will ever succeed in dissolving it if you don't come back? I returned home, threw myself into the armchair near the window, and remained there, I don't know how long, in the dark, with only the glimmer coming from the street lamps down in the square. The silence from the adjacent room, where until a few hours ago you had lived, was filling me with a sense of death. I wept out my sorrow for hours and hours. Forgive me if I tell you this. I was alone and able to cry. At 10:30, exhausted, after getting out your pictures and taking with me your small alarm clock, I went to bed. This little alarm clock that marks the cruel hours of loneliness into which I was plunged, yet keeps me so much company! You, too, I muse, were used to hearing its ticking in your ear whenever you had it near you.

I awoke this morning at 6:30, and I remained in bed until 8:00, when

---

[1] Marta's decision to depart from Berlin had a traumatic effect on Pirandello. The almost daily letters that follow are among the most desperate, full of loneliness and anguish.

[2] An Italian restaurant in Berlin often patronized by Pirandello.

the maid came into the study to light the stove. I had her bring me coffee and prepare the bath.

I've been here at the desk since 9:00. But I couldn't write anything! Two, three times I tried; it's impossible. I look at your picture smiling at me, as if to give me courage. Then I think that this is not true; that this image smiles for itself, and not for me; and then this smile, which is so beautiful, so full of noble grace, turns cruel to me, and my glance reproaches it, while my heart delights in it.

Let's hope that fate, at least one more time before I close my eyes forever, might want to be kind to me and lead you back to me, Marta, so that I may get back one reason for living, which now is missing completely.

I do not know how I'll make it to Solari's in a little while.[3] I don't wish to see anyone. I cannot eat. What do I have to talk about? It seems that everything no longer has any meaning.

Philips[4] called to tell me that Lantz[5] will arrive today at 5:00; Felix Bloch-Erben called to say that Wreede[6] will arrive at 6:00. To speak about business, yes, maybe I could; because it will seem to bring me closer to you, or to look for a way to do so; and also because you advised me to. But we need to bring to conclusion the big business deal that would solve everything, for you and for me.[7]

I am eagerly waiting for a word from you.

I will keep you informed of everything. But it is necessary that you give me the strength to endure. Only you can give it to me.

I'll keep following you with my thoughts as you travel until 7:45. And from 8:00 on I will picture you at home. I see it as if I were there.

And you, do you see me?

Goodbye, Marta. Goodbye.

Luigi Pirandello

[3] Pietro Solari was the Berlin correspondent of the periodical *L'Italia letteraria*. During Pirandello's exile in Berlin he was, with his family, very friendly to the playwright.

[4] Pirandello spells this name Philips or Philipps. He was an employee of the Tonfilm Company in Berlin.

[5] The scenarist Adolf Lantz was employed by Pirandello as helper/secretary during his stay in Berlin.

[6] Fritz Wreede (Pirandello here spells it Whrede) was the director of the Felix Bloch-Erben Theatrical Agency, where the contract that gave Hans Feist the right to be the translator of Pirandello's plays into German was signed.

[7] In all probability Pirandello alludes to the contract for films illustrating famous music compositions, a project from which he expected world success and enormously lucrative box office sales.

{ 290315 }

To Marta Abba
Via Cajazzo 52
Milan   Berlin, 15. III. 1929

My dear Marta,

Yesterday I ended up going to Solari's. I arrived (it was the fault of your dear little alarm clock) a quarter of an hour late. There I found Aponte of the *Corriere*, Bojano of the *Popolo d'Italia*, and Ivo Pannaggi, who was admiring some of Fausto's daubs, which Solari was showing around.[1]

We chatted. The usual gossip. News from Italy, news from here. But I heard a good one. At the Embassy, the day after I went there for breakfast, do you remember? A certain man named Curtius was expected,[2] who is president of I don't know which German institution in Rome—to make it short, a big shot. Aponte and Bojano were invited, to honor him; the Ambassador would have liked me to go back, but since I told him that I could not, he invited, instead, Rosso di San Secondo.[3] Now listen. This man Curtius, showing off as a foreigner in Italy who is up-to-date about everything, at a certain point asks Rosso di San Secondo:

"And when shall we hear again in Berlin your *La cena delle beffe*?"[4]

Ambassador Aldrovandi hastens to remedy the gaffe of the illustrious guest:

"Actually, I heard that Mr. Rosso's *Il piacere dell'onestà* will be performed soon again in Berlin."[5]

You can imagine the hundred thousand colors of Rosso di San Secondo's face. He coughs, tries to smile, and says:

"No; maybe *Marionette, che passione!*"

---

[1] Ivo Pannaggi, a painter and friend of Pirandello, evidently was finding in the paintings of Pirandello's son Fausto some merit that the playwright himself did not perceive at the time. Pirandello loved to paint in the formalistic style of his time and did not appreciate at all what he called the "daubs" of his son, who was following the new wave of the Parisian avant-garde. Eventually Fausto was recognized by the critics and by his father as an original, talented artist.

[2] He is referring to Ludwig Curtius, a German archaeologist who was the head of the German Archaeological Institute in Rome, 1928–1937.

[3] The playwright Pier Maria Rosso di San Secondo (1887–1956) was in Germany three times between 1926 and 1932, where he wrote articles for the newspaper *La Stampa* of Turin. His play *Marionette, che passione!* (1918) made him well known in the Italian and international world of theater.

[4] *La cena delle beffe* (1909) is the most famous drama of Sem Benelli (1877–1949).

[5] *Il piacere dell'onestà* (1917) is a play by Pirandello.

And then, Mr. Curtius:

"Marionettes? Yes, yes, how beautiful, I saw them at the Podrecca, the Teatro dei Piccoli, wonderful!"[6]

I don't need to tell you the ferocious joy with which those two journalists were telling this painful story about Rosso di San Secondo. It almost sounds not true.

At three o'clock I went back home. No letters from anybody. Only a telephone message from Philips, during my absence, about a visit by Lantz together with somebody from Tonfilm, sent by Eichberg[7] to discuss with me the dialogue and music parts of the film with the Chinese actress.[8]

At five this gentleman arrived with Lantz. A fellow with big glasses and a face like a pickle, and a very long neck. He is a musician and an architect. His name is Doctor Tempel.[9] Can you believe it? He has already prepared for Tonfilm four symphonies of Beethoven and two nocturnes of Chopin. My idea, already realized; my secret!

You can imagine how I felt! I had been carrying my idea inside myself for almost a year! I did not want to tell it to anybody;[10] and somebody else—this Mr. Tempel—only four months ago (as he himself confessed to me) came up with this idea and lost no time communicating it to the people at Tonfilm, who will make a mint out of it!

Now the cat is out of the bag, and I don't know what I can do about it. I told Lantz and Philips that I had the idea first; but unfortunately there is nothing I can do to stop this Mr. Tempel—who cannot be accused of stealing the idea—from using it, and rightly so. Only the consolation remains that the way I'd be able to do an interpretation of Beethoven and of Chopin he certainly will not be able to do; but in the meantime he will get the credit for the invention and for the first application of it,

---

[6] The puppets of Vittorio Podrecca (1883–1959) had for about ten years as their home the Sala Verde of the Odescalchi Palace in Rome, which was called by everybody the Teatro dei Piccoli, from I Piccoli, the name of the company founded and managed by Podrecca.

[7] An executive in Berlin of the film-producing company Tonfilm.

[8] The silent-movie actress Anna May Wong.

[9] This is an error by Pirandello, which he will rectify in the next letter: the name is Lempel, not Tempel.

[10] Marta used to recall the "holy naïveté" of the Maestro, who had actually divulged his "secret" idea during several interviews given to journalists of different nationalities! See this idea of Pirandello, which in his dreams was a sure money-maker, in many letters to Marta (280706, 280711, 280712, 280713, 290316, 290323, 290401), some of which are not translated in this volume.

and this credit he will not even be able to use properly: so mediocre does he seem, and far from imagining all the ramifications that can be developed from the basic idea.[11]

The ancients believed that at a certain point the destiny of a man was weighed by Jupiter, who in his mysterious judgment either would keep him afloat or would sink him. To me, not a single thing is going well; and it is useless to fight and be obstinate about yielding to the hostility of Fate.

And yet, upon leaving, you told me: "We must win!"

But you see, now I am here alone: without you, without life. . . .

Adieu, Marta. Until tomorrow.

Luigi[12]

[11] The awkward experiments by Lempel were soon forgotten, but Pirandello unfortunately did not find an opportunity to develop his idea.

[12] For the first time Pirandello signs himself Luigi, without his family name; soon he will use Luigi Pirandello again, then Luigi again, and finally he will sign Maestro until his death. See the entry Signature in the Subject Index.

{ 290316 }

To Marta Abba
Via Cajazzo
52 Milan (Italy)   Berlin, 16. III. 1929

My dear Marta,

My first letter should have arrived this morning, and I think with regret of the pain it must have given you. What can you do for me, and why should you keep suffering because of my sadness and desolation? I must shed all my tears in silence, without bothering you about anything anymore. And that I will do. But I should at least be thankful if the inspiration to work flares up in me again. Then the daytime hours would become bearable. While working I would be certainly less affected by my awful loneliness. Only the hours of the evening would remain unbearable. Yesterday evening I came home from the Aida again at 9:30. I have no desire to go anyplace, neither to the theater nor to the movies; without even mentioning the cafés where, alone, unable to exchange a word with anyone, I would notice more than ever the misery of solitude. This dismay comes from the awareness of my condition, of my age, of the little time I've left to live, and from wondering whether it is at all worthwhile. . . .

But here I am, still troubling you, although I have just said I would not do it again.[1]

Let's change the tone, let's talk about something else! About you, who since yesterday have resumed living in Milan. What did you do? Did you go out? Whom did you see? You certainly petted Bullino a lot. I imagined you in bed, and then when you got up, and then . . . then suppositions about maybe she is doing this, maybe she is doing that. I am almost positive that you did not go out in the morning. You probably went out in the afternoon, but where to? My trouble is this, that my imagination, which still sees you in all the hours of the day, does not know where to follow you. . . .

But I don't want to fall again into talking of anguish. You'll give me your news about what you do, how you spend your days, if you wish to, and in the meantime I watch your portrait smiling at me.

Yesterday Philips came back and somewhat reassured me about that gentleman from Tonfilm, whose name is Lempel and not Tempel as I wrote yesterday. The situation is not as serious as it looked at first. It seems that this Mr. Lempel is a dilettante, whom nobody takes seriously. He has attempted small mediocre projects, little experiments with poor results; and he is certainly not able to do more. He is without doubt on the same track as I am, but he does not have wings to fly. Philips has completely reassured me on this point, and now that I had to unbutton fully with him, he promised that he will put me in contact with the Americans for the full exploitation of my idea. I think he was enthusiastic about it. We'll see. Negotiations are still going on for *Six Characters* and Philips has the greatest confidence that we'll be able to conclude the deal soon.[2] In the meantime it looks as if Eichberg will reach his decision tomorrow, or on Monday, about completing his payment for the film starring the Chinese actress.

Wreede, the director of the Felix Bloch-Erben, came to see me; he wanted to reach an agreement on the new play and repeated to me that there are several details to be settled. But the question of the translator remains still to be solved. I called the lawyer Falkenstein to ask how I should act after his breaking off the contract with Feist; that is, whether I should consider myself free and able to give the new play to another trans-

---

[1] Pirandello will continue to make—and almost always right away break—the same promise not to afflict his beloved with the description of his desperate loneliness caused by her departure.

[2] This refers to the project of filming Pirandello's play *Six Characters in Search of an Author.*

lator. He answered, perplexed, that this would not be without risk, although he thinks that a court of law cannot in any way find me guilty after the terrible translations made by Feist.[3] I therefore advised Wreede to work with Falkenstein at finding a way to eliminate every risk and overcome all difficulties. This too was just what we needed! Let's hope that the Deutsches Theater will take *Ma non è una cosa seria*, with which there are no problems, since Feist has nothing to do with it and holds no rights to the translation of this comedy, which is also free from any agency, since the contractual term with Felix Bloch-Erben has elapsed. Should the play be accepted, a new contract must be signed, which would be handled by Giordani. But right here is another stumbling block: how should I act toward Giordani? I have not yet received an answer about his intentions, and I have here two letters waiting for an answer, one from Paris and one from Warsaw. In the one from Paris Mr. Soupault asks me to whom should he send the money from the royalties on the *Esclusa*, which I assume are substantial, because of the success the novel had in France.[4]

Talking about Paris, this morning I received one of the usual letters from Fausto, full of bitterness. It looks as if Vildrac did not organize things as he should have. He sold a few paintings and some drawings. But very few visitors came to see the show. He hopes he will have more today (Saturday) and tomorrow (Sunday.)

And this is all, my Marta. I am waiting, you can imagine with what anxiety, for your first letter: I hope it will perk me up a little—a spark rekindling my inspiration. I need it so badly!

Addio. Addio.

Yours, always,
Luigi

---

[3] According to the contract in question Feist had the exclusive right to translate Pirandello's play into German; Pirandello claimed that Feist's right had ceased because of the very poor quality of his translations, which were jeopardizing the success of Pirandello's plays in Germany. The litigation dragged on with very unpleasant consequences for Pirandello and made Feist a dangerous enemy—to the point that he probably contributed in a decisive way to the events that culminated in the noisy heckling at the premiere of *Questa sera si recita a soggetto* (Tonight we improvise), on May 31, 1930, at the Lessing-Theater—thus precipitating Pirandello's sudden flight from Berlin on June 12, 1930 (see letters 300601 and, above all, 300603).

[4] Pirandello writes here about his royalties from the publication in French of his novel *L'esclusa*, translated by Benjamin Crémieux and published by Kra in Paris in the series *Vieille Sicile*. This letter is typical of many in this collection in which Pirandello talks with Marta about the legal quagmires he was continuously getting into, all his life, due to the poor management of his affairs and the dishonesty of a number of people around him.

{ 290320 }

To Marta Abba
Via Cajazzo 22
Milan (Italy) Berlin, 20. III. 1929

My dear Marta,

By the time this letter reaches you, you will already know whether I received, or not, the nomination to the Academy;[1] it's useless therefore to speak further about it. In the *Corriere* (of the 19th), which arrived today in Berlin, there is written, after all the news, that the king had signed on the 18th the decree of nomination of the first thirty academicians; therefore the nominating is done; and the *Corriere* has published the name of seven elected scientists, promising that the others will be made known in the following days.

Yesterday evening, coming home from the Aida at 9:30 P.M., I found at the door this telegram from Interlandi:

"Can give you almost certainty. Affectionately. Interlandi."

Almost certainty! Does the *almost* mean that until yesterday my name was still suspended? It is not possible, if the decree for all thirty academicians was signed on the *18th*. *Almost* therefore means that Interlandi esteemed not absolutely credible the word of the person who had given my nomination as certain. But by now the *almost* is no longer there. Either I am in, or I am not. And you will know before I do; as a matter of fact, you know already, while you read this letter.

Is it no? Is it yes?

Anyway, I was right in not leaving.

I would have caught more than an airplane if you—instead of recalling me to Italy for the elections to the Academy—would have called me back to stay again near you.[2] Because now, after three years of living close by you, I feel that without you, although I try very hard to resist, I am dying. I am dying because I no longer know what to do with my life; in this horrible loneliness there is no more sense for me in living—neither value nor purpose. The meaning, the value, the purpose of my life all were

---

[1] Pirandello refers to the Accademia d'Italia, which Mussolini had just established. In the previous letter, 290319, here not translated, the playwright had written about the uncertainty of being chosen among the first nominees to the high honor but had refused to follow Marta's advice to go to Rome as soon as possible to influence the decision with his presence.

[2] This sentence implies that Marta had not only left Berlin in spite of Pirandello's pleas to the contrary, but had also clearly asked him not to join her and stay near her in Italy.

you—in hearing the sound of your voice close to me, in seeing the heaven of your eyes and the light of your glance—the light that was brightening my spirit. Now everything is dead and extinguished, inside me and around me. This is the terrible truth. There is no point in my making it known to you; but it is so. It is my fault, because I allowed myself to be caught up again by life, when I shouldn't have. Now it is no longer possible for me to feel abandoned by it. The more the days go by, the more my anguish and despair grow; and I don't know what will happen to me tomorrow. . . .

Enough. I see that I keep on bothering you, Marta; have mercy on me, and forgive me. I am no longer able to command myself, to prevent my grief from expressing itself, even though I know that you suffer because of it. I'll try not to do it again, I promise; and if I cannot take it any longer, what can I say. . . . I think that I'll do any silly thing. . . . I'll drink a glass of water to quench this thirst! You must forgive me.

That's enough for today.

Luigi

{ 290322 }

To Marta Abba
Via Cajazzo 52
Milan (Italy)   Berlin, 22. III. 1929

My dear Marta,

As I told you in my telegram, I got the communication about the nomination this morning directly from Mussolini himself, with these words:

> I am happy to inform you that His Majesty the King upon my proposal has nominated you to be a member of the Academy in the Literature division.
>
> Mussolini

But already yesterday evening, when I got home from the Aida, I found at the concierge's office a telegram from Interlandi that said:

> Very happy, I embrace you affectionately,
>
> Interlandi

Therefore, without the telegram saying it, I understood that the nomination was now certain.

I received another telegram together with the one from the Duce, which I opened before the latter. It said:

Fraternally happy highly auspicious recognition.

Margherita Sarfatti[1]

To Mussolini I answered in the following way:

Supremely proud Your high recognition, I thank Your Excellency for Your great honor and express again my profound devotion.

Well, I am an Academician of Italy. But I remain, my dear Marta, the very same poor man as before, whom no prize, no honor will ever be able to compensate for the loss of your company, which, alone, would have made me enjoy the honor, and more for your sake than for mine. Do you know what I was thinking, when I received the telegram from Sarfatti and the one from Mussolini? That one from you was not coming, and when, a little while later, one did arrive, it seemed to me *opaque* because it did not carry your name, and the joy it expressed was not from you alone, but was lumped in with that from all your family; it did mean a lot to me, but it was not the *light* that would have shone, if *Marta*—Marta even in the name of all her family—had expressed all *her* joy.

But this Marta, who in the telegram wished that her joy, without her name, would appear to me buried in that of her family; this Marta who left me to go away to her family (I don't tell you so as a reproach, but because, unfortunately, it is for me the awful truth); this Marta who, knowing that I am here alone, cannot think that in this horrible solitude I cannot be happy about the nomination unless I think that *she* is happy because of it; this Marta, look, has not written to me for three days; and she leaves me in the depth of this loneliness without even that echo of life which would be heard in a letter from her. I wait for it every morning, to take from it strength to last and live, through the day, at least until the evening, when the anguish assaults me with fiercer strength, until it suffocates me; I can say at least: "She wrote to me!"; I can say: "She is no longer here; I do not see her at my side; I do not hear her speaking; but she has written to me, she has thought of me. . . ."

I am dying to know what you are doing, what you think, what you are going to do, what you *feel*. . . . Did you go to the theater? How do you

---

[1] Margherita Sarfatti, the Jewish-born author of the influential book *Dux*, was at the time on her way out as Mussolini's lover but still very powerful and close to the Duce as self-appointed czarina of Italian cultural politics.

spend your evenings? Do you plan to go, as you were saying, to the Riviera, to San Remo? Will you go there alone? What hopes do you have for the coming year? Are you preparing yourself? Are you reading something? Did you go to see the Pitoëffs at the Manzoni?[2] They performed the *Three Sisters* by Chekhov. We too wanted to perform it. . . . What a beautiful play it is. . . . How I feel it in this moment! Chekhov is the most desperate of poets, maybe even more than our Leopardi. . . . The grief of Leopardi was intense but noble and intellectual; in him there is at least a certain dimension of thought. Chekhov is narrow, narrow like anguish itself; and he does not think, he lives the despair of life, he lives it not only in himself, but in everybody, he lives it in all the poor human souls, in the life of every day, even in the sun of the beautiful days, even in the flowers of the vain springs. I would love to have the *Three Sisters* here to read it over again; but I am even without books. . . . I did not feel the lack of them before; I did not feel the lack of anything before; now I feel that even the books are not here; I say, certain books. . . .

Do you sometimes think of me? And do you think of what will happen to me, to us? *Me* does not mean anything else. . . .[3]

Will you write to me? Will you tell me everything? Do you want me not to write again?

Addio, Marta. I cannot continue anymore.

Luigi

[2] Georges and Ludmilla Pitoëff, Russian actors who had become French citizens, had interpreted with great success the *Six Characters* in Paris (1923) and at the time were performing at the Teatro Manzoni in Milan.

[3] Pirandello is overwhelmed by the anguish of solitude, by a sense of being abandoned, and by the cruel uncertainty about Marta's feelings toward him. The themes here, that by now for him there is no longer a *me*, but only an *us*, and that life has no sense, value, or purpose but in the love of Marta—interwoven with reproaches of Marta's coldness to him—will continue appearing in the letters, either explicitly or, most of the time, only hinted at and immediately repressed, but sufficient to send a clear, imploring message to the beloved. The explicit word "love," *amore*, is used rarely, which is no wonder if we think about the erotic-sexual meaning of the word and its impropriety in the mentality of a married Sicilian gentleman, as Pirandello always felt himself to be to the end of his days.

{ 290323 }

To Marta Abba
Via Cajazzo 52
(Italy) Milan   Berlin, 23. III. 1929
　My dear Marta,

　This morning at last a letter from you arrived! It's the letter of the 21st and rather long, but signed, as if on purpose, *Marta Abba*—personal and family name—who knows, I might make a mistake, and mix up Marta with another Marta! Why did you want to hurt me, Marta? As if the distance were not enough, why do you make yourself even more distant in your letter, signing personal and family name? Is it impossible that you—being so sensitive—are not aware of what you are doing, and therefore I must think that you did it on purpose, maybe to reproach me, without saying it, because in my most recent letters I signed my first name without my family name. Is this why you did it? Yes, because your first two letters were signed only Marta. But I told you why I did it. If I was wrong, forgive me. It was to feel more like being with you, less distant; to be with you, at least in my letters, *I*, without family name, I, who have nobody anymore in my life who calls me and thinks of me without my family name, or without my qualification of professor, or of teacher, or of father. All right. I won't do it anymore!

　The letters I write to you are the only ones I write in longhand, although I am no longer good at it, being out of practice. But I cannot even think of using the typewriter when I write to you; I'd feel horrible using a mechanical instrument to express my feeling to you. But it seems that you, making yourself so much more distant, no longer Marta—Marta Abba—you are telling me: stop it, I don't want to hear about your feeling anymore; you bother me; leave me in peace. . . . —Is it not so?

　No, Marta, it must not be so, absolutely not; woe to me if it were so! But even if it is so, let me know it. I want you to tell me honestly, because you should not be forced to lie to me, neither for pity nor for any other reason.

　. . . Marta mia, did you see the list of the Academicians? Everybody was dismayed in reading it: Beltramelli,[1] Marinetti . . . ,[2] and Trombetti, who

---

[1] Antonio Beltramelli (1879–1930), a writer of short stories, novels, and books for young people, had been one of the twelve founders of the Teatro d'Arte di Roma with Pirandello but had later joined the list of the "enemies" because of a disagreement.

[2] The prophet of futurism, Tommaso Marinetti (1876–1944), was in a special way on

is a glottologist,[3] and Formichi, who is a linguist, and Romagnoli, who is a translator and a linguist too, all put together with the creative writers; D'Annunzio is not included and not even Ojetti in place of that Beltramelli; and it's better not even to mention how the nomination of Marinetti makes the whole list ridiculous, because during all his life he has aimed his boisterous although harmless guns against all Academies and all museums and libraries and schools. . . . Had I known that my name had to be mixed in among those selected, I would have tried to be left out; because in such company it is better to stay out of the Academy, rather than to be in it. . . . I'm grateful that Di Giacomo[4] and Panzini[5] are with me.

I ran out of paper. Until tomorrow, Marta. Addio.

Luigi Pirandello

Pirandello's "black list." The Maestro hated Marinetti's enthusiastic, bombastic activity of Fascist propaganda.

[3] Alfredo Trombetti, a specialist in linguistics, published studies on the origin of language and comparative studies on languages of different groups. It seems that Pirandello is questioning not Trombetti's merits in the field of scholarship—nor those of Carlo Formichi (1871–1943, a specialist of Sanskrit and English languages and literature) and of Ettore Romagnoli (1871–1938, a well-known translator of the Greek classics)—but the fact that they were nominated in the wrong category, as if they represented Italy's creative literature.

[4] The poet Salvatore di Giacomo (1860–1934) was also a historian of Naples.

[5] Alfredo Panzini (1863–1939), a novelist and essayist.

{ 290325 }

To Marta Abba
Via Cajazzo 52
(Italy) Milan   Berlin, 25. III. 1929

My dear Marta,

This morning I received your four small-size memo sheets of the 22nd—still using those from the Casanova[1] here in Berlin, a memory of New Year's Eve. Strange when I think that four months have passed: at first the days were flying, but since the evening of the 13th,[2] time seems to stand still. The last few days were long enough to make me think of New

[1] A night club in Berlin.

[2] The evening of Marta's departure from Berlin.

Year's at the Casanova as something immensely distant in time—you were all excited, throwing confetti and paper streamers, you were asking me to please carefully save the piglet-shaped balloon, which Cele then blew up, trying to fill it up with too much air: a blow, boom! and there it was, shriveled forever—much to your chagrin.

I hear that you went back to Miss Aillaud's office[3] and that you spent two and a half hours there, leaving then from there more than ever convinced that the place is a nest of evildoers, the hellish cauldron of all the gossip of this filthy world of the Italian theater. You say: "But at least here they know my worth, while there, without knowing how to speak the language, I felt as if I were nobody." My Marta! I tell you, it's better not being anyone anymore—and being worth a lot for ourselves and for those who can really understand and appreciate us—rather than being of any value for those people! On the other hand I understand that in order to think this way you should have an experience and a feeling for life that you cannot yet have. And then, you no longer had in your heart—to keep you here—the feeling that you had before for me, and the confidence you had in me. The long wait made you tired, and you went back to smell again the nausea of that foul sewer, and to wait, there too: but for what? a chance that (given the present miserable condition of the Italian theater) couldn't be anything but uncertain and mediocre. Beware, my Marta, beware! You are not receiving good advice; not because all those who are around you do not love you a lot, but because, for what you are and for what you must be, you need to have around you lofty advice and long-range planning, way above whatever that black pit that is Via Giuseppe Sacchi 9 can offer,[4] where your father took you again to drown you. I know, poor man, he is eager to see you on the stage again; he is afraid that if you keep away from it, you will lose ground; he lives only, you can say, for the gossip inside and around the world of the actors; and he feels as if gasping for air at anything he hears and fears might harm you. . . . I feel so sorry for him; but believe me, Marta, all this is harmful for you.[5]

[3] The office of the Società Italiana del Teatro Drammatico (also called Sitedramma) in the Via Giuseppe Sacchi 9.

[4] The address of the office of Giordani and Aillaud.

[5] In this letter a sense of rivalry between Pirandello and Marta's father becomes noticeable, which will come to the surface from time to time during the following years. See, for instance, letter 300301, in which Pirandello affirms that he is the "true father" of Marta. Pirandello never had any doubt about the best intentions of Pompeo Abba and his whole family as far as Marta's welfare was concerned, but he doubted their judgment as narrow-minded and inadequate for Marta's greatness and deeply resented her family's great influence on most of Marta's practical decisions.

You need to breathe in a different intellectual climate. You need to let your soul breathe as you contemplate different horizons. You are one of the truly "Chosen"; please, please, do not, because of mediocre considerations, disappoint the expectations of your destiny, which is high, and must always be high!

But you can ask me what was I still waiting for in Berlin? What *I* am still waiting for; better, what I *was* waiting for, because I was not waiting *for my sake*, Marta, but *for yours:* for the opportunity that would allow us to go back to Italy da padroni, to "do Art," You (even without me if you did not want me any longer near you, as it was before), the true Art, as it should be done, as you alone can do, da padrona, like a queen; like a queen and a slave, but a slave only of Art![6] This is it: you should be waiting for this, here with me, without impatience; and in the meantime you should be seeing, studying, knowing, enriching your spirit by making for yourself a culture, learning languages, methodically and with willpower . . . —all this without the impatience, the laziness of Cele around, who should go by herself her own way and should leave you alone in your way, which should not and cannot be hers. All this! Money will come, it will come for sure, a lot of it, but we must know how to wait for it—with a firm spirit and always working, as I have done all my life.

You say, well, are you not there?

Me, yes, here I am, Marta. But Marta, how can my soul stay here waiting without you anymore? In this abandonment, with the proof that you no longer have the same feeling as before, and that you wanted—perhaps advised by your relatives—to go away from me, and maybe forever? I AM ALONE! I AM ALONE! I AM ALONE![7] May God protect you, my child,[8] from ever getting to comprehend all the cruelty that is contained in this word!

Luigi Pirandello

---

[6] The myth of Art (written on purpose with a capital *A*) for Pirandello remains, all his life, the Absolute, the substitution for the God he has lost. The identification of Art and Marta is for him the highest possible point—it is, for him, like touching the divine.

[7] This exclamation of desperate loneliness is written in letters twice the size of the others.

[8] This expression referring to a "father-daughter" relationship will become more frequent from now on. While the terminology of fatherly love takes the place of "love" without adjectives, in reality "my child!" sounds very much like "my love!"

{ 290326 }

To Marta Abba
Via Cajazzo 52
(Italy) Milan   Berlin, 26. III. 1929

My dear Marta,

Deprived again today of a letter from you, I received instead a very long one from Stefano, which shows my position in Italy as totally changed, straightened-up—from the upside-down way it was. This as a result of the nomination to the Academy.

Evidently, for such a change to happen, people must have been previously thinking of me as dead—and buried by the many enemies who have been waging war against me. For once not seeing them get their way, and seeing me standing on my feet and alive and made an object of favor and consideration by the Duce: all this was enough to make my enemies swallow their pride, and a great number of people are now opening their mouths who, believing me in disgrace and finished, had not dared to utter a word in my favor anymore.[1]

After some delay, Stefano has been sending me all the telegrams that have been coming to my home in Rome. Mussolini himself, before sending his telegram to the embassy here in Berlin, had sent an *urgent* one to my address in the Via Onofrio Panvinio.[2]

. . . It is moreover absolutely certain that the state theaters will be set up the way I want them, because Mussolini always keeps his promises.[3]

---

[1] Only a few days before (letter 290323) Pirandello had written that had he known who was going to be nominated to the Academy, he would have tried his best not to be on the list. And now, a letter from his son and the standard telegrams of congratulation from important people are sufficient to make him ecstatic and to consider himself victorious against enemies who belong more to his imagination than to reality. The pages that follow appear to be oscillations similar to those of a manic-depressive patient in a moment of euphoria, dreaming with his eyes wide open.

[2] A list of telegrams follows, sent by many personalities of Italian political and cultural life. Another list of offers also follows, including the position of editor of two new journals, and the rumors that he will be named president of the Società degli Autori and that he will be offered the position of a top consultant at the Ente Nazionale per la Cinematografia. Everything is referred by Pirandello as practically sure, but no part of the above-named bonanza ever materialized.

[3] The good fortune seems to rekindle Pirandello's faith in Mussolini, which had been completely shaken before his departure for Berlin (see letter 280922). Mussolini did not keep his promise, and the state theaters as Pirandello had dreamed them never materialized.

We must learn to wait, because he needs time; woe unto those who get tired of waiting. To round out all these blessings, Marchesano[4] writes to me (believing that I am short of money) that he is putting at my disposal 60,000 lire, so that I may return immediately to Italy, telling me to give it back when I have money to throw away. In the meantime the contract for the sale of my villino has been already signed, and around April 20 I'll receive a payment of 865,000 lire, but 230,000 will go to the Monte dei Paschi;[5] with the remaining 635,000 I will take care of my children, I'll give Lietta her dowry;[6] I'll pay off my loans from the Banca Commerciale; I'll get rid, in one word, of every obligation, and still about 40,000 lire will remain in my pocket.[7]

Here it looks like things are taking a favorable course. Everything is happening seriatim: first a series of bad things happened one after the other; now it's the turn of a series of good luck.

. . . Good news, my Marta; but all together they are not able to give me back a breath of life; that breath of life that a word, a glance, a smile from you would give back to me. . . . After your departure—because you did not want to believe in me anymore, and because you went away far from me to go your way and I mine—my soul, Marta, has been wounded without remedy. Your way? Yes, *you can go your way* and you'll make it. But I, mine? Recognition, justice, honors, prestige, authority, earnings: what will they be worth for me, if I no longer have my life, *my life?*

Luigi Pirandello

[4] The Roman lawyer Giuseppe Marchesano, married to a cousin of Pirandello.

[5] The Monte dei Paschi is a financial lending institution that held the mortgage on the villino.

[6] Pirandello had promised, at the time of Lietta's wedding, a dowry of two hundred thousand lire, which he had not yet been able to pay. As a way of keeping his promise, the writer was paying his daughter the monthly interest on that amount; to his sons Stefano and Fausto he was, on the contrary, giving a monthly subsidy of two thousand lire each. The capital received from the sale of the villino represented for Pirandello the longed-for possibility of liquidating in one lump sum the onerous obligation he had imposed upon himself of supporting his three children with substantial monthly payments.

[7] A very small part of the money eventually remained in Pirandello's pocket—a far cry from his previous calculations. In letter 260815 he had expressed confidence in selling the villino for 1,350,000 lire, with one million left to invest after meeting all his obligations. This seems to be the oft-repeated story of Pirandello's dreams about big money. See the entry Villino in the Subject Index.

{ 290328 }

To Marta Abba
Via Cajazzo 52
(Italy) Milan   Berlin, 28. III. 1929

Marta, my Marta, your cry for help on Saturday evening has arrived at this very moment! I knew that when you left and went back to Italy like that you would end up in such a state. All the stronger was my chagrin when I saw you leave and get away from me, because I felt I could not and should not do anything to prevent it—although I knew. At that time every word of mine, every attempt at persuasion, would have had no consequence at all, because it would have looked selfish on my part; that is, that I did not want to let you go for my own sake, so as not to be left in this horrible solitude; and also because it was clear that you had lost your confidence in me and that you thought you would be safer trusting your father's ridiculous Conceit[1] and your sister Cele's infinitely silly conceit. Oh, my Marta, my humiliation for all this! My dejection at not being able to confront you with a convincing reason against your decision to leave— a factual proof, a signed contract, something that could be touched by your hands and give weight and strength to my words!

But it's useless to tell you all this now. Right now you need to be relieved of the despair filling your soul, and to be consoled, my Marta, by the person who loves you and does not live for anyone but you. How can you say that *you no longer are*; that *you do not exist anymore*; that you do not even have your art left; that *your place has been taken*? You *are you*, you exist for yourself, for what you are; for what you are worth, as an artist and as a woman; for all the talents of your inspired soul which, as certainly as they have already been recognized before, will with the same certainty soon impress everyone again; for the gifts of your heart; for your beauty, which is as great as your goodness: you exist for all those who love you and who cannot be happy without you. And why do you say you do not have your art anymore? Don't you have your art in yourself? Even if at this moment you are not practicing it, have you really lost it? It is alive, and it will live again tomorrow on the stage! Who can have taken your

---

[1] The capital letter is Pirandello's. This explosion of emotions reveals feelings toward Marta's father and Cele that Pirandello usually kept well guarded so as not to offend his beloved, who was very attached to her family and oversensitive to any criticism of her relatives. Pirandello will later regret this sincerity.

place? Your place on the Italian stage, for a while, can stay empty, but it cannot be taken over by any other actress, *ever*: because none of them even stands as high as your knee, and you are you, unmistakable, unsuppressable, irreplaceable. You—with your way of being, feeling, thinking, expressing yourself, speaking, moving: which is only yours, and cannot belong to anybody else; which makes you MARTA ABBA,[2] a name signed by destiny and entrusted to glory. But this *Marta* should not be *marta*, this MARTA,[3] without these fits of discouragement, should keep herself worthy of her destiny! And I am here to tell you this; I am here to confirm that her destiny (remember!) *has been foretold*; and Marta should not turn away from that *predestination*! I am her man; the man her destiny assigned to her; I am her Destiny, and I am nothing else; and this is so true, that without this, that is, without you, I am nothing anymore. Do you understand this, my Marta?

Things are now changing. I have WORTH. You know that I have worth. The others thought that I was no longer worth anything. But it is not true; *I have worth*. Everybody will be aware, very soon, how much I am still worth. But I would be worth nothing, really nothing, Marta, if I were not worth anything for you. You are my worth; if I lose you, I lose everything. And then, as I cannot lose you, so you should not want to lose me. It is, for you and for me, truly, a question of *existence*.[4]

Look, Marta. The villino is sold. Once I take care of the children, I am free. And this will happen by the end of April. Please start thinking right now, *seriously*, about YOUR company, which you'll have next September. Think of the plays you'd like to stage—not mine, nothing mine: we'll talk about this point together, maybe we'll discuss it. In September you must have *your* company. Leave to me all the worries for the material realization of it. You, and *only you*, will be in charge. You do not need anybody else but me, and saying me is the same as saying *yourself*, because I am nothing else but *you*; I cannot consider myself otherwise, and you

---

[2] Pirandello writes Marta's name in large letters.

[3] Here Pirandello writes *Marta* in letters three times larger than the others. This repeated play with the format of the words appears childish; children like to write words that are important to them in large letters.

[4] Pirandello thus concludes the passionate argument with which he wants to convince Marta of their existential interdependence—with the clear purpose of avoiding the disaster of losing her, which, he is convinced, would mean the end for him. From this theoretical reasoning, he moves to a practical level; that is, he offers his personal fortune to finance a new company for Marta. In reality, the actress will soon begin her first laborious period as artistic director / manager. Pirandello did not finance her company; it was Marta's father, Pompeo Abba, who invested a substantial amount of money and time in his daughter's venture; Marta had to struggle very hard to get through the season.

too should not consider yourself otherwise: *I*, for *us*, means *you*. After paying in April the rest of my debts to the Banca Commerciale, I'll get from Töplitz[5] in September a new line of credit to be used as the financial base for the new company. I know Töplitz, I know his wife, I know Mattioli, the personal secretary of Töplitz; I have every possible connection with the Banca Commerciale. A line of credit of at least 150 thousand lire will be open for me, unless in the meantime (that is, between now and September) I happen to make the big money I expect from the movies, in which case there would be no need of anything.

But, I repeat, all this must be my responsibility alone. Marta must think of nothing but *her* repertory, her interpretations, her company, and her dresses, not to pay for them, but for the joy of wearing them and adapting them to the roles she plays.[6] Marta must not weep, Marta must not despair, Marta must always think that for her there is always

Her Luigi[7]

[5] The director of the Banca Commerciale in Milan.

[6] Pirandello lets himself be carried away by a fantasy that touches the borders of a sadomasochistic dream. In the dream Marta is the mistress, Luigi her servant/administrator who pays the bills (of course, these are fantasies; Marta's bills were paid by Marta or by her father); Marta is happy and without worries, playing with *her* repertory, with the dresses, etc., while Luigi does all the dirty work for her. How different was the reality! Marta was too proud in her independence, too down-to-earth, and knew the Maestro too well to "buy" the dream, which in her answers she will not even mention, as she does not mention any of Pirandello's "useless chatter."

[7] In the enthusiasm of his amorous offers, Pirandello goes back to using the confidential "Luigi" as his signature.

{ 290329 }

To Marta Abba
Via Cajazzo 52
(Italy) Milan   Berlin, 29. III. 1929

My dear Marta,

Last night I could not sleep—I was still thinking about your words of yesterday, which totally upset me and plunged me into a state of unrestrained turmoil. My mind was running in a hundred directions at once, ideas were constantly popping up and then crumbling: about leaving, seeing you again, shaking you up, bringing you here back with me, talking together about the new company, the actors, that one no, this one yes, the plays to perform, preparations, and in the meantime buying here the stage lights—the most modern and most powerful ones—and learning how to use them. And also about studying, the two of us together, you and me alone; opening up my mind and pouring all my knowledge into you in a few days, to enrich your spirit with all the necessary literary trends; studying French in addition to German, to give you a command of at least two languages beyond Italian, for your tours abroad. All the above *must* happen again, if we are to know how to do things the way they should be done: with perseverance, willpower, without getting lost and without deviations. You should by all means set up for yourself a rigid program, to be followed point by point, with absolute discipline and utmost precision. You spend too much time in front of the mirror, thinking how best to make yourself up. You do not have all that much time to lose: you should no longer do it. Anyway, it is useless; because you do not need it, you are always beautiful without it. You must get up early, always at the same time; and never go to bed later than 12:30 A.M. One hour is sufficient for the morning bath and getting dressed; breakfast follows, then the study of your roles, as you used to do; in the afternoon, languages; but your studies must include also the plays, to grasp their deepest spirit and squeeze out of them all the life they want to have, and the meaning and the value they have; and also all the effects that can be extracted from them in performance—never arbitrary, always legitimate, although personal, because they result from being illuminated by your very special intelligence. There shouldn't ever be time for boredom and for regrets; we should constantly fill up our day with work. Life will not appear empty anymore; we will not have the feeling of having lost it, if every day we find it again within us, awake and ready to nourish our passion for art, which is never satiated, never gets tired, and is never completely fulfilled.[1]

Your cry for help, Marta, has worked as a whiplash also for me. "If Marta needs comfort so badly, I told myself, I should no longer remain downcast in this dejection into which her departure has thrown me!" And even last night, after all the turmoil of the thoughts I just told you about, since I could not lie in bed any longer, I got up. The new play was on the desk,[2] where I had left it for a long time: I finished it in four hours of feverish work. Victory must be ours, Marta, by all means. You must not

---

[1] This rare sharing of Pirandello's inner thoughts about the formation of an artist reveals, at least partly, the secret of his extraordinary personal productivity, based on a strict discipline of work.

[2] Although there are no other precise hints about which play he is talking about, it is almost certain that here *Questa sera si recita a soggetto* (Tonight we improvise) is meant. See in letter 290407 a sentence that seems to furnish direct proof of this.

leave me. We must win with all our strength the war carried on by our enemies,[3] win with our work, win with our courage, win with pride and constancy; and never give up by putting ourselves meekly in their hands. You were advised very badly, extremely badly. You can only get hurt by these enemies. Even if they wanted to do something for you, you would only receive evil; because they don't know and don't want to do anything but evil, and whoever is with them cannot do anything but evil. Marta, I assure you, they will be soon defeated, they will be at our feet. Rise, Marta, against those who advise you to bow your head before them. Even if you would bow it because they offer to crown you, don't do it. The crown they would put on your head would make your brow bleed, and your whole soul would feel heavier than under an actual yoke. They can impose only yokes of humiliation if not of infamy: yokes of degradation. Do not believe anymore in their power. They still play the game, but underneath the mask of tyrants their faces are white, must be white with fear, because they must feel the day of reckoning very close; too much evil have they perpetrated and they must pay for it—and they will pay. Let me come back to Italy. I must go back anyhow; but not the way you went back (you, who surrendered, following the advice of those who intervened to part you from me, thus doing so much damage to you and to me).[4] I must go back after a complete victory here, both in the movies and in the theater, with a great success that might give me back all the prestige in my country, where already, with the nomination, I obtained a victory against all my enemies. The value of the nomination, for me, is all here: political and not literary. It also has a value because it will be useful to me to fight and win again, and definitively; because I won't have a complete victory until my enemies are crushed to the ground.[5]

Courage! courage! courage, my Marta! Write to me, tell me all your thoughts about my letter of yesterday. Addio,

Luigi

[3] The enemies of whom he speaks here are not only Giordani and his cohorts, but also, it seems, something more generic: the enemies as a persecuting entity, which includes all those who do not understand and do not favor Pirandello and Marta. This persecution complex was impressed on Marta to the end of her days.

[4] The bad advisers are evidently Marta's father and sister, whom Pirandello could not forgive for persuading Marta to abandon him in Berlin.

[5] Pirandello's bombastic language about struggling to the end against the enemies, and of total final victory, sounds like an echo of the Fascist rethoric of this time. This language, however, is pathetic, because it is typical of an adult person who reasons in a childish way: only children have enemies like these!

{ 290330 }

To Marta Abba
Via Cajazzo 52
(Italy) Milan   Berlin, 30. III. 1929

My dear Marta,

This letter of today and the one I wrote yesterday will probably reach you together; the reason is that yesterday, after writing the letter, because of the night I had passed without sleeping and working like crazy to finish the play,[1] I crashed into a deep sleep on the sofa here in front of the desk, and I slept until 9:30 P.M. Nor would I have probably woken up even then if the maid, concerned at not seeing me go out for supper, had not come to knock at the door, with a certain amount of panic, since she had to turn down the bed for the night. That is why at 9:30 (and it was almost ten o'clock before I could be ready to go to the mailbox) the letter could no longer leave on time.

My diligence in writing to you every day, however, is certainly not matched by yours, because today is the third day that I have not received anything from you. Surely one word, at least one word you could have let me have, after all I wrote on Saturday! Eight days have passed, eight days! And I do not know what I am supposed to think, my mind goes to so many things. . . . When I think that you wrote to me: "I don't have a word of comfort from anybody, not even from you. . . ." From me, Marta? Comfort from me, after you left me the way you did? When those who are around you, your family, to whom you preferred to go, neither knew how nor could give it to you?[2] While I alone was capable of giving it to you here—and now more than ever, after what happened, after what is still to come—I alone could give you comfort, had you stayed here, as you should have. Your nature is too impressionable, Marta, and your sister Cele more than anybody else is the one who knows how to take advantage of it. You give in, without even knowing it, to her suggestions, which are all harmful for you; she has led you always where she wanted; you have always ended up doing what she wanted. I know that I was wrong both in

---

[1] As explained in the preceding letter, it is probably *Tonight We Improvise.*

[2] In this letter Pirandello courageously faces the touchy theme of the relationship between Marta and her family, which, in Pirandello's opinion, was seriously damaging the well-being of the actress. Later he will bitterly repent his sincerity, which was anything but well received by Marta, and he will blame his "offensive" words for Marta's prolonged silence.

not asserting a firmer influence on you and in yielding completely to you. A serious fault, not as far as you are concerned, because I know perfectly well that what you want is always right and just; but because, when your sister is near you, it's no longer you who are the one who wants, but it's she. So many times I had to give in to her in order to please you, although I knew that wish was not yours but had been put into your head by her, and it was not honest, it was not right. Forgive me, Marta, if all the love I have for you gives me the courage to tell you this. I say it, Marta, only for your sake, not because I want anything. I'll never want anything from you; but it must be *you, only you* to wish, to command, and not others through you. Then yes, with closed eyes I abandon myself to you, like a blind man to the hand of his guide, because I am sure that you, with the soul and the heart that God gave you, will guide me always on the path of honor, even though among stones and thorns; and never on paths where one can get lost, or, at least, where time and dignity can be lost. Your sister is in you, your mother is in you, your father is in you (all good people, may God guard me from denying it, who love you even more than they love themselves, as I have told you before), but they do not understand you, they cannot understand you! Only one thing, unfortunately, they understand very well about you—that you are so enormously impressionable—and they have learned to perfection the art of influencing you with a piece of news, sometimes only with a simple exclamation. They know that you flare up quickly and get all upset, and they make you do what they want.[3] Now, if they only would make you do things that later redound to your advantage! But no, they make you do things that are incongruous. Because I confess to you, Marta, that in my long life and with the contacts I have had with thousands and thousands of people, I never met a more incongruous man than your father. Trusting yourself to him, who acts like he knows everything and never knows anything, you won't be doing anything but inconsistencies and go senselessly back and forth, in a most limited and narrow-minded circle of action, changing direction at every shadow of a suspicion, in the uncertainty of everything. Believe me, it is really so, Marta, I am not exaggerating. Believe above all that I don't tell you these things with an evil purpose, so that you might,

[3] Pirandello here outlines two distinctive characteristics of Marta's character: her easy susceptibility to influence and her short temper, which could be maneuvered by those who knew her well for their own advantage, resulting in her notoriously changeable and contradictory behavior. According to Pirandello, in order to be independent in her decisions the actress should have followed her own feeling, which was naturally good and enlightened, and should have also strengthened her willpower, which was her weak point.

because of this, subtract even an infinitesimal part of affection or respect from your father. I tell you this to awaken in you the faculty you lack most, willpower: *your* will, which must be always *only your true* will, the one that must be born of your own true feeling, in the light of your own intelligence. Do you understand? I want you to be you, and only you, as you feel, as you think, as you believe, you alone. Not I therefore, nor others. You alone. Can't you see that I don't speak for myself?

I am waiting for a letter from you. Until tomorrow,

Luigi

{ 290331 }

To Marta Abba
Via Cajazzo 52
(Italy) Milan   Berlin, Easter day[1]

My dear Marta,

Are you sick? in bed? Yesterday I sent you a telegram to find out. No other supposition seems to me possible; because I cannot believe, after the letter you wrote to me, after those I wrote to you, that you could leave me without one line, without even a formal wish for this Easter, which I am spending here alone, for so many days, in a silence that is driving me crazy.

I don't know how many times I read over again the few desperate words of your last letter. I know them by heart. They do mention that an illness that was latent in you had flared up; but that was an *illness of the soul*;[2] there is no hint, at least in your words, that you refer to an illness of the body. But it must be so; otherwise, your silence cannot be explained.

I'm going crazy trying to remember what I wrote in my letter of the 22nd, which might have caused your latent illness to flare up.[3] Unfortunately my letter was full of nothing but the grief and desolation into

[1] March 31, 1929. In this important Easter letter Pirandello for the first time explicitly uses the word *amore* (love) in describing his feelings for Marta.

[2] The italics correspond to Pirandello's own underlining in the original. The fact that he uses many such underlinings in this letter means that the points he is trying to get across are extremely important to him. The rejected lover is fighting a desperate battle using all his persuasive power to convince his beloved to rekindle her no-longer-burning love flame in her heart!

[3] See letter 290322, in which Pirandello reproaches Marta for going away from him and in which he asks, at the end, full of fear of losing Marta forever: "Will you write to me? Will you tell me everything? Do you want me not to write again?"

which your departure has thrown me: so much so that, I confess, it seemed to me unfair that, while complaining that *you do not have a word of comfort from anybody*, you still wanted and expected such word *particularly from me*—although I was so disheartened and desolate because of you! How could comfort come from me when all my life had gone away with you? When here with me nothing but regret was left, continuously, every single hour, every single minute? The only comfort that could come from me was knowing that there is one person in the world who loves you more than himself, one who does not live, who cannot live without you, who therefore lives for you. And since this person is not *a nobody*, and since this person is *worth something* and is not a rag to pick up with two fingers and throw away, the immense love of this one, who was here only for you, could and should have given you comfort. *If it does not give comfort anymore* the blame is not mine; if you feel *alone and abandoned*, it is because *you do not want me anymore*, you did not want me anymore and you went away. If I were still in your heart, you would have always *me*— and *only me* you should have not reproached for wanting to deny you comfort. *The fact is that you do not keep me in your heart anymore.* This is for me the dreadful truth. Otherwise you would have not gone away. That is why you feel alone. You find yourself faced with a *useless* life because of this. You think that (God forbid!) in dying you would bring grief *only to your family*. To me, no! I therefore do not exist at all anymore for you. You show it with facts, you say it with words, and then you complain that *not even from me* does a word of comfort come. Oh, Marta, your crisis was born from this: from *a feeling that no longer is in your heart.* You scream that *you no longer are, you do not exist anymore*—because of this. You *would be*, you *would exist*, you *would find again your art* and you *would take up again the position that you think you have lost*, if only what is now dead in your heart would come back to life. I am not wrong, I cannot be wrong. Question yourself well, question the depth of your heart, and you'll see that this is it.

When you are convinced of this, it will mean the end of me. But you, who are young, you'll know how to recover.

Luigi Pirandello

{ **290401** }

To Marta Abba
Via Cajazzo 52
(Italy) Milan　　　　　　　　　　　　　　　Berlin, 1. IV. 1929
　　My Marta,

So, really ill? I reached that conclusion after waiting day after day, admitting and then eliminating all other suppositions, and counting the days when you had not written, three, four, five—but is it possible?—six, seven, eight, until I came to Saturday when, in the greatest anxiety, I sent the telegram. It was the day before Easter; such a sad Easter day, rainy and foggy like winter! Solari had invited me over the phone to spend it in his home; I was in a frame of mind you can imagine; I waited the whole morning of Sunday for an answer to the telegram; I was thinking: "Is it possible that she doesn't want me to receive even a good wish? After all the letters I wrote, even if she is indisposed and cannot answer, she will send a telegram and tell me that she is not well. Nothing, nothing, nothing—I was desperate—and at one o'clock I called Solari to beg off from going, because I was not feeling well; with such bad weather I thought it was better to stay home. He insisted, he wanted to know what was wrong with me; just a bad headache, nothing serious; and then, better to go out, it would be good for me; they were waiting for me, they had found just the right roast of lamb, small but good; enough, he kept insisting: and—in order not to betray my real feelings—I got a cab and went. When I arrived, what an embarrassment! There were the two German cousins, there was Aponte from the *Corriere*; they all knew that it was Easter, and everybody had brought chocolate rabbits with little chocolate eggs; because you must know that they usually have rabbits, besides the little and big eggs, and bring them to the children. They enjoy hiding the bunnies around the house, here and there, so that the children will have fun searching for them everywhere, with loud screams of jubilation and surprise when they find one. I found everybody in the house as if they all had gone mad; they were acting searching and screaming around with their little daughter. At first I did not understand what was going on; but then I felt terrible when they explained to me about the custom of the rabbits. I had brought nothing. Thank God, they knew that I was not feeling well and that I did not really want to go. Enough, one way or another the dinner came to an end; at three o'clock I went back home, with the hope that I would at least find an answer to my telegram; still nothing; nothing for the whole day! But already that morning I had reached the conclusion that you were ill—while I was writing the letter with the date of Easter which you must have already received, a letter that, little by little, while I was writing it, became nasty. Please forgive me, my Marta, although it is unforgivable to have written those words while surmising that you were ill; but I should be forgiven, because it was the fury of the passion I have for you[1] that made me write such words, and the torment of being so far away from you, the anguish of no longer possessing your earlier regard. Do you know at what time I received your telegram? At ten to eleven when, getting up from the sofa where I had been lying in the dark, I was getting ready to go to bed, with my soul in turmoil and my swelling heart ready to explode. "I feel better"! What did you have, my Marta? Fever? What other disease, besides the serious one of your wounded and discouraged soul? Are you still in bed? No, I don't want to suppose so; if you tell me that you are better, I want to be sure that by the time you receive this letter you'll have already gotten up; all your illness will be over, and you'll look at everything around you with different eyes, and even at me, waiting here for a good word from you, which might give me back some life.

Now I'll give you the news. I must leave for London with Eichberg in a few days; but I will not leave before I receive a letter from you, even a few lines, which will reassure me of your recovery; I am going to London with Eichberg to sign a contract for two more films; before leaving, tomorrow or the day after tomorrow, I'll meet with the Americans here. I've already prepared my memo, in which I explain my new idea, with the greatest clarity and efficacy;[2] if the idea is accepted, Marta, our fortune is made; we'll do whatever we'll want to do. Pray—you who know how to pray in your heart, like a child—to the Good Lord.[3] Please write to me at once! Even two lines! But tell me everything! That you love me! These two words would be enough for me! For me, they are everything.[4] Addio.

Luigi

[1] This is the only time in the whole correspondence with Marta that Pirandello—evidently under the strain of a violent emotion in receiving the telegram with the news that Marta had been ill, and trying hard to excuse his writing of the previous letter—calls his paroxysm of love "fury of the passion I have for you." The expression "fury of passion" is totally self-explanatory and does not mean a platonic form of love!

[2] Pirandello is still hopeful about the realization of his "secret" project of films illustrating masterpieces of music.

[3] This is the first time that Pirandello writes about praying to the "Good Lord," a

thought that sounds distant from his mentality, which saw in everything the hostility of a blind fate (what he called in Italian "sorte nemica") at work.

[4] It is also the first time that Pirandello openly asks Marta to explicitly declare her love for him.

{ 290402 }

To Marta Abba
Via Cajazzo 52
(Italy) Milan   Berlin, April 2, 1929

My dear Marta,

Two very different letters arrived from you this morning at the same time. One carries the date of *March 22;* it looks as if it was begun, dropped, started over again, and then broken off rather than finished; as if written in the midst of a crisis—exactly the one I guessed at and described—so much so that reading it and seeing the effect my letters had on you at that point (an effect of cruel pity, both for yourself and for me) I had decided to ask you whether you preferred that I no longer write, in order to promote your recovery.

This letter of yours either carries a wrong date, or you kept it, without mailing it, until the 30th. It arrived in fact together with the one of the 31st, Easter day: but it is completely different! As much as the first one is wallowing in low spirits, tormented by cruel pity and swimming with tears, so is the second one upright, spritely, and sharp, almost without a trace of what was written in the other. "By now you should have the letter in which I wrote *about my little indisposition of the day before yesterday which now is over.*"

My Marta, so much the better! But I was able to write all that I wrote—about your courage, your willpower, the confidence you should have in yourself, the wretched suggestions you should not tolerate from other people—exactly because of what you yourself had written to me in your last two most desperate letters, which reached me after a silence of NINE days:[1] the world you had lost, the feeling that you were no longer yourself and that you did not exist any longer, your place taken, nobody giving you a word of comfort . . . —was I dreaming? You did really write me those letters; I read them, read them over again and again; I was like a maniac for nine days waiting for a word from you; and now in comes a letter about what you now call "your little indisposition already over,"

[1] The word "nine" is written in large characters.

arriving together with a second letter, which proclaims your willpower, your boldness, your pride, and that you will never be defeated! I repeat, so much the better, my Marta! But I am struck with amazement, I am not able to put together the two letters;[2] nor can I fully realize what happened to you during all those days of your silence, and then between your earlier desperate discouragement and the confident resurrection of today. Easter? God grant it! For me Easter has not come; it will never come—I say for me as a HUMAN BEING. What does it matter to me by now that my fortunes are on the upturn, with victories that seem to me like a hollow joke? I am dead as a human being, dead and buried; and at the same time I am a human being who is *still alive*, Marta, desperately alive—*alive and yet without life anymore*—there is no misery more terrifying and awful than this.[3]

You ask me not to write anymore about it, not to upset you.[4] I know; I shouldn't do it, so that you won't get all perturbed; but I do not have the strength to impose upon myself the necessary restraint, Marta, I cannot get over my desperation, I cannot suffocate my wild grief. Don't call it selfishness, Marta, it is life that is taken away from me, LIFE ITSELF;[5] it is not "the misery that cleaves to all humanity"; it is LIFE ITSELF, LIFE ITSELF![6] You say: *enough*, Marta. But you don't understand that "enough" means for me NOT TO LIVE ANYMORE? I can be silent, forever silent—*enough* can only mean that for me. There are many ways to die, even when one's actual death does not occur or is not sought. This is what *enough* means: not to be alive anymore. You must understand that this transition from life to death cannot be made except by speaking about it with despair, with desperate resignation (if resignation is possible for some people), and this happens when you so much as open your mouth; or by silently clenching your teeth and letting grief devour your insides until the last fiber of life is extinct. But how can you speak of anything else? I can speak about you. But to speak about you means to speak still about Life, when I am already dead. Yes, even at my death, with Death's own two feet firmly planted on my corpse, I can start talking about you, Marta, and of your life. You must live your life without me, and life must

[2] Pirandello cannot understand the contradictory character of Marta, which moves to extreme moods with the speed of lightning.

[3] What a "Pirandellian Pirandellism!" It sounds like a line in one of his plays.

[4] Marta had therefore written to him not to upset her anymore with "*chiacchere inutili*" (useless chatter) about his love. It is really true; it is a twice-impossible love.

[5] Written in the manuscript in large characters and underlined twice.

[6] Again, written in large characters.

be beautiful, full of joy, and glorious; the sort of life a soul like yours and a heart like yours deserve. And when you do have it, full of joy and shining with glory, you'll think a little of me, Marta, about me who will no longer be, about me who loved you so much, so immensely, as to die from being forced not to talk about my love anymore.

Your poor
Maestro[7]

[7] Pirandello here signs Maestro, which he preferred until the end.

{ 290405 }

To Marta Abba
Via Cajazzo 52
(Italy) Milan   Berlin, 5. IV. 1929
    Marta,

I am in receipt of your few words of Wednesday, 3, still signed *Marta Abba* (although you know how much you hurt me when you sign that way); and then you say you are afraid "that even now, as usual, I won't understand you." No, Marta, I am not able to understand you if you really believe, after my last letters, *that I have not understood you.* I don't know, I really don't know anymore what I am supposed to understand. I have explained clearly all that I thought I should understand from what you wrote to me, from what you said about yourself, and about me. And now you say that I did not understand! What should I then understand? I don't know anymore! *Nothing good,* certainly, for me, if—after saying so—you sign *Marta Abba.* Something good can come to me only from Marta. Marta Abba who wishes me well because I am leaving for London is nonsense to me; because all the good things that can come from London or from America or from Rome or from the whole world have no longer any meaning, are nothing for me, if the *true* good, the *only* good does not come anymore from Marta. I have said this to you, and I have said it over and over again; you surely cannot have misunderstood me; I have always spoken, in every way, clearly. From you, on the contrary, not a single clear word has come to ease me from this torment. I tried to understand what you wanted to let me know through the expression of your feelings, of your frame of mind, of your plans; and by dint of interpretations and suppositions that made my heart bleed, and caused me to shed the bitterest tears of my whole life, I reached the most dreadful conclusion I could ever reach: my death in your heart. I have already written this, and yet you tell me that *also now, as usual,* I do not understand you; and you sign *Marta Abba.* In the name of God, I implore you to tell me clearly what I am supposed to understand! I give you my word, Marta, I swear it on the love I have for you, which is for me the very same as life, I will tear to pieces the letter that you will write to me, a clear letter, so that I may at last understand you and get free of this torment that is driving me mad!

The nature of my feeling for you, Marta, cannot change; cannot become only *affection*, and nothing else, except at the cost of my feeling like dying. Also this, you see, I tell you clearly. A simple *affection*, a distant affection, as noble and disinterested as it may be, if it wants to be nothing but *affection*, affection *only* and that's it, *affection and nothing else*, from you, will be for me like death. *Dead*, yes, I can be dead; I already considered the full horror of this death, and I have been sinking into it—you saw it in my last letters; but it is no longer possible for me to stay *alive*, still sensible to any good that could come from life, of any other kind, even if it were your simple affection. I will not have any good in this world if you take away *the good* of my Marta, mine, *mine*, which means *all my life for you*, because you are all my life. Being all my life does not imply—please mark my words—that you should not go your way in Art by yourself, that I should be always physically near you, no; it's enough that you feel me *near* inside your heart, as before, always *near*; and that when you will not feel any longer that way, you'll tell me, honestly, as a soul as noble and pure as yours cannot but do. This is it. Without false pity. Because I have a strong and proud spirit, and I can close with firm hand the door to life and shut myself up, mute in my grief and in death.[1]

I am awaiting, Marta, I can't tell you with what anxiety, a word from you. Addio.

Your Maestro

---

[1] This letter is fundamental to an understanding of the relationship between Pirandello and Marta Abba. It reveals that the actress, even in the letters that were not preserved, although pressed as heavily as humanly possible to declare with precision her feelings toward the Maestro, purposely maintained an evasive and detached tone in her answers, ignoring his dramatic pleas for a "clarification." In this renewed and stronger-than-ever request, which remains unique in the collection of the letters, Pirandello defines with the greatest clarity what he wants to receive from his beloved and implicitly reveals what his beloved is not giving to him. He also seems to hint again at suicide, a thought that in this period returns frequently to his mind. See the entry Suicide in the Subject Index.

{ 290406 }

To Marta Abba
Via Cajazzo 22
(Italy) Milan   Berlin, 6. IV. 1929

My Marta, little and great,

I don't know how you all of a sudden got the idea that I would be leaving at once for London. I would have given you notice by telegram, which is what I will do at least two days before I actually leave. Can you ever imagine that I would take a chance on missing or receiving with delay even one letter of yours!

. . . The whole world of the movies is going through a revolution. It looks as if the talking film is really a prodigy: they have succeeded in reproducing to perfection the human voice—close up, distant, tuned in all possible ways. Which means that they'll definitely need actors who know how to speak well, and therefore also playwrights who know how to make the characters of the no-longer-silent movies speak. You understand: if the characters of the film from now on are going to speak, not just anybody will be able to make them speak; it will be necessary to employ a writer who knows the art of the dramatic or comic dialogue—a theater writer. They will have to hire the best ones available. The problem of keeping a film international—raised by the spoken word—will always remain to be solved: the English actors will not be able to speak anything but English; the Germans, German; the French actors, French; the Italians, Italian; neither is it possible to resort to translations, because the same actors will not be able to pronounce well the words translated into a language that is foreign to them. There will therefore no longer be any such thing as an international film, but instead English, German, French, Italian films, with significant reduction of the area of distribution, which has hithertho permitted the expenditure of enormous amounts of money for the production of every film. I don't know how they will solve this problem, which involves not only the language, but also the financial aspect. Right now they are all crazy about the miraculous novelty of the film that speaks (*in English*); not only in England are they as if possessed, but also in Germany, because they expect that it will soon speak German; but when it does speak *in German*, how will it be understood by the Americans and by the English people, and vice versa? They don't think about it.[1] They affirm, however, with unbearable arrogance, that the legit-

---

[1] At this time dubbing was not yet known.

imate theater is dead and buried; that soon nobody will care about it, because from now on there will be the talking film, which not only will reproduce the voices, but also will do things that the stage has never dreamed of doing.

This being the situation, I don't know what decisions I'll make on my return from London. Felix Bloch-Erben, in whose hands I put my idea for the musical film, will work to find, either in America or here, somebody who will want to realize it and invest millions. We must get started now, because it seems to me that so far the only way to solve the problem of internationalization is simply by making *sound* films. Sound—and not talking—films. The image, like music, can be understood by everybody; the word, no, because it is only in the language of those who speak it. But a representative of Tonfilm of England, with whom Bloch-Erben spoke today, said that my idea seemed brilliant, but only for a few selected people (as usual!) and not for the masses. "Pirandelo[2] is an exceptional poet," he told him, "whom I personally admire very much; but he cannot be good business." If the other executives think the same way, I can pack my bags and get back home.[3] But Wreede has faith in the deal and requested a three-month option to buy into it.

Stefano writes to me that Bisi has shown a great interest in me, and that he is ready to buy a subject proposed by me and pay a lot of money for it, almost double the amount Eichberg paid: one hundred and fifty thousand lire and maybe more; and that I could contract for more than one subject; also for *Six Characters*. I will think about it on my return from London, and in the meantime I am writing to Stefano to be ready and start negotiating.[4]

I am waiting, I am waiting, I am waiting. Oh, Marta, one word from you would give life back to me! If you only knew how my soul is!

Your Maestro

[2] *Sic*! Probably Pirandello transcribes, making fun of it, the pronunciation of his name as heard from the representative of Tonfilm of England.

[3] This was the destiny of the idea, which was not deemed sufficiently sure to generate a truly popular success. The idea, in very different forms, had to wait many years before reaching the mass market with films like Walt Disney's *Fantasia*.

[4] Pirandello refers to the deal with the Ente Nazionale per la Cinematografia, at the time under the direction of Bisi, who wanted to develop a lively program of film productions. Unfortunately, this hope also fell through.

{ **290408** }

To Marta Abba
Via Cajazzo 52
(Italy) Milan   Berlin, 8. IV. 1929

My dear Marta,

No letter from you today. The one I am waiting for perhaps will come tomorrow.[1] And it will restore my peace of mind. What has been worrying me most for a number of nights is that I cannot sleep anymore. I had so far always found in sleep a respite from all the pains of my life—which have been many—and a certain tonic for my physical health. I'd certainly have gone mad if all the torments of my heart and all the turmoil of my mind had not found rest during the night. Now, for several nights, my eyes remain open in the darkness, and the hours become *enormous;* I shiver and shake and—a frightening thing—if my eyes get veiled by an almost-white drowsiness, my body feels as if it were whining, speaking. Like in the past. . . .

I am not angry with anybody; I rebel against insomnia itself; I make an effort to sleep, forbidding myself to think, to feel; I cannot; the body does not want to; the beast does not get tired and, although whipped, it still does not want to; its blood is all churned up; its heart beats too quickly and does not want to; maybe it conceals a disease that I don't know about yet; but if it cannot help itself, I certainly can't.

. . . Now I have started writing *O di uno o di nessuno*, to make sure that my repertory can start afresh with comedies suited to the one company or the other: *O di uno o di nessuno* seems tailored for Almirante and Tòfano[2]—with no important role for a woman. If my good mood lasts and inspiration helps me, I'll finish it soon. I have written almost all of the first act, but I am afraid that it cannot be developed in less than four.

I see that it is necessary to do so, because I do not know which of the Italian companies now in the process of formation will be able to perform *Questa sera si recita a soggetto*. Here in Germany it will be performed for sure next fall, and not at the tail end of this season, which would mean a great loss. Pallenberg is enthusiastic about it and has taken it for

---

[1] The letter with the longed-for and dreaded answer to his "final" request for a "clear answer" about her love for him.

[2] At the time of this letter, the actor Luigi Almirante was heading the Almirante-Rissone-Tòfano Company.

himself.[3] It will be performed also in England and maybe in America. It is a comedy not meant for Italy. Its production is costly and can be risked only with the probability of many performances.

The same applies for *I giganti della montagna*—I find myself always thinking about it. I am strongly tempted to start writing this other myth of mine, the third and the last—but I must overcome this temptation and go for something practical. I can envision its scenes, one more beautiful than the next; I see its characters, all of them, one by one; I caress them with my fantasy; during last night, a sleepless night, the first scene was done from the beginning to the end; God knows what an effort I had to make this morning, when I got up, to leave it there and open instead the file where there are already 24 typewritten pages of *O di uno o di nessuno*.

. . . Mussolini will get around to funding the state theaters, or the municipal theaters; perhaps earlier than people might believe; he will certainly keep his word; sooner or later he always does whatever he promises. If I'll still be alive, Marta—my time will come. If I don't live, I won't care about anything.

. . . Soon it will be one month since you left, and it seems to me as if it were an infinite amount of time. . . . Perhaps I'll send you, one of these days, a bunch of poems I composed during these lost evenings. They are written for you alone and not for other readers—not because there is anything bad, but because they are only for you. Addio.

Your Maestro

[3] The Viennese actor Max Pallenberg was discovered by Max Reinhardt in 1914 and had an illustrious career, especially at the Deutsches Theater in Berlin.

{ 290411 }

To Marta Abba
Via Cajazzo 52
(Italy) Milan   Berlin, 11. IV. 1929
  My Marta,
After so many days filled with the most distressful suspense (yesterday, desperate, I was no longer able to restrain myself from sending you a telegram), I received this morning your letter of the 9th which *talks about other things*. This means that you want me to reach my own conclusions. As far as whatever I thought I needed to understand—and which made

me feel almost as if I were dying—you wrote to me that I do not understand you at all, and that I have never understood a thing about you also in the past. What conclusion do I have to draw from all this? That I am still alive in your heart? That you are always my Marta? I don't wish for anything else, I am not asking for anything else, my Marta, my little Marta, my great Marta, who does not want to understand (or perhaps cannot understand) that the fact that she, after three years, has left me— what a horrible event—cannot possibly have meant for her what it did for me! I, not you, was the one who felt like the very life had been torn out of me by your departure; with my heart, and my whole soul torn out. And it was I, not you, who was left alone here, in a loneliness that is not only tangible, but also total and infinite—the most frightening loneliness of all. About all this, however, you are silent and you want to hear nothing but silence. You want to say nothing. You talk about other things.[1] So you order me too to talk about other things. So I will talk about other things, Marta; to obey you, I'll talk about other things, but remember that my heart, under the pressure of this silence, will explode, Marta, someday. You really cannot imagine how much I am suffering!

. . . You say I should change my way of life? No, *not at my age;* my life has always been like this; even *when I was twenty it was like this.* On the contrary now, in the sense that you mean, it is much more active. I have never done anything but think of beautiful and noble things; and many times I was successful—but sometimes I was not—in writing them; I've always been unfit for practical life. Therefore I should not bewail my luck—actually I do not complain for myself, but for the others who, although aware of this, pretend not to know, and so expect from me what I cannot deliver. From all the work of forty years, which produced large amounts of money, I have nothing left; other people always took it, it has served other people's interests; I still want to keep on working, always working, because I know that I do not know how to do anything else. I don't know why it is that now they do not want my work to bring in as much money as before; if it did, it would continue to produce money for

---

[1] Marta's final sentence of life or death—so passionately desired and so tensely awaited—actually dissolves like a soap bubble. Marta says that the Maestro has never understood a thing about her, she doesn't want to hear any more of that nonsense, and continues to write about practical things as if nothing had happened. And this is the end of it. It seems sensible to conclude that Marta knew very well how to handle the Maestro. She wanted to keep the status quo in the type of relationship they both implicitly had agreed to, which was convenient for both and which could last only because they had practically, de facto, chosen to live in a nonintimate intimacy.

other people and not for me, because I never enjoyed my money, I never knew what to do with it for myself, it has always been used by me to make other people happy; my only unhappiness now is that I cannot make other people as happy as I could before or even more so.[2]

... Let me go back to Italy. I'll go and talk to the Duce. The state theaters will be set up: you may be sure that they will. Either that, or else municipal theaters, according to my other idea. But we'll somehow succeed in solving, in a Fascist way, the problem of the theater in Italy; and the "gang" will be swept away; you can be sure of that too.[3] The time is ripe. They are fussing a lot about it; but they'll get nowhere, because all they can do is nothing but evil; and they've done already so much of it, that they reached the limit, and everybody has a feeling that this is it! Even Mussolini must feel it. And then it will be our turn. But before that, by September, you'll have your own company. Yours, and not anybody else's. Yours, and not theirs. Yours, and not mine. Yours, yours—yours alone.

Write to me, write to me. Think of me. Be conscious of me. Addio.

Your Maestro

---

[2] This long, candid confession about how Pirandello viewed himself permits a more precise understanding of his inability to administer his vast financial resources wisely. He was honestly convinced that he was living modestly and that he was spending his money "only for others." In reality, during the eleven years of his relationship with Marta he spent large amounts of money on himself. He lived for long periods in very expensive hotels, or rented very expensive addresses in expensive cities like Berlin and Paris; he dined every day in expensive restaurants; he was often seen in night clubs accessible only to people who could afford to pay stiff bills. The "others" he is talking about are only members of his family and his own theatrical enterprises. There is no trace in the letters, nor are there to my knowledge any records of significant donations by Pirandello to charitable or cultural institutions. No trace exists in the letters of any money actually sent to Marta for her struggling company; that is, beyond the very generous offers that remained only beautiful words. The large amounts of money he earned in years of worldwide editorial, theatrical, and film successes, even discounting the enormous slices that were taken more or less honestly by his agents, are certainly equivalent to several millions in today's dollars (1993). Wise handling of his large income should have allowed him to put together, without big sacrifices, the fortune he was always dreaming about and to avoid the many financial worries that afflicted him until the very end of his days (see letter 361121, written just a few weeks before his death).

[3] Pirandello seems to be regaining his faith in Mussolini, which for a while had been dwindling. The language used here repeats in a pathetic way the characteristic tone and the very same sentences of Fascist propaganda, which aimed at presenting the dictator as a man who—whenever it came to the prestige of the Italian nation, as Pirandello honestly believed was here the case—would make prompt and irrevocable decisions, stepping over every obstacle and without regard to any personal interests.

{ 290416 }

To Marta Abba
Via Cajazzo 52
(Italy) Milan   Tuesday 16. IV. 1929
My Marta,

I am writing from London, as you see.[1] I am dead tired, because, after ten hours in the train—from 1:00 to 11:00 P.M.—I got on the ship in the Netherlands and spent the night at sea; I landed at 6:30 this morning at Harwich in England; I could not sleep at all on the ship because I had to take care of Lantz, who was seasick. The sea was really bad; but Lantz was much worse than the sea. I've never seen a man in such a wretched condition. Poor man, he is not in good health to start with, he suffers from kidney stones; the seasickness knocked him out. Suffice it to say, with God's help we made it through the night. But, after landing, we had to continue on a train to London, for two and a half hours more. The Ambassador[2] was kind enough to arrange for me to find dear old Pettinati at the station,[3] and Pettinati accompanied us here to the Savoy, where we are staying in two rooms with connecting bath. I had every right to go to bed and rest. I did not want to. Always up and going, that is my motto! I put Lantz to bed, and immediately with Pettinati we started to make a number of phone calls. First I wanted to call Cochran,[4] as I had promised you. Unfortunately the answer was that Mr. Cochran was out of town and that he would not be back before the end of next week; that is, in fifteen days! This misfortune, however, is not too unfortunate, because I heard that since the demolition of the New Oxford Theatre where we performed, Cochran at present only deals with revue and operetta, and is no longer interested in drama. Had I found him in London, I would have not been able to close any deal with him anyhow. If good luck

---

[1] Pirandello uses the letterhead of the Savoy Hotel in London. The writer, just arrived with his secretary Lantz, hopes to close deals with British producing companies for the filming of his *Six Characters* and other scripts. High on his priorities, and the very reason for which he was sent by British International to the English capital, is to see at last the all-new talking films—not yet available in Berlin—and become familiar with the "miracle" that was to revolutionize the film industry.

[2] Ambassador Bordonaro, a distant relative of Pirandello, was at the time representing Italy in England.

[3] Mario Pettinati, whom Pirandello later nominated as his representative in London.

[4] Sir Charles Blake Cochran, English actor and theater manager, who in 1926 had presented Pirandello's *Six Characters* at the New Oxford Theatre in London.

assists me, perhaps there is hope to sign a contract for the filming of *Six Characters*. Tomorrow, here at the Savoy, I have a meeting with Mr. Sinclair, who is the owner and director of one of the most important production houses here. It seems that he is very enthusiastic. He is talking about filming two versions of the picture, one silent and one spoken. Still, maybe he'll do neither. In the meantime I set up a meeting with Gaumont British.[5]

As usual, reporters came to interview me all through the morning, and photographers too, because already the morning papers were carrying the news of my visit. I don't know how many interviews are scheduled for tomorrow.

. . . I went with Lantz to see our first talking film. I won't tell you what a horror! What voices . . . what destruction of every illusion! The figures looked like ventriloquists: you saw their mouths moving, but the voice was not coming out from there; you could not make out where it was coming out from: a voice that was not human! If God wants it so, and these beasts want to continue like that, it will be the death of cinematography and the salvation and resurrection of the legitimate theater. Hearing images speak will seal the death of the image, and therefore of the screen; and the triumph of dramatic theater! I'll still view three or four of them just to satisfy these people of British International who paid for the trip and the expenses; but for me the one I saw was more than sufficient.

I'll write to you again tomorrow, my Marta, and I'll keep you informed of everything.

In the meantime, good night. My eyes are closing by themselves. It is half past ten, and I'm going to bed.

Think of me! Think of me! Until tomorrow. Addio,

Your Maestro
who loves you so much

---

[5] A film-producing company born as a subsidiary of the original French company started by the pioneer of cinematography, Léon Gaumont.

{ 290421 }
=========

To Marta Abba
Via Cajazzo 52
(Italy) Milan   Berlin, 21. IV. 1929
    My Marta,

Here I am, back in Berlin. I arrived two hours ago. After my first letter from London I was no longer able to write, because I was so busy the whole day that I had not even a moment to breathe; at night, as soon as I got back to the hotel, dead tired, I was overcome with sleep. The purpose that Eichberg and British International had for my trip with Lantz to London turned out to be a big failure.[1] I came back with the staunchest belief that the talking film is the most brutal among all the mistakes the movie industry has ever made; and I am very happy to know that that great little Chaplin is in agreement with me. But all this would lead us to a long discussion we cannot have now. You'll read what I'll write in a long article[2]—the first of a series I'm going to write for Anglo-American Newspaper Service, with which I signed in London a profitable contract: six thousand lire for each article, one per month. I signed another profitable contract for ten short stories (not new ones, but translations of those I wrote and published in the collection *Novelle per un anno*) with another publishing house, which actually owns the English monthly and bimonthly illustrated periodicals: ten short stories per year, which will pay me 150 pounds each, to be divided with the translator. Remember that each pound is worth about one hundred of our lire, and that all this will be earnings on an already existing work. With these two contracts alone I am assured of enough money to live on decently; and I'll have very little work to do: one article of ten typewritten pages each month.

    . . . I haven't yet seen anybody here in Berlin, and therefore I don't know what the news is around here. I found a letter from Stefano, who calls me back to Rome where, he says, he is positive that a very important deal with the Ente will go through. He says that the time is ripe for me in Rome, and that my presence is absolutely necessary. I'll go for a short

---

[1] British International paid the expenses of Pirandello's trip to London with the idea that he might become enthusiastic about the talking film and get ready to write scripts for future productions.

[2] This article was also published in Italian in the *Corriere della sera* of June 16, 1929, with the title "Se il film parlante abolirà il teatro" and reproduced in volume 6 of Pirandello's complete works, *Opere di Luigi Pirandello* (Milan: Mondadori, 1960).

visit, perhaps at the end of this month. But we'll talk about it tomorrow. Now I'm dying to get your news! Are you still in Milan? I need to see you. I cannot exist anymore without seeing you, talking to you, hearing your voice advising me. Until tomorrow! Addio, Marta,

Your Maestro

{ 290422 }

To Marta Abba
Via Cajazzo 52
(Italy) Milan   Berlin, 22. IV. 1929
   My Marta,
   I feel completely disoriented—after so many days without a word from you. I don't know how to compose my heart and my spirit. I feel as if I'm throwing my words into a bottomless abyss—without an echo. Should you never again answer, should I never again be able to get my words to you—how cruel and unbearable that would be for me! Now my words go, they fly, and far away there is your bosom that receives them. What does your hairdo look like, Marta? I did not tell you, the last days you were in the room next to mine—but your round pretty head, seen from behind, with that little tuft of hair in the back, how pretty it looked and how well it suited you! Do you still wear your hair in that fashion? How is your hair styled now? I know all the different expressions of your eyes. All I need is to half close my eyes, and I feel all those looks of yours upon me. Your eyebrows—you make sure that nobody touches them. That blue vein under the eyes, the flare of your tiny nose, the smile on your lips, your milky white teeth. . . . How clearly I see you, Marta! And I am here, so far away. . . . Perhaps far away also from your mind, as one who should never again get close, but rather disappear into time, farther and farther away from your life, which is now present only to other people and to yourself. Who is hearing the voice coming out of your lips! I do not hear it any longer. . . . Ah, Marta, when this thought occupies my mind and grips my throat, I feel I am falling into an infinite despair and I curse my age and my fate, and nothing can console me for my misfortune.
   Enough. I must not begin again to say what you do not want to hear. But how can I rise from this pit? Up, up. If I could only once breathe, draw even one deep breath from the very bottom of my lungs—which have been for so long oppressed. After years and years of unspeakable

misery, they did breathe for a moment; now oppression suffocates them again.[1] Enough.

I did not know that the *Corriere della sera* of the 19th already carried my interview in London with Rizzini, who came to see me at the Savoy. One of the owners of the Aida gave me the news, when I went there for dinner. I don't know whether you missed this interview too. If not, you read what I think about talking films. Notwithstanding my hostile judgment, I most certainly will make a spoken film—but one that will be against the spoken film. Just think about it. It's a most original idea. Man has given the machine his voice, and the machine now speaks; it speaks with a voice that has become its own and is no longer human, as if a devil had taken possession of its body and is amusing itself, while speaking, by commenting upon the action of the silent film with its moving shadows; it calls out to them, pushes them, stops them, suggests to them this or that action; it deceives them, laughs scornfully about them; it reveals a secret, foils a plot; it does whatever it likes. It will be a talking film, but only the machine will speak; the ventriloquistic voice then will not be offensive anymore, because it will not pretend to be a human voice, but the voice of the machine, and everything will be all right. The idea is splendid. I must offer it first to those people of British International, who paid for the expenses of my trip to London. But they will have to pay plenty of money; otherwise, I won't give it to them. With an idea like this today a lot of money can be made. And I have so many more ideas! I never had that many before! But I am no longer well, I do not sleep at night as I used to before. . . . Perhaps it is the last flaming of ideas that will devour me! If you knew, if you only knew what I have had in mind for *I giganti della montagna*! And how well *O di uno o di nessuno* is turning out. . . . My pen has never felt lighter than now; it has wings. . . . When I write I feel as if I were floating in midair, happy; I may never touch earth again. . . .[2]

Did you read *Questa sera si recita a soggetto*? I am looking forward with great expectation to your comments. The poems? I'll send them. But you alone must read them. You alone. Addio, Marta. Addio.

Your poor Maestro

[1] This statement is important to an understanding of how Pirandello viewed his life; that is, as "years and years of unspeakable misery" before meeting Marta, followed by a brief parenthesis of happiness when living near Marta, and finally by "infinite despair" and "suffocating oppression" after Marta's departure from Berlin.

[2] This euphoric creative state is not, this time, in any correlation with encouraging news from Marta.

{ 290425 }

To Marta Abba
Via Cajazzo 52
(Italy) Milan Berlin, 25. IV. 1929

My Marta,

Nothing has arrived this morning either, and my fear is growing that you are still indisposed. I am not well either. I am suffering again with neuralgia of the cheek. I heard yesterday that Otto Kahn is in Berlin,[1] and that he has expressed a desire to meet me. I think, however, that he does not know my address; moreover, I cannot go out with my swollen face. Today I'll eat in my room if I still feel like this. My stomach is also giving me trouble.

But I do not want to talk to you about my miseries.

I already began, and I hope to finish by tonight, my first article for the Anglo-American Newspaper Service: "Will Talking Film Abolish Theatre?" The article must be at least two thousand words long. I have already written about one thousand, and I am far from exhausting all I want to say about the subject. How can spoken film supersede theater, if it wants to be a mechanical and photographic copy of theater?[2] And when it succeeds in becoming such a copy, will it generate more and more desire for the original, that is, for real theater? If film wants to stop being film and become theater, at most it will be neither film nor theater, but something mechanical that will be unsatisfactory either as theater or as film. I don't know why this is not understood by everybody. But it's a general aberration. You'll read the article, if it is reproduced in Italy.[3] It is brimming with spritely humor. And to think that I wrote it when I was so depressed! We must get in our little digs, but cheerfully, with a good purpose. Art can profit from everything, even from human stupidity; satire depends on it. And there are many ways to create satire. When I want to do so, I know where to get the zest for it. And I feel that this time it caught fire.

---

[1] Otto Kahn, one of the richest American businessmen of the time, became an admirer of Pirandello, and later gave great hopes to the writer that he would use his great influence with Paramount in his favor. See especially letter 290430.

[2] Pirandello could not foresee at this time that cinema would soon go beyond theater to find its own aesthetics. True, early films were called photoplays, but they soon got over that. Film did supersede theater for other reasons: stars, many lavish locales, huge screens, massive movie palaces. He could imagine none of this. Only one year later, however, Pirandello already describes the talking film as "a new expression of art" (letter 300527).

[3] See note 2 of letter 290421.

It applies to both the Europeans and the Americans. This devil of an invention of the speaking machine is,[4] after all, very amusing. It all depends on knowing how to use it. You can let the machine say, slyly and subtly, all those things that conscience carefully avoids saying. To observe the conscience of honest and civilized people caught by surprise at the words of a machine that reveals their innermost secrets might make a very amusing show. If only God and people would give me time and opportunity to work! My spirit is inexhaustible and ready, and every day I would be able to start over again and create. . . . But I should not have all these worries that oppress me, nor this unjust war I am not fit to fight—I should be left alone with my work and just receive, at the end, a fitting recompense for all the wonders I would be doing, by the force of one smile. . . .

Enough, Marta. I suffer too much. I have to finish here, for today. Addio.

Your Maestro

[4] See also letter 290422.

{ 290428 }

To Marta Abba
Via Cajazzo 52
(Italy) Milan   Berlin, 28. IV. 1929
  My Marta,
  I've been staring at your image on my desk for a long time, and I can't tell you what I felt, thinking that those lips of yours no longer part in a tender smile for me, and that those eyes do not look at me any longer with such an intense, tender, and modest grace. Your heart is still good to me, still wants what is good for me; but your mouth is full of bitter words, and your eyes do not gaze at me anymore in such a kindly way. If you only could feel how much I am suffering, I'm sure you would have some mercy on me. You don't talk about yourself any longer; I don't see you in your letters anymore and I don't know anything anymore; you talk to me about everything except what I would like to know and what interests me. You scold me—yes, I know, for my own good—but then I feel compelled to excuse myself and to write long, stupid letters like yesterday's,[1] which make me appear small and perhaps even wicked, which I am

[1] Letter 290427, here not translated, is a very long, detailed, and tedious rebuttal of

not; if only, on the contrary, life were not so petty, wicked, and truly miserable to me, forcing me into contacts and actions for which I am not fit, which I somehow get done (very badly) without much thought, just to get rid of the aggravation, thus falling into inexcusable contradictions, so that it is easy to catch me red-handed and believe that I am not sincere. No, Marta; it is the annoyance given to me by things I do not want to do and yet am forced to do; people I don't know how to avoid, although I am dying to get rid of them; the trouble I impose upon myself though I cannot stand it anymore: all this and many similar matters are the cause of the bad conclusions that—if they don't understand me—people can come to about me. The more mistaken, the more contrary these conclusions are to my intentions. If they wished to understand me, then they would feel sorry for me, because truly there is no man unhappier than myself and no man to whom fate has been more hostile and more cruel.[2]

But I do not want to trouble you anymore, talking about myself.

What about my going back to Italy? The more I think about it, the more I feel my soul rejecting the idea. With the kind of people who are there, the very thought of whom is making me sick; with this nature of mine, and with all the care I should take to follow your valuable advice; the brakes I should impose upon myself, the attention I should pay: I'll tell you the truth—now that I no longer see any reason why I should do all this—I don't feel like doing it, I really can't! For whatever slight pleasure I'd get out of it—because I cannot be near you—it does not make

---

Marta's accusations. The "impressionable" actress, under the influence of Miss Aillaud—whom Pirandello hated and despised and who he feared would poison Marta against him—accused the Maestro of overdoing the push for his new plays, of plotting behind her back to give his plays to other people, of being insincere, and so on, to the point of turning himself into an object of ridicule because of his foolishness. In that letter, Pirandello confesses: "I have absolutely no practical sense for living and I never pretended to be or look like a shrewd man, and the final proof of it is that after working so long, I am so poor."

[2] This letter is among the most revealing about the perception Pirandello had about himself during his frequent periods of gloom and despair. Life appeared to him insignificant, miserable, mean, and cruel; his existence seemed meaningless and purposeless, and people around him became unbearable nuisances to him. In the barrenness of such a "petty, wicked, and truly miserable" life, without a religious faith and without human ideals operating as a satisfying substitute for one, the brief period lived near Marta appeared to him as the only oasis, the only truly "good thing" that ever happened to him—unfortunately now no longer existent. Life with Marta had therefore assumed the function of the Absolute Good; the loss of such a supreme good had precipitated him into a state of extreme unhappiness, with the only possibility of relief being death (for him equal to annihilation).

any difference if my life remains what it is here, far away; nothing appeals to me if I cannot be near you. Even if everybody would carry me back in triumph—I am so full of bitterness and so empty of desire for such things that I would interpret it as a mockery. You do not want to calculate, Marta, what I have lost! I had it in my hands, unexpectedly, as a supreme prize, as an inestimable compensation for all the miseries of my life, and when I should least have lost it, I did lose it. You went away, my life is finished. I go through the motions of doing things and talking; I keep on fighting, I write, I keep busy—but it all feels purposeless. There are the needs of daily life, the burdens I have to carry, my reputation, which has also become a burden for me, because I have to make people appreciate and respect it when in reality I don't care at all, just as I don't care about anything else. Believe me, Marta, the only trip for me to take is the one without return.

. . . Why should I return to Italy? I can go to London or to Paris; or, even farther, to America. Give me advice, my Marta! Do you really think that I should go back? I am a foreigner in Italy—people there show recognition and appreciation for me only when an echo of my successes abroad reaches them. It is so, unfortunately! And I am in just such a mood, but I will follow the advice you give me. You are my fairy godmother—the only truly disinterested person, who wants only what is good for me, and whom I can believe and trust. I'm waiting. Addio.

Your most unhappy
Maestro

{ 290430 }

To Marta Abba
Via Cajazzo 52
(Italy) Milan   Berlin, 29. IV. 1929[1]
　　My Marta,
　　Although I did not receive any letter from you today, I am writing because I have something "of the greatest importance" to tell you.[2]
　　I went today for lunch at the Adlon, invited by Otto Kahn, who is now

---

[1] The date of April 29 is probably a mistake. The postmark on the envelope reads May 1—and it seems almost impossible that Pirandello would wait a whole day to mail it. Knowing his habits, it is much more probable that he wrote during the night of April 30 and mailed it on May 1.

[2] Pirandello refers ironically to Marta's request that he should write only about things

in Berlin. As you know, Otto Kahn is one of the wealthiest persons in the world; they say he is the sixth richest. You also know that he likes me a lot. Therefore he wanted me to come for lunch today at one-thirty: the two of us alone. He left everybody. He took me by the arm and led me to the dining room of the Adlon, where he spent an hour and a half with me, until three o'clock. He wanted to learn about all my ideas for the cinema, and when I explained them to him, he was *enthusiastic:* enthusiastic about *Six Characters,* enthusiastic about the musical films, enthusiastic also about my new idea of the talking film with only the machine speaking. He said, word for word: "All these things, besides being magnificent and brilliant, are also great business, and somebody must be really stupid not to understand it. A man so full of new ideas as you are cannot make it in Europe; you must come to America. The two general directors of Paramount are now in Paris; I'll talk to them and I will say there is stuff here to make truly big business with you."

He wanted my address here and in Rome, because the day after tomorrow he is leaving Berlin. Tomorrow morning I'll send the script of *Six Characters* to his hotel.

If Otto Kahn wants (and judging from what he said and from the way he acted with me, you cannot doubt that he wants it), the deal should go through, because he is the person who gives the money to Paramount. If he gives the script of *Six Characters* personally to the two general directors in Paris, and tells them, as he said to me, "This is a big deal," the two general directors will not be able to say no. And if this is the case, we'll go to America to do *Six Characters,* and once in America, once we get in with Paramount, all the rest will come by itself. Who knows, it might make our fortune. But by now I mistrust my luck too much to entertain any hope in my lifeless soul. My soul will not light up again for something that life might bring me, and I know that death is blind. My eyes did have a last light, and it has faded away. . . .

Addio, Marta.

Yours, always yours,
Maestro

"of the greatest importance." Evidently the actress, tired of the repeated complaints of the Maestro, asked him to limit his writing to practical, "important" business, without "useless" sentimental "chatter."

{ 290505 }

To Marta Abba
Via Cajazzo 52
(Italy) Milan   Berlin, 5. v. 1929
     My Marta,

     This morning I received your letter of *March* 3 (you meant *May*: on *March third* you were still here in Berlin, and I wish you had never gone away!). I was afraid you did not want to write to me anymore. Even yesterday, after a few days of dismal waiting, I wrote to you and implored you to answer my letter. In your letter I received today, not even a hint of the anger I imagined would be in you, and which I blamed for your silence. "Dear Maestro, I received your letters, of which the latest was dated the 29th. No news from me, meanwhile I am reading yours." The stone that falls on the grave could not be colder than this.[1]

     . . . In the meantime, yesterday, I received from Miss Aillaud this telegram: "Please telegraph immediately if accepting contract for worldwide

---

[1] In the preceding letters, not translated here, Pirandello had written at length, several times, imploring for "forgiveness" and "compassion" for the "ill-fated letter that must have provoked your anger"—referring to the long, detailed letter 290427, in which he defends his attack against Miss Aillaud and other people in Italy. In letter 290501, he writes: "I clawed at my forehead" in a fit of horror and disgust at finding out from Marta's letter that his beloved had agreed with the hated Miss Aillaud in criticizing and ridiculing his behavior. The present letter confirms the fundamental contrast between the extroverted, impulsive, and changeable character of Marta and the introverted, melancholic, and tormented nature of the writer, who had made out of nothing a whole immense bubble of tragic fantasy leading to a paroxysm of terror—of having lost forever his most precious contact with his beloved. Here again we see that Marta never writes answers to anything related to Pirandello's most pressing requests—for compassion, for forgiveness, for a word, or even only a hint, of love—nothing at all. As if nothing had happened, she just sends practical news, when available, and talks business. For Marta, when a storm is over, everything goes back to business as usual. After all, Marta shows a common sense unknown to the Maestro. She knows that there is no solution to the complexity of her relationship with him. She will continue to give the little she can to a man who, on the sentimental and fantastic level, is convinced he is literally "dying" to receive what she cannot give—and which, on the practical level, even he probably does not really want to get. "The stone that falls on the grave" is precisely the fact that Marta does not answer, does not want to answer, does not care to answer—meaning clearly that she cannot give him what he requests and is therefore sealing his "tomb." Pirandello is also relieved at finding out that Marta will be there for him as she was before. His "hopeless hope" can continue; nothing has changed. He gets so excited at this realization that he ends his letter—changing the somber tone of the beginning into enthusiasm—in a dream, in a pressing invitation to his beloved to come back to Berlin!

film rights *Come prima* for ten thousand dollars Stop Useless counter-request closing being urgent Greetings Aillaud." Ten thousand dollars are worth about two hundred thousand lire. I accepted the offer.[2]

Marta, you tell me that in Milan the weather is bad—gloomy weather that makes you sad. Here in Berlin the weather is splendid. All the trees on the square, all the trees along the canal are in full bloom; the Tiergarten, all green, is a paradise. If you want to go away from Milan, why don't you come back here for a few months, without much luggage, to relax and have fun? Soon in Berlin the theater festival will be in full swing; French companies will come; from Italy Toscanini will be here with presentations from La Scala; it will be a month of great theatrical festivities; being an actress, you have certainly a strong reason to be present. Marta, come! Otto Kahn will be here; big deals will be closed; I'll surely make enough money to be able to go back to Italy with you, when the time comes for you to form your company—which must be yours alone, and you alone must be its head. What kind of proposal do you expect this miserable Polese[3] can make to you—that filthy rascal with whom they made you shake hands? Why do you choose to need such people, who are all wretched creatures, nasty, stingy tradesmen, who can see only their miserable four cents' profit, without even money left over for cleaning up after the show? Marta, don't you really have any faith left in me anymore? I'll rise again; I've already risen; I am still the first; I'll always be the first, and nobody will have the power to take it away from me. *I alone am still able to write great new things.* I still have so many of them in my mind. Nobody is younger than I am! And if I am the first, you must be the first, too, by all means! I cannot take anything away from you, because your glory as an actress is one thing and mine as an author is something else, and the latter does not exclude the former; the glory of D'Annunzio did not detract anything from that of Duse.[4] The Actress, if she is great, is

---

[2] He refers to the play *Come prima, meglio di prima*, which was made twice into a film after the death of Pirandello: *This Love of Ours*, by W. Dieterle in 1945, and *Never Say Goodbye*, by J. Hopper in 1956. In the part of this letter here not translated, Pirandello lists a number of other business deals with film companies and publishing houses, among them the filming by Righelli in Italy of his short story "In Silenzio," which, under the title *La Canzone d'Amore* (1930), ironically became the very first talking film ever made in Italy!

[3] Enrico Polese was an agent who controlled the theaters of Milan for the Suvini-Zerboni and other agencies. Both Pirandello and Marta name him in their letters to Mussolini as one of the enemies who were boycotting their theater (see Alberti, *Il teatro nel Fascismo*, pp. 196, 206, and 207).

[4] Strange, this parallel with the poet Gabriele D'Annunzio, of whom Pirandello in his youth had been very jealous. When D'Annunzio was having his love affair with the famous actress Eleonora Duse, Pirandello was little more than an unknown man of letters.

great by herself as Actress; the Poet, if he is great, is great by himself as Poet. Moreover, I do not want my name to appear with yours, in your company, which must be, I repeat, yours alone, led by you, performing your repertory and not mine: unless it pleases you to still perform, from time to time, a work of mine. Come, Marta, come, come! Take yourself away from that mist of darkness! From contact with all those filthy people! Come to Berlin for the festival; the reason for your trip has been found: it will be the festival. We'll stay here until the end of June. Business deals will be closed; then we'll go to the seashore; during August you'll put together your company; in September you'll perform and I'll go back to Berlin, for the revival of my plays; in October I'll get back to Italy for the Academy. Do you know that the Academicians will have, like the members of the Chamber of Deputies and the senators, free travel on the state railways? Therefore I'll be able, from time to time, when you'll have your company, to visit you here and there for a few days, if you wish it. But now come! come! You need to take only two trunks; for a month and a half or two months, you can get dresses here without bringing them with you. I am waiting for you to tell me "I'm coming!" Ah, what a light would open up in my soul! Marta, Marta. . . .

Your Maestro

{ 290508 }

To Marta Abba
Via Cajazzo 52
(Italy) Milan   Berlin, 8. v. 1929
    My dear Marta,
    I sent you a telegram to find out where to address my letters, and for how long, because in yours—which arrived this morning—you announce your departure from Milan *on Thursday at the latest*. Today is Wednesday, and this letter will not leave before tonight; even if it travels very fast, it will not get delivered in Milan, as express mail, before very late tomorrow, when you certainly will not be there anymore. After receiving your address by wire, I'll send this letter there, and so you'll receive it as soon as you arrive, and it will give you my

WELCOME!

    Also, I had suggested that you come to Berlin for the theater festival! By now my suggestion has already reached you, and I think: "Who knows if she will answer my telegram saying: 'I'm coming!' " But it would be too

Pirandello on the stage of the New Oxford Theatre in London on the occasion of his Teatro d'Arte's performances of *Six Characters in Search of an Author*, in which Marta Abba interpreted the role of the stepdaughter (June 1925).

Pirandello with Marta Abba in Rosario di Santa Fe, Argentina, where Pirandello's company performed at the Teatro Colón (July 1927).

On the opposite page:
(*Above*) Marta Abba (*right*) and her sister Cele on the terrace of the Grand Hôtel des Bains in Lido di Venezia, at the time of the Teatro d'Arte's performances at the Teatro Goldoni in Venice (May 1928).
(*Below, left and right*) Marta's parents, Pompeo and Giuseppina Abba (born Trabucchi), in their fifties at the time of the letters.

Marta Abba as the model Tuda in *Diana e la Tuda*, the first play Pirandello wrote for her (Teatro Eden, Milan, January 1927).

On the opposite page:
(*Above*) At the Grand Hôtel des Bains in Lido di Venezia (May 1928). *From the left*: the journalist Rezzara, Marta Abba, Pirandello, the hotel manager, and Marta's sister Cele.
(*Below*) On the terrace of the same hotel, Cele Abba, Marta, and Pirandello (May 1928).

(*Left*) Marta Abba as the peasant prostitute Mila in Gabriele D'Annunzio's play *La figlia di Iorio*, directed by Pirandello on the occasion of the Volta Convention in Rome (Teatro Argentina, October 1934). The actress is wearing a costume designed by Giorgio de Chirico.

(*Right*) Marta Abba in *La nostra compagna* (*L'ennemie* by P. A. Antoine), a play in the repertory of the Compagnia Marta Abba during the 1929–30 season.

On the stage of the Teatro dei Fiorentini in Naples, on the occasion of the performance of Pirandello's play *Trovarsi*, which opened on November 4, 1932. *From the left*: Giulio Donadio, Marta Abba, Pirandello, and Carlo Ninchi.

Poster for the
April 15, 1933,
performance of
*Six Characters
in Search of
an Author,*
presented by
the Compagnia
Marta Abba
at the Teatro
Olympia, Milan,
on the occasion
of the tenth
anniversary of
the play's first
performance.

(*Right*) Marta Abba in the play *La buona fata* by Molnár, which was in the repertory of the Compagnia Marta Abba during the 1929–30 season.

(*Below, left*) Marta Abba photographed in her dressing room during the performances of Salomon Poliakov's play *Il labirinto*, which opened at the Teatro Argentina in Rome on April 7, 1927.

(*Below, right*) Marta Abba as Hedda in Ibsen's *Hedda Gabler*, which was in the repertory of Pirandello's company from February to June 1928.

beautiful; and by now, for whatever remains of my life, I do not expect anything beautiful anymore.

Recover, Marta, in that new place that is still unknown to me, your full vigor and your peace; be without sad thoughts, happy and serene. May my wishes for good health and tranquil rest welcome you at the threshold! I'll not write anything anymore that might even minimally trouble you. If I have good news, I'll send it to you; I'll keep any sad news to myself.

Perhaps, if you give me permission, when I come to Italy for a few weeks (not now, later), before returning here, I'll come and visit you for a day, just to see you again. That is, if you will give me permission; otherwise, no. I am dying to see you again, to hear again the sound of your voice, to feel again the glance of your eyes! But I do not want to dream! You say in your letter "down there" and you talk of a "*little village*" where you'll be able to take the same cure as in Salsomaggiore. Where can it be? Why didn't you tell me at once? *Down there* . . . it sounds far, far away . . . it sounds like in Tuscany, where there are many such small resorts . . . *Chianciano* . . . I was there for three seasons, one after the other. But I got there a course in living language. How well they speak in the country around Siena! Times of my distant past. . . . I was not thinking of the theater; I was writing my short stories and, only for myself, a few poems. . . . I was like the prisoner who no longer hopes to get out of his jail. Because at that time life itself looked to me as if it were a prison. And I was just about thirty-eight! My beard was blond, and I had all my hair. . . .[1]

Away, away with these melancholy thoughts! Wherever you'll go, Marta, at this time you'll find the beautiful spring. The grass everywhere, even on the edges of the little country roads, is green, with a new and fresh green; the meadows are full of flowers; and the contemplation of free and open nature is a divine ecstasy—time seems to be frozen and all things seem to be in an astonished stupor. The fresh flowers of your smile will bloom again on your lips—rosy but not red, tender and not burning, sweet and not violent.[2] You need tranquillity. Do not take along books that could trouble you! If I only could invent for you a beautiful fable, springlike, for you to read in the country! With the smile of all the brooks and that arcane peace that descends on the fields at the setting of the sun. . . .[3]

[1] Memories of the years 1905–1906—but all his life was to him like a prison!

[2] Reminiscences of *Pasqua di Gea*, Pirandello's collection of poems of 1890.

[3] Here Marta becomes almost like Petrarch's Laura.

Once, condemned to stay in the city over the summer vacation, I wrote *Liolà.*[4]

Are you going to the country with Cele—or by yourself?

I seal this letter without knowing where it will reach you. I'll write the address on the sealed envelope as soon as I get the telegram with your answer.

Be happy, Marta! Find your serenity again.

Addio,

Your Maestro

---

[4] See the letters of July 14 and 20, 1916, to his son Stefano—who was then a prisoner of war—published in the *Almaracco letterario Bompiani* of 1938, p. 37.

{ 290627 }

Miss Marta Abba
Hôtel Vendome
(France) Paris   Berlin, 27. VI. 1929

My Marta,

Yesterday I did not write because I had nothing to say; to be truthful, today I don't have anything to say either, but it is a great sacrifice for me to spend a day without writing, although I've been thinking of you the whole day—of you in Paris.[1] Who knows how many beautiful things you are seeing! You must be walking around from morning till night, here and there, stores, cafés, theater, business. . . . And, of course, you do not find even a moment to write. Of course, I am not scolding you for it! I understand very well that it must be so . . . you cannot even think of writing because now there is in you a turmoil of fleeting impressions, eagerness to see and do, things shattered in confusion. . . . They fill you and make your day fly by, without even realizing how. Impossible to collect yourself and pin them down. You can do it later.

---

[1] As was to be expected, Marta did not go to Berlin. After a brief stay at Terme di Mirandolo, a small resort in the province of Pavia, she went back to Milan. Pirandello went to Italy at the beginning of June, but in Rome he got disgusted again because of the political situation, and he also became more and more aware of the hopelessness of his emotional impasse. After spending a few days in Milan near Marta, he went back to Berlin. The present letter is addressed to Paris, where Marta was spending a couple of weeks shopping and seeing the theater. There the Maestro hoped to join her soon. Seeing Marta did not improve his mood: evidently she was polite, matter-of-fact, as if nothing had ever happened—but, again, she did not give him the only thing he wanted most!

I do understand—still I'd like so much to know something!

I never wished so much to be insane as I do now. Only madness can give us what fate has denied. Riches, joy. . . . For the insane, the possession of goods is not illusory, nor is the fulfillment of our desires. Happiness is achieved. The baby to whom a poor insane mother gives the milk of her breast might well be made out of just a rag—but what does it matter? She has from that rag truly the whole joy of motherhood, and woe betide you if you touch it! It would be the cruelest of cruelties to say to that mother: "Wake up, you are dreaming!" We all, when we dream, are insane. For the insane the dream lasts even when the senses are awake.

I don't know why, with a pen in my hand, while I was thinking I came up with such considerations. . . . But I have been watching for so long your picture that is smiling at me, here on the small desk. . . . And then, in these days (something very rare for me) I am experiencing the pleasure and the anguish of dreams—and I don't know on what it might depend. Ah, taking revenge, while sleeping, of all decency and all logic of the day! reversing with blessed calm all the so-called most solid truths! admitting with healthy satisfaction the most ridiculous contradictions to those respectable truths! multiplying three by three equals eighteen; four by four, sixty-nine; with the swift certainty of somebody who possesses instinctively the most elemental and obvious knowledge, and practices it, with the greatest seriousness and without making anybody laugh! Now, if a dream is a brief insanity, think that insanity is a long dream, and imagine how happy the insane must be. . . . Insane people, of course, who are not evil. Because woe if the dream becomes evil![2]

I had bad dreams too, and unfortunately they last even when my senses are awake. . . .

Enough.

. . . I am dying because I cannot get away from here! Nobody writes to me, either from Milan or from Rome. I fume, I fret, and being so upset I do not find a way to get back to work.

I talk to your picture when I am alone.

I hear that the cold wave has reached Italy too. Here we have a shower every day. I hope the weather is good in Paris.

Write to me, if you have a minute. Greetings to your father and Cele. Have a wonderful time. Cordially and affectionately,

Yours,
Maestro

---

[2] Pirandello appears still intrigued by the mystery of insanity, which a number of years before had inspired his *Enrico IV*.

{ 290628 }

Miss Marta Abba
Hôtel Vendôme
1 Place Vendôme
(France) Paris   Berlin, 28. VI. 1929

My Marta,

I received your letter of the 25th—I am ecstatic and I thank you for your good wishes with all my heart. Today I am *twenty-six* years old! Soul and body are in agreement to place the six after the two. Can you believe, I got home at 4:20 this morning, after spending the whole night at Angermayer's house, listening on the radio to the dramatic boxing match between the Spanish champion Paolino and the German champion Schmeling. I really did not have any interest in this fight, but all Germany was anxious about the fortunes of their young champion, and, wanting to please, I accepted Angermayer's invitation. It was a most youthful waste of sleep. At 8:30 Elizabeth came—merciless—to bring me my coffee and prepare my bath. After only three and a half hours of sleep I jumped out of bed, and fresh and relaxed I dived into the bathtub. After lunch at the Aida, I slept for an hour on the couch. I do not know how, but people here at the Herkuleshaus knew that today was my birthday; they knew it also at the Aida. I found flowers both here and there, from the owners of the hotel and the restaurant. Also Lantz, Eichberg, Tauber, and Philips sent me flowers. Evidently there must be here in Germany a *Who's Who* that carries celebrities' dates of birth. I wouldn't know otherwise how everybody was aware that today was my birthday.

But let's stop talking about me.

. . . Did you see *Melo* by Bernstein?[1] I can imagine how bored you were at the Comédie-Française, and you'll see how disenchanted you'll be with all the French productions after seeing the German ones. You still could see something fairly good if the theaters of Dullin (the *Atelier*) and of Gaston Baty were still open:[2] not for anything else, but because they imitate the productions here.

---

[1] In letter 280710, Pirandello had expressed his strong criticism of the play *Melo* (1926) by his friend, the boulevard playwright Henry Bernstein (1876–1953).

[2] Both Charles Dullin (1885–1949) and Gaston Baty (1885–1952), leading theater directors of the time in Paris, directed Pirandello's plays in Paris. Dullin had directed, in 1922, the first Pirandello comedy ever produced in Paris, *Il piacere dell'onestà*, and Baty was going to direct *Come tu mi vuoi* in the 1932–33 season.

How long do you plan to amuse yourself in Paris? If you are staying so comfortably at the Vendôme and will remain there probably for the first half of July, I could come to the same hotel—if you don't mind. But I have still so much to fight about here with Feist. He is like an eel, he slips through your fingers as soon as you try to grab him. Enough. We'll see the result of the meeting of the three lawyers. I know from Wreede, who came back this morning, that Reinhardt is enthusiastic about the play.[3]

. . . Until tomorrow. Write. Greetings to everybody. Cordially,

Your Maestro

[3] Max Reinhardt, the German director, was scheduled at this time to direct *Tonight We Improvise.*

{ 290629 }

Miss Marta Abba
Hôtel Vendôme
1 Place Vendôme
(France) Paris   Berlin, 29. VI. 1929

My Marta,

Yesterday evening I had supper with Salter, and all the time we spoke about you and your tour.[1] He told me about the great impression you made on him in the short time he could see you, but which was enough, experienced as he is, to understand all that could be accomplished with you. I spoke about Rivolta,[2] with whom an agreement could be reached to join together the tours in North and South America. He liked the idea. But he said that we should find a way to combine the two tours through Mexico or Havana, just as I wrote yesterday. He could take care of this himself, in agreement with Rivolta. He promised he would write to you in Paris at the address I gave him. You'll show the letter to Rivolta, then the two of them can correspond with each other and deal directly. I heard here in Berlin that this Salter is a very capable businessman, but also somebody you had better watch carefully. It is important, perhaps, to make Rivolta aware of it. Theater merchants are all the same. Slave traders. The honest ones are all stupid; they don't make money, nor do they ever let other people make money. Unfortunately, you must end up

[1] Norbert Salter, a German-American theater impresario, was trying to organize a tour of Marta's company in North and South America.

[2] A theatrical agent who represented the interests of Pirandello and Marta in Paris.

having the swindlers do the job, while you watch out as carefully as possible. You have to state the terms, point by point, with utmost precision, so that no opening for cheating is left, and you should not get on the ship before having deposited in the bank the agreed amount and all possible guarantees: advances and travel expenses. Before signing any contract, you should consult lawyers or other experienced people. But you can count on your father for all that. Before anything else, however, Gallo's report should arrive from America.[3] Salter considers it neither opportune nor prudent to speed up the deal with a cable, which would arrive before his letter. Gallo himself will send the cable, if the deal seems good to him; although always, in big business negotiations, it is well to take it slow and easy and think things out before making up one's mind.

I am going crazy here because of the time these lawyers are making me lose uselessly—they can never find a way to agree on the details of the meeting. Something is not convenient for one lawyer, something for the other, so they keep putting off the meeting, day after day. They were supposed to get together tomorrow, Sunday, but today Felix Bloch-Erben wrote to me that he had to leave Berlin tonight, and that it will be necessary to put things off until Tuesday or Wednesday. You'll see, on Tuesday or Wednesday, Feist's lawyer will not be able to attend, and will propose Friday or Saturday, and so on, week after week. I cannot take it anymore! Meanwhile, if the agreement is not reached, I risk missing the upcoming theatrical season, which is going to be a triumph for me, with at least four of my plays in the theaters of Berlin. My *Lazzaro* will go to London at the beginning of July. I got the news in a letter from Miss Aillaud, which arrived this morning with a check for ten thousand lire. The letter is very short. She says that she does not know anything about the film to be produced by Fox[4] because Miss Cutti has not answered as yet; she says that De Santis has hired the actor Riccione, but that she objected and insisted on Ricci for the role of the Son[5] and asked which leading actress he is thinking of hiring for the role of the Mother; she reports, as I already said, on *Lazzaro*, which is being produced in London, and she encloses the press release of the theater that will present it and concludes by telling

[3] Fortunato Gallo, theater impresario.

[4] Pirandello refers to the deal with Twentieth Century-Fox for the film *As You Desire Me*, which was eventually produced three years later, in 1932, by the director George Fitzmaurice, with Greta Garbo in the main role. See footnote 1 at the beginning of letter 290720.

[5] The actor Renzo Ricci (1899–1978) did actually perform in the Italian production of *Questa sera si recita a soggetto*, directed by G. Salvini in 1930.

me that I'll receive, under separate cover, an acting copy of *O di uno o di nessuno*—another copy has been already sent to Almirante.[6]

This is all the news.

I am waiting for you to tell me about how long you intend to stay in Paris, and if I'll be permitted to join you there. Otherwise, where do you plan to spend the summer, so that I may stay near you to work and finish the new play. Meanwhile, my best regards to your father and to Cele.[7]

All the best, with affection,

Yours,
Maestro

[6] The actor Luigi Almirante had been the father in the famous original production (1921) of *Six Characters* and performed in many plays by Pirandello, joining later, in 1934, Marta Abba's company.

[7] Marta's father and Cele were in Paris with Marta.

{ 290716 }

To Marta Abba
Via Cajazzo 52
(Italy) Milan
Berlin W.10, 16. VII. 1929
Hôtel Herkuleshaus
Friedrich-Wilhelmstrasse 13

My Marta,

After your departure, Paris seemed like a desert to me.[1] I went to lunch with Fausto at the Crémieux's. At 2:30 I returned to the Hôtel Vendôme, paid the bill, went upstairs to my room, and closed the luggage; in coming downstairs, I saw the closed door of no. 5: closed, my life. Impressions that cannot be controlled.

I left at 4:20; Fausto accompanied me to the train station, in his turn looking so very sad at remaining all alone in Paris.

My first thought in the train was that at the same time you were also in a train, on a different track that was taking you farther and farther away from me, and that this would have lasted until 10:30 in the evening. Far away, farther and farther away. . . . Then at 10:30 I pictured you arriving in Milan, I saw you getting out from the station, then in a cab, then arriving home; at the door of Via Cajazzo I left you and, back in

[1] Pirandello had joined Marta in Paris at the very beginning of July for a few days and was now again back in Berlin.

my train, I saw myself alone continuing my journey—my journey to Berlin.

As soon as I arrived in Berlin I immediately got on the phone with everybody. First of all, Salter. No answer yet from America. He told me about the letter from Rivolta and how he had answered. He asked about you and whether you had a good time in Paris. Conclusion: still nothing certain except his goodwill to conclude the deal and his promise to inform me at once, as soon as he receives any news from Fortunato Gallo.

Mrs. Lantz called me and said that her husband would be back from London on Wednesday afternoon, and, please, I should not leave again before his arrival because he had *many things* to communicate to me. It might be Joe May's stuff, which might interest me.[2] Tomorrow evening we'll know what it's all about, and I'll pass it along to you.

Fritz Wreede (the owner of the agency Felix Bloch-Erben) phoned me to say that the three lawyers had already settled on the terms of the legal agreement for the solution of the contract with Feist. I then called my lawyer to find out what these terms were, and Dr. Frankenstein gave me an appointment for today or, better, for this morning at 11 in his study in Behrenstrasse 23. I was there, and here are the terms: payment of two thousand marks, one thousand at once at the signing of the agreement, and one thousand at the date of the first performance, which is foreseen for the beginning of October, and then 15 percent on half the royalties due to the Agency Felix Bloch-Erben. The contract is very burdensome, especially for this outrageous figure of 15 percent, but since it will be paid by Wreede and not by me, Frankenstein advised me to accept the agreement just to get rid of such a greedy person, who could still give me a lot of trouble. I'm still burdened with the payment of two thousand marks; this money, however, will be advanced by Wreede against my royalties and gradually recovered from them, so that I'll hardly be aware of it. The important point is that I am now free for the new season. Max Reinhardt wants to have a meeting with me to agree on the interpretation of points of the play;[3] the conference will take place before the end of the month; that is, before my departure. He'll come from Vienna just for this meeting. Meanwhile Meinhard[4] is preparing two more plays, one of which will be certainly *Ciascuno a suo modo*. I cannot tell you how much kindness and warmth he shows to me. He arranged for me to find a large bunch of flowers in my room and a present—a magnificent walking stick with a big

[2] Joe May, Austrian producer and director.
[3] The play is, as already mentioned, *Tonight We Improvise*.
[4] Carl Meinhard, actor and director, owned the Theater am Nöllendorfplatz in Berlin.

ivory head and a golden ring with an engraved dedication and with also the ferrule made of ivory—and two hundred cigarettes. He waited for my return, and today he left for his castle in Bavaria, after inviting me to spend August at his place. I thanked him and I told him that it was impossible for me to accept because I have to go back to Italy.

I was disappointed at not finding my usual apartment at the Herkuleshaus free; they gave me for the same price a magnificent apartment on the first floor, with two large rooms, double bed and bath, but I felt more at ease upstairs, although I have to recognize that here it is much better.

Enough until tomorrow, my Marta. I am writing, as agreed, to Miss Aillaud. I am waiting for your news with great eagerness. Meanwhile I send you my best greetings,

Your Maestro

{ 290720 }

To Marta Abba
Via Cajazzo 52
(Italy) Milan   Berlin, 20. VII. 1929
   My Marta,
   . . . Let us speak of the new play.[1] As you know, it had been combined with *I giganti della montagna*; now I must free it, almost drag it out from that mountain, and see it *whole and alive*, by itself, and no longer as part of the other. I must make a big effort of concentration—which is not easy. Now a whole play—from the beginning to the end, free from any foreign element and organic in itself—must be developed from what I had thought would be good as part of one play, out of which part only a few scenes, albeit the most important ones, had to be drawn. Will I be able to accomplish that? I must succeed, whatever the cost. I will put to work all my mental energies. It must become a masterpiece for my Marta.

---

[1] The new work written for Marta and inspired by her is *Come tu mi vuoi* (As you desire me), which became the most successful of all Pirandello plays ever performed in America. Its Broadway production and film rights brought big profits to Pirandello and to the Shuberts. As appears from the present letter, Pirandello created the play from a part of the original total conception of *I giganti della montagna*. At this point Pirandello tells Marta about his decision to give immediate precedence to the writing of *Come tu mi vuoi* over *I giganti della montagna*, because he wants to provide Marta as soon as possible with a play made to order for her company. *Come tu mi vuoi* had its world premiere in Milan, at the Teatro dei Filodrammatici, on February 18, 1930, performed by the Compagnia Marta Abba—while *I giganti della montagna* remained unfinished.

Here, since yesterday, it has gotten ferociously hot. Last night I could not sleep. I still have a lot of trouble in settling the quarrel with Feist, and I can't wait to get away and free myself from all concerns of every type that are troubling me and do not give me a moment of rest. Ah, how unhappy is my life, Marta, to the last! to the very last! And I have only a few years to live. . . . Enough! Let's not talk of such melancholy matters. Warm greetings and all the best from

Your Maestro

{ 290721 }

To Marta Abba
Via Cajazzo 52
(Italy) Milan   Berlin, 21 (Sunday). VII. 1929
My Marta,

. . . I want you to understand this clearly, my Marta: I am here, as before, as ever, ready to do all you order me, ready to approve all you do and all you order me to do, ready to approve all you do and think, because what is good for you is good for me, because I know that what you do is always right, since there is nobody in the world more unselfish than you are, and, lastly, because you never got tired of proving to me the love you have for me. I am writing the new play and it will be only for you; if it is not for now it will be for later; or it will be for now, if you wish it. I'm waiting for an indication from you.

The days go by, all the same one after the other, and here nothing gets done. Yesterday, at fifty-two, the brother of Reinhardt died of a heart illness, and with his death Reinhardt lost his right arm. It is a disaster also for me because Reinhardt, being in mourning, will not be able to come to Berlin anytime soon and settle things with me for the new production.[1]

You cannot imagine how irritated I feel about everything. I'm so sick of life I cannot tell you! After all, so alone, what am I doing here?

It's better to stop, not to afflict you with my troubles.

Cordially,

Your Maestro

---

[1] Pirandello's fears were unfortunately well founded, and the consequences of this death were much worse than he could at this moment foresee. Max Reinhardt was unable to go through with his plan of directing Pirandello's *Tonight We Improvise*, and the fact that he was not the one to direct the play—in the very special circumstances that developed in Berlin and which exploded at the time of the premiere—was probably a decisive factor in the disastrous outcome. See letters 300601, 300603, and 300605.

{ 290722 }

To Marta Abba
Via Cajazzo 52
(Italy) Milan   Berlin, 22. VII. 1929

My Marta,

. . . Meanwhile you can be reassured about the date of delivery of my new work: it will be in your hands certainly before the deadline you specified—and may I succeed in being worthy of you and of your great Art! I have already started with the writing. The first act will be stormy. I must make the sincerity of this woman believable and justify her pretense,[1] *in depth*. This woman, not only unselfishly and because of her loving nature, but also *because of herself* and of the conditions of her soul and of her life, must be able to become another person, *sincerely*: to be *the other*, truly *alive*; so that, when the *other* actually arrives, lifeless, *dead* in her soul, her sacrifice can appear, in front of this *dead woman*, the sacrifice of life, a true and powerful sacrifice, and not the consequence of the discovery of a deception—which after all never existed, if the husband had been aware of it even before. Do you understand well what I am trying to say? Leave it to me: I am already in it. Follow me into this depth, into which we must descend with courage. But I would love to have you close to me! I've never felt as unhappy as I am now. I'm really touching the lowest point of my desperate loneliness. I swear it to you, Marta, that I pull myself together only because I think that *I have to work to finish this play for you.* I set it as a task, in order to find a reason to live. But I'll go down into the very depth of despair, in this work, which will be my greatest. If I don't move people to tears with this play, it will mean that all their hearts have turned to stone.[2]

I would like to scream for help; but to whom?

Enough, Marta. Addio,

Your Maestro

[1] The pretense of being somebody else. Pirandello clarifies here his intention of making out of the protagonist of *As You Desire Me*—Elma, the dancer from Berlin who tries to become Lucia, so as to build a new life for herself and her lover—not a deceiver, but a symbol of a "powerful sacrifice" of genuine life on the altar of convention and meaningless "truth."

[2] This discussion of *Come tu mi vuoi* is one of the clearest examples of the important part Marta played in the creation of key roles in Pirandello's plays of this period. This letter reveals the secret of the success of that touching play—born from such an abyss of pain and despair.

{ 290913 }

To Marta Abba
Via Cajazzo 52
(Italy) Milan   Berlin, 13. IX. 1929

My Marta,

When my train arrived yesterday morning, I found Lantz at the station.[1] . . . Lantz had not rented an apartment for me—although he had checked out a number of them around here. He had not felt like making a decision without knowing whether I liked his choice; therefore, for the time being, I went to the Herkuleshaus, where, to tell you the truth, I feel at home, because the hotel employees know and respect me, and they take good care of me. It is very expensive, I know, but the location is beautiful, quiet, and without annoyances of any kind. I think it will not be worth while to move from here, since soon I have to depart again for Russia or for Italy. Anyhow, should I change my address, I'll give you notice in advance.

The very long and very boring trip has exhausted me; I spent the night almost without sleep. All yesterday afternoon I was in bed, but I was so overtired that I could not fall asleep. I made up a little bit tonight, but now I have a terrible headache. It will pass!

I found here again an infamous article against me by Feist in a socialist newspaper, which obliged me to take legal action for slander, with plenty of proof to back it up. He says that I cheated him, that it is not true I broke with him, but that he broke with me because by now my plays are worth nothing—either in Italy (where nobody performs them anymore) or in France and the other countries of the world, and so on.[2] This outrageous publication has left everybody indignant here and has hurt him more than me, but, of course, by obliging me to sue him, he has suc-

---

[1] Pirandello is again in Berlin, just arrived after a summer spent helping Marta with the many preparations for the organization of her new company—which was to tour Italy during the 1929–30 season. After a period of several months of almost daily letters following Marta's departure from Berlin, there are therefore no letters for the whole month of August and the first two weeks of September.

[2] See the article by Willi Hirdt, "Tra moda e morte: Presenza di Pirandello nel teatro tedesco," in *Scena illustrata*, 122/3 (March 1987), especially pp. 33–34, to understand the buildup of anti-Pirandellian clouds in Germany—due to the great increase of nationalism and the general malaise preceding the Nazi takeover of power—which exploded into a storm at the opening of *Tonight We Improvise*, just a few months later, at the end of May 1930.

ceeded in nullifying the agreement concluded with my payment of the two thousand marks. He has obtained what he wanted in order to hurt me; that is, to go to court and obtain a prohibition of the performance of my works in Germany during the next season. Both yesterday and today, I went with Lantz to my lawyer's office to figure out how to bring legal action without at the same time hindering the performance of my works. . . . In the meantime the legal action has been initiated—I am absolutely sure I'll win and I'll force him into public disgrace. He knows he will lose, he knows he has been lying; he acts only for the purpose of damaging me, like the mad rascal that he is. He has trampled on his own dignity as a human being. But let's not talk about him anymore. He makes me sick!

. . . Please try to go to Salsomaggiore soon, and then to the country; take care of yourself, be calm, and don't worry about anything. Greet all your family from me. Cordially,

Your Maestro

{ 290927 }

To Marta Abba
Via Cajazzo 52
(Italy) Milan

Berlin, 27. IX. 1929 (or 28? I don't know! I don't know whether it is Friday or Saturday either!)

My Marta,

. . . So you'll open your season on the 19th in Varese; you haven't told me yet with which play.[1] I'd love to be informed about everything regarding whatever you have already decided for your tour—places and dates—so that I can follow you, at least in my thoughts. And I'd like to know for each place, in order, the plays you'll perform. This way, always in my thoughts, from far away, every night, I'll listen to you performing. I'll see you living your roles. This distance will be a misery for me! During the three years we were together, didn't I not get tired a single night of hearing you performing! Of all the pleasures of life that art can give, I never experienced a pleasure equal to the one you gave me! Perhaps I am asking too much, but, because you care for me, I hope you will comply. I do not have any other comfort left but this, in this horrible solitude in which I

---

[1] Varese was the first stop of the tour of Marta's newly formed company.

feel myself now, and in which I'll feel myself even more, as soon as you start getting again fully involved in performing. Do not forget me, my Marta, for the love of God! Remember that, from far away, I'll be always near you with my whole soul, I'll be there on the stage, in the wings, to delight in your voice, to follow each gesture, each movement, each expression of yours; to laugh if you laugh, to weep if you weep.[2] No human creature has ever attached his own life to that of another creature as I did to yours, Marta. Always remember this.

How pleased was I at your asking for news about *your* most recent play *Come tu mi vuoi!* I am still working on the second act, which I want to be more beautiful than the first. I have the feeling it is getting better and better. I must stop very often because something very strange is happening to me; I see the creatures of my fantasy *so alive, so independent from me*, that I am no longer able to contain them inside the composition I have to put together with them; they slip away on their own; they tend more than ever to get away from the roles assigned to them and to do something else, to talk about something else—the most surprising things, which are born from chance, from a change in mood, as happens to us all in life. Sometimes it costs me an incredible effort to get them back, almost by force, to their action in the drama. Who knows what would come out if I would yield to their whims and let them act the way they want, whatever they want. . . . [3]

So, besides fighting with the others from whom I receive so much trouble and so many disappointments, I must also fight with my characters. But I do like this fight, and above all the thought that I do it for my

---

[2] Pirandello describes with rapture the memory of the high points of the happiest three years of his entire life—those he spent near Marta during the tours of his company (1925–1928)—enchanted as in a dream behind the wings, lost in the bliss of watching his beloved while she was performing, and identifying himself with the character and mumbling in a low voice the dialogue of the plays he had created. Pirandello's untiring stage fever had roots in his youth, as appears in the letter of December 4, 1887, in which the young Pirandello writes that he could not enter a theater "without experiencing a lively emotion, without feeling a strange sensation, an excitement of the blood" through all his veins. There he also writes: "That heavy air you breathe there, heavily smelling of gas and paint, inebriates me; and always in the middle of the performance I feel overcome with fever and I burn. . . . I never enter alone, but always accompanied by the phantasms of my mind, people bustling around . . . living in my brain, who would want to jump straight onto the stage" (Providenti, ed., *Epistolario familiare giovanile*, p. 22).

[3] This rare example of Pirandello's "living aesthetics" is very significant and valuable because it translates his theories into a vivid existential record of his unique creative process.

Marta is enough to make me like it—for my Marta who, I hope, eventually will be very happy with it.

. . . I am concerned about the insomnia you complain about. You need to sleep, you need a full night's sleep to restore the forces you use up during the day (and who knows how much energy you burn up, studying your parts plus all the anxieties and the concerns of the imminent enterprise!). The password, remember? is . . . *tranquillity!* I wrote to Almirante for the first time only yesterday, saying that I could not accept the distribution of the roles the way he had done it, and that if Tòfano does not take the role of Tito Morena, I'll take the play away from him.[4] I am waiting for an answer, and I'll keep you informed.

Meanwhile, my Marta, all the best from your

Maestro

---

[4] Pirandello is referring to the play *O di uno o di nessuno* for the Teatro di Torino.

{ 291011 }

To Marta Abba
Via Cajazzo 52
(Italy) Milan   Berlin, 11. x. 1929
My Marta,

How is it that you don't write? Right this moment, when I am in such anguish because of you, knowing that you are in the midst of disappointments and difficulties? At least one word! Since last Sunday you have written nothing, nothing at all, and it's already Friday! I know nothing about how things have turned out, whether the break with Marcacci[1] is definite, what's the situation with your company, what you did about finding a substitute for him, whether you'll go to Varese on the 14th to open on the 19th. . . . No news at all! I don't know what to think, how to find a moment to rest! You would certainly have written if something had been settled. Since you haven't written as yet, I must assume that everything is still up in the air . . . and you can't imagine in what a state of turmoil my heart is![2] I cannot possibly leave because that scoundrel

---

[1] An actor who was supposed to be hired for Marta's company.

[2] Pirandello is very upset because of Marta's silence, just a week before the opening of her season in Varese; his trouble is compounded by the fact that he has no cash on hand, as appears in the rest of the letter. This letter is important as a means of documenting his many sources of substantial income, which would have been more than sufficient to live

Righelli, who arrived two days ago in Berlin, has not yet come around: he owes me six thousand marks, equal to thirty thousand lire![3] I'm sure he won't be able to give me the whole amount at once, but he'll have to give me something at least: I won't allow him a minute of peace if he doesn't pay. He promised over the phone that he'll visit me tonight at the Aida. I haven't as yet sent my monthly check of two thousand lire to Fausto (and it is already the 11th); I owe two weeks' rent; and I must have enough money left for my trip. I calculate that *more than one hundred thousand lire are owed to me*, forty from America, thirty from Righelli, thirty from the publisher Hobbing, who hasn't yet put on the market the two books that were already proofed and printed; without counting fourteen thousand more that should come from Bemporad, for the publication of *O di uno o di nessuno* (already finished), and from Mondadori for that of *Lazzaro* (also already finished). It is a terrible moment everywhere. There is no way to get a cent; nobody wants to pay! And with so many credits that I have, one surer than the next, here I am with just a few hundred marks in my pocket—I cannot leave if they don't pay! A million delays and legal complications make it impossible to get cash from the treasurer of the province of Rome for the sale of the villino, although it is already concluded. Stefano writes to me that payment will not be completed before the middle of November, because around the 20th of the current month, they will pay the first 450 thousand lire; on November 15, the remaining 450 thousand. The villino was sold for 900 thousand lire. But we will get only 865 net, which (after paying off the mortgage held by Monte dei Paschi) will be reduced to 625. After giving the promised checks to the children, and paying *all* debts, nothing will be left for me, but I'll get myself free from all my past; thank God, *I will not owe anything to anybody*! I consider this achievement as my greatest stroke of luck since I was born! I would not have to repay immediately the forty-odd thousand lire I owe to the Banca Commerciale, and I could pay off the debt with half of my royalties, as I am doing now. In that case, from the sale of the villino that amount would remain available for me, for the needs of the moment. My income from the theater, with three new plays soon to be produced, will be so great, we hope, that soon, if I devote half of it to payments, I will be able to pay off the debt. But there

---

very comfortably; it also winds up the sad chapter of the building and sale of his villino in Rome, which brought him probably the largest lump sum of money he ever had in his life (roughly the value of $1 million in 1993 dollars)—all gone before it was even cashed.

[3] The film director Gennaro Righelli owed Pirandello money for a film script he had not actually been able to produce. See letter 300322 and the Name Index under Righelli.

is the interest, which is high, and which would weigh me down for the whole time until the final payment. It would be better to pay it all off without delay and be free of debt. The credits I have will have to be paid to me, sooner or later, and the income from the theater will be paid to me, and I'll breathe freely at last. Money will pour in from everywhere: America, Russia, Germany, France, England, Spain, Hungary, Austria, Poland, Italy. The recovery will be complete. And Marta must be liberated with me once and for all. Freed from all the narrowness and all the miseries of the wretched world of the Italian stage, she will continue, if she wishes, to work as an actress, but as absolute *Signora* and *Padrona*, and she will have everything she wants—her liberation, too: at last! Then I'll walk away from life happy, because I'll have done for my dearest daughter what I had to do: very little, actually nothing compared to the abundance of life she gave and will continue giving to my art, and compared to the priceless comfort she graciously gave—during the last few years, with complete self-denial—in compensation for the always hostile fate of her poor

Maestro

{ 291212 }

To Marta Abba
Hôtel Bonne Femme
Turin   12. XII. 1929[1]

My Marta,

. . It's imperative that you be liberated from all these wretched and distressing trifles, and that you be allowed to breathe the pure and inspiring air of Art! No more bickering around you! Somebody else should take

---

[1] This letter is written on the letterhead of the Hotel Corso Splendid of Milan. Pirandello, after leaving Berlin on October 17, briefly visited Marta in Milan, then went to Rome for the inauguration of the Accademia d'Italia and other business. After another visit to Marta at the end of the month, he left for Vienna, where he hoped to set up a European tour (which never materialized) for Marta's company; he went back to Berlin to take care of the matter of his future production of *Tonight We Improvise* (which was to open on January 25, 1930, in Königsberg), returning to Italy again to help Marta out with the Italian premiere of his play *Lazzaro* in Turin (December 7, 1929, at the Teatro di Torino). The letters that follow, many of which are not translated here, are addressed to hotels in various Italian cities, wherever Marta was performing in her fatiguing and precarious tour, and are primarily concerned with business related to the productions, the hopes for new contracts, and repetitious lamentations.

over the burden of leading you to the haven of financial profit without any loss! Don't have any doubt that you'll get there: *you most certainly will.*[2] What matters most is that you should be well, without any of the preoccupations that might distract you from dedicating yourself to your art and from studying, and might distract your intelligence from the care that you alone can give for the good success of your shows.

Nobody better than myself is in the position of knowing and appreciating your divine intelligence: I have a proof of it in the comparisons I can make. If you only could see how pitiful the role of Sara looks when interpreted by Melato![3] To me, she looks like a washerwoman! Being accustomed to you, it is excruciating to see my drama interpreted by others. A hundred times better if it dies—forever—and if nobody speaks about it ever again. . . . With you, Marta, it looked as if it were definitely mine, even more than mine: *yours and mine*; now it doesn't seem to belong to anybody . . . , as if it did not mean anything anymore. . . . You were Fulvia for me, you were Ersilia, you were Signora Frola, you were the stepdaughter, you were Silia Gala, you were Evelina Morli. . . . [4] *They are all dead; and I am dead with them.*

I feel, Marta, I swear, I feel *truly dead.* In Turin, in your room, leaning against the wall, the last evening, while taking leave from you, I had the precise feeling of my death; its shiver is still running through my spine.

Perhaps you did not perceive what happened. Had you been aware of it, you would probably have had a word of pity for me, or, rather, of sympathy.

Enough.

. . . I must stay here, at this torture.[5] It will open, it seems, at the beginning of next week; on Monday, maybe, the theater will stay closed for the dress rehearsal, and we'll open on Tuesday night. On your way to Piacenza on Monday, you'll be able to, or rather you'll have to, pass through Milan. So I'll see you then, and right after that, on Wednesday morning,

[2] From these words it is clear that the tour of Marta's company was operating in the red, causing serious worry to Pirandello and to Marta.

[3] Pirandello refers to the production of his play *Lazzaro* in Milan, which was about to open in a few days with the actress Maria Melato in the role of Sara, compared with the production of the same play in Turin, in which the same role was interpreted by Marta.

[4] Pirandello names the main roles of his plays brought to life by Marta's interpretation: Fulvia Gelli, in *Come prima, meglio di prima;* Ersilia, in *Vestire gli ignudi;* Signora Frola, in *Così è se vi pare;* the stepdaughter, in *Sei personaggi in cerca d'autore;* Silia Gala, in *Il giuoco delle parti;* Evelina Morli, in *La Signora Morli, una e due.*

[5] Pirandello was in Milan to assist—as he had done in Turin for Marta—in the preparation of the production of his *Lazzaro,* whose failure he foresaw.

I'll join you for a few days in Piacenza. I'll bring you up-to-date on every-thing. Then, if I feel up to it, I'll go to Rome to renew the battle; I'll make every possible effort to speak to Mussolini about establishing the regional theaters. I must somehow find the energy for it; help me, Marta; I would like to do this good deed before leaving the stage! I do not do it for myself; I do it for our country, for the nobility of our art, for you, Marta, who will remain when I won't be around anymore!

Your Maestro

{ 300227 }

To Marta Abba
Via Cajazzo 52
(Italy) Milan

Berlin W.10, 27. 11. 1930
Herkuleshaus
Friedrich-Wilhelmstrasse 13

My Marta,

Here I am again, sitting at this desk, with your picture in front of me and your little alarm clock trying to comfort me with its ticking. My two windows open on the light-spangled Lützow-Platz, and, down below, the sad, silent canal under the Herkules Bridge, and the big, skeletonlike trees. . . .

Why did I come back to Berlin? I don't know! I don't see a reason for anything anymore.[1] But I do not want to talk to you of the condition my spirits are in. . . .

---

[1] During this prolonged stay in Italy, Pirandello had been accompanying, as much as his beloved would let him, Marta's company (which is why there are no letters for more than two months). During these peregrinations, he came to realize with increasingly icy clarity and intolerable chagrin that Marta—preoccupied with the extremely demanding work of managing her company—was miles away from even thinking about the type of love he was longing for. Marta herself, on at least two occasions (in Ferrara and in Lucca), had told him clearly that she no longer had the strength to "keep him alive" in the way he requested (see letter 300303). This inexorable awareness had driven him to the recent crisis of depression, perhaps the most violent of his whole life, during which only the personal intervention of Marta, who ran to visit him as soon as she realized the seriousness of his mental condition, saved him from almost certain suicide (see letter 300301). Pirandello, still desperate and bewildered, once again tried to find safety in flight, without a definite plan. Providenti (*Mnemosine*, pp. 12 and 45) points out this trait in Pirandello's psyche: "Flight is his permanent state of mind; he escapes in 1887 from Palermo to Rome"; "It is a continuous flight from himself that makes him go to Germany in October 1889 . . . to

I arrived this morning at nine, very tired from the long journey—after tossing the whole night in my berth, without falling asleep even for a minute. At nine I found that good soul Lantz at the station, and he brought me up-to-date on everything. The situation, both of the theaters and of the movie industry in Berlin, is at this moment frightening. More than six theaters went bankrupt and are now closed, among them the Renaissance (Hartung's theater); the Schauspielhaus (that is, the State Theater) is in crisis, Jessner fired, with a deficit of five million marks, and also the three theaters of Barnoski are on the brink of bankrupcy. Reinhardt is managing to eke out a living with only one theater.[2]

In the provinces things look better. The success of *Questa sera si recita a soggetto* in Königsberg is really extraordinary and the echo it has had all over Germany is enormous. I'll go to Königsberg on the evening of the 4th, stay there the whole day of the 5th, and I'll come back to Berlin on the 6th. It seems that they will give me a hearty welcome. Meanwhile rehearsals of the same play are in progress in Frankfurt.

Around the 10th of next month, I'd like to go to Paris and stay there for some time. I have no more peace. The destination of my traveling should be infinitely farther away, to find peace, since I cannot stay near you.[3] Paris, New York . . . even there, yes, the other world . . . earning, earning a lot, a lot, a lot of money . . . to defeat a hostile fate . . . and, after winning, to say: "Here it is, I won, enough! . . . I can go now!" Because nobody wants me to stay.

I am anxiously waiting to hear from you what you decided, where you'll go after Milan. . . . I need your itinerary, to follow you at least with my thoughts. Did you remain at the Regina or did you go back home? I send this letter to Via Cajazzo, so as not to make a mistake. Tell me where you prefer me to send my mail.

For the love of God, please write! It's all I have left. . . .

Your Maestro

---

the foreign university" (Bonn); he flees from Italy to Berlin with Marta in 1929; he now flees from Milan—turned intolerable because of Marta's (both physical and moral) absence—to Berlin, "like a fly without a head"; within a few months he will depart suddenly from Berlin after the humiliation of *Tonight We Improvise*, and two months before dying he will again feel the urge to flee from his home in the Via Bosio without knowing where to go (letter 361025). Pirandello is staying now, for about twenty days, at the Herkuleshaus in Berlin, during which time he will go to Königsberg to receive a big welcome for the great success of the world premiere / preview run of *Tonight We Improvise*. This extraordinary success made him practically certain that the play would be a big success at the opening in Berlin—making him blind and deaf to the change of atmosphere in the capital city that was foreboding disaster. From Königsberg he will go back to Berlin on March 7, and will then go for a week to Paris, and come back to Berlin probably on March 18.

[2] Pirandello describes some of the effects of the political and economic crisis in Germany that was preparing the ground for the Nazi takeover.

[3] Pirandello does not miss an opportunity to repeat to Marta that the true and only reason for his depression was the fact that Marta did not want him to stay near her—especially while she was extremely tired and busy with her tour through a great number of small provincial cities. In the letters of this period there are many clear hints at suicide as the only possible liberation.

{ 300228 }

To Marta Abba
Via Cajazzo 52
(Italy) Milan Berlin, 28. ii. 1930
My Marta,

I am like a fly without a head; I don't know where to turn, nor what to do; hours go by, while I'm sitting here at the desk, thinking of so many things . . . if anybody, in hiding, were here spying on me, he'd think I was doped. On the contrary, I feel within myself such a turmoil of thoughts and feelings, that anybody—if he could experience it personally for just one moment—would feel himself being swept away into the whirling spiral of a storm and seized by such a fit of dizziness as to go insane from it or even die. I still succeed in resisting, and I keep steady. I'll keep steady to the last. And if I should die—don't be afraid—I'll be able to die, *as a person who knew how to suffer so much.*[1] Let's talk about something else!

Let's talk about you, my Marta. First of all, live without any trace of worry, and never swerve by so much as an inch from being yourself. Believe me, Marta, this is the moment of your victory; but on the condition that you remain *what you are.* You won because *that is the way you have been!* Don't fail, therefore, to keep on being yourself. Do not let anyone try to change you with mediocre and stingy advice; do not lower yourself by compromising with anyone; do not beg for anything; do not try to get into anyone's good graces. Go forward, walking proud and sure in your

[1] Marta Abba was referring to this excruciating inner pain of Pirandello when she repeated, until a short time before her death, that the principal reason for her decision to publish these letters was to make known to the world "how much the Maestro had been suffering."

way, which is *yours alone*, and cannot be otherwise, because you—and you alone—must teach yourself to follow your own path, doing everything your own way, as it befits Marta Abba!

. . . I tell you these things, not because you need it. I know your pride and the awareness you have of yourself and of your worth; I tell you this, because unfortunately those you love most are not always capable of understanding and, without meaning it, they often advise you wrongly and steer you into doing things you'll have to regret later. Don't ever believe, my Marta, for God's sake, that I have any *personal* animosity against your relatives; if I was frequently in opposition to them it was only *for your own good*, for this personal interest that I have for your good, the way I want it, as I feel that it is worthy of you—only so and not otherwise! Your relatives are the best people on earth, but they do not have the intelligence to understand you and to assist you in your *difficult* path; they would like to make it *easy* in their way, without understanding that you cannot go ahead through narrow and easy streets; you'd lose yourself in the valley, while you are supposed to be climbing to the hilltop! How can you expect them to have the stomach to follow you to the top, born as they are for the plains? I get scared every time I hear your father say to you: "Leave it to me," and I hear him give advice to you, although I know that it is given to you always for a good purpose—but *good*, as he means it, cannot be good for you! Your good is something else, so much bigger, so much higher! And I, who understand it so well, am forced to stay far away from you. . . .

But it doesn't matter about me, about what I suffer, so far away. What matters is that you go forward, always, and without the help of anybody. Forward, forward, and always higher, higher, and higher!

. . . Perhaps tomorrow, if I have the courage, I'll start working again. There is no other salvation for me. But you must give me the courage. May you have, my Marta, all the good things that your Maestro wishes you always, always, and all the love of your poor

Maestro

{ 300301 }

To Marta Abba
Via Cajazzo 52
(Italy) Milan

Berlin, I. III. 1930
Saturday

My Marta,

... I no longer have any personal interest of my own; all my interests are identical with yours, because my present ambition—and the only purpose for which I drag on this horrible existence (horrible because far from you)—is this: to strive with all my forces (and they are still many!) to make you rich and in control of your destiny, in Art as much as in life. You are performing, my Marta, a play in which you shout with all your soul and demonstrate that the *true truth* is not that of actualities, but that of the spirit.[1] Now, in our case, the *true truth* is this: that I am your true father, and that you are my creature, my creature, my creature, in which all my spirit lives with the very power of my creation, so much so that it *has become your thing and you are all my life*.[2] And the *true truth* is that I am not old, but young, the youngest of all, in my mind as well as in my heart; in my art, as well as in my blood, in my muscles, in my nerves. In the interest of facts that can lie, somebody else can deny these true truths; but you can't, my Marta; you must be always living in this truth of the spirit! I am you, as you desire me, and if you do not want me anymore, I—by myself—I am nothing anymore, and living is no longer possible for me.[3]

I'll go this afternoon at 4:30 to see Felix Bloch-Erben and I'll find out about the condition of my affairs in Germany. The performances in Königsberg[4] continue to be an enormous success and will continue for

[1] Pirandello refers to *As You Desire Me*.

[2] This is possibly the passage that most vibrates with emotion, in which Pirandello, right after surviving the crisis that had driven him extremely close to suicide, expresses in the clearest way his fatherly love for Marta, whom he considers as a creation of his spirit and incarnation of his art, to the point of repeating three times the words "my creature."

[3] Pirandello refers again to the words of the title and to the meaning of the content of the play *As You Desire Me*. There is an almost mystical sensuality in all this reasoning, an erotic tension toward a union that is never fulfilled, something ineffable and decadent that manifests itself in the last works of Pirandello, especially in *I giganti della montagna*, of which he seems to anticipate some of the themes.

[4] He refers to the preview run of *Tonight We Improvise* (its premiere in Berlin was still in the planning stage).

the whole month of March, which is unheard of, since it is a provincial city. It's exceptional that more than eight or ten performances of a play are given in an outlying area. Mine has been in performance for a whole month and will continue for one more month.

. . . My presence in Rome at this moment would certainly have been very useful. But a crisis occurred which I would have never expected, and which threw me suddenly off my course. I no longer made sense out of anything, and if you, my Marta, had not come, by now, I believe, I would not be here anymore! Useless, now, to go over again what happened.[5] I see you seated near me, on the morning of my departure, in the compartment of my wagon-lit, and this is enough to cheer me up. . . . Life is made of moments. . . .

Write, write to me, my Marta, even a little bit, but write and keep me informed of everything; where you are . . . what you are thinking about . . . what you are doing. . . . I don't want to know anything else! May you receive all the love of your

Maestro

[5] This passage is the most explicit reference by Pirandello to the crisis of despair—which evidently happened in Italy a short time before this letter—during which he found himself at the brink of suicide; Pirandello acknowledges that Marta's rushing to his help was the only factor that saved his life.

{ 300303 }

To Marta Abba
Via Cajazzo 52
(Italy) Milan   Berlin, 3. III. 1930
    My Marta,
    . . . The news you send me—for the very fact that you thought of sending it to me—gives me pleasure, but it is certainly not the kind of news I would like to receive. I want *your, your* news, of you, Marta, about your days; I want to see you, to follow you, to feel myself near you! I picture so many things, I hear your voice, I know every expression of your face, all your gestures and your movements, how you turn your eyes and how you glance as you talk to one person or another; I could tell you everything about yourself, every slightest motion of your soul, every deeply concealed fold of your thought, the whole "momentariness" of life that goes through you without the time to register even in yourself or to appear for one instant in your awareness. But you don't tell me anything and I

don't know anything. I continue my imagining in emptiness: "will it be so?" or "will it be true?" In the morning I think: "she will be still in bed," then I say, "here it is, perhaps she is getting up now." But I don't know where you have your breakfast, whether in the hotel or in the store[1] or in some restaurant; I don't know if and when you go to rehearsal; until the evening, when you go to the theater to prepare for the performance, I am no longer able to *see you,* and you can hardly imagine how much I suffer because of it.

. . . I hear about the performances of *Come tu mi vuoi.* Why did you believe, my Marta, that it would have displeased me if you had changed the bill for Friday? If you did that, for me it was good. Never again have such worries about me; all that you decide about my drama is fine with me, always; it belongs to you; it must only serve you and nobody else; you are the absolute mistress, and you can give Nulli all the orders you wish, for this or any other play, as seems best to you.

. . . Tomorrow evening, as I told you, I'm leaving for Königsberg and I'll stay there only on the 5th; on the 6th I'll be back in Berlin. In the conversation on Saturday with Felix Bloch-Erben, we decided to give up having Reinhardt, who is too busy, direct the play, and to give the job to Martin[2] of the Volksbühne, which nowadays is in first place among the theaters in Berlin. Martin will come with me, on Tuesday evening, to Königsberg to see the production of my play directed by Müller, which they say is very beautiful. They are preparing a great welcome for me there, but I don't know how I'll respond to that welcome, being in the mood I'm in. I feel completely exhausted; so much so that good old Lantz doesn't recognize me and does nothing but ask why I am like that.

I received a very long letter from Crémieux, full of good news. I must go to Paris before the 13th, and stay there for a good while. The productions of *Questa sera si recita a soggetto* with Pitoëff, as well as that of *La vita che ti diedi,* have been settled. I'll go and see them, but believe me, my Marta, that *nothing* can bring me back to life—whether I go there or I stay here—if within yourself you truly feel that you cannot give it to me: it was *fatal* for me, it has *cut me to the quick* what you told me in Ferrara first, and then in Lucca, before leaving. . . . You cannot imagine what a horrible effort it has been costing me ever since—this dragging myself through life—this life that is no longer life; even more so because,

[1] The store of Marta's father.

[2] Karl-Heinz Martin (1886–1948), artistic director of the Volksbühne after 1928, ultimately did not take over the direction of *Tonight We Improvise* either.

since then, you have not made a move that would be a reprieve from that—for me—capital sentence. . . .[3]

. . . If work has no longer the power to perk me up and to distract me from this continuous torment, I am lost. May you receive, my Marta, all the good things that are wished for you by

Your poor Maestro

[3] Here Pirandello explains what had precipitated the frightening crisis that had brought him to the verge of suicide. Marta had told him, in Ferrara and Lucca, clear as a bell, that she did not feel anymore that she wanted to fulfill the function of "giving him life" (she had plenty of other preoccupations; with all the problems of her company, she was dead tired and could not take any more of Pirandello's interminable "useless chatter" about a love problem that had no solution). The relationship between Pirandello and Marta reveals here its desperate impossibility: a concrete, matter-of-fact woman like Dulcinea, with her hands in her apron, and a more-than-ever moonstruck Don Quixote, staring into emptiness with wild eyes.

{ 300304 }

To Marta Abba
Via Cajazzo 52
(Italy) Milan   Berlin, 4. III. 1930
   My Marta,
   . . . Yesterday evening the Swedish journalist Thorstad, who purchased *Lazzaro* and *Tonight We Improvise* for Denmark, Sweden, and Norway, came to see me. He told me that he found out that it was Mussolini himself who prevented the Nobel Prize from being awarded to me in order "not to cause dangerous jealousies in Italy" (it is evident that he was referring to D'Annunzio) and requested "that it be assigned to Deledda, which would not create any rivalry." He said that this had left a terrible impression in Sweden, and he is sure that the next prize will be awarded to me, for which there is very favorable support. As the Berlin correspondent of the leading newspaper of the Swedish press, he will write in this vein the long interview he had with me yesterday evening. I told him I would not move a finger to get the prize, and he answered that other people will move their hands to give it to me.
   We'll see. Then, maybe, my luck will change! But we also need America! I am ready to go to America! Anywhere, anywhere. . . .
   Write to me one word, one word, my Marta, that can comfort me! And may you receive all the love of

Your Maestro

{ 300310 }

To Marta Abba
Teatro Fiorentini
(Italy) Naples   Berlin, 10. III. 1930
    My Marta,

I received this morning, at 8:30, your telegram—sent at 0:35 A.M., evidently after the performance—in which you promise *you'll write* to Paris. I'll stay in Paris only four days. I'm leaving tomorrow morning at 8:30 on the Train bleu, and I'll arrive on Sunday evening at 11:30. I'm staying the 12th, 13th, 14th, 15th, and I'll leave again for Berlin on the morning of the 16th. I am going only to be present at the premiere of *La vita che ti diedi* and to come to an agreement with Crémieux and Pitoëff about *Questa sera si recita a soggetto*; I'll take care of other business of mine in France with the publishers Gallimard and Kra, and settle my arrangements with the agent Bloch and the Society of French Authors. At this moment it is not convenient for me to leave Berlin and Germany. The echo of the success in Königsberg is increasing daily, and what I have been awaiting for a year and a half seems imminent; that is, the great revival of my plays here. Everybody is telling me that it would be crazy to turn my back on it now, after waiting so long. More than ten German theater directors went to Königsberg to see *Questa sera si recita a soggetto*. Meinhard will go on the 15th to bring the show here to Berlin. I must therefore be back from Paris by the 16th to work things out with him. After that I'll go myself to Hamburg and Leipzig. Angermayer was telling me yesterday that he would buy the play for one hundred thousand marks, confident that he would make a good profit. One hundred thousand marks are half a million lire. But Angermayer says that I'll earn much more than that, given the warmth of the press and what is being said about the play: half a million marks—not lire! All three hundred theaters in Germany will want to produce it, between now and next fall. Even cutting down such hyperbolic figures, the fact remains that I would be making an enormous mistake if I abandon the field, after sowing, just at the time of the harvest. I must be back in Berlin on the 16th. Therefore I'll leave the two trunks here at the Herkuleshaus, and I'll go to Paris with just a piece of luggage for four days. A visit to Paris will do me good.

As you see I am writing as a reasonable man who can do his accounts. Don't believe it. I have hell in my soul. I was on the brink of committing the insanity of leaving because I cannot stay put in any place; but it is useless for me to flee; I should flee only from myself and go away from life; I cannot live like this anymore! You can't imagine, Marta, how much I am suffering. I myself do not know how I manage to bear this awful pain. Every time, after the strongest spasm of torture, I fall into an infinite dizziness; motionless, incapable of moving even one finger. Someday enough strength will be left to me to stretch out my hand and deal the death blow. . . .[1]

Enough. I am waiting for your letter in Paris before the 15th. You should have plenty to write to me. . . . After that, I'll be back here at the Herkuleshaus.

Receive all the love of

Your Maestro

[1] Pirandello's deep depression continues, the futility of "flight" appears more and more evident, and thoughts of suicide are again formulated with details that reveal the extraordinary intensity of the crisis he had been experiencing since his trip to Italy.

{ 300312 }

To Marta Abba
Hotel Univers
(Italy) Naples   Paris, 12. III. 1930[1]
My Marta,

I am, as you can see, at the Vendôme, and I occupy room 5, the same one you had, and I sleep in the same bed in which you slept during your Parisian vacation. This way I feel a little less far away from you. Here in these rooms I have your picture of that time, with the two big straw hats, the white one and the black one—which suited you so well—and the white and pale blue dress with the mantelet. . . . I see you here lying down on the couch of green *peluche* near the little desk I am now writing at, facing the drawing-room window . . . , I see you while you talk to that hateful Torre,[2] who is eating you up with his enamel eyes of a swindling fake magician, and I cringe when I notice that you are smiling at him in a different way from the way you smile at good old Camillo Antona-Traversi. . . . My trouble is that I notice everything and I suffer because of everything . . . though I really should give no importance to things that

[1] Pirandello uses the letterhead of the Hôtel Vendôme in Paris. He is in the French capital to be present at the premiere of *La vie que je t'ai donnée*, performed by La Petite Scène at the Salle Iena and directed by X. de Courville.

[2] Guido Torre represented Pirandello's interests in Paris for a couple of years.

have none for you . . . but when devotion is so complete and absolute and when a person doesn't live except through the life that is given him by another person, if even a minimal part of this life fails him for one moment, this is what unfortunately happens! This is why, Marta, you should forgive me and not feel offended. It is pain and not reproach; it is a confession of a weakness and nothing else. I deserve your compassion, which you can grant me only if you understand the reason of my suffering.

. . . I'll stay in Paris until the evening of the 18th, and on the 19th I'll go back to Berlin. I'm sure I'll get some business done. But it is imperative that I know what you are doing, otherwise I lose my bearings, I don't see and don't hear anything anymore, just as if nothing any longer existed. . . . I don't want to know how the theater is going, what you are performing; I want to know about you, I want *to see you*, through the hours of the day, what you are thinking about, what you are busy doing, whether you meet anybody, whether you are alone with your father or if Cele is with you, how is this Teatro dei Fiorentini. . . . I know nothing about nothing, and I feel as if I were lost, blind, deaf . . . absolutely unable to do anything. I send you my most cordial greetings,

Your Maestro

{ 300316 }

To Marta Abba
Grand Hôtel Univers
(Italy) Naples   Paris, 16. III. 1930
    My Marta,
    I received your letter of the 13th, and I am more and more worried at
the news you give me about your health. No doubt it is nothing serious,
but it is also obvious that all your symptoms reveal a great loss of your
physical energies, plus the abuse you have made of your vital forces and
the urgent need you have for some rest and relaxation.
    . . . You cannot imagine, my Marta, the impression I got from the last
words of your letter; this tiredness of your spirit added to that of your
body, and I do not know whether it is cause or consequence! I would
like to make a million suggestions. . . . You know, my Marta, that I live
only for you, I am yours; I am always at your disposal, always; if you wish,
when you wish, I can rush to you; I don't want you to be so tired and
upset and without any interest in life! Life, all life must be for you: it's
your right! My Marta, courage! courage! Remember that I am here for
you, all for you: somebody who is still *somebody . . . somebody* who is
still nothing anymore without you! Until tomorrow. With all the love of
                                                          Your Maestro

{ 300324 }

To Marta Abba
Grand Hôtel Univers
(Italy) Naples   Berlin, 24. III. 1930
    My Marta,
    . . . This alone is my torment, that I do not hear anything anymore
from you. And believe me, my Marta, this torment is such that I don't
know how long I'll be able to stand it. My spirit has been taken over by
such a frightful darkness that I see my end near and unavoidable. There
is no human force that can stand what I am suffering. . . . I don't know
why I must go on suffering like this. . . . I don't have a moment of peace
. . . wherever I turn, thorns and bitterness of all kinds. . . . I would be all
right if I had at least your letters with some comfort. . . . But nothing!
You don't write; or if a few times, in a hurry, you do jot down a couple of

words for me, it is to speak about other subjects, and never of yourself. . . . What conclusions should I draw from all this? I find myself facing a wall. The only solution is here in the drawer of my night table.[1]

Before you sent me those newspaper clippings, I had learned from Stefano's letter, received the same day, that the papers in Rome had shredded *Lazzaro* to pieces—with the exception maybe of Checchi, on the *Tevere*—and that the performance had been very bad, a real *dog*; I knew also about the *Giornale d'Italia*, which, however—maybe by mistake—carried a long, favorable article, signed by Luigi Antonelli, when the Almirante-Rissone-Tòfano Company performed *O di uno o di nessuno*, at the Teatro Argentina. What do you want me to do, my Marta? I don't see what I could have done to cause so much resentment against me. I worked; I gave four dramatic works in one year to the dramatic literature of my country. If they are alive and vital, time will prove me right. My plays will remain, and my country will be blamed for not having been able to appreciate them and for having offended me unjustly. By now I am accustomed to these offenses, and they hurt me no more. I am suffering for quite other reasons. . . .

. . . You do not answer the many questions I asked you in my letters. . . . And yet I was speaking about very serious matters, and I expounded to you considerations that deserved to be taken into account. . . . Not a word! And, I repeat, I don't know what you are doing, where you are going, whether you will continue after April 15 . . . nothing! And I live only for you! What do you think my life can be like these days? What makes you think that I care how they persecute me?

The worst is that I am no longer able to force myself up out of this hole and go back to work. I worked at *Coquette* because it was for you![2] Here everybody is very busy with *Questa sera si recita a soggetto*. . . . I look at them, I make an encouraging big smile with my lips . . . inside, I feel nothing . . . let them keep on . . . let them do whatever they want. . . .

. . . My Marta, receive all the love of

Your Maestro

[1] The acute depression continues, and with it the longing for an end, that is, suicide. Here he talks about an instrument of death, probably a revolver he kept in the drawer of his night table.

[2] Pirandello had worked for a long time to adapt and rewrite completely the Italian translation of this play by Preston Bridges and George Abbott for the use of Marta's company—setting aside his own pressing creative work. See also letter 300402.

{ 300325 }

To Marta Abba
Grand Hôtel Univers
(Italy) Naples   Berlin, 25. III. 1930
My Marta,

Your letter of Saturday arrived this morning at 8:30 and brought me these bits of news: you started rehearsals of *Vestire gl'ignudi* for the evening to be given in your honor in Naples; as usual, at rehearsal you caught a bad cold; you took a Calmin to fight a sudden bad headache that has been bothering you on and off for some time; in Naples the sun comes and goes; you are happy about the good news I gave you in my special delivery of the 20th, and you cannot see yourself in a film anymore because you are too ugly and worn out![1] Very well! Assuming you are as you say, tell me, Marta, as ugly as you are, as worn out as you are, do you wish to throw yourself away? Do it! I am here with open arms to receive this ugly and worn-out thing into which my Marta has turned! And the beautiful part of this is that I would not give an inch of her little finger in exchange for all the most beautiful women in the world, if ever there were any! Shall we make this magnificent bet, that you pull yourself from Naples, and I receive you with open arms here in Berlin? I'm afraid I would smother you with hugs, so great is the longing I have for you! I am just joking, of course.

. . . You see what the problem is, my Marta? You do answer from time to time, in passing; you do not bear in mind my letters, what I write to you in them, what I ask you in them; and so I feel as if I were talking to the wind and not to you; that my voice is lost in the desert, and I remain frustrated and disappointed without ever knowing anything. You should answer, at least once, to the point and let me know that I have in you, always, my same Marta as before. As far as I am concerned, Marta is always in me, always the same one as before. She cannot change and will never change.

Yesterday evening I was at the Kammerspiele to see *L'Ennemie*.[2] Here it is. I'll describe it to you. In the production, no brilliant idea. A ceme-

[1] This summary of Marta's letter corresponds to the typical content of her correspondence: concrete news, no "useless chatter," and no answers to Pirandello's specific questions.

[2] This play (1929) by André-Paul Antoine, referred to by Pirandello in the Italian translation as *La nostra compagna*, was performed in Germany with the title *Die liebe Feindin*.

tery, mournful. Many graves painted on the backdrop, in a mannerist romantic style, with weeping willows, funeral urns, and a sorrowful sky, also mannerist; other tombs, in relief, three-dimensional, one at the left, older, with a golden railing, columns and architrave: the grave of the Sailor; and the Sailor himself has climbed up and is lying on the architrave, raised on his elbow and with his head braced on his hand, as you can see in sculptures on certain sarcophagi. The other tomb, that of the husband, is at the right, with a small railing all around the blooming flowerbed. The Husband wears a tailcoat; nobody knows why. He speaks with the Sailor, from down there, seated on a garden chair, while the other man is still hanging on up there. Then the Sailor, clinging to the protrusions of the tomb, descends, and do you know what happens? The lights go out, from above some scenery is lowered—the way we did with the garden in *Six Characters*—you hear the pulleys screeching; the scenery is put together quickly, with just a small spiral-shaped wooden column, like those the photographers use, and on this small column the Fiancée is leaning, on her elbow, in a position suitable for a romantic photograph of the 1880s, like the ones you still see—faded away—in certain old family albums. The acting style fits the different scenes: not as a *caricature*, but absolutely as a *parody*; parody of the Fiancée, parody of the Wife, parody of the Lover-Vampire; parody, at last, of the old hypocritical Mother. I can't tell you the *brutality* with which the parody of the Lover-Vampire was achieved! But it was *parody*, and as such it was funny and could pass. The elements of the set, simple and obvious as they were, were lowered from the ceiling once from one side, another time from the other: in a word, nothing pretended to be realistic; even those set pieces were parodistic. There is no way to compare it either with your interpretation or with your production. Quite a different thing! But in her way, parodistically, you can't say that Lilì Darvas did a bad job. The costumes were very beautiful, especially that of the Wife—pearl gray, with a small feathered hat set on the high hairdo, all curls and ribbons. The robe of the Lover-Vampire was raw green, black stockings, black culotte, most unbecoming, and a bright red wig; octopuslike gestures, legs up in the air, and everything in sight: stuff for . . . a burlesque, you can imagine! Since it was not intended to be serious, it could pass. The men, especially the Husband and the Lover, were admirable in their acting. The Husband was one of the best actors in Berlin, whose name I can't remember; it is a Russian name;[3] he is probably the best character actor on the German

---

[3] Richard Romanowsky, who played the role of First Dead.

stage, and he will perhaps play the role of Sampognetta in my *Questa sera si recita a soggetto*, but I don't know why he was wearing a tailcoat. The Lover, in the middle of the second act, appears in a very elegant sport suit, tight gray trousers, white waistcoat, white spats, gray top hat, and a binocular case for the races hanging from one shoulder. In the third scene he is in very elegant black silk pajamas with a red rose on the chest. And this is the way he appears at the end from the tomb at upstage center. The audience laughs, but then it applauds very little; they obviously consider the play a farce in several scenes, and its success is very mediocre. It is really presented as an elegant farce. Nothing more than that.

Are you satisfied with this report I gave you? My Marta, how much I love you![4] Allow me to say it! I would never have done it but for my Marta. I don't know why, but today I feel light-headed. I also have good news about what is being prepared for me here. I'll keep you informed.

Until tomorrow, my Marta. Write, write to me! And receive all the love of your

Maestro

[4] This is one of the very few times in which Pirandello writes plainly and explicitly: "How much I love you" (*quanto ti voglio bene*)!

{ 300402 }

To Marta Abba
Hotel S. Lucia
(Italy) Salerno   Berlin, 2. IV. 1930
   My Marta,

At last I have received your letter of Sunday 30. I am still in bed, very ill and extremely weak. It seems useless to express all the pain your words have caused me by the offensive interpretation you chose to give to my eagerness to receive your letters and your news; of the desolation I experienced in never getting an answer or a sign of pleasure, or interest, or participation, or curiosity, or sorrow, or, in a word, of even a minimal interest in the many things I told you, I shared with you, I described, I reported in my letters—not even a hint at having received *Coquette*,[1] not

[1] See footnote 2 to letter 300324 about *Coquette*. Pirandello had given up many precious hours of his own work to adapt that mediocre play for Marta's company.

even a hint about the great suffering I went through;[2] nothing, nothing, nothing; the most absolute lack of interest—as if you had not even read my letters. And only now, with a tone that wounds me through my soul, you ask me whether I am happy to hear "what you were doing and what you had done in Naples," as if I had asked you and I wanted to know *with an evil intention,*[3] and not just to feel less far away from you by getting all the news that you used to send me before. If you believe that your skimpy letters, written occasionally, without a lively and true *spirit of presence* in anything you wrote, did not give me a reason (not to scold, because I never did that) to feel obliged to express my keen pain at such undeserved behavior: what do you want me to tell you, my Marta? I must be wrong to feel as I feel, and you must be right to write to me as you write. But can you seriously believe that I could have been disrespectful to you, when you remind me *to whom* I am writing? I believed I was still writing to that same Marta to whom for so long I have been writing and to whom it is not possible for me to be disrespectful—because she is to me the highest and noblest among all creatures on earth.

After this, I don't know anymore what to tell you. My weakness is so great that I feel really finished, and I don't even know how to get up again from this bed.

Addio.

Your Maestro

[2] Pirandello had described in his previous letters, here not translated, the severe pains of his most recent pleurisy, from which he was just starting to recover. See also letter 300405.

[3] Marta's letter was probably reacting, as to an insult, to the requests of Pirandello, who on several occasions had repeatedly insisted that she should describe all the details of her day so that he might visualize every instant, no matter how intimate, of her life (see 290920, 300312, and 300324, in which he writes "to see" in large characters). The actress, by nature very touchy and extremely suspicious about everything, had interpreted such requests as disrespectful and requested that he should remember, when writing his letters, *to whom he was talking.* The above, possibly adding the expression found in letter 300325, "I'm afraid I would smother you with hugs, so great is the longing I have for you!" seems to be the probable cause for Marta's "offended" reaction.

{ 300405 }

To Marta Abba
Teatro Savoia
(Italy-Sicily) Messina   Berlin, 5. IV. 1930
    My Marta,

At last here I have a letter that is truly *yours*, one of those you used to write before, all charged with visual liveliness, with bright expressive flashes that *make me see you*: alive, *present*, in every word! This is how my Marta writes; this way I recognize her as the same person as before, and not in those faraway *absent* letters she wrote me from Naples, without telling me anything, without letting herself be visualized. . . . How can you think I can be deceived when I read your letters? How can you think that a person who lives by the sun can ever not be aware when a cloud passes and darkens it? I don't know what cloud passed, but one certainly did pass; my sun grew dark, and so much cold came into my soul—so intense that it still hasn't disappeared. . . .

Now from Salerno the sun has risen again, and a compassionate ray of its warmth comes to me as an act of mercy. My Marta, may you be thanked and blessed for this mercy that puts me back on my feet and helps me to keep myself going a while longer, alone as I am in this hostile life that is stinging me from all sides.

I hear about the big celebrations in your honor in Naples, and I am so happy! How I wish I had heard you sing *Quann'ammore vo' filà*, dressed in white with the red background of the curtain, in the splendor of the theater. . . . I can imagine the delirious applause, and you, shining, bowing, encoring . . . a triumph! My bosom swells with pride, and I feel the same happiness you must have felt in that moment when we become aware that a spark departing from us—something that WE ARE—fills up an audience and sets it afire. You, who are a woman, you must have certainly felt it even more. . . . It might be the weakness of my present health—I am weeping with tenderness imagining how you must have looked, small, smiling creature of grace and love, in so much glory, in the delirious admiration of everybody. . . . Oh, my Marta, and I was here, without being able to enjoy all that . . . you will climb higher and higher and who knows how high you'll go, and I'll be so far away . . . where nobody will be able to reach me ever again. . . . But this is life: this is your Destiny, and I am happy about it for you, my Marta, believe me—me, who always had this luminous vision of you that just now has made me cry with tenderness and joy. . . .

I am truly incredibly weak. I sent you a telegram saying that I was better, but it is not true. I am not better. I got out of bed because I could not take it anymore. But my weakness is such that I can't stay on my feet. If I stand up, I start panting. My heart was shaken up pretty badly. The doctor found some pleurisy, which explains the pain—a dry pleurisy, in three places, one above the shoulder blade and two under the left arm-pit, which hurt a lot if pressed; and another one in the middle of the back. Let's hope they will clear up with this application of heat. But I have no more fever and, as I already told you, I got out of bed. I am lying on the couch with my folder, to write to you. I switched on the lamp on the desk—it shines on your picture, which smiles with a divine smile. . . . I must close this letter to get it mailed. It will bring you my "welcome" to Messina, where I am addressing it. Meanwhile, good night, my Marta; and think of the great love of your poor

Maestro

{ 300406 }

To Marta Abba
Teatro Savoja
(Italy-Sicily) Messina   Berlin, Sunday 6. IV. 1930
    My Marta,
    . . . I attribute the nonarrival of your second letter to the evil of dis-tance. I think that, after writing the first, you probably received my other letters full of complaints and the one in answer to your last from Naples, and consequently your kindly attitude toward me might have changed—without thinking that those letters had been written before, and that therefore, the conditions having changed, they should no longer have been taken into account. But the evil of distance is exactly this: what was written *before* arrives always *afterward*; we read it, and without taking this into account, we change our attitude; what is already past in the mind of the writer becomes the present in ours when it arrives today—unwittingly setting us back to the earlier mood. . . . With this in mind, reading your last letter and feeling reborn at each word of yours, I wished I could have destroyed with my thought particularly that one that I wrote in answer to your last one from Naples, which might have reached you the same day or

the day after you wrote from Salerno;[1] I don't know how much I would
have been willing to pay in order to prevent it from being delivered to
you; on the other hand I could in no way allow those letters to fall in the
hands of others or be lost, and so I had to alert you that I had addressed
them to the Hotel Santa Lucia; in a telegram, open to everyone, I could
not tell you to destroy them, and so I had to grin and bear the pain that
you would pick them up and read them, at the cost of uselessly embitter-
ing you and, for me, risking a change of your attitude toward me.

Didn't it happen like that? Isn't this perhaps the reason why you did
not write the second letter? What a nuisance and what a torment is this
distance, when one has the nuisance and the torment of being obliged
to rummage through all the explanations of whatever might have
happened![2]

. . . How much I'd love to be in Sicily with you! Who knows whether
I'll ever have a chance to go back there again! This declining life of mine
is by now entirely dependent upon wild hopes, which I cannot even mention. . . .[3] But the pressure of my work will not allow my life to collapse.

I am feeling better. If this sun continues, I'll be soon on my feet. My
heart gives me less palpitations, and these painful spots above the
pleura—which, as long as they continue as they are now, are not serious—will soon clear up. I'll go back to work. I thought about a new play
that could have as its title *Quando si è qualcuno*.[4] Strange! I originally
thought of the title in German: *Wenn man jemand ist—Quando si è qualcuno* is a translation. Too bad I cannot also write it in German by myself. . . .

. . . Until tomorrow, my Marta, with all my love,

Your Maestro

---

[1] He refers to his letter of April 2—still on the way when Marta wrote the soothing
words that arrived in Berlin on April 5.

[2] This convoluted letter is a typical example of Pirandello's confused anxieties about
Marta's changing moods and possible extreme reactions to his never-ending complaints.

[3] A veiled hint at the *extreme hope* of his life; that is, to live near, or better, with Marta
for good—which he was not even allowed to mention to Marta.

[4] This is the first mention of the conception of Pirandello's last autobiographical play.

{ 300409 }

To Marta Abba
Teatro Savoia
(Italy-Sicily) Messina   Berlin, 9. IV. 1930
My Marta,

. . . For you who live your days *in the present*—the way they are: sad or
so-so, all taken up with the things you have to do; being the way they are,
unpleasant or so-so—the damage is less. I do not experience—except as if
from a distance—this sense of time that passes and feels as if it did not
touch me at all and as if it were not meant for me. It gives me the impression that everything is past, and that I am as if dead, and therefore, if I say
something . . . oh no, *I said it* . . . and if I do something . . . no, *I did it*
. . . the people I see, *I saw them* . . . if they talk to me, *they talked to me* . . .
and so on. . . . It is a frightening experience: to see the present as past!
But I recognize very clearly the reason for this very strange phenomenon,
which without doubt would be interpreted as an obvious sign of mental
illness if revealed to a psychiatrist. My life is present only in you, who are
so far away. I live here, therefore, as if at a great distance from my own life
and from myself, like in a kind of a past. What is far in respect to space
becomes far also in time . . . and therefore *I said, I did, I saw, she was*
talking. . . . Just like that!

When shall I get back from this distance?

When will my life be back in the present?

. . . .

Maestro

{ 300412 }

To Marta Abba
Grand Hôtel
(Italy-Sicily) Messina   Berlin, 12. IV. 1930
My Marta,
Yesterday, three things:
1) went out for lunch
2) went to a tea party at Mrs. Stern's
3) saw *Fiamma* by Müller.

. . . The contract between Felix Bloch-Erben and the director of the Lessing-Theater was signed. *Questa sera si recita a soggetto* will be performed at the end of May in Berlin under the direction of Hartung, with first-class actors and actresses chosen among those who are available. It looks pretty much sure that we'll have Valetti for the role of Signora Ignazia and Sokoloff for that of Sampognetta. And since one thing follows another, do you know what we'll have in a few days here in Berlin? Another revival of *Sei personaggi in cerca d'autore*, not directed by Reinhardt, who is now in Vienna, but in a new production by the Theater in der Klosterstrasse.

It will be a real trumpet blast for all German theaters: like a reveille. Of course the call was heard first in Königsberg, but the reveille must sound from Berlin, and it will sound loud indeed. The time has come.

And now I'll tell you about the third of the things I did yesterday, because it is the one you might be most interested in: how Käthe Dorsch interpreted *Die Flamme*.[1]

What a disappointment, my Marta! Enormous disappointment as far as the actress is concerned; disappointment also about how the work is understood, performed, and produced here—I felt like throwing up. I was not wrong at all imagining that they would stress the brutal part of the play. Both Ilonka—called in during the first act by Fasal when the client Employee comes—and Gasti appear on the scene almost naked, worse than naked: quite lewd. I can't tell you what Fasal looks like! They all speak a coarse slang, as befits that kind of low people, a language I would have not been able to understand had I not known the play as well as I do. Of course, this slang is lost in the translation (and therefore the translation I worked on was at many points incomprehensible), but the stronger color given to the dialogue is all to the damage and not at all to the advantage of the play because it gives it a disgusting vulgarity that is sickening and unbearable. Ilonka speaks like a Hungarian woman who has learned that Low-German slang, and this makes people laugh a little, but it is a disgusting laughter. Everything is disgusting: gestures, acts, words, attitudes. Dorsch obtains in a cheap way the effects of her conflict—between her brutal instincts and her aspirations to motherhood— by jumping back and forth from one to the other without any transition. I would have loved to have you here on that stage, to teach these people how to act, how to give sense and value to the role being performed, even when the playwright himself did not so much as dream of doing so, and

---

[1] A play (1922) by Hans Müller that was considered for Marta's repertory.

what a *truly great* actress can do, interpreting a role like that! While making this comparison, I could measure, my Marta, all your greatness. I certainly did not need to make that comparison for myself, but it was useful to measure the high level at which you are when compared with a Berlin star like Dorsch, and, since you are so much superior to her, in what esteem you would be held should you ever perform in Germany.

Before the performance, at 5:30, I went to a tea party at Mrs. Stern's. She is a Jewish young lady, about forty, with dark hair, short, very vivacious, jumping like a rubber ball between outbursts of laughter and a continuous entanglement of words; pleasant as a whole, being without any false poses of intellectuality; cordial, warm, friendly to everybody. She looks like an enlarged caricature of her little eight-year-old daughter, who also is jumping in the drawing room in front of everyone, so that you cannot tell anymore whether the mother acts like the daughter or the daughter like the mother. Both gave me a festive welcome. And the people there! Actresses, actors, critics, journalists, truly the entire art world of Berlin. The wife of Fritz Lang—you know, the director of UFA—was very kind to me. He was not there, being out of town on a trip. His wife seemed enthusiastic about the script of *Six Characters*, already published in German, and told me she had sent it to her husband to read. Among the actresses, I saw Bergner, Greta Noger, Valetti, Höflich, and many others whose names I don't remember; among the actors, Kortner, Forster, Pallenberg, George, Klöpfer, Deutsch, Curt Bois, and many others; I spoke with Kerr,[2] who is very happy about the coming performance of *Questa sera*, and with a great number of newspapermen from *Die Zeit*, *Berliner Zeitung am Mittag*, *Vossische Zeitung*, and from almost all the newspapers of Berlin. I could hardly get away at 7:30. Lantz was radiant with happiness because he says that all this will be helpful. But I was dead tired. Enough, until tomorrow, my Marta. All the best.

Your Maestro

[2] Alfred Kerr, the leading theater critic of Berlin.

{ 300415 }

To Marta Abba
Teatro Biondo
(Italy-Sicily) Palermo   Berlin, 15. IV. 1930

My Marta,

This morning at 8:30 Elisabeth brought the following three telegrams with my coffee:

"Immense success—amazing production—audience enthusiastic—greetings—Nulli"

"Reporting magnificent success of performance thanking you for giving your play to Teatro Torino—affectionate congratulations and regards—Gatti"

"Happy for your immense success and also for us dear Maestro best wishes—yours Biliotti"

. . . It looks as if it was a wonderful success, at least judging from these telegrams. It remains now to be seen how the newspapers will react, because that's where the real enemies are, and not in the audiences that love me. But I have already thoroughly chastised the critics in my play, whipping them to the blood as if they were asses, and they will carry the scars for a long time.

You will see, my Marta, that everywhere the miracle that happened with *Six Characters* will happen again for *Tonight We Improvise*. The play has been picked up almost everywhere in the world, and everywhere with great success. I saw it in Königsberg, I had a proof of it. Over *Six Characters* it has the advantage that it is *amusing, quite clear,* and *easy to listen to,* passing continuously *from one surprise to the next.* Here in Berlin Hartung is enthusiastic and is telling everybody that this production at the Lessing-Theater will be the most important enterprise of his life. And to think that those people at Sitedramma[1] and that unspeakable Mattioli and that equally unspeakable Ramo of ZaBum hung on to this work for seven months without wanting to do anything with it![2] Now they will gnaw their fingers to the quick at the echo of this immense success. God has punished them. They had their salvation in their hands, and they drowned. All the enemies will bite their nails. I am always the youngest of all, and as long as I live I'll always be the youngest of all, because God put

---

[1] The theatrical agency controlled by Giordani.

[2] Evidently the Italian distributors / possible producers of Pirandello's plays had no faith in this latest strange and unconventional parody.

this TRUE eternal youth in my blood and in my heart and in my brain! I have still so much to do and to say, to astonish the world; and all the big beasts will be scorned for eternity by my *I giganti della montagna.*[3]

Now I have to give you another piece of good news. Here in Berlin the rumor about Metro-Goldwyn-Mayer's invitation to go to Hollywood spread at once; the same representative of Metro-Goldwyn—or I don't know who else—might have been responsible for that; it was certainly neither Lantz nor Philips, who is now in Paris. The fact remains that the news spread, and Lantz said it is no wonder, because in the film world everything gets around at once. Enough. Yesterday afternoon Hollywood's United Artists' representative, who is Hofmannsthal's son,[4] came to see me here at the Herkuleshaus and made other proposals. United Artists, in sharp competition in America with Western Electric and Metro-Goldwyn and Paramount, knowing that these companies had opened branch offices in Paris (the one for which Fontana came to you to ask for pictures of yourself), immediately opened another branch of their own here in Berlin, with very strong main offices and dependent offices in Paris, and also in London and in Italy (Luporini) and in Spain. In one word, the conquest of Europe. Because they want to produce talking films, they need (as I had foreseen a year ago) dramatic authors and dramatic actresses and actors! My Marta, the time has come! This is our chance to go from one big money deal to the next, from Paris to Berlin. Hofmannsthal saw your smiling picture on my desk and asked who was that *wundervoll* actress; Lantz was here with me, and you can imagine how he spoke (he, not I) of Marta Abba; naturally, later I spoke, too. We spoke about the filming of *Six Characters*; he took along the already printed book of the scenario, prepared with Lantz, to read at home. In the meantime I sent a cable to Metro-Goldwyn with my answer: fifteen thousand dollars for three months, thirty thousand for six, with the obligation that at least one script will be purchased and paid for extra during the first three months, and a second one if I should have to stay in Hollywood for three more months. Between now and September, it will be possible to close a few more deals by remaining in Europe, in Paris or in

[3] Pirandello was convinced that his *I giganti della montagna* would stand in the history of dramatic literature as his greatest masterpiece. Pirandello is in a manic phase, building a big dream castle of a fantastic worldwide success (including the trashing of enemies, victory over his adversaries, etc.) on the fragile news of three conventional telegrams of congratulations on the premiere of his play *Tonight We Improvise* in Turin, Italy. The reality would be quite different!

[4] The son of the Austrian poet/playwright Hugo von Hofmannsthal (1874–1929).

Berlin, with United Artists or with Metro-Goldwyn. My Marta, it will mean riches, you'll see, and all our troubles will be at an end.[5]

Until tomorrow! With all the love of

Your Maestro

[5] This letter is full of hope for an imminent future of renewed worldwide theater successes and for great wealth from contracts with American movie producers. The much-longed-for economic independence and the consequent "triumph over his enemies" appears to Pirandello to be around the corner.

{ 300417 }

To Marta Abba
Teatro Biondo
(Italy-Sicily) Palermo   Berlin, 17. IV. 1930

. . . I talk to you about all these things because, if I talk about something else, you say that I write "volumes of useless words."[1] But in these "useless words" is, after all, my whole life, and all the rest has no importance for me unless related or capable to give some value to the vital substance of those "useless words." Success . . . fame . . . all the "useful" earnings that can come out of it—and will come—without those "useless" words would become nothing but ashes.[2]

I started again to write with so much fervor! *I giganti della montagna,* my Marta, will be a truly gigantic work. I have thought things . . . things. . . . But I don't know how they can be produced, I don't say in Italy, but even here. . . . Great things! Prodigious! I took the story of *Il figlio cambiato* and I transformed it splendidly to serve as drama: the drama that the heroic countess is carrying around, at the price of her life. The transformation has come out so well that also this time, as for *Come tu mi vuoi,* I must force myself to overcome the temptation to make out of it a work by itself: it would come out magnificent! I'll talk to you about it tomorrow. But I have thought and I am thinking of many other things. It would be a real pity if I should die right at this moment! But I'll not die, I'll not die! I touch wood! Easter of Resurrection, help me! Help Marta, to whom I send all the love of her

Maestro

[1] In the previous part of the letter, Pirandello had been talking about business. Marta continues to ignore Pirandello's explicit and/or veiled messages requesting at least a hint of a response.

[2] From this and other similar passages it is clear that Marta used to react with firm

common sense to Pirandello's insistent demands for a response to his requests for expressions of love. The experience of a five-year-old relationship had taught Marta to ignore completely his sentimental outbursts and pathetic requests, or, at the most, to answer advising the Maestro to abandon a theme by now irrevocably closed—and therefore to be classified as "useless words."

{ 300418 }

To Marta Abba
Teatro Biondo
(Italy-Sicily) Palermo   Berlin, 18. IV. 1930
  My Marta,
  I've just come back from a rehearsal of *Six Characters* at the Theater in der Klosterstrasse. I made incredible efforts to restrain myself! I was feeling as if I should interrupt not only every scene, but every cue. Had I had a free hand, I would have done everything in a different way. You understand, I was seeing you before my eyes, your interpretation, your face, your expressions; and in my ears and in my soul I was hearing your voice. Moreover, they were not following the revised text of my play—as we performed it at our Teatro Odescalchi—but the first edition, without the new finale. The work seemed to me as if it had been mutilated. But it was too late to propose changes; I just gave a few suggestions for the finale and for the interpretation of some points that were unclear. The suggestions were accepted and at once rehearsed with excellent results. Lantz, who was with me at the rehearsal, assures me that the work—as it is now performed—has a very powerful *Wirkung*; that is, a most powerful effect, and I was satisfied with that. But he has never seen your interpretation and does not know how the play came to life in our production. Here they have another mode of interpreting, another sensitivity; therefore they give a different coloring to and place another kind of emphasis on their cues—especially on the dramatic ones—and it is easier to leave it up to them, even if we feel our stomach go sour. The actress who then played the role of the Stepdaughter, remember? Her name is Kinz; the name of the present one (what a coincidence!) is Kainz.[1] But I don't believe that Kainz is worth Kinz. We have to say, however, that the latter is not vulgar at all. I've never seen Kinz. But here the newspapers wrote—at that time

---

[1] The play on words is based on a mistake. In reality the names of the two actresses are very different: Franziska Kinz and Gertrud Kanitz. Pirandello corrects the latter's name in letter 300419.

and even again three months later—that "after Marta Abba no German actress in the role of the Stepdaughter will have a chance." No German actress? No actress in the world!

At this time, my Marta, (it is 5:00 P.M.) perhaps you are already in Palermo and, passing by the Teatro Biondo, you already picked up my letters. . . . I close my eyes and see Palermo, I see the Hôtel des Palmes where last time we were together.[2] Your good mother was with you, and Cele too, who this year, poor girl, will have to spend Easter with the bitterness of the great sorrow she went through. . . . [3] You too will spend Easter away from home; but you'll not be as lonely as I'll be. I'll be working, and I won't be feeling so lonely anymore—while working and thinking of you. I am feeling inspired in my work, as I was telling you yesterday: truly inspired. And I am happy; only my health is not doing well; this devil of a spot on my left lung doesn't want to give up. I went to the Theater in der Klosterstrasse and came back home in a taxi, and I did not catch cold. Don't be afraid; I am taking good care of myself, and I do not intend to leave my skin in Berlin: it would be too horrible, without even being able to see you once again! . . .

Until tomorrow, my Marta!

Your Maestro

[2] Pirandello's company had performed at the Teatro Biondo in Palermo, November 3–23, 1927.
[3] Cele had just broken an engagement.

{ 300420 }

To Marta Abba
Teatro Biondo
(Italy-Sicily) Palermo   Berlin, 20. IV. 1930

My Marta,

. . . I am afraid that the Easter festivities in Sicily will not draw people to the theater (as they do in other regions of the Continent). The Sicilians are fond of feasting, but they celebrate by shutting themselves in the family, inside their homes, leaving theaters and coffeehouses empty. Moreover, I believe that on Holy Saturday, in the churches, they celebrate the Resurrection as a theatrical spectacle, with a Holy Sepulcher that opens up wide in the middle, and Christ springing out of it like a jack-in-the-box, with a little flag in his hand and the winged angels who fall astonished on the floor, one on one side and the other on the other—and the bells ring, and everybody kneels down singing hosannas. At least, when I was a boy, that's the way they did it; I found so many things changed, every time I went back for a short visit: also this theatrical Resurrection might have changed, or at least I hope so, because it attracted so many people, like a true theatrical show, so that all the churches were incredibly crowded, and nobody even thought of going to the theater.

Yesterday Lantz, accompanied by his wife and his son Robert, who had gone to the theater to see the premiere of *Six Characters*,[1] came around later in the evening to tell me how the performance went: excellent! great success! Sold-out theater; great applause; they called for the author; the author was in bed with the little dogs dipping their teeth into his shoulders; the animals, however, feeling the warmth of the bed, had already gone to sleep. They are still sleeping this morning. If one of them just begins to wake up because I make a bad movement, it yawns at this beautiful Easter that I am spending in bed all alone; just as the sky, veiled by mist, yawns at the window; as this open door of the studio yawns . . . and this continual drop of water falling into the sink from the faucet that does not shut off properly. . . . Oh, my God, I can't take it anymore. . . . Let's talk about cheerful things! The telephone already rang three times on the little desk of my studio, and I let it ring. Yesterday I had given orders to Elisabeth not to let any phone calls through, because I cannot answer from the bed. But today Elisabeth is not there because it is the feast of Holy Easter; who knows who is left at the concierge's switchboard, who probably doesn't know about my order of yesterday, and I'll receive this spate of good wishes by phone, until somebody shows up to whom I can renew my order that nobody should bother me with the phone. My God, I hope I won't have to stay in bed much longer, with so much that I have to do! It is this cursed weather, so damp, so squalid and pernicious that makes me sick. If only a little sun eventually would appear to dry up this deadly humidity in the air and to give a little spring warmth, not only could I get up, but also go out! Out in the open air! On Tuesday the rehearsals at the Lessing-Theater[2] will begin, and I would like to be there and see how Hartung directs, and meet the actresses and the actors that were chosen . . . can I stay here frying in bed? Nobody can be convinced that my frenzy is hurting me more than those little dogs. . . . I am waiting for a little sunshine; you certainly have so much of it over there, my

---

[1] The revival of *Sei personaggi in cerca d'autore* at the Theater in der Klosterstrasse.
[2] Rehearsals for the production of *Tonight We Improvise*.

Marta: send me a few rays of sunlight, nice and warm, in a happy letter! Here they are; I apply them to the place where it hurts, and I am recovered. I get up and go to rehearsal.

Write to me, my Marta, please do write! If you only knew how much I need your letters. . . . But you, too, you are so busy. . . . No, don't worry about me, write to me when you can, but don't leave so much time between letters. . . .

. . . It is 5 P.M. Your answer to my telegram of good wishes hasn't arrived yet. I seal my letter and I send it to be mailed. I hope tomorrow I'll be able to give you better news about my health. Meanwhile, once again, all the best with all the love of your

Maestro

{ 300425 }

To Marta Abba
Hôtel des Palmes
(Italy-Sicily) Palermo   Berlin, 25. IV. 1930
      My Marta,

This weather drives me to despair: it doesn't stop raining, and I am staring at the rain, behind the windowpanes of my studio, and at those poor big trees along the canal that cannot manage to dress up in green, although it is almost May. Along the branches they have so many buds, which are in danger of withering; they are waiting, in order to open up, for a glance of the sun, which is not coming—it doesn't want to come. Addio, spring! We'll jump from winter to summer. But if at least this damned humidity would pass! The poet Heinrich Heine sang:

> In Germany there is no summer
> summer is a winter
> painted with green . . .

But, in spite of its being almost May, you cannot yet see even a first hint of that green coat. . . . Everything is bare: dampness, mold, and the blackness of the rain washing all this dampness and all this mold. . . . I cannot take it anymore!

Hartung has put off for one day his return from Heidelberg; yesterday I was supposed to talk with director Saltenberg, and he didn't show up; he called up and promised that he will come today between 1 and 2 P.M.

here to the Herkuleshaus to submit the list of the actors who seem to him the best suited for the interpretation of the individual roles of *Tonight We Improvise*. I have no choice but to trust him; since I do not even know the name of all the actors, I can neither judge nor choose a priori. I'll be able to give a judgment on the selections he made only at rehearsal—but the weather must change so that I can be present at those blessed rehearsals! They will start next Monday (today is Friday) at the latest, and since there isn't much time left, Hartung is determined to rehearse also during the night, after the show. Can you imagine: I should be feeling really well, and on the contrary. . . .

But I don't want to trouble you with these useless complaints about the miserable weather and my bad health. . . . Perhaps you too are having plenty of trouble with your season in Palermo, but I hope I am wrong! I want to think at least of you happy in the sun. . . . Yes, I want to breathe deep when I think of you, by God's grace far from these mists!

I am working at *I giganti della montagna*. The idea of using the story of *Il figlio cambiato* as the core of the drama has solved all my problems. Now I am composing this *Il figlio cambiato* in verses, almost in the form of a fable, and I'll take from it as much as I need for the performance that the company of the contessa is to give for a short while in the first act— before the poet Cotrone and his *scarognati*—and again, briefly in the third act, to the Giants. Since you know neither the whole plot of the work nor the characters, it is impossible for you to understand. It is better that I don't tell you anything, and that the whole play comes to you new when it will be finished, and I'll be able to read it to you to get your opinion. If your eyes shine, if your mouth smiles, if your face is moved . . . this is the only prize for me, for which I am still writing. . . . I'd have been dead a long time ago; I was already dead after *Ciascuno a suo modo*. If I am still alive and writing, I owe it only to you. And therefore everything belongs to you. Everything, even if you do not interpret some of my work. What does it matter? It belongs to you anyhow![1] I always write it for you, for you to like it, even if you do not perform it, as it was in the case of *O di uno o di nessuno*, as maybe it will be also for *I giganti della montagna*, which probably will not find a way to be performed in Italy because of the necessary production expenses.

. . . It is almost one o'clock. I'm ordering my food. But I have no appe-

---

[1] Pirandello did, in fact, leave Marta the rights (and royalties) to the plays inspired by her. This passage—together with other, similar ones from this correspondence—was used by Marta to prove in court her rights when they were contested by the Pirandello heirs.

tite. Perhaps at this time you too are getting ready to go to breakfast . . .
but I cannot see you. . . . Enough, until tomorrow, my Marta!

   With all my love,

                                                                    Your Maestro

                            { 300429 }
                            ==========

To Marta Abba
Grand Hôtel des Palmes
(Italy-Sicily) Palermo   Berlin, 29. IV. 1930
   My Marta,
   This month of April, which seemed to me endless, will be over tomorrow; can you imagine how long the month of May will seem to me, since
I'll be spending it here without a break! In June at last you'll be in Milan
again—free—and I'll come back, and we'll plan together what to do
during the next year. Perhaps I'll have to go to America; who knows,
maybe you too will go, either for a tour or alone, if we sign a contract over
there for *Six Characters* (this time a real one, with all the legal para-
phernalia). Otherwise you'll have your tour in Europe, according to the
itinerary I prepared for you, and I'll go alone to America for my last big
harvest, if God gives me the strength. We'll do all we can to get you out
of Italy this year—so as to make your name known in the world and thus
put to shame all those small country lice, who have greatness before their
eyes and cannot see it. When the echo of distant triumphs sounds in
their ears, only then will they recognize the voice they did not want to
hear while it was speaking to them from close by. You are still young, my
Marta, and what happened to Eleonora Duse will not happen to you: she
ended up missing ten years of life in art; when already old she went back
to the stage, but in order not to starve to death she had to leave her
country and go around the world all the way to America; before being
glorified and almost sanctified, she had first to die—and certainly a horrible death amid the smoke and the noise of the machines in a city across
the ocean.[1] You are young, and you'll be able to enjoy the triumph that
you will soon enjoy—*not in your own country, but in the world*—and then
you'll pay back all the evil that your country did to you during the most
difficult years of the first conquest, with the good you'll have done for

---

[1] Eleonora Duse died alone in Pittsburgh on April 21, 1924, where she was performing
Porta chiusa.

your country, spreading everywhere the glory of your name. Someday or another, my turn will come to leave my bones—God knows where; only then perhaps will Italy mourn the writer she will have lost, the writer she fought against and embittered to the very last, to whom nothing was given except with clenched teeth and balled fists. I will be sorry then not to be able to raise my head from my coffin to spit in the faces of my posthumous admirers.

Let's drop this topic. Thanks be to God, I do not need that glory, either posthumous or present, to come from my country. I don't care about Glory, with a capital *g*—it's only a cosmetic consecration! I never looked for it, I never did anything to get it, I never posed as a statue on a pedestal;[2] I walked the paths of life, a man among men. The richness of my soul, the power of my brain, and the enormous capacity for feeling with my heart were enough for me. This has been my true, *living* glory! And having found *you*, so that I was able to see it alive. What does all the rest matter to me?

I am here now with this new company that the Lessing-Theater has formed for my play. . . . Expectation is already enormous all over Berlin. Interviews become more and more frequent.

Let's hope that everything will be all right.

. . . Until tomorrow, my Marta! In your last letter you wrote to me: "See you soon." I wish it were true—good-bye . . . until tomorrow! How many days must still pass!

Always all the love of

Your Maestro

[2] The thoughts expressed in this part of the letter will appear again in Pirandello's play *Quando si è qualcuno.*

{ 300430 }

To Marta Abba
Grand Hôtel des Palmes
(Italy-Sicily) Palermo   Berlin, 30. IV. 1930
    My Marta,
    I'm right in the midst of the most intense frenzy of work, and I'm feeling like a god. My health is back and is fully sustaining my effort; should I die at this moment I wouldn't mind—I'd be dying on my feet, in the midst of work! Creation and rehearsals: rehearsals that are *alive,*

because the work is extraordinarily alive—how alive cannot even be guessed by simply reading the text: as soon as you touch it, it vibrates, it moves, it jumps, it splashes, and one doesn't know how to contain it because it finds in itself new surges of development, and there is no time to run after it. I immensely enjoy discovering that right here is a hint to pick up, and over there an unsuspected track. . . . I feel as if I wished to re-create it all, moment by moment—it is all born so prodigiously, almost without interruption, like a miracle of vitality. It must be seen with the actors and with all the scenery and lighting effects that Hartung has created—wonderful! It will be a marvelous treat to behold. I am helping out with all my strength, without getting tired. I cut, I add, I mix all my life into it, with my fantasy in flames and my heart in a tumult.[1]

Then, back home, other work, different. The giants of the mountain who are really developing gigantically. It's a pity that you do not remember that little story of mine, *Il figlio cambiato*—or maybe you never read it! If you only knew how it has developed, how it has become a part of the "myth"! It is the story of a mother who believes that her son was exchanged when he was a six-month-old infant. All over South Italy there is a popular belief that during the windy and moonless winter nights certain witches, called the women, fly through the air; they enter the houses through the chimneys and the dormer windows, and they take babies away from the side of their sleeping mothers; or they braid the child's hair on its head in a way that cannot be undone, and woe unto you if you should touch those braids with a comb or cut them with a scissors; the child would die. Or they pass their thin forefingers over the closed eyelids of the little creatures, and the next morning the baby opens its eyes and they are crossed, or, worst mischief of all, they exchange children from one mother with another; that is, they take away a beautiful child and leave there an ugly one, and bring the beautiful child to the other mother in exchange for the ugly one. This happened to the mother in my story. And from there I drew the plot of the play. People made this poor mother believe that her beautiful son was taken by the witches to a royal house, and that therefore her son has grown up as the son of a king: a king of a northern country, like Iceland or Finland. Now it happens that one day a young prince arrives on the coast where this mother lives; he is ill, he needs the sea and the sun to get well. They say that this young prince is a king's son, who was sent to Italy incognito to get cured. The king-

---

[1] This first part of the letter describes in a vivid way a moment of inspiration, exaltation, and artistic creation, which can be considered a concrete, authentic example of Pirandello's aesthetics of life.

dom is far away, gloomy with fog and ice, and troubled with envy and political passions. But here is the serenity of an eternal spring, the resonant laughter of the sea, the voluptuous warmth of the sun. One day the news comes that the king is close to death in the capital of his kingdom. The young prince must go back there, to receive the crown upon the death of his father. You already guess that—since the first moment of that young prince's arrival—the mother has been convinced that he is her son who had been kidnapped when he was in swaddling clothes. She has nursed and brought up a little monster, whom everybody mocks as "the king's son" and who is going around with a gilded cardboard crown on his big gangling head. Now a conflict arises between this little monster and the young prince, who is condemned to go and die on the throne if he leaves the country of the sun; between the two is the mother, who succeeds in keeping close to her the one whom she believes to be her true son and lets the little monster go to the throne.

That summarizes the fable. I am handling everything like a legend, in almost dreamlike, lyrical scenes. And it seems to me it's coming beautifully. I am happy.

. . . I am sending to you the first copy of *Come tu mi vuoi*, which has just arrived from Milan. The book, as you know, is dedicated to you.

Until tomorrow, my Marta! Now and forever with all my love,

Your Maestro

{ 300504 }

To Marta Abba
Teatro Massimo
(Italy-Sicily) Catania   Berlin, 4. v. 1930
My Marta,

. . . Here at last we have good weather. It is even warm, at least during the day. At the Lessing-Theater rehearsals are continuing, but I was not able to attend. Lantz came to tell me that some actors were changed who at rehearsal did not prove to be right for the roles. Tomorrow, if my swollen cheek is a little better, I'll go. Rehearsals start at 10 A.M. and end at 5 P.M. I'll take care of myself. You understand, my Marta, that so many things depend on this production in Berlin! In September, at the opening of the season, all Germany might start to perform my plays again. And here the theater, with all the money it brings in, can really make you rich. I cannot just mark time, taking care of my health, while so many interests are at play. My body must go back to being obedient to me; otherwise, what am I doing in this life anymore? Up, up, and to work![1]

.   .   .   .   .   .

Your Maestro

[1] This passage makes clear how important the production of *Tonight We Improvise* was in Pirandello's plans. It must therefore be kept in mind if we are to understand his reaction after the troubled premiere.

{ 300505 }

To Marta Abba
Hotel Bristol
(Italy-Sicily) Catania

Berlin, 5. v. 1930
and
6

My Marta,
Yesterday I started with the date and address of this letter, but literally *I did not find one minute* in the whole day to write it. I got up about one hour later than usual, at 9:30, because of this pain and swelling of my cheek. I had just finished taking my bath and at 10:15 I had just settled at my desk, when Hartung called from the Lessing-Theater to solve a problem that came up during rehearsal. I had to go immediately to the Lessing-Theater by taxi, and I stayed there until 2:30. Back at the hotel, I had just ordered my usual lunch when a call from Philips announced that in fifteen minutes he would pick me up because Lasky from Paramount had set up an appointment with me at the Adlon at 3:00.[1] I did not have time to eat. Before the lunch could be sent up from downstairs, Philips arrived with the taxi—and we had to go without delay. At three we got to the Adlon. Lasky, who is like a king, asked us to come in at once. The conversation and the negotiations lasted from three to six. At 7:30 Lasky was scheduled to leave for America. I dealt with him as equal to equal, as king to king. By dint of clear and precise refusals, after endless proposals and discussions, I obliged him to yield on all points. I had heard from Philips that on that very morning Lasky had received a long cablegram from New

[1] The producer of American movies Jesse L. Lasky (1880–1958) was at the time vice-president of Paramount.

York that told him to sign a contract with me. I have reason to suppose that Otto Kahn (one of the most important stockholders of Paramount) had been working very effectively over there. Over and over again, our conversation was interrupted by bellboys who announced one visit after another; there must have been a waiting room full of people, since it was the last day—actually the very last moments—of Lasky's stay in Berlin. Lasky was putting off everybody so as to continue the negotiations with me. I tell you, three hours: almost to the last moment before his departure. And I did not give in. I accepted only when I obtained the assurance that at least *two* scripts will be purchased by Paramount. But the contract contemplates *four* scripts, for a total of sixty-seven thousand dollars; plus a payment for three months at one thousand dollars per week for expenses and a round-trip ticket, with the obligation of staying part of the three months in New York and part in Hollywood. The date of departure will be in August or September, as soon as I'll be notified by the administration of Paramount. Moreover Lasky showed great interest in the filming of *Six Characters*, which I decided to exclude from the contract, because it should be the object of a separate contract. When we parted he told me that he would read the script of the film during his trip home and that he would write to me on the subject as soon as he disembarked in New York. I do believe that I'll get the contract also for *Six Characters*. In the meantime Lasky himself, yesterday before leaving, ordered that the news of the contract signed with me—for four scripts and my trip to Hollywood to find materials for further original works—should be released all over the world. This morning the news has actually appeared in all German newspapers, and it will appear, I'm sure, also in the Italian ones, because it was released by United Press, which is an international press agency. Today it is the talk of all Berlin. But I heard that Gilbert Miller, one of the major owners of theaters in New York and an importer of European plays to America,[2] at present is in Europe. Miller has ties with Paramount and has already bought two of my plays (I think they are *Questa sera* and *Come tu mi vuoi*). At the moment he is in Hungary to buy Molnár's new plays. He will be here in Berlin in a few days. I'll see him and I'll propose a tour for you in North America, in cooperation with Paramount, for next season. That way you too will go to America, my Marta! I'll concentrate all my energies on doing everything possible to

[2] Gilbert Miller was the American impresario who realized Marta's dream, making her a successful star on Broadway and changing forever the course of her life—but too late (1936) for Pirandello!

succeed in this effort. We'll go together, we'll work there, and we'll come back loaded with money and glory.[3] What do you think about that, my Marta? In all this I see nothing but you, I do not think but of you: of you alone, and of nobody else. All my love,

Yours,
Maestro

[3] Pirandello reiterates his cherished project: to be near Marta in America far away from the Italian world, to earn enormous amounts of money in the movie business and make Marta a great international star, so as to go back to Italy da padroni and organize an ideal theatrical company with Marta at its head, without financially depending on anyone in the realization of an exclusively artistic program.

{ 300507 }

To Marta Abba
Hôtel Bristol
(Italy-Sicily) Catania   Berlin, 7. v. 1930

My Marta,

I am still surprised at the speed with which this new adventure of my wandering life has happened. I feel as if I were being tossed on a sea hit by all possible winds, on a rudderless little ship as light as a nutshell and with all the sails torn. I still have an anchor; that is, you. Woe betide me if this anchor should fail me. But the harbor, where is the harbor?

I'm enclosing two of the hundred newspaper clippings in which my departure for America is announced. As if Germany were Italy, now even here they reprimand the German movie industry for not taking advantage of my presence in Berlin for over a year and for allowing the Americans to lure me away. Now the same reproach is extended to all Europe. Away from Italy, away from Germany, away from all Europe: to America! What a destiny is mine! They make me go away, and then they say: "What a shame for us to have caused him to go away!" And when I am not there anymore, they will say: "What a shame for us not to have kept him near, to have sent him far away, farther and farther away! So far away that eventually he disappeared from everybody's sight!"

But let's not talk about melancholy matters. As long as I have you, I have everything, and this horrible loneliness of my personality in the world does not frighten me. On the contrary, it gives me pride and power.

I went back to work. Tonight I have to go to the reception of the International Students Association. It seems that also the minister of culture will come. Today an official commission of about twenty students from every possible nation came to discuss arrangements for the reception; they told me several times: "Maestro, you are younger than all of us!" Of course! It is God's will that I die, in a short while, very young.[1]

You won't believe the number of invitations I receive from all over. I don't go anywhere. I tell Lantz to answer that I am ill and that I need rest. After all, it is the pure truth.

. . . Until tomorrow, my Marta. With all the love of

Your Maestro

[1] "Very young" (*giovanissimo*) is written in large letters. Pirandello's rebellion against his ailing body's evident old age is so profound that he invokes the will of a God he does not believe in to affirm the eternal youth of his spirit!

{ 300514 }

To Marta Abba
Hôtel Minerva
(Italy) Rome   Berlin, 14. v. 1930
My Marta,

. . . Perhaps at your opening night you saw Peppino Marchesano,[1] who probably came to greet you backstage. . . . In his way, he loves me. And he loves you very much, my Marta. But I know that he does all he can to separate you from me, as if I were not already far away enough. Nobody wants to have mercy on a man who is dying in his horrible loneliness. They know that you have affection for me and mercy on me; they know that you defend and support my art; and they do not get tired of screaming after you: "But when will she stop helping him? When will she finally let this Pirandello die?" They would be ready, however, to glorify me, as soon as I'm dead—after doing all they could to see me dead. But not you, my Marta! You will help and defend me! You! You won't make me die!

I need so badly not to feel so alone in life! I need a soul who under-

[1] Giuseppe Marchesano, a Roman lawyer married to Pirandello's cousin, shared with the other members of the Pirandello family the desire to hasten as much as possible the end of the relationship between the Maestro and Marta. Pirandello was afraid of Marchesano's influence on Marta while she was performing in Rome and wrote this letter to warn her and to implore her not to give in to the pressure of his family.

stands me, a heart who feels some *true* affection for me! I cannot live anymore without it. And I have so little time to live! Will Italy ever repent her fierce ingratitude to her best children! And you too, my Marta, who are destined for great things, you will feel this very same bitterness and will regret you were born Italian.[2] May God not let that happen!

You deserve to be adored, not only for your greatness, but also for your goodness. Again, all the best for you, best wishes, and with the deepest gratitude of

Your Maestro

[2] The hostility that Pirandello and his work met in a number of Italian theater people, especially among the critics, caused deep resentment in his extremely sensitive soul. During the worst periods of his depression the playwright translated those feelings into a persecution complex, which he extended to the whole nation, accusing almost everybody in Italy of a lack of understanding and/or malicious hostility. It is probable that the memory of the Maestro's bitter expressions against his own country influenced Marta Abba's decision to leave her treasured letters to the custody of an American institution. Marta's own feelings were deeply hurt by the way the so-called friends of Pirandello treated her after the Maestro's death: according to her recollection, she was abandoned by almost everybody in Italy, and she was met with great hostility when, in the 1950s after her divorce and her return to Italy, she tried to resume her acting career.

{ 300517 }

To Marta Abba
Grande Albergo Minerva
(Italy) Rome   Berlin, 17. V. 1930

My Marta,

. . . "Be happy, Maestro, the world is yours!" The world, my Marta? And what can I do with it? If *you* think this way about me, knowing how I feel, ah! then yes, more than happy—it makes me delirious with joy if you say *that it is mine!* Otherwise it is a meaningless expression of good wishes. The world . . . a path that leads to a goal . . . a sweet home of my own, which is this goal. . . . [1] But so, without a path and without a home, wandering and alone, alone and wandering . . . the world, the world . . . looks like so much but is nothing! Less than nothing, my Marta!

[1] At this point the most profound of Pirandello's desires is revealed; that is, the longing for a home full of love, with Marta at his side. Later (see letter 321125) the same dream will escape the usually reserved pen of the Maestro when he affirms that he could conceive of rebuilding a home for himself only with Marta.

"Useless chatter!"

. . . I hope that *Tonight We Improvise* will be a great, enormous success; the play is shaping up magnificently out of those most laborious rehearsals. Fritz Lang is looking for me to produce the film of *Six Characters*, if possible here in Berlin. One of these evenings we'll get together. They say that he is speaking about this project with great enthusiasm. But I keep my reserve. I have the feeling that the filming of *Six Characters* will actually be done in America, when I'm there. And I have the idea that you too must be there.

As soon as I lift my eyes from the paper, my eyes go to the bust portraying me, of which the sculptor Isenstein gave me a plaster copy. I put it on the little shelf of the great big stove that is in my study—do you remember?—in the corner by the door. With this plaster bust, the stove looks like my tomb, and I see myself as if in a cemetery. A merry sight! The bust, however, is very beautiful. I'll give it to you on my return, if you want it. I accepted the gift with you in mind, as I did the seal of Königsberg, the gold medal of America, and many other things that belong to me. . . . If they have a value, they have it only because they are meant for you.[2]

Enough. Until tomorrow, my Marta. I started to study English, one hour each day. And what about your French? Talk to me about yourself. . . . Addio, with all the best wishes and all the love of your

Maestro

[2] Marta in fact received those gifts from Pirandello, and she used to treasure them and show them to visitors and friends. The plaster copy of Pirandello's bust was sent to Princeton University with the correspondence and exhibited on the occasion of the gala reception in Marta Abba's honor at Prospect House (November 9, 1986).

{ 300518 }

To Marta Abba
Grande Albergo Minerva
(Italy) Rome   Berlin, 18. V. 1930

My Marta,

. . . Today is Sunday, and there is rehearsal from eleven in the morning to four-thirty in the afternoon. You have over there in Rome two shows! To throw away one's breath, spending one's very soul. . . . What an enormous effort it costs me to make people understand, in a language that is not mine,[1] what I wanted to say—these German actors are very good, but they make you sweat up seven shirts before they understand one thing and before they get the intended effect! I must also hold back a bit so as not to offend the sensitivities of Hartung, who is directing the rehearsal. It is very difficult when I have to correct him too, when he has misinterpreted and taught in a wrong way how to say a line or make a movement. Moreover there is a difference in temperament. Here they scream when we would murmur, and murmur when we would scream. In this I have to let them act as they please; it is a question of temperament, and since the play is presented here, it is necessary that the work reaches the German audience with those tones that are their own, although so contrary to our interpretation.

. . . Enough. Until tomorrow. I repeat every day these words, and the days pass, my life passes, by dint of repeating until tomorrow, until tomorrow. . . . But what never passes is the love of

Your Maestro

---

[1] Pirandello had a good knowledge of German from his period of residence in Bonn as a university student (1889–1981), but after decades of distance he had forgotten a great deal. He could converse in French and eventually learned enough English to get by. In several letters he insists that Marta must study languages (letters 290330, 300421, 300523). He is generous with praise for Marta's hard work and success in performing in French (letter 311009). He supports with enthusiasm Marta's serious study of English in London (letters 350128, 350130, 350225, 350304) and is ecstatic at her triumph in her first performance in English (letter 360727).

{ 300522 }

To Marta Abba
Hôtel Milan
(Italy) Salsomaggiore   Berlin, 22. v. 1930
  My Marta,

. . . Yesterday I was very busy the whole day—I hardly had time to breathe. As soon as I got up I wrote a new scene for *Tonight We Improvise*—one more, for which I saw the necessity during rehearsal. It came out very well. I just made it to get it translated, page by page while I was writing it, by Kahn, who was here since eight o'clock. At eleven we were through, and we immediately hurried to the Lessing-Theater by taxi. You might as well say that for several days since these rehearsals have started, I have had no lunch. We eat a small sandwich or something like that, standing during breaks, which do not last more than ten minutes. For me this is a serious matter, because in the morning I only drink a small cup of coffee, and therefore I remain without food from one evening to the next. Moreover I drink so much coffee and I smoke so much, that when evening comes—fatigued as I am and with a burned stomach—I feel no desire to eat. I do not know how I manage to keep going. The nervous energy helps. And my physical resistance is truly prodigious. Unfortunately, however, I am always in low spirits. . . . Back from rehearsal at five in the afternoon, I had a very long meeting with Mr. Farley from Paramount, who this morning left again for Paris. I already told you that this Mr. Farley traveled to Berlin just to see me and come to an agreement about the scripts. I had to fight his American mentality, which is so different—if not opposite—from ours. Feeling strong because of the contract, I declared that they cannot oblige me to write for their so-called *vedettes* as if I were a tailor who must cut a suit for a client: a suit fitting Mr. Chevalier, another suit fitting another imbecile of the same kind. I am a poet, and they must think of finding the most suitable actors for the characters of my fantasy. We discussed for over two hours. Mr. Farley kept saying that that was the American system; I kept replying that the American system is beastly, because it sacrifices the writers and kills the actors, condemning them to play *always* the same types, without ever changing; so that eventually audiences get tired of seeing, over and over again in their stereotyped poses, Garbo or Swanson, Pickford or I don't know whom else; for example, Dolores del Rio. After finishing this endless discussion, we talked about the scripts. This one yes and that one no

. . . —two more hours! Finally, at 9:30, he left loaded with books: fifteen volumes of short stories, novels, plays. He told me that he will send them back to me from Paris after selecting the four subjects that, according to his opinion, are best suited to the American taste. I repeat, I am strong because of my contract, and they must grin and bear it. But I foresee a lot of trouble ahead. You wouldn't find more stupid people anywhere than in the movies! Mr. Farley is actually one of the least stupid, and I must add that he went out of his way to be very kind and respectful. Enough. We'll see what he will choose. He is condemned to reading for life, poor Mr. Farley!

I am very happy with the rehearsals. But shall I make it, alive, to open-ing night? Until tomorrow, my Marta! I am waiting for your news. You are getting closer to home . . . and I am always far away, but always near you with all my love.

Your Maestro

{ 300524 }

To Marta Abba
Hôtel Milan
(Italy) Salsomaggiore   Berlin, May 24, 1930
My Marta,

I kept on working through the night. At 3:00 I began to see at the two windows of my study the first transparency of dawn, like a mystery that was attempting to disclose itself from far, far away, uncertain whether the revelation eventually would be fulfilled. The black houses on the other side of the huge Lützow Square appeared like profiles of mountains against that first shimmer, and I had—I do not know why—the same feeling about this dawn as I had of another one, by now so remote, that appeared through the glass of a train window while I was traveling, and far away on the horizon was seen, still black, a range of hills. A feeling of mysterious and most profound pain. Pain of all life condemned every day to reawaken from the forgetful sleep of night. The benefit of sleep was denied me tonight, and the journey . . . wasn't my life one long journey without arrivals, without rest? Seated in front of my writing desk in an alien house, far away, here I am, without a home of my own upon this earth anymore, deprived of my own bed in which to sleep . . . and the dawn, as from the glass window of that train that had been running all night, surprised me tonight from the windowpanes of my study, sleepless, as it did then. Will the work I have done ever compensate for the pain that this dawn has given me, as I drown the bitterness of my individual fate in the universal bitterness of this most useless mortal life?[1] But let's not make matters worse with useless thoughts. And now, my Marta, you also travel; you're also fated to travel unceasingly, and you've already made so many trips since we left each other in Milan. While I remained here, you traveled from Milan to Naples, from Naples to Messina, from Messina to Palermo, from Palermo to Catania, from Catania to Rome, and now from Rome to Salsomaggiore.[2] Will we get back to Milan and see each other soon?

I don't know what the devil happened with this damned Bellotti, who has once again thrust himself into the middle of things to cause trouble, as is his nature. I received from Nulli a brief letter from which, since I don't know the facts, I cannot understand anything. As far as I can make it out, Bellotti, returning to Milan, repeated everything your father had told him against Nulli. You see what kind of services you get from this Mr. Bellotti? I have no knowledge of what grave matters your father might have talked to him about in order to rouse in Nulli such a fierce reaction: he mentions cowardly lies and shameful slander and declares that he's firmly determined to prevent your father from continuing to defame him. I enclose the letter so that you may know how to behave. One thing is certain, that this Bellotti is a dangerous person. Because whatever your father might have said to him while letting off steam against Nulli, he didn't have to go and relate it to Nulli and so make trouble or who knows what kind of devilry. Why does anyone have to be so wicked? Why do you and I—who work, who suffer so many torments for our art, and throw into our work all our blood—have to then be the victims of such people, who are all around us and, not content to suck our blood, cause trouble, bitterness, create obstacles, and leave us not a moment of peace? I am still fighting with that scoundrel Pilotto, and, on June 15, I must be in Rome to argue in the appellate court, since it seems that Pilotto won in the lower court because of the testimony of that Judas, Chellini, who had sworn before the court that I had promised to

[1] This powerfully poetic and sad passage, one of the most inspired of the correspondence, was selected by Marta Abba for a public reading in the original Italian at Princeton University, during the gala evening given in her honor for the donation of the letters. The eighty-six-year-old actress, sickly and confined to a wheelchair, repeated her stage magic, eliciting a moving ovation even from the many who did not understand the language.

[2] Pirandello here outlines the itinerary of Marta and her company during the theater season that was soon coming to an end.

pay the penalty to Pilotto. I'm certain that the two cronies made a deal to split the money. But they are in for a surprise! I will not pay. Now you too are having trouble and expenses because of that Nulli, and you too found Bellotti to be a Judas. And life goes on—the world is merry and gay! Please inform me how things stand, so that I can give tit for tat to this Mr. Nulli. I am ready to intervene in any way possible, as soon as I have knowledge of what's going on. But why, in God's name, must things of such little importance be so dragged out in life? Artists' lives must be kept sacred, and like something sacred, respected! Let the others drown in that misery; we need to breathe a different kind of air!

Enough! I am waiting for your news, my Marta! My poor, unfortunate Marta, you, too. . . . Oh, get rid of all annoyances! When will this day come? Until tomorrow. With all my love, my total love,

Your Maestro

{ 300525 }

To Marta Abba
Hôtel Milan
(Italy) Salsomaggiore   Berlin, 25. v. 1930
My Marta,

. . . I confess that I am full of anxiety about this opening, which is coming up next Saturday evening. The expectation is great, as you can see from the press and from the reservations at the box office—something completely unusual here in Berlin so early before the show. Here the opening nights (as, by the way, also in Paris) are mainly by invitation. Now at the box office sales are so brisk that there is already talk of stopping them for fear that there won't be seats enough for the invited guests. Do you understand? It is the clearest demonstration of the great public interest, which here usually—outside the circle of the routinely invited guests—begins the day after the premiere, when the reviews published in the newspapers are read. My anxiety originates from the bitter certainty of being by now *a foreigner as far as my country is concerned,* and that therefore I must conquer *another country* for my art. Everything depends on this premiere, to which a great solemnity will be given by the presence of the minister of culture and the inclusion in the official program of the *Kunstwoche.* The success will give back to me all the theaters of Berlin and of Germany. I notice during rehearsal some defects of understanding on the part of Hartung, which I promptly try to correct. Rehearsals are now held even during the night, after the show, and we get home at four in the morning. The actor I like best is Andersen, who plays the role of Rico Verri. But Lennartz is good too. The actors are all more or less responding, but my apprehensions are for Hartung, in spite of the fact that he is considered one of the best German directors. He is pigheaded, and I have a very hard time putting my advice across.

. . . With all the love of

Your Maestro

{ 300527 }

To Marta Abba
Hôtel Milan
(Italy) Salsomaggiore   Berlin, 27. v. 1930

My Marta,

I just got back this minute[1]—it's 19:30—from the Lessing-Theater, where I was attending rehearsal since this morning. My head is like a balloon and I'm falling apart from tiredness. I haven't eaten all day. I've only been smoking, smoking, smoking—my throat is dry and my lips taste bitter. Upon my arrival at the hotel, I find your letter; as soon as I see it, everything is forgotten; I am no longer tired; I open it and I read it.

. . . The present moment is very difficult in all German theaters, just as all life is very difficult now in Germany. There is no money around; the crisis is all over! The theaters are plagued by the so-called *prominents*, famous actors who exact such fees and such percentages on the income that it becomes impossible to run a theater. Even with sold-out houses, it's impossible to cover the expenses, and theaters either go bankrupt or have to close. This is the real situation. And in such circumstances it becomes impossible to talk business with theater directors and producers. In spite of such difficulties, I still hope to succeed. And I hope that the success of the play at the Lessing-Theater will help a lot. I am thinking only of you, I am hoping to triumph only for you, my Marta! Only, only, only for you! I want to bring you good news at my return.

. . . The *Italian* film will be done abroad, and this is one of my greatest hopes to get you out of Italy: it will be done part in Paris and part in America. The future of dramatic art and also of the playwrights is now there—believe me, we must direct ourselves toward a new expression of

[1] This letter is 300527 bis in the Italian edition.

art: the talking film. I was against it: I changed my mind.[2] But we'll talk at length about all that. Do not make any commitments. Until tomorrow, my Marta! I am going to the Aida for a bite, and then I'll go back to the theater for the night rehearsal. All the love of

Your Maestro

[2] This is the first mention in the correspondence of Pirandello's "conversion" to the talking film and of his recognition of film as an art in itself, independent from theater (see letter 290425).

{ 300601 }

To Marta Abba
Albergo Italia
(Italy) Brescia   Berlin, 1. VI. 1930

My Marta,

Well, as per my wire, it was a stormy evening. It felt like being back at the premiere of *Six Characters* in Rome all over again.[1] The tempest of that night, however, was unleashed by noble passions—it was the violent clash of the young generation against the old. Yesterday night, on the contrary, it was the obscene fury of a bunch of queers that broke out as instigated by Feist,[2] by his infamous cousin, by other people of the Reinhardt group and other enemies of Hartung and Saltenburg. Before the show in the foyer of the theater, these obscene people openly tried out the whistles they had taken along. Many ran backstage to break the news, and panic spread among the actors. Andersen, who was playing the role of Rico Verri, was panic-stricken more than anybody else. Lennartz was on the contrary heroic; she defended and sustained the play to the end, leading the audience to a vehement and passionate response. Unfortunately the play laid itself open to the criticism of the enemies because of the very bad direction. I talked about it yesterday. The very spirit of the work was lost in Hartung's complete misunderstanding of it; its sprightliness was gone, each detail appeared disconnected, wriggling by itself without com-

[1] The famous tumultuous opening of *Six Characters* in Rome took place at the Teatro Valle on May 10, 1921.

[2] Feist's revengeful anger was caused by the fact that Pirandello had dismissed him from his job of translating his plays into German. The long story of Pirandello's unpleasant relationship with Feist is well documented in many letters of this collection. See the Name Index, especially in the Italian edition of this correspondence.

posure, like the detached cut-off tail of a snake. Those who knew the play because they had read it could no longer recognize it in that performance. All meaning, all value had disappeared. Everything seemed arbitrary; nobody, also because of the actors' panic, understood why all those scenes followed one another without connection, crazy. It looked like an orchestra in which, after throwing out the conductor, each instrument had started playing by itself. And the whistles of the audience were also playing on their own, as if they were splashing around in an unspeakable joy. Looking from my box, I had a wonderful time. At the end, the reaction of the great majority of the public (more than three-quarters of the audience) took over, and then a deluge of applause exploded—a hurricane of ovations: but only for me, for me and Lennartz, who, as I was telling you, was heroic, because she was the only one who did not lose her bearings, and the audience wanted to reward her for that. I could not count how many times they called for the author: they never finished! The ill-meaning people, after doing the intended damage, had gone away; then it appeared clear how few they were, because the theater remained full and everybody was standing and shouting cheers and getting sore hands from applauding.[3]

As you can imagine, I did not get any pleasure from that demonstration. As far as I am concerned, my play had been killed by Hartung. Since the stage had failed me, I felt unarmed and defeated. For me the winners were those who whistled. I would have whistled too, instead of bowing to that applause and to those ovations, which were intended to cheer but were hurting me.

See, Marta, I had every reason to feel uneasy. I had anticipated the uproar. I had also thought of Feist; I had been warned that something was brewing against me and against the play. I did not want to do anything to prevent it, so as not to lower myself down to the level of those dirty

[3] According to Pirandello's version of the events, Berlin's newspapers were in general biased both in criticizing the new play and in reporting with plenty of detail the turmoil that had troubled the performance; moreover, they hardly mentioned the extraordinary applause and the ovations accorded to the author at the end of the show, thus succeeding in stamping an official label of "disastrous flop" on the premiere. On the reasons for such negative, united, and partisan reportage by the press, see letters 300603, 300605, 300606, and 300607. Pirandello's version of the events is in strong contrast with the version given by most historians, whose conclusions are evidently based on the German press of the time, mainly on the newspaper reviews. See, for instance, an echo of this attitude even in the relatively recent article of 1987 by Willi Hirdt, "Tra moda e morte," *Scena illustrata*, 122/3, pp. 33–34, and Michele Cometa, *Il teatro di Pirandello in Germania* (Palermo: Edizioni Novecento, 1986), pp. 287–317.

rascals. I needed the backing of a good production in order to defend myself and go against the public, as I always did—and that was not there. I had only the weapon of the serenity of conscience left, and I preserved it whole, to the last, to the point of rejecting with disdain, down inside my soul, that final triumph, made to my person and not to my work—which was horribly wounded and failed.

This is Berlin. I felt as if I were in Italy. I don't know where I should go. Hatred follows me everywhere. Perhaps rightly so: I should go away from life, this way, chased away by the hatred of those triumphant cowards; by the incomprehension of the dummies, who are in the majority; and as a punishment for so many of my sins that you, with your noble spirit, have always reproached me for.

Enough. Arrivederci, I'll see you soon, my Marta! I hardly have the courage to tell you once more all my love.

Yours always,
Maestro

{ 300602 }

To Marta Abba
Albergo Italia
(Italy) Brescia   Berlin, 2. VI. 1930
   My Marta,
   I received your letter of the 30th. While reading it, at first I could not understand why you called me selfish;[1] then I realized that it was in reference to that note of D'Amico about the soiree in your honor in Rome. Who was thinking about that anymore! But, my Marta, do you really think that I was *so selfish* as to dare to keep a great actress like you shut up exclusively inside the circle of my art—as if I had not been the first to recognize the diverse talents of your rich artistic nature? Wasn't it I who advised you to make your debut in Rome with Bontempelli's *Nostra Dea*—so sure was I that you would succeed in the test of a challenging role like that, instead of that dull and silly role in Giovannetti's *Pauletta*?

---

[1] Right after the disaster of *Tonight We Improvise* and the consequent shattering of so many dreams, Pirandello received a letter from Marta accusing him of being selfish. The oversensitive Maestro, already in a tumultuous state of mind because of his play's fiasco, now goes through a painstaking and painful defense of his behavior, which summarizes for us the many things he had done for Marta and exposes his disturbing persecution complex.

And wasn't I the one who worked so hard to prepare for you a worthy text for the performance of Ibsen's *The Lady from the Sea*; I, finally, who did the same for Müller's *Die Flamme* and for Passeur's *Suzanne*? I who wrote to all Italian playwrights, starting from D'Annunzio (to whom I had hoped never to write)[2] as well as to the minor ones, asking them to send us plays to perform? I who forced you to perform, against your will, *Marionette, che passione!* by San Secondo, in order to get a new play out of him; I who suggested that you perform at least one play by Praga; and didn't I advise you to make your debut in Milan with a play by Rocca? I who for a whole year have been looking around for plays worthy of you, without being able to find a single one, as was the case with the many scripts we read together in Milan when we were lining up the repertory for your company? How can you believe such un unjust thing about me, that I do not want you *to get around*? Get around, yes, but *high up*, in the beautiful, in the noble art, in the true and great art, so that you do not lose this coat-of-arms of nobility, which makes you *unique* and which must unmistakably form your artistic personality and engrave it into the history of the theater? This I think and feel for you, because I know all your *present* greatness; and then I get annoyed about what that spiteful D'Amico has written, not because of mean and shabby selfishness, but because, together with the other critics, he is still holding off on assigning to you the place that you deserve in the Italian theater. What is he waiting for? He is waiting, like everybody else, for you to leave Pirandello, *and then* he will assign you the place you deserve . . . *in the Italian theater*? Let these great Italian theater people come forward! Let them tell you once and for all what you should perform, if you leave Pirandello. Then if Pirandello gets mad because you do not perform his works, then yes, Pirandello is the most disgusting egoist! But when talking about an evening in your honor in which you performed *Scrollina* by Torelli *and not a work of mine*, Mr. D'Amico spews out his poison by denying your present greatness and hoping that you will leave Pirandello so that you might "occupy the place you deserve in the Italian theater," then Pirandello is no longer selfish, Pirandello is simply angry, my Marta, at this misrepresentation of you, of what you are worth *now*. The poison of D'Amico has bitten me only because of you. And this is so true that now I feel terrible that you continue to present my plays with the idea that they hurt you! That is the greatest pain anyone can inflict upon me; that is, that I hurt you, and I cannot, I cannot possibly tolerate it! If you feel

[2] It is well known that Pirandello deeply disliked Gabriele D'Annunzio.

this way, if you suffer because of it, you must immediately throw all my repertory into the sea, my Marta, and you'll make me happy, because the mere thought that my plays are a burden to you is unbearable; away, away, away, with the whole thing! I don't want my Marta to suffer anymore. If I am that selfish, I do not want any of my works in your repertory next year—not even one. My daughter, my creature must take command by herself, she must be herself, because she is great, *already now* great, because she made Pirandello live on the stages of Italy and of the whole world; she will be equally great *tomorrow* making other authors live. The wrong they do to my *great* daughter is that they say that she must *wait until tomorrow to become great*, when she will no longer perform Pirandello. This is not *right*, it is not right because it shows two things: underestimation of Marta Abba and spite against Pirandello, and a wicked desire to set Marta Abba against Pirandello, to separate her from me and make me feel even more alone. So be it! My Marta *must no longer suffer* because of this great anger against me and my art. I'm really hurting you, my Marta, I'm hurting not your *greatness*, but the *recognition of your greatness*. I couldn't help noticing the injustice of your accusation, but I tell you (and I already told you on another occasion) that—since I am so much disliked and hated by everyone (I don't know why)—it is better, yes, it is better that from now on you leave me aside. For a person who loves as I love you, it is a joy even to die. I am not selfish, unfortunately I am not selfish, my Marta! I am for everyone, and nobody is for me. I am alone. With all my love,

Yours,
Maestro

{ 300603 }

To Marta Abba
Albergo Moderno Gallo
(Italy) Brescia
Piazza Duomo   Berlin, 3. VI. 1930
     My Marta,
     Here the uproar of the press is not less violent than that of the audience at the premiere, on the night of the 31st. I dared to touch their god—do you understand? Max Reinhardt—right during the celebration of his anniversary festivities. Everyone has come to see in Dr. Hinkfuss's role a

satire aimed at the god of German theater directors, Max Reinhardt, and this explains the storm unleashed against me. Give it to the impious person, give it to the foreign iconoclast, to the desecrator of the temple! Away with him! Away with him! Away with him! They literally chase me away, by dint of their insults and abuses. All this tumult, in the theater as well as in the press, is without any doubt well organized: Feist, I found out, has been employed by Reinhardt as head of press relations for the last five months. Together with Reinhardt's entourage he was the one who launched the attack. He gave everybody to believe that in Doctor Hinkfuss I intended to portray Reinhardt, whom today all Berlin is celebrating. Therefore the performance of my play—right on the same evening when a big banquet in his honor was taking place in the Marmorsaal—was interpreted as an incredible insult, all the more offensive because perpetrated by a foreigner. The dedication of my work to Reinhardt not only could not destroy the wicked insinuation, but was interpreted as outrageous shamelessness and arrogance; and they saw a proof of all this (something I could not even imagine) in the person of Hartung, who is considered here the rival of Reinhardt; that is, the defeated rival who was deprived of his theater, the rival chased away from the Renaissance Theater exactly because he dared to compete with Reinhardt. Do you understand? I had no idea of all this; I am just finding out now, while I am still stunned by an assault that took me by surprise. Never believe, my Marta, that I got all upset about it. Not at all! Because this god Reinhardt is not a god for everybody, not even here in Berlin; he has the press on his side, but not the public. On his own home ground, the Deutsches Theater, at the premiere of Unruh's *Phaea*, which was given eleven days ago *and failed* right at the beginning of the anniversary festivities,[1] the audience

---

[1] The three-act play *Phaea* by Fritz von Unruh had its premiere on May 13, at the Deutsches Theater, and continued there until August 18, reaching a total of 110 performances. Pirandello does not say that Reinhardt himself was implicated in the organized boycott of *Tonight We Improvise* in Berlin. As a matter of fact, it seems certain that Reinhardt did not have anything to do with it. The German director was touched when he found out that Pirandello had dedicated his new play to him, sincerely wanted to direct that production, was sorry when circumstances made it impossible for him to keep his commitment, and always showed a very friendly attitude toward Pirandello. At the end of 1930, Reinhardt started planning a new production of *Six Characters* in Vienna, which opened in August 1931 (see letter 310108). The German director showed his admiration for Pirandello on several occasions; for instance, see letter 320427, in which Pirandello reports that Reinhardt went to his box to congratulate him for the opening of *Pensaci, Giacomino!* in Rome, and letter 340429, in which Pirandello transcribes Reinhardt's telegram inviting him to be present at the opening of his *Six Characters* revival in Vienna.

shouted "Pfui Reinhardt! Pfui Reinhardt!" which is worse than "Down with Reinhardt," because in *pfui* there is a sense of spitting. The audience, most of it, *was on the contrary with me* on the evening of my premiere; only the conspirators whistled and made noise, and then became silent when, at the end, great ovations exploded from the whole standing public that called for me, shouting, "Och Pirandello!"; that is, "Long live Pirandello!" more than twenty times. And now every night audiences fill the theater and have a lot of fun and clap so hard they hurt their hands, undisturbed. The play triumphs every night, as it did in Königsberg. But I feel uneasy in being considered, in a foreign land, as involved in a personal battle that I never even thought of fighting, and that was wickedly invented and set up by a rascal whom I had never judged capable of doing what he did.

. . . With all my love,

Yours,
Maestro

{ 300605 }

To Marta Abba
Politeama Fratelli Marcenaro
(Italy) Como   Berlin, 5. VI. 1930

   My Marta,
   . . . Here in Berlin a certain awareness of the wrongdoing begins to surface, not in the public that was always on my side, but in the newspapers. Nobody remembers such an aggression against a writer. It was a wild and ferocious pack of mongrels, in which the lowest feelings, hostility, fury for revenge, partisan hatred, contrasts of artistic and political tendencies, were all mixed—socialist and Communist newspapers attacking on one side and Catholic and rightist newspapers attacking on the other. The change has begun since it became known that the most famous German writers, with Thomas Mann at their head, meeting in the house of Hanns Heinz Ewers (you have met him, but I haven't as yet) intended to publish a formal protest; the idea, however, was abandoned because Felix Bloch-Erben convinced them it would do me more harm than good. The protest reached me anyhow, but in a private form: I received flowers and letters, letters, letters, without end, which poor old Lantz is now answering. The *Vorwärts* began to rise in my defense— notice, it is a socialist newspaper; but then came the *Neue Zeit*, a right-

ist paper, to ask for a reckoning of the incredible scandal in the name of German culture and civilization; and the majority of the newspapers from the province, from Hamburg, Dresden, Cologne, Frankfurt, Munich, and, most of all, Königsberg—where the play was a triumph—are revolting against Berlin. In Königsberg, as a protest, the play is being revived, and that theater is announcing another play of mine for the next season. The scandal will eventually turn against those who promoted it, and everybody says that I'll have as clamorous a revenge. But I have a bitter taste in my mouth, and I'm drowning in nausea. I know I should be above all this, and I know I must be aware of what I am worth, but this experience of human wickedness has given the last stroke to my disgust for life. I feel I am definitely alone; I feel I cannot expect any comfort from my country; I think about so many other things, and I ask myself why I must still go on suffering like that.

But I don't want to fall again into yesterday's sadness, which made me tear my letter to pieces.

If I am still useful for anyone, here I am. I must not fall like this. I must force myself, above all, to overcome the nausea of work. What I don't have is an opportunity to tell the sorrow of my heart to somebody who might comfort me and help me to keep going, by giving me a reason for it in spite of myself—a reason that is really strong enough to outweigh so much pain.[1]

Today in the afternoon I'm having a long conference with Felix Bloch-Erben. Tomorrow Philips will arrive from Paris. Through him I expect news from Paramount. What a beautiful perspective, now, going to America to fight against the stupidity of the movie crowd! It's better I should stay right here. I see so much darkness everywhere that this letter also risks ending up in the wastepaper basket if I continue. Enough, enough, my Marta; I have no other comfort before me except that of seeing you again in a few days—your heavenly eyes and your radiant brow.

I wish it were tomorrow! All my best wishes and all my love,

Yours,
Maestro

---

[1] Pirandello here admits his great weakness and desperate need of psychological help. Pirandello's need to communicate with someone—always obvious all his life, and manifested in the letters of his youth, those from Bonn, and those to Antonietta and Lietta— here becomes the lament of a blind man who is begging for a helping hand and a word of love in order to keep going.

{ 300606 }

To Marta Abba
Politeama Margherita
(Italy) Como   Berlin, 6. VI. 1930
    My Marta,
    . . . The defeat is due to the wickedness of the enemies and not to the
work of art. The public knows that very well, and even the enemies know
that. They thought they were triumphing, but they must recognize that it
is not true. They maliciously wrecked one performance, and they enjoyed
putting out a light so that they were left screaming against me in the
darkness. But, on the contrary, voices are now rising from every corner,
shouting them down and making sure that I am seen in the right light.
You mention the critics, but the real plot was hatched right in their nest
by Feist, as head of Reinhardt's press relations. In the audience he could
not do much: he sent a gang of homosexuals like him, rich people who
paid for their regular admission ticket in order to acquire the right of
ostentatiously waving their whistles and of blowing them. The true audience eventually overwhelmed them, and the evening ended with an
enormous demonstration in my support; more than twenty curtain calls,
one after another, and the whole theater was standing. The critics did not
report a word about that; they talked only of the disturbance stirred up by
those few rascals and borrowed from them the opportunity to hurl themselves at me. Feist had sown his poison exactly there—saying that my
work was against Reinhardt, as I told you yesterday. But please, let's not
talk anymore about such dirt, which I have already washed off me. Performances at the Lessing-Theater continue, and they will continue for a
while. Audiences have fun, applaud, and do not understand what the
scandal is all about. The theater seasons here are not like at home. Now is
the time of the Berlin Theater Festival, the focal point of the season, and
my work has been included in the official program of the festival under
the high sponsorship of the minister of culture, like Toscanini's concerts.
Reinhardt presented at this festival his major novelty, *Phaea* by Unruh,
which was a flop, and precisely the failure of that centerpiece, directed by
the guest of honor Reinhardt, decided the fortunes of my play. I am just
finding out now! For the last eleven days since the failure of *Phaea*, in the
theater circles of Berlin the word was circulating that also *Tonight We
Improvise* had to fail. The death sentence had been pronounced. Any
success would have been interpreted as a condemnation of Reinhardt

during the celebrations in honor of his anniversary. But all Germany, I repeat, is against Berlin. Nothing was lost. All major German cities, Hamburg, Frankfurt, Leipzig, Munich, Dresden, and Cologne, will present my play during the next season. Felix Bloch-Erben fully assured me about that point. But I will not set foot anymore in Germany, where such an outrage could happen.[1]

We'll decide together what I'll do next—or better, you will tell me, since I have only you. I must go first to America. At the cost of whatever bitterness, it is necessary that riches come to us, and they will come. Then we'll see. You exhort me not to look defeated. No, my Marta! Can you imagine! I don't feel at all defeated; I feel offended, wounded, nauseated as a human being because of this wicked and foolish spectacle of human cowardice. That, yes! Only thinking of you, humanity becomes noble again in my eyes. You are there, a human and divine creature; this is enough to make up for humanity's evil and cowardice! And only because of you I am still standing and I am not disgusted at being a man. Thank you, my Marta. I'm kneeling on the ground in front of you,[2] with all my love!

Your Maestro

[1] For further information and documentation on *Tonight We Improvise* in Germany see Cometa, *Il teatro di Pirandello in Germania*, pp. 287–317.

[2] Pirandello attributes almost divine qualities to Marta, using reminiscences of the Christian concept of redemption through one innocent divine savior.

Letters of 1930 from
Paris, Berlin, London, and Rome

PIRANDELLO left Berlin, probably on June 13, for Rome, where he had to appear before the court of appeals for a civil trial that had been brought against him. He spent about five weeks in Italy, part of it close to Marta, and left again, probably on July 22, for Paris to meet the American impresario Lee Shubert. The meeting had as its result the immediate acquisition, at a high price, of the U.S. rights to four works including *Come tu mi vuoi* (As you desire me), which would go on to become the biggest success ever of any work by Pirandello on Broadway and the subject of the well-known film starring Greta Garbo.

Evidently Pirandello's deep depression had not even started to heal. The visit to Marta in Italy had confirmed the terrible realization that "the former feeling" on the part of Marta had really ceased to exist. The letters in this group are among the saddest of the whole collection and often repeat expressions of longing for death and even for suicide.

In Paris Pirandello lived at the Hôtel Vendôme from his arrival on July 23 until his return to Italy, via London, in the middle of August. The absence of letters between the middle of August and October 10 suggests that Pirandello spent the rest of the summer close to Marta, vacationing and working with her on organizing the next tour of her company. When the letters begin again on October 10, Pirandello is in Rome for the elections at the Accademia d'Italia, and Marta is in Venice, preparing the opening of *Penelope* by Somerset Maugham. Once again the letters stop for a month and a half, between October 18 and December 5, when Pirandello and Marta are both in Milan. Marta has a difficult time getting her theater season started, and Pirandello is remaining to take care of several pieces of business. Marta does not want him to stay near her too long; Pirandello must leave, heading toward Paris in search of a new location for his exile and of a permanent center for the very promising development of his international deals—which unfortunately find formidable obstacles because of the economic and social crisis in Germany and the Great Depression in the United States.

{ 300727 }

To Marta Abba
Albergo del Cav. Uff. Enrico Abba
Caspoggio
(Italy) (Sondrio) 27. VII. 1930[1]

My Marta,

This very fruitful trip will be extended perhaps all through next week.

As you know, I signed a contract with Shubert for four plays, two already written—*Questa sera* and *Come tu mi vuoi*—and two still to be written—*I giganti della montagna* and *Quando si è qualcuno*. He paid for everything, trusting my name. He personally released the news here and in London and in America that in New York there will be this year a Pirandellian season, at which the author will be present. After signing the contract, I wired to Cochran in London the following: "Sold today Shubert two new plays of mine *As You Desire Me* and *Tonight We Improvise*. Please telegraph if deal interests you for London. Greetings. Pirandello."

This morning I received the answer:

"Extremely interested delighted to hear from you kindest regards from my wife and myself. Charles B. Cochran."

Therefore on Wednesday morning I'm leaving for London, where I am almost sure I'll close the same deal.

. . . With all the love of your poor

Maestro

---

[1] This letter, written on the letterhead of the Hôtel Vendôme in Paris, belongs to a group of eleven letters written from the French capital—with the exception of one written from Berlin—between July 23 and August 13. After leaving Berlin for good, Pirandello will continue his voluntary exile in Paris, beginning in October. The occasion for the present visit to Paris is an appointment with Lee Shubert, the impresario who controlled a substantial share of the theaters on Broadway and all over the United States.

{ 301215 }

To Marta Abba
Via Aurelio Saffi 26
Milan (Italy)

Paris, 25. 12. 1930
5, Avenue Victor Emmanuel III

My Marta,

. . . But another news from you, besides that about the poor progress of the season, gives me pain and worries me more; that is, the news that you are not well! Stress and tiredness hang together: tiredness of the body, exhaustion because of hard work, and weakening of the nervous energy can be very damaging to your health; even more serious is letting yourself worry about things that are going wrong. If you had the reassurance and the comfort of seeing your things go well, you would feel less tired, and your health would not suffer so much. I know that, and I am suffering because I am not able to do anything to remedy all this. Let's pin our hopes now on *La buona fata*! But do not let financial worries bother you; you should not have such worries at all: I am here to take care of them.[1] I have close at hand more than one big contract, which should be signed very soon, and you know, my Marta, that money for me has now only one attraction, that of giving it to you, all of it, for the only joy that is left in my life is that of earning it for you alone.

Do you think that I spend too much money?[2] The apartments are here very expensive, and I must keep a decent place for the people I deal with. I do not do it so much for myself, believe me, because I could live anywhere and in any fashion as far as that is concerned. After all, I do not spend money on anything else. Every night at 9:30 I am home.

. . . I am not really well. I do not eat, I do not sleep, and the pain in my shoulders is coming back. Patience! Until tomorrow, my Marta! Be healthy, please, and always think about the love of

Your Maestro

---

[1] From this sentence it is evident that the many promises of financial help Pirandello had made to Marta were only nice words. In reality Marta had to worry a lot about how she could keep her company afloat.

[2] Marta had noticed that Pirandello was spending large amounts of money for his daily needs and had mentioned it in her letter, probably trying to help him avoid his perpetual problems with money (while he was dreaming about many millions of dollars from America). The amounts mentioned in letter 301210 (here not translated) for the rental fee of his Parisian apartment and the services are very high, and the restaurants where he dined every day were expensive. The Maestro had chosen for his living quarters an address in one

of the most central, elegant, and expensive areas of Paris, accessible only to the very rich. Notwithstanding that evident reality, Pirandello was still convinced that he was living modestly, that he was hardly spending any money on himself, and that all his money was going to "others." And he was promising everything under the sun to Marta, counting on possible future income, *before* having the cash in his pocket. Marta's financial losses were covered by her father, who acted as administrator and invested significant amounts of money and time in Marta's company.

{ 301217 }

To Marta Abba
Via Aurelio Saffi 26
Milan   Paris, 17. XII. 1930
                                             5, Avenue Victor Emmanuel III

My Marta,

. . . I am spending days and nights in a sadness I cannot describe. At 9:30 P.M., after a bite of supper, I come back home and at 12:00 I go to bed, after remaining for two and a half hours in a chair, like a discarded puppet, to consider this misery of my life that is coming to its end in such desperate loneliness. I don't feel like reading, I don't feel like writing, I don't feel like doing anything. I am really ready for death—if someone or something doesn't come to rouse me from this lethargy.

Enough. Love me a little, my Marta, for all the love I always had and I still have for you.

Your poor Maestro

{ 301226 }

To Marta Abba
Hôtel Bonne Femme
Turin   Paris, 26. 12. 1930
                                             5, Avenue Victor Emmanuel III

My Marta,

. . . I received good news from Cutti and copies of the newspapers that talk about *As You Desire Me*. In Philadelphia the play was a hit.[1] The adaptation of the text and the production itself are getting the last

[1] Philadelphia was at the time one of the usual tryout cities for productions on the way to Broadway. *As You Desire Me*, produced by the Shuberts with Judith Anderson in the

touches, and the play in New York will be perfect. All the newspapers talk about the power of the drama and praise especially the third act, which they call "magnificent." It seems that Anderson is excellent. I enclose her picture, cut out from a Philadelphia newspaper. It seems that Cutti together with Philips is preparing for my visit to Hollywood, and that she is dealing with two other film outfits. She promises further news, also by wire, and she asks for photographs.

. . . Shall I make it? It all depends on my overcoming myself. My health is not that great. I don't eat, although I do try. Enough! One way or another, it will pass. Write to me, my Marta, let at least some life come to me from you. All my love, as always, from

Your Maestro

---

leading role, had its premiere on Broadway at the Maxine Elliott Theatre on January 18, 1931, and continued for 142 performances—the only hit of any Pirandello play on the U.S. commercial theater circuit.

{ 301231 }

To Marta Abba
Hôtel Bonne Femme
Turin
                                                     Paris, 31. XII. 1930
                                                 5, Avenue Victor Emmanuel III

My Marta,

I want to write once more, the last time with the date of this year, 1930. Who knows whether I'll be able to write by the end of 1931: I have the feeling I'll be dead by then. But I don't want to talk about melancholy thoughts.

. . . Today I'll be working all day. I am writing a very strange, long story, perhaps the most original of all my short stories. And I'm having fun writing it. Last night I kept writing at my desk until one-thirty; and I spent a very restless night. Tonight, the last of the year, I'll be at Crémieux's, who invited me. At midnight, while drinking, I'll fly with my thought, and I hope our good wishes will meet. With whom are you going to be? If I could, I would kill them all—of course, with the exception of your parents—all of them, only because they can be near you while I am so far away. You'll see their faces, and not mine; you'll talk with them, and not with me; you'll hear their voices, and not mine, and you'll touch their glass with yours and will exchange the ritual good wishes. I'll be, if at all, just a thought—who knows how distant—among many others that will be near you, or, worse, among only a few of them.

Forgive this giving vent to my feelings, my Marta! If you only knew how much I am suffering. . . . You cannot even imagine! But I must hold out in this nonlife as long as my vital forces assist me. I feel that all my energies for working are getting fired up again; I will still produce new and powerful works. I will die while working, the way I always lived. I must make another fortune again, and I'll do it. Big contracts are coming through. And you'll see; I'll go to America. And I'll come back with a fortune. Then we'll tour the world, Europe and America. And you'll stay, great and happy, somewhere; then I'll die. This is not a plot for a dream: it is the truth.

I must close this letter to get it mailed before midday. I want you to have it tomorrow, on New Year's Day, with all my good wishes, once again, my Marta! May you be happy, my Marta, anyhow and wherever you set your happiness, even at the cost of my death!

With this wish I kiss your beautiful baby hands, and I send you all my love,

Your Maestro

Letters of 1931 from
Paris, Milan, and Portugal

THE LETTERS OF 1931 report the triumph of *Come tu mi vuoi* (As you desire me), first in Turin and then in Chicago and New York. Pirandello is going through a period of euphoria. Broadway is conquered, and Hollywood is soon to be conquered, too. The dream of piling up a great amount of money quickly appears to be nearer to realization than it had ever been. The day in which every economic worry is finally over—and even the financing of an independent theater for Marta becomes possible—seems right around the corner. The Broadway success of *As You Desire Me* induces Metro-Goldwyn-Mayer to buy the film rights for the then-enormous amount of $40,000 and to start negotiations for the production of a series of films based on Pirandello's short stories, novels, and plays, including *Six Characters*. Moreover, negotiations are making good progress in Paris for a contract providing for the systematic diffusion of his literary works all over the world. This deal promises a guaranteed steady high income and finally getting rid of inefficient and greedy agents. The Max Reinhardt production of *Six Characters* in Vienna and several requests for Pirandello's plays from prestigious theaters in Paris promise a renewal of activities in the German-speaking countries and a development of the French market; even the Comédie-Française is considering opening its doors to Pirandello, an honor very seldom granted to non-French living playwrights.

The wave of success spurs the playwright to plunge into his creative activity again. Although weakened by constant hemorrhages and by a serious heart attack—and all but recovered from his depression—the Maestro gives himself up completely to work, which now flows "swift and colorful." He is determined to bring *I giganti della montagna* to completion as soon as possible, being convinced that with this play he is reaching the peak of his artistic creation. At the very bottom of his heart, however, a secret hope is still alive—that the imminent availability of large sums of money might create a situation in which Marta would no longer refuse to live close to him. A new hope of being close to Marta seems to be coming also from the producer Lee Shubert, who is now making big profits with Pirandello's hit, *As You Desire Me*, on Broadway and seems to be interested in a tour of the United States, with Marta starring in title roles of Pirandello's plays and the author present as an added attraction.

In the midst of so much success, Pirandello appears extremely vulnerable to the moods of his beloved. He spends two of the "most horrible days of his life" because Marta is angry over one or two indiscreet expressions in one of his letters. When the actress leaves Paris after a monthlong visit, once more Pirandello remains annihilated and confused. In his sad messages he also adds an insightful, although evidently biased evaluation of her physical, moral, and professional talents. Marta is described as *the* modern performer, totally dedicated to art, free from any contamination of commercialism, and therefore the only true hope for an artistic resurrection of the Italian theater.

In the middle of August, Marta's rather serious illness upsets Pirandello, who abandons everything in Paris and dashes off to Genoa to assist and encourage his beloved, who is afflicted with exhaustion and depression. In September the author accepts an invitation to go to Portugal, where he is evidently enchanted with the "regal honors" he is made the object of. In November the letters of 1931 are brought to an abrupt end with an excited invitation for Marta to take over a leading role in Paris. Performing in French in a major Parisian production represents a unique break, which will speed up Marta's rise as an international star.

{ 310101 }

To Marta Abba
Hôtel Bonne Femme
Turin (Italy)   Paris, 1. 1. 1931
                                    5, Avenue Victor Emmanuel III

My Marta,

. . . How did you spend your New Year's Eve? Where? With whom? Did you think of me? Something strange happened to me. At a certain point in the evening, while I was listening to the conversation those three people were having around me,[1] I heard inside myself, as if somebody were calling me "Maestro!" with your voice, my Marta. So much so, that

---

[1] Pirandello was with his agent Torre, the secretary of his agent Calvet, and Paola Masino, Massimo Bontempelli's friend.

I instinctively looked at the clock. It was five past eleven. Well, my Marta, it was perhaps truly your thought that was calling me, because between France and Italy there is a time difference of exactly fifty-five minutes; so that in Italy it is midnight sharp when here in France it is five past eleven. But did you really think of me at midnight sharp? Perhaps you were in your dressing room after the performance. I hope you will let me know in order to find out whether last night at five past eleven I really felt an instance of telepathy.

I am not feeling well. I lost weight. For the last five days I've been suffering again from circulatory trouble, which had left me alone for the last twenty years. I am losing a lot of blood and vital forces. If it continues, as seems to be the case, I must see a doctor to get some remedy for so much loss. Enough. This is the least of my troubles! If I only could get into a cheerful mood! Let's hope that your good wishes will bring me luck, my Marta. With all the love of

Your Maestro

{ 310103 }

To Marta Abba
Hôtel Bonne Femme
(Italy) Turin

Paris, 3. 1. 1931
5, Avenue Victor Emmanuel III

My Marta,

. . . This morning I received a comforting telegram from Cutti announcing that *As You Desire Me* was a hit in Chicago. Now Chicago is the most important city of North America after New York, perhaps even richer than New York, although it has three-and-a-half million inhabitants, while New York has seven. The great success in Chicago means a lot financially, and that's reason to rejoice. Cutti seemed to be very happy. In the telegram she says that she also spoke with Lasky from Paramount, and that she will write. The whole tone of the congratulatory message is most promising. Let's hope for the best. I'll send you the rest of the information as soon as I receive the letter. You know that Torre is an amateur magician or psychic—whatever you want to call him. He says that he drew my chart and that this year "will be my year."[1] Perhaps it is

---

[1] Whether coincidence, clairvoyance, or simply an astute reading of recent successes and knowledge of pending contracts, Torre was right: during 1931 Pirandello will earn substantial amounts of money—in good part due to the success on Broadway of *As You Desire Me.*

a sign that I must die, because I believe that only then my luck will change. But I wouldn't mind if, before that, fate would permit me to earn great amounts of money—although not for myself.

Enough. Until tomorrow, my Marta. I am waiting for an answer to all my questions. With all my love,

Your Maestro

{ 310108 }

To Marta Abba
Hôtel Bonne Femme
Turin (Italy)
Paris, 8. 1. 1931
5, Avenue Victor Emmanuel III

My Marta,

. . . You must forgive me, my Marta, if I often trouble you with my complaints about not receiving any letters or news from you; my complaints are not reproaches; they are the expression of what I'm suffering, being so far away, without seeing you, without knowing—for days and days— anything about you. You must have compassion and understand why I do that—and imagine the extent of my grief. You say that I "do not believe in anybody." That really *is* a reproach. What do you mean I don't believe? If I did not believe, what would I be living for, so far away and all alone? I can still hold out in this life only *because I believe.* And your advice to stay in Rome "among people who still love me" sounded to me like a mockery! Should I concentrate on the implications of your advice, perhaps then would I recognize the terrible folly of feeling as I do and of living the way I do . . . or not living![1]

. . . Here it has begun to be extremely cold, and the never-ending smog is oppressive and intensifies the discomfort. Last night at the Crémieux' I met the German wife (second wife) of Lucien Luchaire, who gave me the incredible news that Max Reinhardt is preparing a second production of

[1] The words "or not living" are written in larger letters. Marta had written suggesting to the Maestro that he should go back to live in Rome with his family, who really loved him. At this moment, however, Pirandello was more than ever infatuated with the idea of his exclusive love for Marta. Moreover, he was feeling alienated from his children, who did not conceal their embarrassment about the relationship of their beloved father with a young actress—younger than they were—while their mother was still alive and confined in a mental institution. The meditation on the "whole meaning" of Marta's wise advice (which, by the way, only a couple of years hence he will accept and follow) would have made him clearly aware of Marta's message; that is, that he belonged with his children and not with her.

Six Characters in Search of an Author at the Theater in der Josephstadt in Vienna—saying that he has discovered a deeper meaning in my play. It is really incredible, but Mrs. Luchaire assured me that she read the news in the *Vossische Zeitung* and that she will send me the newspaper so I can read it myself.

Enough, my Marta. I leave you with this, and with all my love,

Your disappointed Maestro

{ 310109 }

To Marta Abba
Hôtel Bonne Femme
Turin (Italy)   Paris, 9. 1. 1931
                                                        5, Avenue Victor Emmanuel III

My Marta,

. . . You write that you saw Bontempelli and Masino, who talked to you about the sad condition of my health. I am wasting away, my Marta, because I am in low spirits, and my soul has fallen apart and won't ever get together again. Neither other people nor the adversities of destiny broke my spirit: it has fallen apart because . . . but how can I tell you why, if you tell me that I should go back to Italy . . . and to Rome . . . and that you want to see me serene, "because in any case I have already lived my own life"? No, my Marta, it is better that I stifle my despair in this knot of anguish that is closing my throat and that I don't say a word anymore. Fortunately I have some old portraits of yours, with which I can trust myself, without opening my mouth, only looking and remembering . . . if I must die soon, as I wish for myself with all my heart, it will be sweet for me to die so, in silence and far away.

. . . Here in Paris I saw the actress Bovy[1] of the Comédie-Française, who sent me an invitation because some time ago somebody told her that she was going to interpret *Come tu mi vuoi*. . . . She is a very nervous, intelligent-looking small woman—the most modern among all the caryatids of the Comédie-Française with Cécil Sorel at their head. It would certainly be a great honor to have one of my plays performed at the Comédie. I played the great man with suitable modesty, and I told her that I would talk about it with Crémieux. Some play of mine will eventually be performed, because there is really a great emptiness in all that is

---

[1] Berthe Bovy, a Belgian actress born in 1887, had been a member *sociétaire* of the Comédie-Française since 1919.

presented in Paris today, as is the case, by the way, everywhere. Perhaps I'll go soon, but my plays will remain as the only ones that truly said something new. And, better, when I will no longer be around, everybody will recognize that. Then, Marta, you too will think more than ever about all the love that your poor Maestro had for you until his last breath.

[*unsigned*]

{ 310112 }

To Marta Abba
Hôtel Bonne Femme
(Italy) Turin

Paris, 12. I. 1931
5, Avenue Victor Emmanuel III

My Marta,
    . . . I received a telegram from Cutti calling me to New York in the name of Shubert to be present at the premiere of *As You Desire Me* on the 17th of this month. I should therefore leave at once. Shubert offers, besides the round-trip, one thousand dollars a day for *a few days*, maybe one week, but he doesn't specify anything. He says only "for a few days," and Cutti advises me to accept in view of the pending contracts for films. She wants an immediate reply, but I must think it over thoroughly, not only because of my poor health, but also because of the ongoing negotiations I am involved in here in Paris, for both theater and cinema. One thousand dollars a day is a goodly amount; just five days of that would mean a hundred thousand lire, of which I would spend not even one third. There would also be the enormous overexertion of the round-trip. Before deciding I have to think over a world of things. In the low spirits in which I find myself, plus being troubled and disturbed by what you just told me . . . I don't know, I have the feeling that a storm is gathering around me and wants to uproot me and sweep me away. . . . May God help me! I never felt so unable to grasp the roots of this shaken tree—which is my life—from which the winds have already taken away all the leaves, and only the wrenched trunk remains, and the knot of the sturdy twisted branches.
    Pray for me, my Marta,[1] and have mercy, for all the love of

Your poor Maestro

---

[1] This is a very rare request for prayers to Marta, who was a religious person. Also the invocation "May God help me!" a few lines above, is most unusual in the personal writings of Pirandello, who did not believe in a merciful God.

{ 310125 }

To Marta Abba
Teatro Verdi
(Italy) Cremona   Paris, 25. 1. 1931
                                                    5, Avenue Victor Emmanuel III

    My Marta,

    . . . I don't say that I am afraid, but I am a little concerned that, one day or another, I, too, may be attacked by the flu,[1] being so weak, because all Paris is sick with it, and depressed from this continuous fog and rain, and I would need to be taken to a hospital, because not even a dog would be here to take care of me. But let's hope that I will escape it, because, after all, although not young (at least you do not want to believe me so—worse, for you I am of "a certain age") I too have, like you, a healthy and vigorous constitution. You don't know that, discovering myself by chance suddenly in a mirror, the desolation of seeing myself looking the way I do each time kills in me the amazement of not remembering how I look. And only then—because of those looks that I discover but that *while I live and while I feel* I cannot keep in memory—I experience a sense of shame in my still very young and warm heart. I believe that other people should see my heart, *where I live*, while they see me wearing this sad mask of old age, that is, an appearance *I do not remember*: and all misunderstandings and disillusions come from there, and people have a respect for me for which I have no use and which often wounds me as cruelty does.[2]

    . . . With all the love of

                                                              Your Maestro

  [1] Marta had just recovered from a bad bout of influenza.

  [2] Pirandello candidly confesses his inability to accept serenely the physical and social consequences of old age and, implicitly, his inability to discover the spiritual riches that reveal themselves to a person who consciously grows into advanced age in harmony with himself and with the total reality of life.

{ 310127 }

To Marta Abba
Hôtel Firenze
Como (Italy)

Paris, 27. I. 1931
5, Avenue Victor Emmanuel III

My Marta,

I have received your express letter from Bergamo, and I can't tell you with what tenderness of all my soul I read the prayer you made in Alessandria to dear God, with whom you had reached a "perfect agreement," without a flock of doctors or anybody else around: that He might help you—when you were running a fever of 39.5 degrees centigrade—as He alone could do it, and give you courage and strength to let you perform that evening despite your illness! My Marta, you—who could receive in your soul the idea of such a miracle and, without listening to the arguments of prudence and fear, trusted yourself to it and wanted to try it out—you are a divinely holy little girl, to whom no grace can be denied. I read your letter with a trepidation that could not have been greater if that night I had been in the wings spying on you while you were performing on the stage with a temperature of almost forty degrees. The miracles worked by a fairy godmother are nothing in comparison; those were miracles to laugh at; you were performing the real miracle in yourself! A miracle of the spirit over the flesh liberating you from the disease! My Marta, with such a soul, who on earth can be worthy of you? Somebody who has been fighting for courage all his life, and who continues to fight and suffer to gain courage, tells you so. The life to which destiny condemns us is unfortunately unworthy of such victories. But, with your generosity, you do not experience spite; on the contrary, you have so much compassion for life as it is, and you say that we must accept it the way it is, and try to make the people laugh with some cheerful story— those people who are suffering and who after so much suffering want to have some fun ... cheerful stories! Ah, my Marta, Molnár can write them. He with his three wives and every night getting drunk— for whom everything goes well—tomorrow maybe he'll even have a fourth wife, when he'll get tired of wearing the horns that Darvas[1] is putting on him

---

[1] Lilì Darvas, actress and wife of the Hungarian playwright Ferenc Molnár, is here presented by Pirandello as the lover of actor Hermann Thimig. Pirandello tries to explain his inability to write cheerful comedies, comparing his tragic sense of life with Molnár's easygoing, popular appeal.

with Hermann Thimig, and about which he does not care as long as Hermann Thimig performs well with his wife in his cheerful comedies that bring him piles of money . . . one needs a happy nature like his. But, even if I should write a cheerful comedy tomorrow, do you know what they would say? That it's no longer me, and they wouldn't give it any importance.[2] I did write some cheerful comedies, in my own way: *Così è (se vi pare), L'uomo, la bestia e la virtù, Questa sera si recita a soggetto* . . . the public did laugh; I cannot make it laugh any other way. *Quando si è qualcuno* . . . and also *I giganti della montagna*, after all, will be a kind of humorous tragedy. . . . But casual laughter? It can be only for those who see everything superficially and passing by. . . . To my shame I have a penetrating look and two devilish eyes. You know them well.

Yesterday I was invited to lunch at the *Journal*, where all the *Presse latine*, that is, all the journalists from the newspapers of the Latin world were meeting. The president of the banquet, the director of *Paris-midi*, boasted about my presence and invited everybody to toast "the greatest dramatic author Europe has now, who is honoring Paris with his presence"; everybody stood up and gave me a great, never-ending ovation. With a hand in my pocket I was pressing your letter with all my might, in which you tell me that you "are proud of your Maestro." What's the meaning of glory, if you cannot give it away as a present to someone? I was enjoying it only because it would give pleasure to you, who have your own glory, which I too enjoy, much, but much more, infinitely more than mine. And then you are not only glorious, you are good, and you are beautiful, and you are a woman, and young; while I . . . enough! Take care, write to me, talk about yourself, and have all the love of your

Maestro

[2] Pirandello developed this line of thought in his play *Quando si è qualcuno* (mentioned three lines below), which was on his mind at the time.

{ 310208 }

To Marta Abba
Grand Hôtel Mediterranée
Pegli (Genoa)
(Italy)   Paris, 8. ii. 1931
                                                          5, Avenue Victor Emmanuel III

My Marta,

At last I have received your letter from Pegli, without any date—but it must be the 4th—either sent or delivered with delay, enclosing the article by Panseri: "Revelation of Marta Abba." You can imagine, my Marta, with what joy I read it. It is true that whatever other people say about you, it always seems too little to me in comparison with what I think. But it is also true that this recognition by Panseri, in its spontaneity and because of his courageous statements, gives me great satisfaction, and you were right to write him the way you did. Not only the recognition from Italy, my Marta, but from the whole world soon must be given to you—complete and triumphant. You must be proclaimed the greatest and most original actress in the world, above all those who used to be, and above all those that will ever be. Then I'll be satisfied; I always have recognized you as such, not because of the affection I have for you, but because of an objective judgment and after seeing all the so-called major actresses of every country. None even comes up to your knee! Your natural expressive power, your talent for illuminating every deeply concealed fold of thought or of feeling, the spontaneous and unforeseeable originality of every pose and of every movement on the stage, every glance, every gesture, every tone—all of which you find without searching, not only by divine intuition, but by the illumination of your sovereign intelligence—make you unique in the world: Marta Abba.[1] I'm reading in the American newspapers the hymns of praise that all the critics are writing about Judith Anderson for her interpretation of *As You Desire Me*; all the newspaper clippings are full of her pictures, and you can't imagine the irrita-

---

[1] Both "*unica*" and "Marta Abba" are written in larger letters. This passage is a synthesis of Pirandello's "objective" judgment about the dramatic art of his beloved. As it appears from many reviews of the time, Pirandello's opinion was not shared by many critics, who saw Marta's acting as generally good but sometimes flawed by histrionic exaggerations and a certain harshness. See, for instance, Renato Simoni, *Trent'anni di cronaca drammatica*, vol. 3 (Turin: Industria Tipografica Libraria, 1955), passim. Pirandello was very bitter at the critics and interpreted their judgment as biased. See, for example, letters 310330 and 330209.

tion I experience, because for me *Come tu mi vuoi* is yours, and I can't see anyone but you in it, and this other person I see in your place seems to me to be an intruder. All these critics who are talking about "a great creation" make me laugh, and I would love to shout to them: "If you had only seen my Marta!" I really can't wait for you to go and show the miracle of *true creation* to those gentlemen, the American critics and the entire public, who will be astonished. Strangely enough, the honorable Ludovici's wife, who is an American writer and in these days is visiting Paris, yesterday told me that this Judith Anderson, of all American actresses, is the only one who can somehow come close to you—and she thinks that Anderson physically looks a little bit like you. As a curiosity, I'm enclosing a picture of her. Perhaps, very farfetched, here and there: but my Marta is beautiful, really beautiful, and this one is not. . . .

. . . I am glad to hear that your mother is with you, and also Bull, and that you now have a beautiful car that takes you from Pegli to Genova. . . . Ah, if only there were a little place for me in it. . . . Enough. Always think, my Marta, of the great love of your distant

Maestro who is always near you

{ 310210 }

To Marta Abba
Grand Hôtel Mediterranée
Pegli (Genoa)
(Italy)

Paris, 10. 11. 1931
5, Avenue Victor Emmanuel III

My Marta,

I wish you were inspired to write to me more often, because the need I always have of your letters, as of air to breathe, at this moment is greater than ever, and I'll tell you why.[1] I do believe that I am composing my masterpiece, *I giganti della montagna,* with a fervor and a trepidation that I can't express. I feel I have climbed to heights where my voice finds unheard-of sounds. My art has never before been so full, so varied and unpredictable: so truly like a feast for the spirit and for the eyes—all like shining pulsations and as fresh as dew. It matters little if you will not

---

[1] There follows a vivid and revealing description of Marta's inspiring presence in the creative process of *I giganti della montagna.* Marta's minimal enthusiasm for this drama was responsible for the slowing down of the writing in its final part. As is well known, when Pirandello died five years later, the play had not been completed.

perform this work, either because you think it is not for you or because you won't be able to do so for whatever reason. This is a secondary problem. What not only matters but is also absolutely necessary for me at this moment is to think that I'm writing for you. I wouldn't be able to write one more word should your divine, inspiring image abandon me for one instant. I follow this image of you, in the situations in which I placed it, and little by little it finds for me the words and creates for me the scenes, and carries me ahead—suggesting, showing me what the other characters must say, what they must do in order to answer to its vagaries, to placate or increase its anxieties, to make out of the contrasting characters the supreme harmony of the composition. Without being aware of it, from so far away, perhaps not even thinking a little bit about me, taken by other thoughts, by other preoccupations, you are doing my work. Now I wonder what would happen if you were more alive to me, alive as you were before, when you used to think more and care more for your Maestro, who without your thinking of him (I say at least your thinking of him) cannot live any longer. Ah, my Marta, I absolutely must think that you are the same for me in order to continue to work as I am working. If for one moment I feel certain that you have already detached yourself from me with your mind and with your heart—and I have become just like anybody else, from whom you are far away and to whom from time to time you give an indifferent thought—then everything dies inside me. I feel my soul and my breath falling apart; every light goes out in my brain, and my hand falls on the paper, motionless as a stone. Help me, help me. For God's sake, my Marta, don't leave me, don't abandon me, I am in my last moments: I need you, I need you so much, I need to feel you are the same and close by, the same as before. . . . Write to me, make yourself heard; I have all my life in you; you are my art; without your breath it dies. You are creating, and you do not know it, with all the power of your art, with the tones of your inimitable voice, with the splendor of your eyes that find the look for every passion; you are creating with the ardor that has come to me from your mind, from your heart, from all your person, so that I might transfer it into the work that I am writing through you and that is not mine but yours: *your creation*. Keep on helping me until the very end, my Marta; do not abandon me; think that not only I would die, but also your work. It is not possible for you not to be, as true and sole author, in everything I am still doing. But I am the hand. The one who dictates inside is you; without you, my hand becomes a stone.

Yesterday I had a little fever and perhaps I have it today, too; I took some cachets of Fevre, and I am careful; but it's nothing: *I am working!*

I don't need anything anymore when I work: I need only you. If I receive a letter from you today, I will immediately be well. I believe that, even if I should die, if a letter arrived, I would rise from the dead. I am so alone, so alone, my Marta, and you cannot imagine the kind of evenings I spend. As soon as it gets dark, anguish overcomes me. . . .[2] But I don't want to upset you uselessly. Addio, my Marta. Write to me! Answer somehow to all the love I have for you,

Your Maestro

[2] The lengthy argumentation that takes up almost the whole letter is one of the best examples of Pirandello's skillful use of the rhetoric of persuasion in this correspondence. The Maestro unceasingly makes an appeal to Marta's most sensitive spots, from her sense of pity and duty to her pride, her responsibility for her exclusive and decisive role in Pirandello's creative process and in keeping him physically and spiritually alive. The letter ends on a touching note, with a desperate appeal against the background of a dark anguish and remorse for upsetting his beloved!

{ 310216 }

To Marta Abba
Compagnia drammatica "Marta Abba"
Teatro Niccolini
Florence   Paris, 16. II. 1931
                                         5, Avenue Victor Emmanuel III

My Marta,

I've just come back from supper: it is 9:25, for you in Italy 10:20; it is Monday; I know that you are performing *Come prima, meglio di prima* in an evening of reduced prices. I imagine that at this moment you are in the second act, remaining on stage for the whole second act: I see you, I listen to your voice, I can follow you, line after line: your voice, of which I know every inflection, is resounding in my soul. My eyes fill up with tears: not only because of the sweetness coming to me from the sound of your voice, but also for the anguish that in this desolate loneliness the memory of the time when I was near you gives to me—and I could never get enough of listening to you from the wings, do you remember?[1] And now I am so far away! I haven't seen you for so many months, I haven't heard your voice, and I don't know anything more about you than the little bit you tell me in your letters. When I think of all that did happen—

[1] Pirandello used to remember those hours "in the wings" as the happiest of his life.

that I had to detach myself from you, from my own very life, to reduce myself to what I am now, a dark and empty shadow of myself—such despair overwhelms me that . . . ah, no, my Marta, enough, enough! I must not fall again into writing to you about those things. . . . Forgive me! You are always the same Marta as before, even if so far away. And if all that has happened, it is a sign that it had to happen that way, because it seemed right to you. And soon perhaps you'll tell me that the time of my martyrdom is close to an end, and that I do not deserve to die so hopelessly and in this anguish, because you do not wish that, because you have mercy on me, and you do not want that! In this hope I am working without pause so that my work may win over everything, overcome every obstacle, uproot every prejudice, shout my everlasting youth as a victory over the years![2] Again, Marta, you'll see, I'll assert myself as the strongest of them all, and the youngest; I alone am young; I alone am alive; all the others are old and rotten corpses. You'll see what *I giganti della montagna* is like! It has everything, it's an orgy of fantasy! The lightness of a cloud passing over the depth of an abyss; powerful laughter exploding among the tears, like thunder in the midst of storms; and everything suspended, everything seeming to be flying and vibrant, electric; no comparison with whatever I have done so far; I am touching the peak, you'll see! But it's you, only you that are touching it, my Marta! With all your soul, which rejoices in me and creates inside me that sense of a fable in which all the characters breathe, and the words bloom like flowers that seem astonished at being born. There is somebody, my Marta, who is living your life, and you don't know it. Your *true* life!

   . . . All the love of

Your Maestro

[2] Pirandello reveals the profound longing that is still keeping him alive: to triumph on the international scene and reach such financial levels and such prestige as to be able to provide for the actress conditions of work and glory that would place her among the top world stars of the theater and the movies. This new situation would induce his beloved to accept his living nearby in the common realization of the final project of an art theater, completely independent from the Italian theatrical "dunghill." Besides these perspectives of personal ambition and professional success, Pirandello also uses intimate and touching arguments to win Marta's heart, such as making an appeal to her compassion as a woman and boasting about his "perennial youth."

{ 310220 }

To Marta Abba
Hôtel Cavour
Florence (Italy)   Paris, 20. ii. 1931
                                                    5, Avenue Victor Emmanuel III

My Marta,

. . . Money from America has started to arrive, already more than fifty thousand lire of royalties—from Chicago alone, and only through January 17. There are still two weeks to be accounted for in Chicago; and then New York, where the box-office take really grew. The drama critic of one of the most important newspapers over there writes: "If this play does not have a long run, I'll throw down my pen and no longer be a critic." This means a lot, my Marta, because a "long run" for America means months and months, and going the way it's going, there is enough to put together a substantial nest egg. Sixty-four thousand lire have also come in from the new contract with Dutton for the publication of four volumes of plays—that's from America also. Of course, I saved it all; that is, I deposited it in the Chase Bank, which is an American bank, with a branch in Paris—a very solid bank. And I deposited everything in dollars, without exchanging it for francs or lire. I promise you, my Marta, that I'll be a millionaire at the end of this year, and not only a one million millionaire, because it is not risky to suppose . . . but I do not want to make you too many promises. I am working! You'll see what a revenge! It has started with America. It will be everywhere. But you must help me. . . . I owe all this to you . . . because if it were not for you, I wouldn't care about anything . . . the real danger is for me to fall back into my depression and the lack of interest in anything, in which I've been for about a year and from which only now, through my work, I am getting out. But do you see? It is sufficient that a letter from you is later than usual to make me fall back again; and each time the effort of getting up again is more painful, until I won't make it anymore and I'll let go forever. . . . Useless to go on, if I am already dead. In me and for me, I am not alive.

Write to me, therefore, my Marta, to prove that I am still alive in you, without even saying that, talking instead about yourself, replying, as you had promised, to my letters, before I left—do you remember? You should think about all the love that I had, have, and always will have for you.

Your poor Maestro

{ <u>310222</u> }

To Marta Abba
Hôtel Cavour
Florence (Italy)   Paris, 22. II. 1931
                                        5, Avenue Victor Emmanuel III

My Marta,

Today, Sunday, only one mail delivery, at 9 A.M. No letters. I hope tomorrow! At 10:30 a telegram arrived from Cutti from New York, which I transcribe for you:

"Sold picture rights Metro-Goldwyn fortythousand dollars Comemivuoi stop Per contract Shubert you share onethird must have your telegraphic acceptance immediately Regards Cutti."

. . . *Forty thousand* dollars is a most exceptional price, even in America, which demonstrates the exceptional success the play is having over there. Usually, the price paid for any script by a renowned author doesn't go over fifteen or at most twenty thousand dollars. *As You Desire Me* has earned twice as much from Metro-Goldwyn. Unfortunately, of these eight hundred thousand lire I receive only one third, because that's what the contract says that I signed with Shubert about the four plays: one third to me, one third to Shubert, and one third to the translator; that is, 13,333 dollars, equal to 266,660 lire. Naturally I telegraphed my acceptance. By now the royalties must be more than 200,000 lire. As you see, I am well on the way to the million: we are in February and I have almost half of it. Meanwhile Shubert is preparing his second production, with *Tonight We Improvise* in another theater. It will be the Pirandello year over there in America. What I could not get in Italy with four new plays I'll get in New York, and it will mean millions; because you'll see that, with this great success, following the example of Metro-Goldwyn, now other movie companies will move; Brock Pemberton will revive *Six Characters*, on which he already made a deposit; perhaps I'll have to go to America, and I'll come back with a fortune, which I'll owe only to you, because I would never have written *As You Desire Me* without you, just as I would have written nothing at all if you had not given life back to me. We'll think together about what to do with this fortune. Meanwhile I'll save it here abroad, in a safe place.

I am dealing with an important international agency, directed by a certain Desiré Schwarz, for the exclusive world management of my narrative works, novels, short stories, and editions of my complete works, including the theater, translated into all languages, and their use for the cinema, which would give me a sure guarantee of at least one million francs per year; I'll pay the agency 10 percent on the first million; 20 percent on whatever will go over that amount within a year. This way I'll do as Shaw did in England, and I'll be free of any financial worries for the time remaining for me to live. I will not handle this business directly; a lawyer from here, expert in this kind of business, will be in charge. The contract will be prepared with great prudence: a one-year trial, after which a renewal for another year, and at the end of this second year, if the results will be satisfactory, a commitment for five years. I would like to hear your opinion on this. The management of income from performance royalties is not included in the contract. It covers only the cinema and the translations and publications of my work in various languages. Just to think that every short story translated and published in America is worth one thousand dollars, and that I have about three hundred of them! My work has so far never been properly managed by someone who would know how, as the work of Shaw has been, who has written much less than I have, and who meanwhile is twenty times a millionaire, exactly because he had in McDonald the man who knew how to manage his work. If I have finally found one now, I could at last be at peace and keep on working without any concerns of this sort.

I have filled your head with numbers, my Marta, but I believe that you'll be happy about it, because this money will be useful not only in giving me peace, but in allowing me to work freely and do beautiful and great things, worthy of you! We don't have any other ambition! Still always Art, but without the humiliation, with leisure and freedom. My dream is that you will have a theater of your own, where you can perform how and when you wish whatever you choose; and then rest; perform three or four months, not more; Teatro Marta Abba. Help me; I'll get there, and soon! It will be sufficient that you think a little about the love of

Your Maestro

{ 310225 }

To Marta Abba
Grand Hôtel Cavour
Florence (Italy)   Paris, 25. II. 1931
                                                        5, Avenue Victor Emmanuel III

My Marta,

. . . I was horribly sick the whole night long; I felt that I was going to die any minute. My heart was throbbing like a tempest in my breast and did not allow me to breathe; all my blood was surging to my head; and in my whole body I felt a frenzy I cannot explain. I could neither stand nor lie in bed, not even sit in the armchair; at a certain moment I had the feeling that the end had come. . . . I must absolutely forbid myself to work in the evening. . . . But you understand me: I get home early at 9:30, and what do you want me to do alone in the house? There is the desk with the pages of *I giganti della montagna* spread around . . . to escape from my loneliness I allow myself to be tempted. . . . Last night I worked until one in the morning. I was so overexcited that when I got up from my desk to go to bed—knowing that I would not be able to fall asleep at once—I tried to read a few pages of a German book about the poet Rilke. I wish I had never done that! I was frightened at experiencing a phenomenon that had never happened to me before: all the lines, all the printed characters were literally dancing under my eyes, as if the electric bulb at the top of the bed were shaking, but the lamp was steady, and the lines of the book were dancing. Very upset, I sat up in the bed, and then the thumping in my heart began and my breathing started to fail. . . . Enough! I was very sick until six in the morning; then tiredness overwhelmed me and I remained prostrate until 8:30; the doorman—who every morning brings me the coffee with milk and the newspapers— woke me up: I could cheerfully have sent him to hell! After drinking the coffee, I threw myself on the bed and I remained there until ten, but without being able to sleep. Now I have a face like a corpse and such a weakness that I cannot even lift an arm. That makes me feel bad, because today at four o'clock the representative Schwarz of the international agency Copyright, about whom I talked to you in my last letter, is scheduled to come for the signing of the contract. The contract was prepared by one of the best lawyers in Paris, and I'll also have the assistance of my theatrical agent Alfredo Bloch, a specialist from the Society of French Authors—since I have been elected a full member I have the right to such assistance. The terms are excellent. I'll pay 10 percent if the yearly earnings are one million; 15 percent on anything over one million up to three million; after three million I'll pay 20 percent. It is a colossal work of promotion worldwide. What so far has never been done for me, will be done: the whole body of short stories, novels, theater, will be translated into all languages and published everywhere; all the subjects that can be used for the movies will be developed. One person will go to America expressly for me. With this agency, a French author, who doesn't have even a tenth of the reputation I have, François Mauriac, has earned in one year more than four million: his last novel was translated within a few months into sixteen languages. Schwarz assures me that there is a chance to make plenty of money with my novels alone. My guarantee is that the more he makes, the more I make, and that if the yearly earnings should stop at one million he would end up losing money on the deal, because his expenses for the translations and the promotion will go beyond the one hundred thousand lire of his percentage. He is therefore encouraged to make me earn more, because his earnings begin after the first million. But when you think that Metro-Goldwyn paid eight hundred thousand lire to film *As You Desire Me*. . . .

Enough, my Marta! I'll keep you informed on that matter. But write, write to me, don't leave me without a word and without advice from you. Ah, if only I had you near me at this moment! Until tomorrow. Everything is for you, everything for the love of

Your Maestro

{ 310317 }

To Marta Abba
Hôtel Minerva
Rome (Italy)   Paris, 17. III. 1931
                                                  5, Avenue Victor Emmanuel III

My Marta
. . . Did you really leave by car on Sunday night? I could not sleep until almost Monday morning, imagining you traveling the whole night from Florence to Rome, tired from two Sunday performances, jolted the whole long way, with your father at the wheel, who, God forbid, at any moment could be overcome by sleep. . . . I was tossing around in my bed trying to show you how to avoid imaginary dangers, and my heart was pounding and my breath was failing. In order to overcome the agitation and the

worry, I kept telling myself that perhaps those anxieties were out of place because probably you had not left, having received some news from Cele . . . for instance that she had time to wait for you in Rome without your fatiguing night travel. In one word, a lot of frantic nonsense. Now I'm waiting to hear from you how things actually went, whether you really left, whether everything went well, if you saw Cele, and above all if you suffered a lot after the overexertion of the two Sunday performances in Florence. I imagine that in Rome, after Cele's departure, you got a good rest, because that evening you had to perform, of all things, *Come tu mi vuoi!*

. . . Since my children live in Rome, and also Marchesano is there— who probably will come to see you and to talk to you with his usual unpleasant brusqueness about things that annoy me—I implore you, my Marta, to keep me apart, in your thought and in your heart, from every- thing concerning my family or that Marchesano might tell you about because of his false interest in my welfare. Do not pay attention to any- thing; do not confuse me with the others. Think only about one thing, that I have no other good in life but the one that can come from you; all the rest is my death. You won't desire, like the others, my death. Act toward these others the way you think best, and if these others do not behave as they should, don't get angry at me, and explain everything considering that it is, after all, natural: you are for me what you are: life; and they, if they continue to be as they are, they are, for me, death, and the one who must defend me from them, if you want me to live, is ex- actly you: I mean, defending me inside yourself, keeping me separate, without giving any importance to them and to what they say. I feel really uncomfortable, knowing that you are in Rome, and I can't wait for your short season at the Teatro Valle to be over.[1] I hope that everything will

---

[1] This passage is very important for understanding the difficult and delicate relationship between Pirandello and his family during his exile. Marchesano, a lawyer accustomed to getting his way with great shrewdness and without much ceremony, was perhaps the most dangerous and most convincing speaker for the whole family, which was against any rap- port between Pirandello and Marta. They were convinced that such a relationship had, among other things, a dangerous influence on the health of Pirandello and on his deter- mination to live far away and alone at a time when he badly needed the assistance and the proximity of his dear ones. Common sense suggested the obvious solution of terminating the impossible relationship with the young actress and getting the old parent back among his own family who loved him and felt powerless, knowing him to be in bad health, far away, and alone. Pirandello is restless and anxious because he knows very well that Marta is impressionable and ready to respond to such an argument, especially if presented as the only reasonable way to take care of the Maestro. Pirandello wants to warn her and make

go well and that you can get some rest in Rome, and some fun, if, as is the case here in Paris, the weather is good again and spring makes its festive entrance into Pincio and the Villa Borghese with the pink peach blossoms and the white almond blossoms. Until tomorrow, my Marta! Especially in Rome above all think, every minute, about all the infinite love of your

Maestro

---

clear that reality is something else, that for him only the love for Marta counted, and all the rest, that is, anything that could come between him and "his life," was for him "death," including in this last category even his family.

{ 310330 }

To Marta Abba
Grande Albergo Minerva
(Italy) Rome   Paris, 30. III. 1931
                                                  5, Avenue Victor Emmanuel III

My Marta,

I have your letter of the 27th, and although you tell me so many sad things of your own soul because of the undeserved spite of the Roman critics, I am happy with your resolution finally to escape and to make yourself free! Yes, my Marta, away, away! During these two months that are left to spend in Italy, practice the French language, start talking—it does not matter if badly as long as you begin to get into the habit of it. For the time being French will be enough; then we'll start here in Paris to study English together, the two of us! I am happy![1] Set yourself free of

---

[1] Pirandello's rare confession of happiness is caused by his hasty interpretation of what Marta wrote under the influence of unfavorable reviews received in Rome (see also letter 310208, footnote 1)—in a moment of discouragement because of the thousand troubles she had to face as company director / manager. Pirandello read in those expressions a final decision by Marta to leave Italy and dedicate herself to a career abroad. Pirandello jumps to conclusions and is now dreaming of having Marta close by again, in the new, bigger Parisian apartment that he is planning to get just for the purpose of being able to have her as a guest, with all the luxuries to be provided by his new wealth. From there they would move together toward a new international glory—the U.S. tour by Marta's company proposed by Shubert (letter 310325) being a first grandiose step in that direction. This dream, besides being based on Pirandello's jumping to conclusions and not on what Marta had actually said, was to collapse also because of the disastrous effects the Great Depression had on the plans of the Shuberts.

everything and everybody and trust me! We'll accomplish great things! I do have the fever of work; all the powers of my spirit are at the boiling point. But without you, I'm like a pole without a flag. You must be my flag: Marta Abba, all over the world. People must know only you, you alone; my theater must live only in the light of your name; and then it will disappear with you, so that my name will remain inseparable from yours, which will have given it *its true life*; and it will be *your glory*, all over the world, although it was martyrdom in Italy, where since Dante to the present time every glory has always suffered martyrdom. There is no conflict between the glory of a poet and the glory of an actress; they are two different and separate glories that can proceed one next to the other, without one detracting from the other; creating on the stage is not a lesser glory than creating on paper or in bronze or on a canvas; and he who creates on the stage and acquires glory for that creation can well stay next to the one who on his own has conquered glory on paper. You remain Marta Abba, the great actress, whether you perform Tolstoy, Pirandello, or Molnár. Irving remained Irving, performing Shakespeare. These types of glory are different and separate.

. . . My Marta, woe be to us if we accept the reality that other people give to us! Haven't you read *Uno, nessuno e centomila*? And don't you remember what Enrico IV says in the second act? Everybody must create *his own reality* by himself and in himself; if you pay attention to the one other people give you it is enough to make you crazy and not to live anymore. Make yourself free and breathe free; in the freedom of your honest feeling and in your straight and noble mind you do not have to give an account to anyone but yourself, and that's it. Do not confuse yourself with those small people, do not be taken in by petty judgments, and don't be worried about them! Until tomorrow, my Marta! Write to me, write! Think about me, about all the love of your

Maestro

{ 310401 }

To Marta Abba
Compagnia drammatica Marta Abba
Teatro Fiorentini
(Italy) Naples   Paris, 1. IV. 1931
                                                 5, Avenue Victor Emmanuel III

My Marta,

. . . I'm writing with a fever![1] Today I had a two-hour conversation with Shubert, who is taking along your pictures to America; he wants lots more pictures to start an advertising campaign in all the newspapers. . . . Shubert wants you to surround yourself with actors of the first order—the best in the Italian theater—so as to present a magnificent show: beautiful people, well dressed, and who know how to act. He definitely wants your tour to be a landmark. Looking at your picture he could not stop uttering exclamations: "Fine! Fine! Fine!" He said that the company, with you and me, should be in New York on September 10 to start the tour on October 1. Twenty days of preparation are not many; it will be necessary to work hard. The contract will be for three months with an option of three more months, after the first three, because Shubert wants to reserve the right to take the company to Latin America, after North and Central America. All expenses will be paid by him. For you there will be twelve thousand lire per day, out of which the actors and actresses coming with you from Italy will be paid. But the precise and complete plan must be made by us. Please be thinking about which actors we should approach, and what should be the pay for each of them, choosing the best. There must be seven, including both men and women, for the main roles. Whom would you consider? It is necessary to start thinking at once about the choice. Once chosen, we'll think how to approach them. I'm waiting for you to tell me, my Marta. This is great luck from every point of view, and a great revenge, an enormous satisfaction, which should repay you for all you had to suffer this year. You'll see how all of them will die of envy as soon as the news breaks! But we should not have any mean feelings of spite against all those miserable cowards; we must look high up and collect all our strength and put all our soul into fulfilling this great task, truly worthy of you, my Marta! It is a great door that is opening. It's up to you to enter, as a queen! I am happy, happy for you.

[1] This letter is 310401 bis in the Italian edition.

... Be healthy, cheerful, don't worry about anything, and think only about all the love without end of your

Maestro

{ 310422 }

To Marta Abba
Via Caracciolo 14
Naples (Italy)

Paris, 22. IV. 1931
5, Avenue Victor Emmanuel III

My Marta,

... Your announcement of a month's extension of your season in that cursed Naples did not reassure me; on the contrary, it makes me afraid it will stretch out until the end of May my torment in feeling you so alienated from me—precisely as it happened last year while I was in Berlin. And then you say that you are not "Mediterranean," that you are not "solar," that you are not a "southerner" the way I see you, admire you, and want you! It is certain that your father, who during the best part of his youth for so many years lived on the Mediterranean Sea, in giving you life put all the impetus and the ardor of that sea and of those southern lands into you, into the blue of your eyes and into the flame of your hair, into all the gold of your flesh—without knowing it, unconsciously—and created you Mediterranean and solar. As soon as you plunge into the Mezzogiorno, you become excited and you do what you wouldn't do elsewhere. I know it, I feel it, and I would rejoice the way I would at an exaltation of my native blood and of my soul if, I repeat, I would not become aware—as I do—that on the contrary you alienate yourself from me, instead of feeling me closer in that blue and in that flame. "Don't make me hate Naples!" I wrote to you; and here I am, hating her, while I would like to love her, as I always did love her, for all the love that city has always had for you and for all the welcome she gives you—because she feels that you are solar, made out of her azure and out of her flame. I am happy for that: I feel you there in the south as if you were in my home; but I wish that you too would feel me near you, to enjoy these festivities, and not so far away.... Forgive me, I beg you, my Marta, for this outcry, because this week I have been suffering so much.... You forgive me, don't you?

... *Maestro*

{ 310427 }

                                                        Paris, 27. IV. 1931
                                              5, Avenue Victor Emmanuel III

My Marta,

The night before last, as soon as I got home from the post office in the Rue de la Boétie—where I go every time I mail letters to you—a violent fever broke out, which forced me to go to bed for the whole night and the following day. Already when I was writing I became aware that I was getting sick. But the illness, I know, is definitely coming from my soul, which has no more rest; it is not from my body, and the fever attacking me with such violence is a cerebral fever, one of those that cause insanity. In reality during the night, the fever was accompanied by a kind of hallucinatory delirium—so disconcerting and painful that I won't describe it so as not to upset you. All day yesterday I remained in bed, totally depressed; today I got out of bed, because it was a passing fever, and nothing else, as if it had been a discharge of a tempest in the spirit—piled up because of so much suffering and so much work—the absolute uselessness of which, in a moment of frightening gloom, suddenly appears evident.

. . . Do not pay attention, I beseech you, to what I am telling you now, nor to what I wrote in my last letter. My soul is truly deranged; I don't know why, I see, I feel myself abandoned by you, and it seems to me that I'm going insane. I couldn't say where this premonition comes from, but it is so; I feel that my breath, my warmth, my life, are failing. . . . I am sick, really sick, without any spirit and without strength. Forgive me!

. . . They shall fall! They shall certainly fall![1] And if tomorrow, as will certainly happen, an Italian theater will rise again, it will not be able to do so without me because, if an Italian theater exists in the world, it exists with my name on it. I will not move a finger, I will not take a single step. But tomorrow, I'm sure, they will come to me; they have no other choice but to come to me, because of all I have done, and because of the position I have taken and will maintain to the end. There are already several signs of rapprochement. . . . I know that S. E. Rocco, the minister of justice and president of the International Society of Culture in Paris,

---

[1] In a long paragraph, here not translated, Pirandello rambles against his "enemies" and expresses his disappointment at some expressions in Marta's letter in which she regrets the fact that Pirandello had taken a position against that powerful group.

on his own spontaneous initiative as president, has written to Stockholm that the Nobel Prize should be awarded to me. I don't know whether I'll get it, and this is, for the moment, of secondary importance; the important fact is that Rocco acted in the name of an international cultural society, being also a cabinet minister in Italy and among the most influential members of the Fascist government. My position is improving daily, always more, not only financially, but also, in a special way, morally. You will see what will happen here in Paris next year after America. The theater is me, it's still me, all over the world. If some plays that have value are successful here as in other places, it is because they were born from my theater, and everybody recognizes that. . . . I'm delirious, forgive me if I tell you these things, my Marta; I tell them not because they are not true, but to reach the conclusion that nothing matters to me—nothing, nothing—if you are not there; if you do not trust me; if—while I am waiting for you here in Paris, God knows with what anticipation, to talk to you of so many things concerning your great future, as I see it, how it will be—you talk to me of your *via crucis* that must continue . . . and you think. . . . No, no, my Marta! Take away from around you all those small things, those miserable and depressing concerns . . . you are great, and you must stay *high up! high up!*[2] And you must have faith in the great things that are coming, that must come! All enemies will fall and will gnash their teeth in the dust, which will become the mud in which they will be buried. As you have so far triumphed over all these small miseries, so will you also triumph in your great challenges all over the world. Your triumph must be worthy of you. Somebody tells you that, somebody who never made up sentences but produced facts, who really knew, by dint of suffering and working, how to impose himself upon the world.

. . . With all the love of

Your Maestro

---

[2] The words *alta! alta!* are written in large characters. Pirandello in his delirious rambling repeats some of his favorite clichés about grandeur and about crushing his enemies.

{ 310501 }

To Marta Abba
Via Caracciolo 14
(Italy) Naples
                                                                    Paris, 1. v. 1931
                                                        5, Avenue Victor Emmanuel III

My Marta,

The very fact that my letter of the 25th has caused you so much pain and so much anger is sufficient to justify the punishment you inflict on me by sending it back, and I beg you once more to forgive me! Perhaps, if you had waited for the next couple of letters informing you about my mental perturbation and the very sad condition of my health at that time, you would have, if not excused, at least forgiven me, because forgiveness is something that comes from the goodness of your heart, and your heart is the best existing upon this earth, as your soul is the most honest. It is right that, while suffering the afflictions that come from other people, you reject those coming from me, because if you can expect troubles from anybody, from me, no, you should not, and it is really unforgivable that I gave you some and continue to give you more. Before shredding into tiny pieces the letter you sent back—so that I too might punish it—I decided to read it over again in order to become aware of the mental state I was in when I wrote it. After this perturbation of night deliriums accompanied by fever, I am starting now to mistrust myself and I'm feeling extremely frightened. Among the many things that were bound to provoke your anger and your dislike (and I wrote you more, unfortunately, in the succeeding letters, which now I recognize to be similar to those, and are the fruit of the unhealthy fright with which I am presently afflicted) I could see—*for my tranquillity* and not as an excuse, which cannot have any value to you—that in the whole tone of the letter, if not in the things I was telling you, my Marta, this love without end that I have for you was never, not even for a moment, belied; that is, this feeling I have to the deepest roots of my being, that without you my life wouldn't be possible anymore. Only in the name of this love, only for the consciousness of this feeling, do I have the courage to beg for your forgiveness, as a prize that you might grant to me, closing your eyes to the pain I gave you.

. . . As far as the lapse in judgment of having publicized your tour is concerned, which you told me was "outrageous," it was certainly not my intention to displease you, my Marta! In the two conversations with

Shubert the tour was "*decided on,*"[1] if not worked out in all its details (because it could not be at that time); I announced what is *true* and *unquestionable*; I said that Shubert *has proposed* to do this tour. Who can deny that? And I believed that to make that known would give you pleasure, and not pain, after the spiteful attack on you by the Roman press. Was I wrong? If you believe so, once more please forgive me, considering that my intention was completely different! Negotiations, on an established basis, are now going on; the proposal *was made*, the date *was decided, an amount of money* was mentioned, there was *the option for three more months* in the eventuality of going also to *South America*. What else was announced that does not correspond to the honest truth? Then why "poor judgment," and on top of that "outrageous"? Even admitting that the negotiations can fail, the fact of the *proposal*, not from your side or mine, but from *Shubert himself,* remains, and nobody can deny that; if you do not trust me or what I tell you, there are two witnesses, one of whom is not even a friend of mine anymore, Torre, and the other is Allatini, whom luckily I was able to take with me to the second conversation with Shubert, not trusting Torre anymore, since Shubert does not speak a word of French and speaks only American. Calling witnesses for what one says—isn't that the saddest thing that can happen? It means admitting the possibility of not being believed, and this is the humiliation I experience, so much more painful, because all I do is meant for your good, as the only thing I am aiming at: I have no other aim, no other intent! I tell you that so that you may *always* forgive me even if I make mistakes, *always* remembering the endless love of

Your Maestro

[1] The word "stabilita" is underlined twice by Pirandello.

{ 310503 }

To Marta Abba
4 Parco Margherita
(Italy) Naples

Paris, 3. v. 1931
5, Avenue Victor Emmanuel III

My Marta,

You can't imagine how much good your telegram has done me! On the evening of Thursday the 30th (as a precaution I had been home the whole day, watching my diet) I was looking out through my glass door at the almost deserted avenue under the constant and oppressive drizzling, when I saw—in front of my balcony that has low iron railings overlooking the avenue—an old woman coming from the country with a bucket full of lilies of the valley hanging from her arm, obviously to sell at midnight to the gentlemen leaving the theaters and the cafés. That's because there is a charming custom of giving a sprig of lilies of the valley, with its four perfumed little white bells, as a good-luck charm, on the night of April 30, to greet the beginning of May or, as the ancients would say, the Kalends of May. At once I opened the window; I went out on the balcony and called to that old woman because I too wanted to buy my sprig of lilies of the valley as a good-luck charm. I put it into a small vase, and although I had the feeling that my fever was rising, I decided to wait for midnight while reading. When it was exactly midnight I took the stem of lilies of the valley and went to offer it to your portrait in my room, inserting it into the low part of the leather frame so that the four perfumed white bells would reach the height of your smiling face. This picture is one of the many that Badodi took of you in Milan and is to me the dearest: that most youthful one, with the black dress trimmed with white, the jacket open, the beret à la Rafael, and your two hands at your waist. I won't say all the good wishes I gave you with my heart. My fever was already high; I went to bed; I got very restless and then the delirium began. From time to time I lifted my head, and by the light of the bulb that had been burning the whole night, I was looking at the stem of lilies of the valley inserted into the frame of your portrait, and you cannot imagine what a comfort and what a solace were coming from those four fresh little white bells near your face that smiled as if pleased by them. The whole night passed that way. At 7:30 I called the doorman for a lemonade with the phone that is on my night table: I was burning. A half-hour later the wife of the doorman came—a good old lady from Nice who takes care of my apartment; she brought in the lemonade, the newspapers, and the letters of the first mail delivery (first and only, because here on May Day there is a general strike). There was only one letter, and supreme irony, it was one of mine sent back, accompanied by a couple of your words of justifiable anger and just punishment. By now, my Marta, you have already forgiven me. Your telegram, received this morning, tells me that clearly. But the whole day of May the first and all yesterday I have been tormenting myself thinking over the many bad things I have kept writing to you, feeling abandoned by you, I don't know why, perhaps because of this inflammatory illness that has affected my brain. I stayed in bed; Allatini came to visit me, and also Caprin, here on a mission from the *Corriere della sera*; I did not want them to say that I am ill; I tried to show that I was not. I had Allatini write under dictation, I talked for a long time with Caprin; I wrote myself, letting them bring to my bed the necessary implements. This effort that I made was helpful; today I feel better; I got up, but I'll stay home. It's raining, raining, always raining. . . . I don't have any more pain in the liver; my bile must have been moving in these days; the diet has been helpful. I'm weak and tired; but you'll see that soon, if I have a little bit of calm, I'll recuperate. Saint Marta will help with her forgiveness. But I am unforgivable for the troubles I'm giving her, so much more because I do not live except of her and for her; and if she punishes me it means death for me. But it won't happen anymore, my Marta; I swear it on all the endless love of

Your Maestro

{ 310512 }

To Marta Abba
4 Parco Margherita
(Italy) Naples   Paris, 12. v. 1931
                                       5, Avenue Victor Emmanuel III

My Marta,

. . . Come and relax in Paris, where you can prepare for other enterprises worthy of you after some rest and distraction from the troubles that have oppressed you for so many months. If you come with your father and your mother, since I have a place here in Paris, I do not see anything improper in the fact that all of you stay with me as my guests. But I have sworn not to give you even the slightest displeasure, and if you command that I do not insist, I'll obey and do as you wish. You could think it over a little while; I do not see anything wrong in that, and I'd be happy;[1] but perhaps is it your father who doesn't want it?

. . . I'm feeling a little better. I spent the night with less agitation, but I cannot say that I spent a good night; I read a lot. If you only knew how many things are going through my head! How many things I'd like to do! My fantasy has never been so lively. It would be a pity if my health

[1] Pirandello had been insisting on having Marta in his apartment as his guest. He wanted that so badly that he was ready to move to a larger apartment in order to accommodate the whole Abba family comfortably. Marta preferred to avoid annoying gossip and probably liked enjoying more independence from the overwhelming hospitality of the Maestro.

should fail me, if I should die without seeing my Marta again! I have no other desire. Last night I was thinking about those scripts I want to write for your tour all over the world, performing alone, without the need of anybody else, as Ruth Draper is doing;[2] she is having great success in Paris performing her monologues in English. Yours would be something different, much newer and more powerful, with scenery and nonspeaking masks. A trunkful of puppets, a crate of scenery and lighting equipment, a director and a makeup specialist: that's all. I am sure it would make your fortune and liberate you from everything and prove to be the only way to solve the nonunderstanding of the Italian language, because with a few lines of translation into the various languages we would give an explanation of the content of your actions on the stage—and addio Italy! All the theaters of the world would be open! And the whole box-office income would be for you alone. Your debut could be organized here in Paris. Think about that, my Marta, and think always about your Maestro who is always here for you, does not think of anything but you, lives only for you, and without you would be dead.

[unsigned]

[2] The American actress Ruth Draper (1889–1956) earned an income of about $5,000 a week with her one-woman shows.

{ 310515 }

To Marta Abba
4, Parco Margherita
(Italy) Naples   Paris, 15. V. 1931
                                                  5, Avenue Victor Emmanuel III

My Marta,

. . . Victory is certain. Between the one who is always intent on destroying and the one who is, on the contrary, always intent on creating, who do you think will eventually win? Destruction cannot be victory. They will believe they knocked you out, but, on the contrary, they'll have smoothed out the ground for the rebuilding that you, by keeping on with your creating, will be ready to do. The new theater in Italy—the one I have created—has still to rise, and it will rise; it matters little if I am no longer there; you will be there, without me, and that is enough. Perhaps it's a good thing that I won't be there. In Italy it is customary to wait for death before awarding honors. And because they ill-treated me so much, they'll have to make up for a lot and they will do so. When that time comes, those who fought most against me will not be merry. And you will rejoice at their defeat. Admitting that with the termination of your company in May none of my plays will be performed in Italy, do you believe that, with that, Mr. Giordani and the whole gang, including the press, will win out? Pirandello can do without Italy; Italy, if she wants to have a theater, cannot do without Pirandello. She will have no more theater. This is the definition of the problem. I live abroad, and theater dies in Italy. America will have plays by Pirandello, France and England will have them, all countries but Italy will have some, too. It will become known, and people will say, as it is already noised about, that theater in Italy is dead. Her only great author is international, lives on the stages of the outside world. This way Mr. Giordani, suppressing me in Italy, will be victorious. And do you think that he won't pay? I won't be there anymore, but you can be sure that he will pay.

    . . . With all the love of

Your Maestro

{ 310520 }

To Marta Abba
4, Parco Margherita
(Italy) Naples   Paris, 20. v. 1931
                                          5, Avenue Victor Emmanuel III

    My Marta,
    I am rather upset about the distressing information that this lawyer from Shubert has given about the theaters and even about the movies in New York and all over America at this moment of frightful financial crisis in the United States: the crumbling of the stock market, bankruptcies of financial institutions, unemployment, strikes, and so on. I reminded him that the box-office take of *As You Desire Me* at the Maxine Elliott Theatre had been excellent for six months; he assured me that it was *most exceptional*; this year all the other theaters belonging to Shubert have had a very bad time; so much so, that he will close the season with a very considerable loss. The Maxine Elliott is one theater; Shubert owns sixty-five in New York alone. At this moment, he concluded, the situation is extremely serious in all America. I talked to him about the tour that Shubert himself had proposed for next October. He was not informed

about that. He asked me what conditions had been proposed, and as soon as I mentioned the amount of six hundred dollars a day, he started scribbling calculations on a piece of paper and in a couple of minutes concluded that, to make a profit on such conditions, Shubert should have a weekly take of between ten and eleven thousand dollars, which to him seemed extremely difficult, even for an exceptional company.[1]

. . . Think of all the love of

Your Maestro

[1] The Shubert organization was deeply affected by the Great Depression and was not capable of honoring its commitments to the production of the other Pirandello plays for which it had acquired the U.S. rights. Legal complications followed, which seriously damaged Pirandello's chances of realizing his "American dream" and contributed to the collapse of his great financial hopes from America.

{ 310531 }

To Marta Abba
26, Via Aurelio Saffi
(Italy) Milan

Paris, 31. v. 1931
5, Avenue Victor Emmanuel III

My Marta,

. . . I don't know whether in Milan the weather is hot; here in Paris it is deliciously cool; and I wish you would decide at once about your departure. But unfortunately I know what an invincible force of attraction your home and your family—impassable borders of your world—exert on you. I who have no more home, I who have no more family, I who have crossed forever all the borders and am alone in the world with Art as my only companion, and with all my feelings and desires being enemies of my peace, in this loneliness—I feel I am calling you without hope. You will come with your family, closed within the borders of your world; your home, also when you are far away, is always present in your mind. I am like the Sailor in *The Lady from the Sea*.[1] But away with all these melancholy thoughts! However it may turn out, I am always and all for you, I have only you in the world for whom I still feel like staying alive, and it

[1] A play by Henrik Ibsen, published in 1888. When the sailor comes back—after years of absence—to claim Ellida (who has gotten married in the meantime), she decides to do "the right thing," that is, to stay with her husband, whom she does not love. Pirandello's hint is clear. Marta has opted for life with her family in her own narrow world while rejecting Pirandello, who is offering total love and freedom from conventional family ties.

will be enough for me to see you again, my Marta, and from the light of your eyes I'll receive the purest warmth of the purest joy.

Come soon. . . . I am waiting for you! Always with all the endless love of

Your Maestro

{ 310611 }

To Marta Abba
26, Via Aurelio Saffi
(Italy) Milan

Paris, 11. vi. 1931
5, Avenue Victor Emmanuel III

My Marta,

. . . Here in Paris we'll think about whatever is still needed to make the two rooms and the living room—those belonging to you in the new apartment—more beautiful, and to give them the finishing touch.[1] But, who knows, perhaps—as far as your home is concerned—for the time being there won't be any need to worry. Are you by any chance really sure that you'll go back to Italy so soon? So many things are on the brink of happening! So many doors will open, and we should not let our future chances be restricted by our immediate desires. Yes, you should study— in a special way—the French language. But you will learn French quickly, staying here in France for a couple of months—I don't say in Paris when the worst heat will come—but either at a beach in the north or in the hills. There are delightful places, and you'll talk only in French with everybody. It is absolutely necessary that you be in command of French, and no teacher is as effective as the use of the living language where the native tongue is spoken. Here you will eventually learn French, and you won't waste your time; on the contrary, you'll acquire a great asset for your future. As far as general culture is concerned, study only what helps you and not more; the mind gets fat and becomes as heavy as a belly; then good-bye freshness and spontaneity! We must nourish ourselves with foods we can assimilate and that are appealing to our spiritual appetite. Otherwise we get indigestion from stupid and useless pedantry. Keep away from that![2] You should interest yourself in a culture that is

[1] Marta had not yet finished furnishing her rooms in the Abbas' new residence in the Via Aurelio Saffi.

[2] The still-active dislike for the pedantic method of philology Pirandello had to follow

appropriate and substantial, without spicy sauces, but with tasty ones. It would be enough if you had the patience to last for a year, one hour each day, with a program well defined in its parts. I'll give you an outline. But you'll have to dedicate one hour a day, without fail; and never give up! You make me laugh when you speak of your "past youth. . . ." It's up to you to bloom again in one minute: it is sufficient that you want it, freeing yourself from every oppression. . . . I am at your service, all for you, as you wish, always. Thinking of you? I am doing nothing else, my Marta, I have no other thought but that of you, continually—it has become all my life, and you can see that I have succeeded in excluding all considerations of myself even when I think of you who are all my life. In reality, since you no longer want me near you, I do not live anymore; I do not live except to think about you from far away as being the only source of my life. Therefore you must love me, and if you tell me that you love me, you will make me happy. You are the first, the most beautiful, the purest, the most just, the holiest among all women: a divine prize for all that life could cost a man in work and suffering. Good-bye, my Marta—in a few days, maybe Sunday (I can't believe it!), perhaps Monday. . . . I am waiting for your telegram, I'm impatient, full of expectation! Ah, my Marta, it does not seem true to me! You'll find me with all my love,

Your Maestro

---

during his early university studies in Germany—against which he had already protested in his letters from Bonn—is noticeable here. See Providenti, *Mnemosine*, p. 11. In his simplified pedagogy, Pirandello shows very modern insights.

{ 310718 }

To Marta Abba
26, Via Aurelio Saffi
(Italy) Milan

Paris, 18. VII. 1931
5, Avenue Victor Emmanuel III

My Marta,

This morning I was waiting for a letter from you that would give me news about your trip and your arrival back in Milan.[1] But perhaps it will come later. You can't imagine how I felt after having had you near me for

[1] The letters start again after Marta's departure from Paris. Pirandello, as usual after each separation from his beloved, is in a state of shock.

a month: completely dead—I do not know where to look, where to go, where to sit; it does not seem to me that there is a single thing worth saying. I must definitely shake off my torpor. Both the day before yesterday and yesterday, getting out from the Quirinal after lunch,[2] I went around a bit looking for a new apartment, and I think I found it in Rue de la Perouse 37, very near the Étoile. It is on the sixth floor, but there is an elevator, and from the study the view is magnificent: the whole square of the Arch of Triumph with the branching off of the wide, tree-lined avenues, and a lot of air and light. The study, can you believe it? has four windows and is furnished with taste; there is moreover another very beautiful room, with a big bed, a bathroom that is larger than my present study, and full of light; plus a stylish foyer, as large as a living room: all for 1,800 francs, plus a 10 percent charge for service (that is, 180 francs, instead of the 300 that I am now paying here), plus 60 francs for the telephone. Electricity is included. I am thinking of buying some linen, so I won't need to rent it; I won't spend more that 1,000 francs—that means that eventually I'll save money, and at least I'll sleep on my own linen: two pairs of sheets, three nice thick towels, ten lighter ones, two bathrobes, and that's it.

. . . . . .

Maestro

[2] A restaurant where Pirandello often had his meals.

{ 310722 }

To Marta Abba
Hôtel Astoria
Via Serra 1
(Italy) Genoa

Paris, 22. VII. 1931
5, Avenue Victor Emmanuel III

My Marta,
What a joy your letter from Campo Fiori, overlooking Varese, was for me! How beautifully you made me see the landscape—with just a few strokes—and gave me the feeling of the altitude! While I was reading your words, it seemed to me as if I were seeing you again as happy as you were on the plane that was flying us from Paris to London—you, a daughter of the air, when your eyelids blinked as if with the rhythm of the wings to express your joy! Ah, my Marta, you do have wings, your

spirit truly has wings, and whoever clips them or puts a brake on them commits a crime. Do you want your Maestro to be happy too? Yes, but only this way, as a reflection, seeing you happy, my Marta! How could I be happy any other way?

I am now waiting for you to tell me where you have decided to go on the seashore, whether to Pegli or elsewhere. My summer vacation will be spent in moving in and watching the trees of the Étoile and of the avenues from the height of the sixth floor, where I am going to live, on Rue La Pérouse, 37, from August 1 on. RUE LA PÉROUSE, 37. Remember. But I'll have time to write it to you many times.

I can't wait to get out of this tomb that increases my sadness so much and makes my desperate loneliness even bleaker.[1] But if I remember that you were here, that you can visualize me here, because you know these two rooms—whereas you do not even know where the new house is located—then I feel sorry to detach myself from the old place. Because for me, who am living only and always on memories of you and on your image, the strongest pain is that of not being able to visualize you in places I don't know, where I've never been with you. It seems to me as if I am getting lost—like someone who doesn't know where he should turn in his search for a cherished person who has disappeared from his sight. Ah, my Marta, I have been experiencing that pain for many years; you do not know what it is, and I hope you will never know! With that, anguish entered my soul forever. I get rid of it only when, from time to time, I see you again. And in this moment, when I have just finished seeing you, I feel it stronger than ever, so much so that my throat is choking me. Enough, I don't want to upset you, my Marta.

. . . Did you buy the Linguafon? What about the English tutor? I'm waiting for you to write to me! There might be a possibility of filming *Vestire gli ignudi* in French next November. Maret, who made the film *Jean de la lune*, asked me about it, and he also asked whether you would be able to do the film in French. I promised I would ask you. But English, French . . . poor Marta, they want you to be a regular linguist!

All this proves that you must leave Italy, because you are destined for the world; you will be *the* international actress. No other actress is as worthy as you are. There is need in the world for a great, beautiful, young actress, and you must be it! For England, for France, for America, for the whole world! Courage, and go, my Marta! I am here entirely for you, but

---

[1] Pirandello had come to consider his luxurious apartment, located on one of the most central and aristocratic avenues of Paris, to be dark and damp.

ready to disappear when you don't need either me or anyone else. Meanwhile I am working on the sketches.[2] *Write and think always about*

Your, your, your Maestro

[2] A series of scripts Pirandello planned (to which he referred with the English word, almost always misspelled!) for the one-woman show that Marta was considering for production as an alternative to her tiring and barely rewarding work as a company director.

{ 310726 }

To Marta Abba
Hôtel Astoria & Bergamo
(Italy) Genoa

Paris, 26. VII. 1931
5, Avenue Victor Emmanuel III
and shortly:
37, Rue La Pérouse

My Marta,

I was hoping to receive the letter that you promised you would write on the evening of Thursday, on your return from the seashore. But I did not get it, and I can't hope that it will arrive with later mail deliveries because today is Sunday. It will get here tomorrow morning—if you wrote it, but I doubt you did. All the time I have been thinking only about those things "that, in silence, talk inside you, and which you wish to communicate to me alone." How many of them I have imagined . . . they kept my soul in turmoil the whole day and a good part of the night! "You want to communicate to me alone": this privilege, for somebody like me who admires and loves your soul as much as your whole person, has given to me first an uplift of pride and joy, then a trembling anxiety that still continues and doesn't allow me to rest. You can therefore figure out how I am waiting for that letter!

You know, my Marta, what you are for me. The torment of imagining you far away—among other people who can have the joy of seeing you, talking to you, being near you while I am here *without life* because I can neither see you nor talk with you, nor be near you—can be mitigated only by the thought that you feel my presence within you and that even from far away you give me life, and that even in your silence you see me and talk to me; in one word, that I am alive and close to you, more than those who see you, talk to you, and are around you. Therefore I was so excited about your promise of communicating to me alone the many things that are speaking to you in silence. My Marta, nobody is or will ever be capable of understanding you as I do, and nobody will ever be able to love you more than I do. Perhaps today upon this earth there is not a single spirit that understands more about life and is able to receive so much of it in himself as I do. And you can say and affirm, without fear that anybody might contradict you, that you own this spirit of mine—all for yourself as your own property to do whatever you want with it; and that now that spirit lives upon this earth only in order to comprehend all life and to give to others the way to understand it and conceive it. This spirit of mine abnegates itself before you, it disappears; or it becomes your shadow on the ground, inseparable. Look at your shadow on the ground, my Marta: it's I who is following you, who is near you; you cannot lose me! And you can talk with your faithful shadow as you can with yourself.[1]

Yesterday Lee Shubert was in Paris for a visit, and I went to see him. On the same evening he left again. He told me that Mrs. Collier, whom we saw in London, is actively working on the tour and that he has the most solid hopes for the success of it; that on August 1, Mrs. Collier will leave for America and that as soon as she arrives she will speed up all the paperwork. We must allow her time, he said—about five or six weeks— and that he is counting on the tour and will keep in touch with me.

. . . .

Maestro

---

[1] In his open statement of supreme and total love, which takes the form of humble self-abnegation—literally at the feet of the beloved—Pirandello seems to indulge in a dreamy kind of masochism.

{ 310803 }

To Marta Abba
Hôtel Astoria & Bergamo
(Italy) Genoa
                                                    Paris, 3. VIII. 1931
                                                    37, Rue La Pérouse

My Marta,

At last I have received your letter, of which I cannot give a precise date because it was started, well, fancy that! on Monday of last week; that is, on July 27, then picked up again, twice, on Friday, July 31, and mailed on Saturday, August 1. I console myself with noticing that, at least intermittently, you thought about me a little bit. But I am happy about the news that you are very well, and if you yourself tell me that you look wonderful, I imagine how beautiful you must be, a joy in the sun—to drive people crazy. I am here under a wintry sky, in the midst of endless rain, with thunder every night, and it's already chilly like fall: summer is finished! If I think of you in the sun, in a bathing suit, almost naked, it seems to me that it can't be true, but only a dream, and if I think that other people can have the joy of seeing you real and alive before their eyes . . . nearby. . . .

I got up; I went to throw myself, with my face on the pillow, on a magnificent leather sofa that takes up the whole back wall of my study, and I spent a quarter of an hour biting my arm.[1] Now here I am again. Calm.

. . . I am happy! I just received your letter of Saturday! You did write it, after your return from Sestri! And this letter is really all from "my" Marta, who thought of me! I am happy. I'll answer tomorrow, at length . . . my Marta, my Marta, do you see? One word from you is enough to put my soul back into my body. Now I am a different person! Until tomorrow! Consider yourself surrounded by the endless love of

Your Maestro

[1] Another typical infantilism, like scratching his face when angry (letter 290501) and the desire to throw himself on the floor and never to get up again (letter 310716).

{ 310806 }

To Marta Abba
Hôtel Astoria & Bergamo
(Italy) Genoa

Paris, Thursday 6. VIII. 1931
37, Rue La Pérouse

My Marta,

. . . The economic situation of all European nations and of America is projected for the next year as disastrous. It is no longer a crisis; it is rather the failure of the bourgeoisie in the whole world. The bourgeois order in politics, in industry, in social justice, in all relationships between capital and workers, in the whole of the so-called civilization threatens to collapse upon its decaying foundations. You notice that at least in France, because right here, with the French Revolution, the bourgeois order was born, and here it has its deepest roots. Everywhere great efforts are made to keep it together, to keep everything from falling apart, but those efforts, for the time being, are desperate and you cannot see from what side help can come. I mean a valid and durable help, and not the ephemeral kind that has been given a little to Germany, a little to England. The future is more than ever obscure and uncertain. It would be necessary for people to understand in time that the so-called technology, the so-called science, as applied to industry, is an awful form of insanity that has launched human life toward the destruction of two categorical necessities: space and time. It is necessary for humanity to repossess time and space in order to find again her peace and her breath. How can you create life without time and without space? Everything is a dizzy escape, a plundering. We must simplify our life and give its roots back to it; crush all its insane complications and make it natural again; destroy all the machines, all of them, and make it so that life may again have its hands, its feet, its head, to think about beautiful things, its heart to feel healthy affections. As it is now, insanity is raging; nothing is ever enough; every resource is swallowed up, all natural energy misused for this general unsatisfactory situation, which is becoming increasingly desperate and delirious.[1]

But why am I talking about this today, my Marta, while you are enjoying a rest in sight of the sea and under the sun? I have no sea, I have no sun, I have no rest: that must be the reason! Tonight, before four, I left my bed to escape the restlessness of the most horrible insomnia; I put my head out of the window to breathe the humid air after so much rain and to look at the dark sky over the city—red, ghostly, misty fumes above the bristling chimney tops. . . . How can people not go insane under such a sky? And I started thinking of you, my Marta, who will have to endure this life for such a long time, while for me it will be over shortly, and I experienced the terrible grief of one who stops because he cannot go on and sees the other person keep going, and going away, farther and farther away . . . but enough of these melancholy thoughts!

. . . Feel inside your heart the endless love of

Your Maestro

---

[1] Pirandello seems to anticipate—although interwoven with the antibourgeois rhetoric typical of fascism—some aspects of today's ecological concerns. He invokes excessive remedies, such as the destruction of all machines, in order to achieve the rebuilding of the human experience in its primordial, natural wholeness.

{ 310819 }

To Marta Abba
Hôtel Astoria e Bergamo
(Italy) Genoa   Paris, 19. VIII. 1931
  My Marta,

I have received your very sad letter of the 16th, mailed on the morning
of the 17th; later I got your telegram of the 18th, evening, which says:
"Wait for today's letter after which please make up your mind always
happy to see you." I'm waiting to obey you. But tomorrow, Thursday,
I'm leaving because I can't take it anymore, knowing how upset you are.
For God's sake, my Marta, react with all the forces of your spirit! The
depression you reveal in your letter is pernicious! You have nothing;[1] you
cannot have anything serious or dangerous. It will be enough that you
rest for a while and that you be calm, without worrying; your very body,
which is alive and vital, will do all the healing by itself—if only those
damned doctors do not interfere (they know only death and ignore life).[2]
But forgive me, didn't you write to me a short while ago in one of your
letters from Genoa that you were "very healthy"? Here I found you to be
in perfect condition, although you did catch a cold, but, after that, from
Genoa you told me only good things about your health; this is the best
sign that nature defends itself by itself, as long as you have, of course, the
kind of care that everybody must have, and rest, a lot of rest, because you
squandered your energies and you had too many worries! But that's
enough, and you shouldn't worry about anything else, for God's sake! Do
not keep on thinking that you are menaced, ill, or exposed to contagion;
do not allow your soul to accept depressing thoughts, for the love of God,
my Marta, don't! These are things that affect all young people! When I
was twenty-six, I myself was endangered; both my sons, Stefano and
Fausto, who are now strong and full of health, had a touch of apicitis:
Fausto in both lungs. Therefore don't be worried a bit, my Marta: take
care, of course, but above all rest and be calm; everything will be over in

---

[1] *Tu hai niente* is written in very large letters. They continue large and diminish in size
little by little in the following lines; they are normal size about fifteen lines below. Pirandello's panic was due to the news that Marta was ill with apicitis, or tuberculosis of the
apex in the lung.

[2] On several occasions Pirandello expresses his low esteem for the medical profession;
this attitude is confirmed by his reluctance to seek medical care even when he was seriously ill. See, for instance, letters 320222, 320607, and 360505.

a few months. And please do not say that from all your sacrifices, from all your struggles, from all your work, after all, you only gained this trifling disease that with a month's treatment will be healed. No, my Marta, you have gained, inside yourself—in the improvement of your soul, in the enrichment of your spirit, in the sense of life you acquired—*your great personality*; and, outside of you, the admiration of all those who know what Art and nobility of behavior and purity of aspiration mean; you have acquired also something you do not want to consider . . . and which makes me cry so much at seeing how you neglect it . . . ah, my Marta, this feeling that I have for you, which, if it has given you many sorrows, has also made a man completely devoted to you who is still worth something, and who lives and thinks exclusively of you and for you. Don't you see, don't you feel that, my Marta? Until soon! Until soon!

Your Maestro

{ 311009 }

To Marta Abba
26, Via Aurelio Saffi
(Italy) Milan   Paris, Friday 9. x. 1931
   My Marta,
   Here I am to explain the reason for last night's telegram, which I imagine must have appeared strange to you! Well, yesterday at 18:00 I was in the offices of the Théâtre Variétés; Max Mauret was having a meeting there with his associates Trebor and Deutsch to discuss with me the casting of *L'uomo, la bestia e la virtù*, for which rehearsals are scheduled to start immediately at the Théâtre St. Georges. They want to cast it with nothing but first-class actors. There is no discussion about the "transparent Mr. Paolino" character; the unanimous choice is Lefort, who created the role of Topaze at the Variétés. The discussion, on the contrary, is quite lively and never-ending about the choice of a leading actress for the "virtuous Madame Perella" character; someone proposes one name; someone else proposes another one, but none of them appears satisfactory; finally Mr. Trebor comes round to questioning me as to whether it was possible to have Miss Abba, knowing that you had interpreted that role in Italy. On the spot I remained speechless—the question had come so unexpectedly. I said that you had never performed in French, but they immediately made me aware that that was not a good reason, because you

could learn your lines, which are not that many, with the help of a good
tutor; as far as the *accent* is concerned, first of all it would not damage the
performance; on the contrary, the *accent* would become a great attraction
when yoked with the name of Marta Abba—and then it could be passed
off as the modification of the voice to express the *virtue* that is characteristic of the role; your coming would be given great publicity, etc. What
could I answer? I certainly could not refuse without even telling you
about it. I said that you had not refused to perform that role in Italian,
given your great versatility, and that you had found in it elements and
traits and attitudes full of new and incomparable humor; but that it was
not really a role for you, accustomed as you are to bringing alive on the
stage much more important ones. They pointed out that everybody knew
your reputation, that the great personality of an actress can reveal itself
in any role, and that the public could be made aware of all this, without
giving up the opportunity for you to present yourself again to the Parisian
public in a role of primary importance,[1] but upon which the responsibility of the whole play is not resting. Because of these considerations, I was
induced by the three directors to send you the telegram with the proposal,
while making clear that I could not know how you would take it and
whether you would accept it. That's all. Now I am waiting for your answer, which I cannot foresee. As far as I am concerned, I would have never
even thought of making such a proposal to you, but since the proposal
was coming from other people, I could not take the responsibility of re-
fusing without at least letting you know. The three directors are enthusiastic about the play and foresee that it will be performed on the stage of
the St. Georges (which is a boulevard theater) *for a whole year.* The role is
what it is. After the first strain of memorizing the French, afterward during the performances everything should run smoothly and without any
effort. The opportunity perhaps should be seized in order to get your foot
in the door of the Parisian scene; then one thing will follow another. Paris
has always been the great showplace of the world, and today more than
ever; France is the only nation that today stands on her two feet, solidly
rich and in good shape. What do you say? It's up to you to judge and to
decide, my Marta! But if you decide to come, you should leave immediately, because rehearsals begin next week and won't last more than one
month. I am only worried about the condition of your health. The
weather is good again, and today it's splendid, but how long will it last?

---

[1] In July 1925, Marta had performed leading roles in Italian with Pirandello's company
in Paris, at the Théâtre Edouard VII.

Winter in Paris is damp, rainy, foggy, without ever seeing the sun—even if not extremely harsh. It's true that Milan's winter is no joke! And here there is the advantage that you would not have to work hard once the first moment is past. But I do not want to listen to all the arguments in favor that are suggested to me by the happiness of having you near in Paris. You must see all the pros and cons of the proposal by yourself and immediately send me an answer, because everybody here is waiting for your decision.[2] With all the endless love of

Your Maestro

[2] Marta accepted the invitation and went to Paris almost immediately, where she rehearsed for about one month and then successfully performed the role of the virtuous Madame Perella at the Théâtre St. Georges until the middle of January 1932.

Letters of 1932 from
Paris, Rome, and Castiglioncello

AFTER THE SUCCESS of the Parisian performances in French, on January 17 Marta returns to Milan. Pirandello, who first tries to conceal his anguish over the new separation, soon bursts into expressions of the "most frightful despair" and into renewed thoughts of suicide. Only the meeting with Mussolini at the beginning of March and the ensuing enthusiasm seem for a while to distract him from the deep depression into which he has fallen again.

The few letters of this year reporting impressions and echoes of three audiences with Mussolini—Marta met him first at the end of January, and Pirandello followed later in March and at the beginning of December—are profoundly revealing of Pirandello's true attitude toward fascism and toward Mussolini as a person. In the letter of February 14, Pirandello expresses his regret for Marta's disillusionment about her audience, during which Mussolini told her: "Pirandello has a bad character." The Maestro describes Mussolini as "rough and coarse human stuff, made to command with contempt mediocre and vulgar people; capable of anything and incapable of scruples." In the same letter, however, he states the need of the "myth we made of him" to govern Italy "in a time as brutal as this." Pirandello had suggested to Marta that in the presence of the Duce she should keep "dry and proud eyes" and take advantage of the nationalistic feelings of the dictator, underlining the fact that, while the theater managers' monopoly was almost totally dependent on foreign plays, her own repertory was proudly Italian and promoting the best Italian playwrights in Italy and abroad.

Marta's visit left a favorable impression on Mussolini, who intervened in her favor for work in films with the production company Cines. Probably due to Marta's visit, the Duce finally decided to reserve time for a long meeting with Pirandello.

In the March audience, Pirandello is encouraged by Mussolini to open his heart. The playwright appears surprised and charmed by Mussolini's show of vivid interest; he jumps at the unique opportunity of exposing in detail his many complaints about the deplorable condition of the Italian

theater and his ideas about the establishment of a state-supported national theater. Mussolini allows him to talk as long as he wants, interrupting only with signs of approval, showing great enthusiasm for the project
and anger against those who had kept it from his attention. For some
time after this audience, Pirandello seems full of energy and enthusiasm.
He wants to realize as soon as possible his dream of a decree from the
Duce sweeping away all the obstacles against the project which had been
piled up by the "gang of enemies."

At the beginning of May, Pirandello is again in Paris, where Pirandellism is triumphant. At the end of the month, after finishing *La favola
del figlio cambiato,* he returns to Italy. He stays in Rome at Via Piemonte
117 until the last week of June, when he goes as a guest to Marta's Villino
Mezzaluna, a small country home that the actress had bought at Lido di
Camaiore, near Viareggio, as a place to rest from her long and fatiguing
tours. The actress and Pirandello spend over a month together, working
at the plans for the next theater season of Marta's company. At the beginning of August, when Pirandello goes to the nearby resort village of Castiglioncello, the letters start again. There he resides at the Villino Conti as
a guest of his son Stefano, surrounded by the love of Stefano's family and
of many friends. At the same time Marta goes back to Milan, Via Aurelio
Saffi 26, to make further preparations for her coming season. By the
middle of September, in the quiet and charming villino, the Maestro finishes the play *Trovarsi* and, by the first week of October, also *Quando si è
qualcuno.*

At the beginning of November, Pirandello leaves Italy again for Paris to
be present at the triumph of *Come tu mi vuoi,* directed by Gaston Baty,
and to receive great honors from the Parisian political and cultural world.

In December the second audience with Mussolini at Palazzo Venezia
hits Pirandello like an icy shower. Mussolini appears ill, yellowish in his
face, old, depressed, almost staggering under the intolerable weight of
uncontrollable events that are threatening to drag the whole world into a
terrifying war. Theater appears to him, in such circumstances, as a secondary problem that can wait for better times. Pirandello remains "with the
blood frozen in his veins" and "anguished because of the frightening impression received."

{ 320118 }

To Marta Abba
Via Aurelio Saffi 26
(Italy) Milan   Paris, 18. I. 1932
    My Marta,

Yesterday I followed you with my thought along your whole trip, worried because of the possible irritations that might have come to you from the luggage, the fatigue of a whole day spent on the train, perhaps alone or, worse, with unpleasant company.[1] I don't know how many times I consulted my watch to figure out where you probably would be . . . already in Belfort, at three; now she will be in Switzerland; now she will cross the Italian border . . . one hour's wait . . . they might have made her step out of the train for customs. When at last my watch indicated 10:45, I drew a deep breath of relief; it was 11:45 by Italian time. I saw you get off the train, I saw you get into the car driven by your father, I followed you home through the streets of Milan. . . . There you are in your room . . . all intent on giving the latest news to your mother, your father, and on receiving some. . . . And I felt so happy for you, because of the comfort you finally were getting from seeing your dear ones and your familiar things around you; family, home . . . those two treasures that I'll never have again.

    . . . When it was 11, I was tempted to make a phone call to Milan 44360, just to hear your voice and get the news of your trip, whether you had arrived safe and sound. . . . I was afraid it would seem too much to you, that I interfere between you and your family as soon as you arrive; I stood fast and overcame the temptation. I was at my desk until 1:30 A.M., without sleeping. . . . I wrote, I read . . . then I went to my room in search of sleep.

    . . . Write to me immediately, my Marta: please! Affectionate greetings to your parents. With the endless love of

Your Maestro

---

[1] The separation from Marta, now back from Paris, is once more traumatic for Pirandello, who finds himself alone again in Paris—with an immense emptiness.

{ 320122 }

To Marta Abba
Via Aurelio Saffi 26
(Italy) Milan   Paris, 22. I. 1932

My Marta,

I just received (it is five minutes before noon) your letter of the evening of the 20th. At the beginning I was alarmed: what is this? But after reading the first few lines I relaxed again.

Follow, my Marta, the impulse of your heart, if you believe that your visit might bring some help to a noble cause, such as the one you are working for.[1] Perhaps through Marpicati[2]—or even without Marpicati—it will not be difficult to obtain an audience. It will be a great satisfaction for you. He will receive you. He will congratulate you on your success, he will ask you what your plans are for the future . . . and the pleasure of seeing you will be such that he won't spoil it with other questions that could lead the conversation to topics that only you, and not he, would like to touch upon; or perhaps you would not appreciate the topics he would like to touch upon. This is what went through my mind, because I know the man. In one word, I don't have any illusions about getting any result. Only the satisfaction of being received remains, and the envy your enemies will experience out of it. It is something, without doubt, but will it be enough if you are expecting more?

The thick network of the combined interests in the world of the theater is intertwined in such a way—since the formation of the Corporation of the Performing Arts—that it won't be possible to break through and penetrate it. He himself[3] has allowed that to happen in order to put himself behind a shield against any extraneous claim. He sends everything back to the corporation, and he washes his hands of it. Giordani cannot be eliminated anymore because of that.[4] He is part of the corporation.

---

[1] Marta had written to Pirandello that she wanted to ask for an audience with Mussolini with the purpose of getting Mussolini's support for her effort to develop a company dedicated to art and to promote the best Italian repertory, against the monopoly of the "gang of enemies" who were only interested in the commercial aspect of the theater and favored foreign plays.

[2] Arturo Marpicati was at the height of his political career, occupying many positions of great power and prestige in the Fascist party and of chancellor of the Accademia d'Italia. See an important documentation of Marta's visit to the Duce in Alberti, *Il teatro nel tempo del Fascismo*, p. 55 (see also pp. 29, 30, 36, 55, 56, 203, 215, 341, 343).

[3] Mussolini.

[4] Pirandello is explaining the reason he is not hopeful about Marta's visit to the Duce,

Since the union of theater owners and managers has elected him as their representative, he is ex officio a member of the Corporation of the Performing Arts, as he is also ex officio a member of the Council of the Società degli Autori. . . . This being the situation, how can you have any illusions? However, my complete lack of trust should not stop you from taking all the steps you feel you should take. If there were, I don't say the certainty, even a probability that you could obtain what you wish by abandoning me, I would tell you: don't bother anymore with me, go along with the others, leave me alone; but you will not be able to go along with the others, because you are noble, you are honest, you want to see justice, you love art, and the others hate you, as much as they hate me and don't want me around. With them, I would feel weak and defeated, even if they offered me the baton of command, while I feel strong when I am alone, and the more alone I am, the stronger I feel. That's why I told you yesterday that, fortunately, after the daily chronicling of events, there is history. We must loathe the chronicling. All the critics are in it. But the work, if alive, remains in history. There is no need for such a work to be written; any noble work, a proud achievement, an act of courage, anything like that will overcome this petty chronicling and gain for itself respect and admiration—even if for a short time, if not forever, even for one moment—if it can serve as an example, or as an incentive, or as a condemnation for all the good-for-nothing and cowardly people.

Marpicati, after all, I believe will be able to advise you very well, since he is very close to what's going on. He is a good friend, you can talk to him; you may make him aware of so many things that he probably doesn't know; and you can learn from him things we do not know, what kind of wind blows up there for us. . . . You can tell him that I had in mind to write to him and find out about those things and that, when I get a chance, I'll do it, but that for the time being he can confide in you.

My Marta, I am in an atrocious frame of mind. I can't keep on living like this . . . I am suffering too much; I don't see any reason to live and suffer like this. My own company the whole day alone has become intolerable to me, and I can't wait to get rid of myself and finish it.[5] I don't feel like working, I don't feel like doing anything. All the fire that is still in me, so much of it, serves only to burn my soul, and no other purpose. And isn't it better then to extinguish the fire of my life forever?[6]

Your Maestro

---

who had personally allowed Giordani, Pirandello's archenemy and head of the "gang of enemies," to obtain a position of great power in the new corporation.

[5] It might seem ironic that only a couple of paragraphs before, when writing about his

repugnance to "joining" the despised "gang," Pirandello had affirmed: "I feel strong when I am alone, and the more alone I am, the stronger I feel."

[6] This unexpected long argument in favor of suicide is probably prompted by Marta's recent departure from Paris and the consequent recrudescence of the sense of loneliness in the Maestro—thus opening again the wounds of his never-healed depression.

{ 320126 }

To Marta Abba
Via Aurelio Saffi 26
(Italy) Milan   Paris, 26. 1. 1932

My Marta,

I received your letter of Sunday evening, after your visit to Marpicati. As far as I am concerned, I found out that on the evening when I gave my talk on Verga "he"[1] went to see a performance by English actors, although he had sent word to the Academy that he was not coming to my talk "because he felt very tired." He was punished, because that night the English actors were performing a play by Vosper[2] that, according to the admission of the author himself, is "Pirandellian"; as a result, trying to escape from a talk by the real Pirandello, he ended up with a work by a false Pirandello. Come on! What salvation can I hope for my art in my country from a man who has chosen to set his artistic expressions and aspirations at the level of Gioacchino Forzano's plays?[3] Better not to think about it anymore. After all, to tell you the truth, after the very sad experience I had with the Teatro Odescalchi first, and then with the famous project of the state theaters, I have given up thinking about it.[4] Now, however, either spontaneously or at the suggestion of someone else, this idea of getting an audience with him was born in you, and certainly, for you, it is something else, and "anyhow a good thing," as Marpicati told you—although I can't see how, beyond the simple satisfaction of being received. If that's enough, nothing else is necessary, as I have previously

[1] Mussolini.

[2] Frank Vosper (1899–1937), English actor and playwright. The play was probably *Marry at Leisure.*

[3] Pirandello despised Forzano's pompous and superficial style, which for him had become a symbol of the worst aspects of Fascist cultural rhetoric. Mussolini loved Forzano's work and gave him unconditional support.

[4] Pirandello here summarizes his disillusion in relation to Mussolini, who had not acted to provide the necessary funds to keep his Teatro d'Arte alive and had not kept his word about setting up state-subsidized theaters under Pirandello's artistic direction.

written; if something more comes out of it, it will be up to you to be satisfied with it or not, according to what you, or he, will feel about it. Anyhow, it will be good for the enemies to know that "Marta Abba was received by the Duce."

I don't want to give you any more pain, replying to what you say about my mood, which you call, improperly, "harmful nervousness." I wish that were the case! But you know very well that that is not it. I have no more nerves left. I have the blackest and most frightening despair that has ever happened to a man who is still "alive," alive for only one thing, in which all his life is concentrated! That's what I have, and I feel I can't last; I feel that it's no longer possible for me to resist this horrible urge that is forcing me to finish myself off once and for all. I have detached myself from everything and from everybody; I was holding on to life with a very thin thread of hope, which now has been inexorably broken. Change, move? Where do you want me to go? How can this feeling change?[5] It's the end. . . .

Maestro

[5] The feeling will change soon, when Mussolini will personally listen to Pirandello and, for a while, give the impression of seriously wanting a reform of the Italian theater, in which the Maestro was supposed to play a major role.

{ 320206 }

To Marta Abba
Hôtel Isotta
(Italy) Genoa   Paris, 6. II. 1932
　　My Marta,

. . . I've read—as you can imagine with the greatest eagerness—what you tell me about your visit,[1] about the impression you received of it, and the discouragement that overcame you because of it. Whoever does not accept—because he cannot accept—all that is today perpetrated against moral and spiritual values has a "bad character."[2] You too, my Marta, have a "bad character" if you intend to keep on acting nobly and honestly; on the contrary, you have a very good character if you go along with all their swindles; if you bow to all overbearing actions, accept all abuses,

[1] With Mussolini.
[2] Pirandello is referring to Mussolini's words to Marta during the audience, that is, "Pirandello has a bad character."

submit to the yoke, go wherever they want, and do whatever they impose on you, then yes, Marta Abba will have a beautiful character. Pirandello has a "bad" one because—called upon to honor Giovanni Verga—he has the courage publicly to denounce the person who was the reason that for such a long time prevented the Italians from honoring Verga as he deserves.[3] Pirandello has a "bad character" because, treated as he was by his own country, he got "all honors," as he[4] says (I would like to know which ones, perhaps the Accademia d'Italia, with Marinetti, Formichi, Angiolo Silvio Novaro, and company?);[5] but afterward—excluded from any active appointement to important offices; excluded from the theater; excluded from the Società degli Autori; made the target of a relentless attack by a criminal who has destroyed the Italian theater[6]—he was forced to flee abroad so that he could make a living. "Bad character" indeed, this Pirandello—who in the meantime continues to speak highly of him, exalting him as a savior of his country, as a constructive genius to whom Italy owes everything—while Italy cuts off Pirandello's livelihood, harasses him with taxes, and lets him risk starving to death. Come on! I feel the need of exalting his myth, even though he tells me that I have a "bad character."[7] I hold on to this character of mine with the greatest pride, whatever sacrifice it might cost, even the sacrifice of my very life. One day it will be known what this "bad character" was all about. Enough. My Marta, don't worry about anything and don't be afraid at all. You'll see, everything will change soon. As your success is certain, so must your faith be certain, too. You cannot fail. Calm your anxiety and your restlessness. Here everybody—Antoine, Kemp, Boïssy, Ray, Strowsky, everybody!—remembers you with the greatest and most sincere admiration. And they ask me when you are coming back. . . . I'm waiting for more news from you! Lift up your spirits, relax, and be sure about yourself as also about the endless love of

Your Maestro

---

[3] In a public speech on Verga given on December 3, 1931, at the Accademia d'Italia Pirandello among the general scandal had denounced his archrival Gabriele D'Annunzio—generally considered as the champion of the Fascist regime and enjoying Mussolini's greatest favor—as responsible for establishing a "style of words" (*stile di parole*) in the Italian literary world, in opposition to Verga's "naked and strong" art (*stile di cose*). This speech exemplifies Pirandello's ambivalent attitude to fascism and explains one of the reasons why Pirandello had several enemies in powerful positions, who also boycotted his theater. See Gaspare Giudice, *Pirandello* (Turin: UTET, 1963), pp. 453–54.

[4] Mussolini.

[5] Pirandello evidently did not feel that those people were worthy of the honor and was strongly critical of Mussolini's choices for the Accademia.

[6] Pirandello here refers to his archenemy Paolino Giordani.

[7] Pirandello felt that Mussolini's regime was a minor evil for Italy compared with the total chaos that he was sure would follow without him and therefore felt an obligation to "exalt" his myth and support him in public.

{ 320211 }

To Marta Abba
Hôtel Plaza
(Italy) Rome   Paris, 11. 11. 1932

My Marta,

I've received your letter from Genoa, written from the Teatro Paganini before your departure. I am still in bed, but more because of prudence than for any other reason. Paris is covered with snow, shivering in a polar cold wave, which was announced the other night by such a violent storm that the panes of my whole window right below the roof seemed to be on the edge of popping out at any time, letting the wind rush into my room, breaking and messing up everything. Then, after the storm had subsided, it began to snow, and the next morning, that is, yesterday morning, Paris woke up all white, chimney tops, roofs, trees, streets, and cold, so cold that I don't know how many more blankets I'd have to put on my bed to take shelter from it. Since there was not enough heat, I got somebody to bring an electric stove into my room, and with all this, my robe and the plaid on my shoulders, my hands still feel like a piece of ice, so that I can hardly hold the fountain pen. Just to think that two days ago it looked like spring had already begun! The weather has gone insane, like humanity!

. . . As soon as I get out of bed—I hope tomorrow—I'll get back to your play, about which I have never stopped thinking. Getting deeper into the play, I see that just as it will not be possible for him to become "everybody," so it will not be possible for her to become "one"; because of that she will not be able to "find herself" only in her love for him; nor will he be able to find it in himself to be "many" in order to fill all her life, which cannot be "one."[1] I'll also think, as you suggest, about the work for Ruggeri.[2] But I must find again the courage to get back to work, but my

[1] In this sentence Pirandello summarizes the central theme of the play *Trovarsi*, which at the time he was writing for Marta, about the dilemma of the actress required to "live" many lives on the stage and at the same time to be "one" for someone she loves in real life.

[2] Pirandello had already mentioned his first thoughts about *Quando si è qualcuno* in

soul is so depressed. . . . My present life is choking me; I feel an invincible disgust toward it. Only you, my Marta, can work the miracle of calling me back to Art; only for you could my inspiration flame up again.

I'm happy that the examination by the doctors had excellent results. It could not be otherwise. But also your soul needs to be kept up. Be calm and full of confidence, my Marta, certain at least of the endless love of

Your Maestro

---

letters from Berlin and now seems to pick up again the thread of those thoughts. However, he does not mention *I giganti della montagna* anymore, which he had announced as almost finished a few months before from Paris, in the middle of the negotiations with Shubert. Evidently at this point Pirandello thought of the actor Ruggero Ruggeri as the natural interpreter for *Quando si è qualcuno.*

{ 320214 }

To Marta Abba
Hôtel Plaza
(Italy) Rome   Paris, 14. II. 1932
    My Marta,
    . . . I am very sorry that you show so much regret over a disillusionment that I had foreseen and that I was expecting.[1] The man[2] is just as I described him to you, believe me, and therefore does not deserve your regret: rough and coarse human material, made to command mediocre and vulgar people with disdain, capable of anything and incapable of scruples. He cannot bear to see around himself people made of a different stuff. Whoever has scruples, whoever doesn't bend, whoever has the courage to tell the truth fearlessly, such a person has a "bad character." Notwithstanding all that, I recognize that in a time in our contemporary political and social history as "brutal" as the present one, a man like him is

[1] Pirandello here talks about Marta's disillusionment after her audience with Mussolini. The thoughts developed here are essential to an understanding of Pirandello's apparent contradiction between his private sharp criticism of Mussolini as a person and of the Fascist regime on one hand and his public statements made both in Italy and abroad, strongly supporting Mussolini and the regime, on the other. It is evident that Pirandello had no thought about the possibility of fighting a regime that he deemed, after all, to be a lesser evil than other forms of government, which in his opinion certainly would have been born from the Italian political chaos.

[2] Mussolini.

necessary, and it is also necessary to maintain the myth that we have made out of him and still believe and maintain our fidelity to this myth as a necessary hardship that—in certain times—it is useful to impose upon ourselves. We shouldn't therefore have regrets, nor expect from him what he cannot give. He has demonstrated what and for whom his inclinations are, and what his aspirations are (even in the field of the arts). Bearing the offenses that those inclinations and aspirations inflict on our self-esteem is the true proof of the unselfishness with which we keep faithful to his myth.

.   .   .   .   .   .

Maestro

{ 320216 }

To Marta Abba
Hôtel Plaza
(Italy) Rome   Paris, 16. II. 1932
    My Marta,

Last night I received your letter of the 13th. I am again in bed because of an inexplicable thing that suddenly happened to me at about 10:30, while I was sitting at my desk reading. Without warning I felt as if I were suffocating from a continuous explosion of gas inside my body, which was relentlessly pressing at my throat and preventing me from breathing or was actually pushing my heart up against my throat, and it was roaring so loud as to almost deafen me. I was congested; I tried to get up but I fell—my legs did not support me anymore; I pulled myself together enough to throw myself on the bed, where I remained until about two o'clock with my clothes still on, believing that I would die of suffocation at any moment; the continuous flow of gas that was shaking me all over was a frightening experience. I had hardly eaten anything for supper; it should not, therefore, be indigestion; certainly something had decayed inside—I have no idea what—and this putrefaction was causing that strange, frightening phenomenon;[1] I got up, went to the bathroom, and took some bicarbonate; I also drank some cognac; it helped a bit, but I still feel a great pressure in my chest, which hampers my breathing; also my arms are aching, especially at the shoulders and elbows, and my heart is pounding crazily in my breast. It feels like being poisoned by this gas

---

[1] Pirandello describes the symptoms of a heart attack.

that presses against the heart and the lungs. I could not sleep the whole night long. Now I feel a little better, so much so that I can write, but still, from time to time, the flow picks up again and overcomes me. I think that one time or another I'll die this way, alone, during the night, like a dog, and my only regret will be that of not seeing you again, my Marta, for the last time. Enough. Let's forget these melancholy thoughts.

. . . . . .

Maestro

{ 320222 }

To Marta Abba
Hôtel Plaza
(Italy) Rome Paris, 22. II. 1932
My Marta,

Your last letter of the 18th is full of worry about the condition of my health; when I read it I really regretted that I had written about it to you, thus causing you so much concern. I am not well, that's certain; it is also possible that my heart suffers from too many anxieties of my spirit— which never has a moment of rest and is oppressed and depressed and signals its condition with each ailment of my constitution because of a bit of badly digested food or a little cold, but what remedy do you think there is for that? What would all the doctors of the world be able to do? When the disease is life itself, from such a disease one can only recover by dying. And I have never believed in physicians and medicine. I know how to take care of myself, you may be sure of it—if a treatment is possible, and I always succeed in getting back on my feet, one way or another, after a fall, still without the need of a cane and even less of crutches, standing straight up. My heart, let's be honest, has every right to feel tired. One day or another, it will give up, and then good night! I wish it would not bother me too much until I go. I am smoking less, and please don't believe that I drink, my Marta; I keep a few bottles for guests, not for me; as a rule at lunch and supper, I drink mineral water; perhaps I should exercise more, but I've never been able to walk without a purpose. Enough; let's not talk about that anymore, and please be reassured, my Marta, that I am better.

. . . . . .

Maestro

{ 320310 }

To Marta Abba
Via Aurelio Saffi 26
Milan

Rome, 10. III. 1932
Via Piemonte 117

My Marta,

Yesterday I had lunch and a long conversation with Marpicati. I exposed clearly and without any rancor the situation that has been created around me, not only materially, but also morally, and I made clear to him that if that doesn't change, it is not possible for me to come back to Italy. He saw my point and told me that that situation will have to change, because the Duce doesn't like the fact that I live abroad and especially in Paris.

He said that on Saturday or Sunday he will talk to him at length, informing him thoroughly about everything, and that, if it can be arranged, he will ask for an audience for me, so that I can personally explain how things are. . . . I spoke with Marpicati also about you and about your visit to the Duce. I did not know that you had written to him (I mean to the Duce) requesting another audience; I know that you want to talk about things you did not have a chance to say the first time around. Marpicati agrees with me in thinking that there is nothing to be expected for the time being and that therefore any attempt is useless. It's a miracle if you can get him to understand the situation and if he leaves it alone, but it is absolutely useless to hope that he will do anything about it.

I've been here only for a few days and I've already had my fill of sadness for all that I see and hear. I feel oppressed by something indefinable. I who have nothing to reproach myself about; I who have nothing to ask; I who want only to work, work, and nothing else, as I've always done— I feel haunted by a shadow that impalpably hangs over me, takes away all sense of serenity, and makes me very uneasy.

Enough. I expect we'll somehow come to some conclusion. I hope to receive some news from you. I'll keep you informed about everything. Meanwhile receive all the endless love of

Your Maestro

{ **320314** }

To Marta Abba
Via Aurelio Saffi 26
Milan   Rome, March 14, 1932

My Marta,

I received your letter of Saturday, and you can imagine the joy it gave me—all the more overwhelming and profound because it was completely unexpected. I delayed one day in answering because my audience with the Duce was scheduled for yesterday evening, and I wanted to inform you of its outcome in this letter. Magnificent. I was received with utmost cordiality and permitted to talk about everything for about one hour. The audience had been scheduled on purpose at the end of the day's list because, being the last, it could then go on longer than all the others.

"Ah, Pirandello, at last I see you again! I'm happy to find you healthier and younger than ever! Sit down." These were his first words. I quickly noted, at the end of his first question, "What do you propose to do?" that he truly wanted to get into talking with me about *interesting and precise* things, and not confine the discussion to generalities and small talk, without any real interest. And then I began to tell him everything I had on my mind to tell him—everything—from *A* to *Z*—I poured out my insides— with the feeling as I spoke that all I was saying was *right*, with the appropriate tone, *proud and serene*, as if everything were being looked at dispassionately and not dictated by a personal interest or by a petty resentment. So much so that he allowed me to talk and talk, without ever interrupting me, except for brief exclamations of approval—"it is true"—"you're right"—"without a doubt"—the eyes sharp and shiny and fixed on mine, and the beautiful intelligent smile on his lips, clearly showing his enjoyment at hearing me speak. You can well imagine, my Marta, all the things I said to him in one hour of conversation; I left out *nothing, nothing*. It would take too long to explain everything in detail from the beginning to the end; I will relate it in person to you when I return to Milan. It is enough for you to know now that at one particular point, when I spoke to him about my plan for the ten regional theaters, which I had presented to the Società degli Autori to be forwarded to him, he angrily banged a fist on the table, exclaiming: "Please believe that this project was not forwarded to me! I will ask the Società degli Autori for an explanation." And he quickly jotted down a note. He wanted me to explain my project in great detail, and at the end he said to me: "I truly believe that this is the best way to solve the problem of the theater in Italy. Do not doubt it, Pirandello, I will study this project and I'll let you know what I think." These were his last words. I left the interview very happy with him and with myself. And you will also be happy, my Marta, when I relate all this to you in person, step by step. Meanwhile I handed over to Marpicati the notes you sent me for the honor to be conferred upon your father, and Marpicati promised me he will get busy immediately, and that he is sure to obtain the honor. I wrote to Bordeaux in the tone you suggested. I must stay here at least until Saturday because Pedrazzini set up the meeting with Marpicati and myself for the end of this week, and I want to go there with two scenarios already finished, "Donna Mimma" and "Esclusa." In the meantime I am rewriting the project[1] so I can send it directly to the Duce with an accompanying letter. I am full of confidence and enthusiasm. I do hope that my coming to Rome will bring such results as to change the course of the theater in Italy.[2] Perhaps I will make a quick trip to Milan to fill you in, and then return to Rome where my presence is extremely valuable at this moment. Meanwhile, send me your news, give my regards to your father and mother, and never stop feeling surrounded by the endless love of

Your Maestro

[1] The plan for the ten regional theaters.

[2] The conversation with Mussolini opens a new phase of great hope and enthusiasm for the prompt realization of long-cherished plans. Suddenly the dream of a decisive intervention by the dictator himself in favor of creating state-supported theaters under Pirandello's artistic direction appears not only possible, but truly at hand. What a contrast to the time of exile in Berlin, when a dejected Maestro was feeling excluded and ill treated by an ungrateful country and, in scorn and spite, was disdaining any contact with the Italian "dunghill"! Now he feels buoyant and plunges without reservations into a whirlwind of meetings at the highest level of Italian politics!

{ 320318 }

To Marta Abba
Via Aurelio Saffi 26
Milan Rome, 18. III. 1932

My Marta,

I received your letter of the 16th. I am in the midst of the most intense work and besieged from all sides. You must be patient, my Marta, and wait for me until Sunday evening, because I badly need your advice before making my decisions. I am leaving on the train you told me about that arrives in Milan on Sunday evening, and I'll inform you there about everything.

I had to reconstruct the whole project of the ten regional theaters, and today Mar. will bring it to the D.[1] I know that the latter, right after my visit, requested it from the Società degli Autori, and I know that the Società degli Autori informed him that they did not have a copy of it anymore. Meanwhile, yesterday morning, as if by some command, Forges-Davanzati, Gino Pierantoni, and Fedele,[2] all three standing at attention, appeared here in Via Piemonte;[3] they invited me to lunch in the country at the restaurant Al piccione and then to visit the new offices of the Società. I won't tell you what respect, what deference they showed me; they were hanging on my every word: "You are a giant, a giant!" Do you understand? They were scared by the command of the Duce. They kept here the amount of my income for the three-month period without sending it to Nulli;[4] they speeded up the payment of my pension, and all three as in a chorus repeated, I don't know how many times during the lunch, "You must stay among us, in Italy; the Italian theater needs you; an active force like yours, an energy like yours should not stay abroad." Evidently they were repeating a slogan they had received from on high. I got out of the situation with free and easy dexterity—courteous and serene. I do my work separately with Marpicati; I work directly with the Duce. Meanwhile I smell the moods of the enemies and I count the friends. I'll talk about all that in person.

. . . I'll send a telegram tomorrow evening confirming my arrival. In the meantime, have all the endless love of

Your Maestro

[1] Marpicati will bring it to the Duce. Pirandello uses abbreviations, probably as a measure of prudence in case the letter went astray.

[2] Forges-Davanzati was the president of the Società degli Autori; Pierantoni was the president of the Corporazione dello Spettacolo; and Fedele was the general director of the Società degli Autori. Pirandello is obviously enjoying the sudden change in the attitude of the highest brass of the Italian theater bureaucracy toward him, caused by the sudden change in Mussolini's attitude. He is now too busy to write even one word of despair in this letter and, in general, in those written during this honeymoon of high hope for Mussolini's personal miraculous "fixing" of the Italian theater.

[3] Via Piemonte 117 was the address of his son Stefano, where Pirandello was residing during his stay in Rome.

[4] Pirandello was in a state of legal war with his ex-agent Nulli, who claimed percentages on the Maestro's income.

{ 320402 }

To Marta Abba
Via Aurelio Saffi 26
Milan   Rome, 2. IV. 1932

My Marta,

. . . Here it seems that the situation is getting really good. The idea of furthering an understanding with Bottai[1] through Marpicati was certainly a good inspiration. I transcribe the letter I received from him right after he spoke with Marpicati. It was written by hand, not typed, and delivered by hand to my home. It reads as follows:

> Illustrious and dear Maestro,
>
> Last night, during a brief conversation, my friend and comrade Marpicati hinted at the belief—which I don't know what rumors might have planted in your soul—about my hostility toward your work in general as a writer and especially as a playwright. Marpicati will tell you, I believe, about my surprise and my pain in seeing attributed to me feelings and intentions that are so distant from the sincere admiration I have for you. I could quote examples of that, even recent ones, but a kind of shame prevents me from doing so—you understand. I hope I'll have an opportunity to see you. We'll talk about the problems of the Italian theater, for which we both care so much. Meanwhile, accept my best greetings. Bottai.

I answered as follows:

> Illustrious and dear Friend,
>
> I thank you for your letter—so clear and kind—which signals the end of a frame of mind that, I confess, was bitter and annoying for me. I too do wish to meet and speak with you—not about the political value of my work as a writer, but about the problems of the Italian theater—being certain that an agreement between my experience and yours could bring some fruit. With my best greetings. Pirandello.

Yesterday, as a result of this letter, I had a phone call from Bottai inviting me to lunch at his home for next Tuesday, *asking my permission* to invite also Pierantoni, as president of the Corporazione dello Spettacolo, and De Pirro, as secretary of the same corporation, so that this discussion

---

[1] Giuseppe Bottai, one of the founders of the Fascist party, was undersecretary and then minister of corporations, governor of Rome, and, from 1936, minister of education in the Fascist government.

about the theater might have a conclusive character. I accepted immediately to make sure that the discussion would happen in the open, instead of behind my back. I'll defend my plan to the last, even more strongly now since I found out that after eliminating D'Amico, they don't have the foggiest notion about what to do, and because of the Duce's wish that every means should be tried to keep me in Italy.

That's the news. I'll go to that meeting armed with great prudence. My tactics will be very simple: those of one who *wants to give*, and not of one who *wants to receive*. It is the country, it is the regime that must want me for something good; I don't want anything for me; I want to give energy, work, ideas, for the good of everybody, in a disinterested way. The good of everybody will be also my good, because it is as well the good of the Italian theater. I believe that the time is really ripe. He has reached the firm belief that at last something serious must be done. He won't fail because of any fault of mine.

This morning I had a long talk with Interlandi, who came to see me at home. He also shares the opinion that I should stay in Italy. We talked about many things and also about the newspaper.[2] On the 9th, the board of the *Giornale d'Italia* will meet to deliberate about the project, which has already been studied by its owner, the honorable Castellino. However, perhaps it's not good to put too much meat on the fire, or at least too much at the same time—so as not to alarm the disillusioned, the jealous, the envious, and the unhappy people. What makes me feel a little disheartened is this livid atmosphere—all soaked in envy, greed, and voracity. One has to look out, in front, behind, and all around; they attack anyone who gains a prominent position, but they fight by means of veiled rumors, instigating fear, throwing discredit all around. The air is therefore pestiferous, and I don't know whether my lungs can stand breathing it for a long time.[3]

. . . .

Maestro

[2] Pirandello refers to the project of starting a newspaper with his collaboration in a position of importance.

[3] This letter is very important for a better definition of the reasons for Pirandello's exile—here it appears clearly that they have not only an amorous component, but also a political one (see, for instance, letter 320122 and 320206). It also provides insights into the oppressive climate under Mussolini's dictatorship, reminiscent of feelings expressed by the Maestro almost four years before, in letter 280922.

{ 320427 }

To Marta Abba
Hôtel Eden
Viareggio   Rome, 27. IV. 1932

My Marta,

At last I've received your telegram with the announcement of your departure from Viareggio and the address where I can write to you.[1]

These have been incredibly busy, dizzy days for me. The Congress,[2] the negotiations. . . . I found the time to be present in the evening at the Teatro Valle, which was really a triumph. The theater was packed in every category of seating, *parterre des rois.* The applause at the end of *Pensaci, Giacomino!* was a great comfort for me, because it made me feel again the fervent approval I used to have from Roman audiences, and to have it back—so full, so warm, so long, so intense, in the presence of the representatives of the whole international theater world—was for me an immense satisfaction, even more so since I found out what was done behind the scenes to take it away from me. Forzano, furious, did not hesitate to run to the Duce and protest so that *Villafranca* might be performed instead of *Pensaci, Giacomino!* Against everybody else, D'Amico, backed by Bottai, fought strenuously against him and against making him look like the principal representative of the Italian theater, while there was Pirandello, who is considered such by the whole world. The whole Federation of the Theater, plus Pierantoni and the party secretary, were for Forzano. Luckily D'Amico prevailed. The interpretation by Tòfano was truly magnificent; the success, also to the honor of the Italian theater, I repeat, was triumphant. There was a procession of visits to my box, beginning with Max Reinhardt and then from all the international members of the Congress. Max Reinhardt requested *As You Desire Me* for Thimig.[3] Tomorrow afternoon, at last, I'll sign the contract with Cines and in the evening I'll attend the performance of *Enrico IV* by the Dutch company De Vries, who came at the expense of the Dutch government to pay homage to me.

---

[1] Marta had just concluded her negotiations for the purchase of the Villino Mezzaluna, a summer home located in the Lido di Camaiore, near the resort city of Viareggio. See the end of this letter.

[2] During the International Theater Congress Pirandello's play *Pensaci, Giacomino!* was performed as the official Italian production, thus prompting a number of Pirandello's enemies to feel envious and enraged.

[3] Helene Thimig, Viennese actress, daughter of Hugo and sister of Hermann Thimig, was the wife of Max Reinhardt.

... I can't wait to breathe a little more freely, and I want to have the joy of seeing your beautiful Villino Mezzaluna. Consider yourself surrounded by the endless love of

Your Maestro

{ 320504 }

To Marta Abba
Costa Fiorita
Lido di Camaiore
(Italy) (Viareggio)   Paris, 4. v. 1932[1]
    My Marta,
    I traveled from Viareggio to Paris together with Bottai and his wife, who came here for the Paris Fair, in return for the visit to the Milan Fair by the French labor minister. I can't even begin to tell you about all the courtesy during the whole trip and about the conversations he himself wanted to have about the theater; he told me that he will be in Paris only for three days and that as soon as he is back in Rome, he will start to phone the construction companies in the various regions which, like the Monte dei Paschi, could take over the burden of financing the construction of the theaters without weighing on the state budget. He is really full of the best intentions. "At your return from Paris," he said, "you'll see that I'll already have made all the preparations for the construction of the theaters, and then, once the financial foundations are laid down and those problems are solved, we'll go together to see the Duce and discuss with him the artistic part of the project; if necessary, we'll call the Counsel of Corporations, after an agreement with the secretary of the party. You'll see, this time we'll come to a serious conclusion; meanwhile I will tackle the problem of a repertory to free the companies from the monopoly."[2] In Paris, as soon as we arrived at the Gare de Lyon, the Italian ambassador came to meet him with the French labor minister, the

---

[1] This letter is written on the letterhead of Luigi Pirandello, 37, Rue La Pérouse. Pirandello had gone from Rome to visit Marta in Lido di Camaiore, and now was back in Paris to take care of many business matters left unfinished at his departure for Italy. The primary purpose of this trip, however, seems to be the closing of his apartment in the Rue La Pérouse, in preparation for his definitive return to Rome. It is therefore a very important step, marking the official end of his exile, after almost four years of keeping his residence abroad. Marta was to reach him in Paris toward the middle of May, and then both would return to Italy at the end of the month.

[2] This was the longed-for answer to one of the main complaints by Pirandello—that

consul, and an army of photographers and reporters; I drew myself aside, but Bottai called me and wanted me to stand near him in the pictures that were taken at his arrival; after that we parted with the promise that we would meet again before his departure, if the official invitations should ever allow some spare time. . . . News: the most serious is the decision that Thalberg[3] seems to have reached of doing the film of *Six Characters* after finishing *As You Desire Me*, about which Lawrence (the representative of Metro-Goldwyn) reports wonders; he says that Garbo's interpretation is *amazing*, and that the film will be *sensational*. There is, moreover, a great interest in me in England, stirred up in great part from America. *Tonight We Improvise*, a translation of *Questa sera si recita a soggetto*, was published in a magnificent volume, and in London two volumes of my short stories will also be published. Here theaters, cinema, everything, is dead. Dullin, after a twenty-day revival of *Il piacere dell'onestà*, left for a tour of the provinces. Yesterday Baty interrupted the rehearsals of *Come tu mi vuoi* because his father is dying in Lyons, but Crémieux is enthusiastic about the rehearsals he has seen and foresees a roaring success. Rehearsals will resume as soon as Baty comes back, and I hope I'll be able to be there. . . . It seems that the condition of the French film industry is disastrous, and the results of the election will only make things worse because the banks are against a leftist government and will deny now more than ever any credit to the industry.

. . . Here the weather is horrible; it is not cold; on the contrary, the air is tepid, almost like spring; in one word, like at home. I'm expecting you and your mother with open arms, and I can't wait for your arrival; I do need your advice to wind up my affairs here. By no means can I now lose my contacts abroad; there is a great revival of interest in me in all countries; everywhere I am the only one who is *truly alive*, and the time of the really great harvest is starting right now; I must not confine myself to Italy, cutting myself off at this moment. Affectionate greetings to your family, and all my endless love for you from

Your Maestro

---

the monopoly of theater owners and managers was enslaving all Italian theater companies, imposing a purely commercial, almost exclusively foreign repertory, thus killing any chance of developing an artistic Italian repertory.

[3] Irving Thalberg, director of Metro-Goldwyn-Mayer.

{ 320804 }

To Marta Abba
Villa Mezzaluna
Costa Fiorita
Lido di Camaiore
(Viareggio)[1]   Castiglioncello (Livorno),
                                                                      4. VIII. 1932

My Marta,

I've received your telegram and your letter; but I had already heard the news through a phone call from Nicola de Pirro in Rome. Also yesterday, I subsequently received a letter from De Feo, which I transcribe:

> Illustrious Maestro,
>
> With great regret I just received the following telegram from Metro-Goldwyn-Mayer: "Immensely sorry incapable of timely sending magnificent filming *As You Desire Me* by Pirandello stop Your telegraphic request arrived ten days ago does not allow to prepare copy in time and ship it for arrival Europe and Venice at desired moment stop We plan sending it anyhow as soon as possible very happy great writer might check how film was realized."
>
> Thus one of our greatest hopes has failed! We count always, illustrious Maestro, on being able to have you in Venice. I wanted anyhow to com-

---

[1] After departing from Paris with Marta, Pirandello resided on the Via Piemonte in Rome with his son Stefano. At the beginning of the summer, from June 25 to the end of July, he was a guest in Marta's Villino Mezzaluna at Lido di Camaiore; Pirandello and Marta had planned to be in Venice together for the film festival, where they were counting on the great success of the film *As You Desire Me* with Greta Garbo, which had been just released in the United States. At the time of this letter, Pirandello is in Castiglioncello—not very far from Marta's villino—as the guest of his son Stefano and intent on finishing his play *Trovarsi*. Andrea Pirandello, the grandson of the writer, wrote to me in a letter of April 26, 1991: "Castiglioncello meant the Villino Conti and this was the cheerful home where Stefano and his family used to go for vacations. We spent the whole summer there, and Pirandello stayed with us sometimes for months—to our great joy. Those were very long summers, because for both my grandfather and my father it was an extraordinarily intense time dedicated to creative work. There was the kind of cheerfulness that is born where there is a fervor of creation and where there are children. Pirandello was quite happy during those months, although he did pass moments of pain and discomfort. . . . And then Castiglioncello meant the dozens of artists, writers, painters, musicians, and people of culture who were always together with Pirandello outside the hours of work. The Villino Conti was the meeting place for dozens of people every late afternoon and every evening."

municate the above to you. With devout and grateful thoughts, yours,

Luciano De Feo.

As you see, all the malignant rumors about the failure of the film in America are false, and on the contrary your supposition—that Metro-Goldwyn had not had the time to send the film to Venice—is correct.

... Here I got back to my intense work schedule, in order to finish quickly *Trovarsi*. ... Here the place is truly delightful: a paradise. Such silence! Such tranquillity! Enchanting natural beauties, much, much better than Viareggio, Camaiore, or Lecco—I tell you, a true paradise. I spend the whole day working, in view of the sea. In the evening I see a few people, D'Amico, the painter Corcos, the painter Bartoletti and his wife, Pasquarosa, Pavolini, and a few more. Tomorrow Bontempelli will arrive. Tell me whether you are going to Milan, and give me your news, my Marta! Although it is so beautiful here, I cannot forget Mezzaluna! and all your affectionate hospitality! Back to work. Best greetings to your mother, Cele, and your father. ... All the endless love of

Your Maestro

{ 320822 }

To Marta Abba
Villetta "Mezzaluna"
Costa Fiorita
(Viareggio)   Castiglioncello (Livorno),
                                                  22. VIII. 1932

My Marta,

I believe that I have found, through one of your suggestions, the finale for the play.[1] Donata, alone in front of the mirror, seeing herself again in the dress and the makeup of that scene, recalls the line of the play that brought about her "liberation," and then relives the whole scene of the third act that signaled her triumph in the theater. The other actors appear inside the room, but only as images of her recollection, as "personified voices" of the other actors, while from a distance behind her, the arch of the alcove widens into a proscenium and the bed curtain opens up as a stage curtain. The scene of the recollected play must be brief, condensed, and powerful; the *true* theater audience should applaud, because little by

---

[1] Pirandello is talking about the play *Trovarsi*, which he was writing and in which Marta was to play the main role, the actress Donata.

little the hotel room has transformed itself into a stage, into the stage of the theater where she had performed. If by any chance the *true* audience does not applaud, no problem—we'll pipe in the applause from beyond the arch of the alcove, so that it will appear also recollected. With this applause the evocation is over, and Donata finds herself alone in front of the mirror, still with her mask as an actress and empty-handed.

I believe in this way I found what was still lacking in the third act: the touch of inspiration. And I owe it to you.

. . . Colin has been here for two days, as usual talking all the time of many things and never reaching a conclusion. Now he would like to go to Viareggio to greet you, and I would like to take advantage of this occasion by accompanying him and bringing by hand Donadio's letter, while tearing this one up, but I am still in doubt because I do not know what trains leave for Viareggio and whether we are still in time to catch one that would arrive at a decent hour. Then I think that perhaps you would not like to see me again within such a short time of my last visit; perhaps you would prefer never to see me again.

I feel like just dropping everything and going back to Paris for good. That way at least there would be the distance in between! To suffer this warmth with ice in the soul; to continue working, when I do not see any more reason for doing it or even for lifting my arm to pick up a pen; to open my mouth and say things that do not make sense anymore . . .[2]

It's better that I let him, Colin, go alone to Viareggio and that I give him this letter for you. I hope to see you soon, my Marta; give me your news; best greetings to your family—and receive all the love of

Your Maestro

---

[2] It appears that the time spent near Marta during the month of July had only confirmed to Pirandello that no change had taken place in the "feeling" of the actress toward him, thus exacerbating the deep wound of his unrequited love.

{ 320904 }

To Marta Abba
Via Aurelio Saffi 26
Milan   Castiglioncello, 4. IX. 1932

My Marta,

. . . And now let's come to our play. Reading between the lines I had the impression that you did not like the third act very much, or that at least you kept to yourself many unfulfilled hopes about it, and many suggestions that you have given up passing on to me. But I really would not know what else to do with it. I confess that it pleases me as it is, and I see that it has pleased everybody here, as much as Strenkowsky and Cele over there. Let's hope for the best. I fully approve whatever you say about costumes and makeup. The scene of the imaginary drama takes place, according to my idea, in the hall, or rather in the room of a grand hotel, occupied by the protagonist (as in the case of Donata), with the difference that the protagonist in this scene is a great adventurer, and the scene takes place in the summer during a great feast in a hotel.[1] The protagonist has her lover enter her room, while downstairs—in the hotel garden— people are dancing; his wife has come to catch them by surprise, and then the protagonist throws her out. What was above all important for me was the following: that the character performed by Donata that night in the theater is a woman who can have a true love, in absolute contrast with Donata, who can't. And I would like Donata's last line—when she gets up from the vision of the performed scene—to be spoken with the perfect conviction of a conquest, with the sincere pride of a triumph of the spirit: "And this is true! . . . And it is at the same time not true at all. . . . True is only that we must create ourselves, and create other things. Only there, then, do we find ourselves."[2]

Although it did cost me much trouble, I am after all happy, my Marta, for having written this play—almost inconsistent in the plot (as it was supposed to be, after all) and yet so clear and eye-catching in every movement of the spirit. It is really uniquely for you, made for your art, which consists of fervor and intelligence—luminous and clear, vibrant and penetrating. Nobody except you will be able *to live it* on the stage; it is absolutely yours, without the slightest possibility that any other actress might make it hers.

[1] See letter 320909 for a discussion of the play's focal point.
[2] *Trovarsi* means exactly that, "to find oneself."

. . . I finally gave in and bought at half-price the FIAT car offered to me by Senator Agnelli: a splendid 524 L, for 16,500 lire, to be paid in two installments six months apart. So I'll come to Milan by car, if I can find a chauffeur. Before that, however, I'll drive back to Rome with a temporary chauffeur that the agency in Livorno will provide for me. Enough, I've now become a rich man. But I always remain, with all my endless love for you,

Maestro

{ 320908 }

To Marta Abba
26, Via Aurelio Saffi
Milan   Castiglioncello, 8. IX. 1932

My Marta,

I am really worried about your situation and the condition of your spirits—so exacerbated right on the eve of the new upcoming enterprise that is so important for you and for your artistic future.[1] You need to gather together all your energies; your mind should be free from every concern; your soul should be serene, and your body strong and ready. How is it that your family does not understand that? Why don't you understand it yourself—with your intelligence? You talk about an abyss that inexorably opens up in front of you—but how? Where, my Marta? Within your family? In the secure haven of your home where—although you are not understood, although you are not paid the attention that everyone owes you, although, because of silly touchiness or thoughtless assumptions, you do get hurt—still you cannot deny that you are loved and that everybody takes the kind of care for your interests that nobody else can ever take in equal measure? I don't understand what kind of decision you want to make, for which you believe you need so much courage; a decision that, if you do not find that courage, "will become much harder and *increasingly* serious for you." As a principle, my Marta, decisions should never be taken in a state of anger; on the contrary, with the greatest calm and careful consideration! Passion blinds, you know, and you never know where you may end up. You have your head well set

---

[1] Marta was scheduled to start rehearsals in October for the debut of her new company with the world premiere of *Trovarsi*, which took place on November 4, at the Teatro Fiorentini in Naples.

on your shoulders, enough not to lose it and suddenly find yourself in a dangerous position, from which it might later cost you God knows how much difficulty to retreat. Be very careful, my Marta, and think it over— think it over calmly; somebody about whom you can be confident that he will never fail you tells you that. I would like at least to be of help in this, in giving you that unshakeable point of reference, that sense of security for your uncertain and troubled soul; the certainty that if tomorrow, God forbid, you should find yourself in danger, at the limit of endurance, in the midst of vicious conflicts—you'll always have me in your corner; and therefore you should not think that a decision, if put off, may get increasingly serious. I'll not die that soon, unless I am killed by a too strong and unbearable grief. Do not believe—in the situation in which I find myself—in the golden dreams that you wish me at the end of your letter! What golden dreams can I have, if I must stay away from my only life? God knows how I manage to resist, inside myself, without showing anything outside. Work has helped so far; I hope it will continue helping, but if tomorrow I should not see any longer the reason and the purpose of it. . . . Enough, now it's your life, my Marta; but I consider my life to be so dependent on yours, that—knowing you to be in the midst of such a conflict, of such turmoil—I am in equally great turmoil myself. Last night I could not sleep, thinking of you. Right now I'm tied up with moving, which must be done today; tomorrow at five in the afternoon I'll be in Rome; on Tuesday I'm going to Cines and I'll talk with De Zuani; on Wednesday I'll leave for Milan. If I can't go by car because I still do not have a chauffeur, I'll leave by train from Sarzana and I'll be at your place on the morning of Thursday. I hope I'll find you calmer, my Marta; if not, I'll do all I can to calm you down. Don't be afraid that I may fail you at the opening in Naples, or at the last rehearsals of *Trovarsi*. Can you imagine! I would rather drop everything in Paris. However, the opening at the Montparnasse must be soon, if not imminent.[2] They are already rehearsing; if these rehearsals are a continuation of those at the beginning of the summer, they should be pretty well along; anyhow, today I sent a telegram to Crémieux and asked him to let me know the precise date of the opening. So I'll know what to do about my departure. . . .

Be perfectly calm, my Marta, everything will be all right; bear up and have confidence, and never think that it is an empty word when I tell you to feel completely secure in the endless love of

Your Maestro

[2] In letter 321108 Pirandello will announce the "magnificent success" of *As You Desire Me* at the Montparnasse in Paris.

{ 320909 }

To Marta Abba
Via Aurelio Saffi 26
Milan   Castiglioncello, 9. IX. 1932

My Marta,

I've received your calm letter of the 6th, and I read it over again three times—such was the effect of your rare, noble, and yet sorrowful serenity. If only we could always watch from above the events and happenings of our life—as sad and unlovable as they can be—and not somehow lose the will to keep on fighting!

. . . I am going crazy with the final scene of the third act of *Trovarsi*, which is still not coming right.[1] I don't want to get discouraged; it will come, by dint of trying and trying over and over again! This poor play received so many blows on its wings by getting out of the nest and trying to fly that now its wings are aching and wounded, and—still trying to take off and fly—it keeps fluttering and does not succeed. Such a thing never happened to me before. And yet I remember that I wrote *Come tu mi vuoi* when I was near you, following your tour around from place to place, putting the finishing touches on it in the Albergo al Parlamento in Florence; and yet so often I felt death in my heart in Florence while I was writing the last act. But perhaps I succeeded because—although I felt death in my heart—I did not make the mistake of reading the play to you piece by piece! The creation of a work is such a delicate process that it should not be shown until it is complete, because its living elements, in the act of intertwining and settling down among themselves, are so sensitive that they recoil or slow down at the slightest contrary impulse; they

[1] Here follows a very interesting passage, in which Pirandello explains frankly how every intervention from outside his own fantasy instead of helping was hindering his creative process, even in a case like *Trovarsi*, for which he had requested an intervention from the very human model from which the drama was drawing its inspiration; that is, Marta. In contrast to his habit of talking only in generalities about his work before it was finished, this time Pirandello had consulted with Marta several times about the basic plot and its development, had discussed the lines of the dialogue, and had read her the first two acts, which he had finished before completing the whole play. It had been an error, because that dialectical, fragile, but logical and theatrically moving flow born from his genius—revealing the connections and the psychological contrasts among the characters—had suffered a disturbance that had interrupted it, and now the work had trouble "finding" its own conclusion; that is, revealing its vital totality to the dramatic imagination of the creator. Pirandello's labor in the creative process was therefore an individual one, even though often suggested by incidents that happened in real life.

no longer find their spontaneous contacts; they risk breaking up and not finding their definitive and correct connections anymore. Now this has happened several times in *Trovarsi*, and the first one now who cannot *find himself* is me! But I keep trying, and you'll see that in the end I'll find myself; and then I'll make haste to send you the play—finished. For a few days, you can wait. The stage design is not difficult for Strenkowski, and the concept of the movements and of the lights does not need much study or long preparation. After all, the play is one of the simplest: the difficulty is in finding *the absolute*, with a woman who is an actress and wants to be a woman and as a woman doesn't find herself and risks not finding herself as an actress, then finds herself again as an actress, but doesn't find again the man who makes her a woman. . . . Well, because the absolute truth—unacceptable in life—is what Salò says in the first act: "either woman, or actress," which is what I've always been saying, that for me "either you live life, or you write it." But Donata is young, is beautiful, and wants also to live. . . . Her drama is this, and so much more complicated, because she is not able to close her eyes, and when she does, she runs the risk of dying and not seeing anything anymore. . . . How can she *find herself* that way? She loses herself and doesn't find herself again; or from time to time she loses herself, and does find herself again; and then *like all other women* . . . —and nothing more absolute! This lack of an absolute makes it impossible for Donata to be a *heroine*; it's the crisis of an actress, which is not overcome, because she doesn't want just one thing or the other, but wants both together, which is not possible if not *relatively* and therefore without a true conclusion. I must find a temporary conclusion, and a beautiful one! I'll find it.[2]

I am waiting, my Marta, for you to tell me whether you will be staying longer in Milan. It would be easier for me to come and see you in Viareggio. Still nothing from Cines. I am waiting for Mario Labroca to get back from Venice. Write to me! With the endless love of

Your Maestro

[2] Pirandello affirms his persuasion that the *absolute* is necessary to create a true tragic heroine; that is, the sphere of the very essence of human nature in which, in the formidable choice proposed by the existential dilemma, the character makes an irrevocable decision and suffers all the extreme consequences of that choice. Evidently a crisis that is common to the experience of many actresses—who do not know how to combine the stage and real life, and keep wanting both without coming to a final decision in the existential choice—might make a good play but cannot touch the sphere of the absolute. Such a crisis cannot create a heroine who suffers in the necessary conclusion the irrevocable consequences of her existential decision. The conclusion of a play about a common unresolved crisis can therefore remain only at the level of a successful momentary theatrical expedient.

{ 320912 }

To Marta Abba
Via Aurelio Saffi 26
Milan   Castiglioncello, Monday, IX[1]

My Marta,

I've received your special delivery letter of Saturday. I was moved by the interest you show in my work, making it your own—your own trepidation, your own heartbeat, your own life! I want to reassure you at once. The work is going forward. The blocking is overcome, the obstruction is cleared. It was enough for me to read the three acts to Massimo Bontempelli without any preliminaries, with a tranquil mind, and it happened, the same as it happened to you when you narrated the content of the play to Strenkowski: everything appeared clear—of a marvelous clarity and transparency—not only to him (which pleases me very much) but also to me, to the point of making me get again the idea of it, precise and whole, like a fruit to be plucked when fully ripe. And now only the work of actually picking this fruit is left, one or two days of work to commit to paper what I've already seen alive. The final scene is brief and of extraordinary effect. I am sending you for Strenkowski the description of the setting for the third act, so that he can work on the realization of what I want for the final scene. The setting for the whole third act is this: "Room in a plush hotel in a big city. Alcove at the rear, with the arch ornamented by a damask curtain that conceals the bed—accessible by climbing a step. In the front of that there is a drawing room, with a great sofa in the middle, a table in matching style, and armchairs. On the table a big lamp with a dark purple shade. On the left wall is the connecting door. On the right, the door that communicates with the next room, occupied by Elj. (Right or left *of the actor*.) This scene must be in strong contrast with the two preceding ones: dark, heavy, overcharged with dense colors as much as the others were cheerful, bright, and luminous. Now, for the final scene; that is, the one with Donata alone, seated in front of the mirror and beginning to take off her makeup—while in the act of taking off her false eyelashes, she evokes the vision of the theater and of the scene that gave her the final triumph—I would like to get this from Strenkowski: that Donata's vision becomes reality in that hotel room; that is, that this hotel room, so to speak, widens out, not only through the lighting effect of an unnatural vision, but also materially, to become a wider room, as for

---

[1] The date is September 12, 1932, as it appears on the postmark on the envelope.

a stage, with its imaginary audience in front of it, which is after all the real audience of the theater. Do I make myself clear? This can be handled easily and especially in the background, where the arch of the alcove is located with its damask curtain. Quietly, that means in silence and very slowly, the curtain must be opened, like a stage curtain, and from there the unnatural light of the vision should enter, while the arch widens on both sides starting from below and revealing from high up in the middle an architrave like a proscenium, more or less like this:

Closed arch   *Open arch*

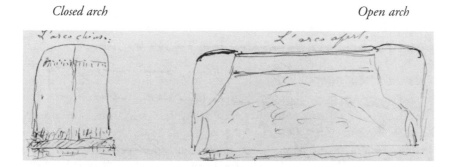

In the background the dark orchestra of a theater during a performance should become barely visible; but it does not matter if nothing can be seen in the semidarkness—all the light must be projected onto the stage. At the end of the vision, with a silent but very quick movement, I would like to have the widening disappear in one stroke, and at once the hotel room returns, narrowed, oppressive, without any other light but that of the purple shade of the table lamp, with the purpose of focusing the whole scene on Donata seated in one of the armchairs, alone, with empty hands, but with her head raised at the sound of the applause that is echoing in her ears.

The scene of the vision is strong, dramatic, almost a single monologue, with effective pauses and changes of tone, as if Donata, in certain moments, would no longer be sure of the words of her lines and would like to remember them, or to review them aloud and find the tone again, which eventually she gets right, and then picks up her performance for herself as she performed it in the theater. The effect, I hope, will be magnificent, or rather, I'm sure that you, with your art, my Marta, will make it magnificent.

I hope to be finished with it tomorrow. Meanwhile I sent the first two acts to Rome to get five copies typed. The day after tomorrow I'll send the third; and as soon as I have the five copies of the play, I'll send them to you in Milan, minus one set that will be for Mondadori, who will have to publish the book early in November.

. . . Write to me, my Marta. Courage and serenity. With all the endless love of

Your Maestro

{ 321108 }

To Marta Abba
Hôtel Excelsior
(Italy) Naples   Paris, 8. XI. 1932[1]
    My Marta,
    I've received your telegram with your good wishes—you can imagine how dear to my heart I found them—and with the beautiful news that the success of *Trovarsi* continues. From my telegram you have already heard about the magnificent success of *Come tu mi vuoi* in Paris. I'm writing now my impressions of last night's performance—both about the acting and the directing. Jamois performs with real passion the role of Ignota, and as everybody agrees, this is her best interpretation of a character in her entire career as an actress. I liked her a lot in the first act, much less in the second, and a little more in the third. But there is no possible comparison with the greatness of my Marta, even in the act she interpreted best; that is, in the first. I won't talk about the abyss that separates her from you in the great scene of the second act. That divine enthusiasm of yours, that impetuosity, and that fervor! Here detached chiaroscuros, deliberate impetuosity, and equally deliberate toning down: a scenic and not spiritual movement. When I heard the whole theater applauding her, I thought: Ah, if all these spectators could hear my Marta in that scene! In the third act, especially because of the well-thought-out movements worked out by Baty and the arrangement of the groups on the stage, she succeeded in infusing a certain dramatic impetus into all her lines, getting some very persuasive effects. Baty's direction is really beautiful. He succeeded in creating the atmosphere of Berlin in the first act in a truly

---

[1] The letters from November 8 through November 25 are written on the letterhead of Le Chateau Frontenac, 54, Rue Pierre Charron, Champs-Elysées, Paris. After helping out during the rehearsals and attending the premiere of *Trovarsi* in Naples on November 4, Pirandello is now in Paris where he has just seen, on the night of the seventh, the premiere of *Come tu mi vuoi*, directed by Gaston Baty. Marta is still in Naples, where the success of *Trovarsi* continues.

prodigious way. Ignota's entrance with the bunch of drunks was most impressive. Jamois's dress is beautiful, white, all rustling with silk, very wide, with black appliqués. The play of the lights, magnificent. The whole choral part was in powerful relief, but this is all due primarily to Baty. Roger Karl was an excellent Salter, and Vitray a very efficient Boffi. The applause was endless and most insistent, the attention of the public intense. I was in the director's box, and at the end I leaned out to express my thanks. Denis Amiel, Gantillon, S. T. Bernard, Bourdet, and other authors and critics came to the box to congratulate me; Bourdet, enthused, said that *Come tu mi vuoi* is my masterpiece. But now we'll have to hear the critics. The moment is certainly not favorable, with this violent tension in relations between France and Italy and with the xenophobia (that is, the hatred for everything foreign)[2] rampant. But there will also be friends. The success will be primarily of the public. But the crisis is deeply felt and the depression of the spirits and of the whole Parisian life is truly frightening.

. . . Last night everybody was talking about you. Everybody remembers you, full of admiration. Best greetings to your parents, and for you all the endless love of

Your Maestro

[2] This definition of *xenophobia* is Pirandello's.

{ 321125 }

To Marta Abba
"Compagnia drammatica Marta Abba"
Teatro Comunale
(Italy-Sicily) Trapani   Paris, 25. XI. 1932

My Marta,

. . . We did not rent the apartment in Via Po,[1] because I wanted to leave everything open until my return. The idea of having a home again, I confess, is intolerable to me, like a prison. I'd be able to have a home only with you. It is not possible for me otherwise.[2] And then, this continuous instability—which gives me at least the sense that everything is

[1] Pirandello was looking for a permanent residence in Rome, planning to live with the family of his son Stefano.

[2] This is the only explicit confession in the letters of his dream of "settling down" with Marta for the rest of his life. A couple of lines later, another important confession

precarious in this life, and that tomorrow might be what today is not—is a hundred times better. And let's keep it so, as long as it lasts; that is, as long as my forces assist me.

You ask me, my Marta, whether I have fun in Paris and how I spend my time. I spend the whole day in the hotel writing, correcting proofs for the publication of my complete theatrical work in ten volumes, and only in the evening do I go to a theater or to the movies. But so far there is little or nothing deserving to be seen. The biggest hit in Paris is *Come tu mi vuoi*: as they say here, *sans blague*.[3] I received many invitations to receptions, as I told you; today, the last, at the Society of French Authors, where President Kistemaekers gave a truly magnificent speech in my honor and presented me with the medal of *sociétaire*. But you know that all these feasts, if they flatter my vanity, eventually bore me to death and tire me. After the formalities of the reception, there was a banquet in which the most famous playwrights of France took part, and the banquet was over—think about that!—at four in the afternoon. Tonight I have dinner with the Danish director Carl Dreyer, about whom I already talked to you. In your letter you do not tell me anything about the results of *Trovarsi* in Palermo, but I suppose it went well; at least I wish so. Here Crémieux found the play as fresh as if written by a twenty-five-year-old playwright, and this gave me pleasure. Because, with a pen in my hand, I still feel truly very young.

. . . I'm waiting for your news in Rome. Meanwhile, my Marta, always feel the endless love of

Your Maestro

---

follows—that the hope of a change in Marta's attitude toward him, even if very remote, had not died in him.

[3] Literally "no kidding" or "seriously," that is, without any doubt.

Oil portrait of Marta Abba by the painter Primo Conti (1928).

Marta Abba in her early thirties.

Marta Abba during her stay in Berlin (1929).

Marta Abba photographed in Rome (1927).

(*Above and on opposite page*) A series of photos of the actress Cele Abba, sister of Marta, taken at the time of the letters.

Marta Abba on a sailboat off the coast of Venice in the Adriatic Sea (Lido di Venezia, summer 1934).

On the opposite page:
(*Above*) Marta Abba during her summer vacation in Castiglioncello (1934).
(*Below*) Marta Abba in the backyard of her summer home, the Villino Mezzaluna in Lido di Camaiore near Viareggio.

Marta Abba (*left*) in the Broadway hit *Tovarich*. The actress played the leading role of a Russian noble emigrée in Paris who works as a maid. *Tovarich*, an adaptation by Robert E. Sherwood of the comedy by Jacques Duval, opened on October 15, 1936, at the Plymouth Theatre, and had a run of more than 160 performances.

{ 321206 }

To Marta Abba
Compagnia drammatica Marta Abba
Teatro Savoja
Messina
(Sicily)   Rome, 6. XII. 1932
                                                    Via Piemonte 117

My Marta,

. . . I was supposed to write, as I had promised, after my visit to the D.,[1] but, I confess, I did not have the courage to do so. I got an impression from him that literally froze the blood in my veins. After the recent triumphal feasts of the Tenth Anniversary,[2] I expected I would find myself in the presence of a giant (because such is the image that people abroad have of him); I saw, on the contrary, in front of me a sick man, with a yellowish face, gray hair, hollow cheeks, almost lifeless, and not only so in his depressed body, but also, and even more so, in his spirits. As usual he received me kindly at the time assigned for the audience and asked immediately, "What do you have to tell me, dear Pirandello?" I answered that I was coming because of my duty as a citizen to report to him the meaning that France had expressly wanted to give to the honors that had been rendered to me with so much solemnity, and the message that all French intellectuals had charged me with bringing to Italy. I added that I was aware of the political reasons why Italy could not be pleased with such feelings and such testimonials but that, nevertheless, since I had received that charge, I esteemed it to be my duty to make them known to him. He let me speak to the end without interruption. He did not answer at all. At this moment, France is his obsession. Evidently, it was a great displeasure for him that France had treated me so well. In politics, today, whatever France does to Italy can only be evil. Therefore, silence. I then spoke about the two charges that I had received from the Italian foreign minister, one to go to the North Pole, that is, to Norway; and the other, almost at the same time, to the Equator, that is, to Egypt. He smiled faintly and told me that it was better for Italy that I go to Egypt. After that I talked to him about my project of the theaters, of which I had heard nothing since Bottai had resigned. At this point he started to talk to

[1] Duce. Again, Pirandello abbreviates the title of Mussolini to make it unrecognizable should the letter fall into the wrong hands.
[2] Ten years of Fascist rule in Italy.

me in a way I would never have expected. What he told me is really of an exceptional gravity. The political situation of the moment in the whole world is tragic; it has never been more tragic; anything can happen at any moment, and the probability of war is also imminent. Those were his words. Only general problems must be faced at this moment; the particular ones of each state in Europe and in the world, although very necessary, must take a second-row seat—all of them. As far as performing arts are concerned, the people must be satisfied with those that can be given for the masses, in the stadiums and the cinemas. For all the rest, we must wait for better times. He then wanted to hear about my plays. He had been informed about the success in Naples of *Trovarsi*. I talked to him about *Quando si è qualcuno*, which was supposed to be performed in Rome, and why it was not produced in Italy. "Is it because of the usual interference of the Suvini-Zerboni?" "No," I answered, "it is because of the present conditions of the theater. I have nothing to ask or to expect from those people." And the conversation ended there, nor could it end otherwise, after what he had told me about the state of the events in the whole world. We greeted each other with the usual kindness on his side, and that was all. I am still anguished by the frightening impression I received. I do not add anything else, my Marta.[3] Today I'm expecting Cele for lunch; yesterday she could not come, and on Sunday she couldn't either, because she had other invitations. Write to me, please, let me know something about you; the world seems lifeless to me. Have all my best wishes, and all the endless love of

Your Maestro

---

[3] Pirandello ends his letters of 1932 with this "frightening impression" of the visit to the Duce and this apocalyptic news about the world situation received directly from the highest Italian authority of the time. The dark clouds on the international horizon will stop many projects in Italy and will contribute to destroying Pirandello's dreams of enormous riches from abroad, which he thought were practically in his pocket.

Letters of 1933 from
Rome, Paris, and Castiglioncello

THE LETTERS in this group are characterized by expressions of tiredness, impatience, and disillusion caused by a thousand delays on
the part of Pirandello's immediate collaborators and by the growing international tension (1933 is the year of Hitler's ascent to power).
Pirandello's prospects of immense earnings outside Italy, which only a
few months before appeared sure, do not materialize, largely because of
the effects of the Great Depression in America, the political upheaval in
Germany, and the growing hostility against fascism in Great Britain and
France (the latter being the refuge of most Italian anti-Fascist exiles and
the object of Mussolini's increasingly bitter hatred). Pirandello's work for
the realization of the national theater continues, but in his heart doubt
slowly replaces enthusiasm. He begins to suspect that should Mussolini's
government appropriate significant amounts of money for the theater,
the usual profiteering by the usual exploiters would nip the reform in the
bud. The relatively frequent proximity of Marta, who comes and goes
following her company's movements, and the gleam of hope that soon at
least one national theater might be realized at the Teatro Argentina, all
seem to distract Pirandello from his latent depression, which in moments
of deeper disillusion never fails to surface again.

The year 1933 begins with Pirandello in Rome, tired and angry because
of serious financial damage caused by his agent Saul Colin's incompe-
tence, but still hopeful about the establishment of the national theater at
the Teatro Argentina. Back from Sardinia, Marta spends a good part of
January in Rome, performing with mediocre success. The Roman critics'
conceit and their refusal to recognize Marta's greatness make Pirandello
furious. In February Marta goes to perform in Turin, and Pirandello
leaves for Paris in the hope of getting rid of his agent Colin, who appears
to him to be one of the major causes of so much frustration and so much
damage. In the middle of March Pirandello again is in Rome, where
everything is stagnating in the lethargy of bureaucratic inefficiency. The
Maestro almost immediately leaves Rome to catch up with Marta, who is
now performing in Milan.

In May Pirandello goes to Bologna for the Writers' Congress, which this year assumes special importance because Mussolini, it is whispered, wants to use it for an attack on Giordani's monopoly of the theaters and against the abuses of the critics, accused of irresponsibly damaging the theatrical industry. Pirandello is fully involved in that struggle, which seems finally to be on the verge of bringing about the longed-for breakup of the monopoly. However, his contact with Italian political reality causes him to lose any remnant of faith in Mussolini and in the system. He comes to understand that his triumph against the monopoly would not change much the real situation of the Italian theater, because the state subsidies would land in the pockets of exploiters and not in those of authentic artists.

In June Marta goes to Rome to star in the film *Il caso Haller*, directed by Blasetti. The actress/manager is still exhausted because of the past theater season and the difficult negotiations for the next—she ends up with the heavy administrative burden of putting together the Compagnia Stabile San Remo Marta Abba, financed by the Commendatore De Santis, manager of the Casino di San Remo. While Marta is filming in Rome, Pirandello commutes to the capital from Castiglioncello, where he resides again at the Villino Conti for the summer. There, in sight of the sea, surrounded by Stefano's family and many friends, he works with enthusiasm on *I Giganti della montagna*, hoping to finish it before his trip to South America, scheduled for August 17.

The fact that only a small number of 1933 letters are preserved is due mainly to the fact that Marta was for long periods of time close to Pirandello. Moreover, during this year Pirandello was greatly involved in the Italian political maneuvers. We must also admit the possibility that some letters might have been lost or suppressed for reasons about which it is only possible to speculate. It is difficult, however, to admit that the playwright did not write to Marta about his triumphs in South America. On September 20, at the Teatro Odeón of Buenos Aires, *Cuando se es alguien (Quando si è qualcuno)* had its world premiere in the author's presence; on the twenty-sixth of the same month, Pirandello gave a lecture on Ariosto and Cervantes at the Teatro Solis of Montevideo.

After the great South American tribute, Pirandello remains in San Remo for about a month to help Marta out in the rehearsals of the Italian premiere of *Quando si è qualcuno*, which the Compagnia di Marta Abba presents on November 7 at the Teatro del Casino Municipale of San Remo.

In May 1932, with the closing of his Parisian apartment, Pirandello ends his residence abroad. From that time on he provisionally lives, when he is in Rome, with Stefano's family in the Via Piemonte and during the summer at the Villino Conti in Castiglioncello. During the late fall of 1933, Pirandello decides at last to settle down in Rome with Stefano and his family in the house at Via Antonio Bosio 15; the writer occupies the apartment upstairs, while Stefano's family lives downstairs. This event of great importance marks the end of Pirandello's voluntary exile and his definitive reentry into the orbit of his family. As it appears from the letter of January 8, 1931, Marta herself had already advised the Maestro "to stay in Rome with people who still love you." This advice was greeted by the Maestro as "a mockery." Only two years later, however, Pirandello's attitude has changed to the point that he decides to abandon forever his voluntary solitude and to get back into the life stream of his family and of the political-cultural Italian world. About life with grandfather at Via Bosio, the playwright's grandson Andrea Pirandello wrote to me the following: "Pirandello lived with us, dined with us, had supper with us, spent many hours of the day and of the evening with us, had fun with us, and also many times lingered in Stefano's study to converse energetically. And there was the other way around, when not only Stefano climbed upstairs to see his father, but also Ninnì went up to see Grandpa, and so did we. . . . Pirandello was happy to have found this haven; he did not suffer the terrible loneliness of certain periods in Berlin or Paris anymore. Although still suffering, sometimes cruelly, because of Marta's absence, he could write to her that life in Rome annoyed him because he was bound by so many obligations, being one of the most important personalities of his time. Moreover, certain aspects of family life also bothered him" (letter of April 26, 1991).

{ 330209 }

To Marta Abba
Teatro Vittorio Emanuele
Turin   Rome, 9. II. 1933

My Marta,

. . . I hope that the remaining two performances at the Pergola of Florence gave you the same satisfaction as the first. It was high time, after the bitterness of Rome![1] But believe me, my Marta, the air of Rome, as far as the theater is concerned, has become unbreathable. The conceit of those so-called drama critics, their priestly pompousness, the "absolute" of which they feel they are the custodians—and each judgment is something for which they have to give account only to God after having weighed and considered it over and over again in every way, in the spasmodic anguishes of their conscience—are clumsy to such a degree, that every soul of an artist, if it is even a little bit alive, cannot take them anymore.

Notwithstanding all that, I believe that your season in Rome, although financially most unfortunate, will produce beneficial effects, because after all the *acknowledgment* of the critics did happen, with the highest grades; and if they recognized that, you may be sure that from now on you'll be *a great actress*; until then, no! Unfortunately the world is that way, and for the person who doesn't want to take it as it comes one thing only is left to do: to go as quickly as possible, as I am preparing to do myself—I cannot really take it anymore.

. . . Meanwhile I am working on the preparation of a complete plan for setting up a Teatro Nazionale di Prosa in Rome.[2] We propose to use the Argentina as is, just eliminating the boxes; that is, reducing the boxes to

---

[1] As announced in letter 330103 (here not translated), Pirandello met Marta—returning from Sardinia—at the dock in Civitavecchia and remained near Marta during her company's performances in Rome. Notwithstanding disastrous financial losses in Rome, Marta for the first time obtained the "official" consensus of the critics establishing Marta Abba—although with reservations regarding some interpretations—as "a great actress." The letters begin again after one month, when Marta leaves the Italian capital to continue her tour, first in Florence and then in Turin.

[2] The big plan for many new theaters to be built in the major Italian cities, thus constituting a network of state-supported theaters, is now reduced to a last hope of transforming the old Teatro Argentina into a national dramatic theater. Pirandello is anything but optimistic about this last possibility. And, as usual when something does not go his way, he thinks of fleeing—again without a plan.

a series of balconies by taking away the dividers and making the space capable of holding at least 1,200 seats—to be sold at the same price as a movie ticket. The plan, from the financial point of view, is already completed; I am now preparing the artistic plan based on the notes I already took. When everything will be finished, I'll go to Alfieri and we'll go together to see the Duce. It is the last attempt I'm going to make to stay in Italy; if this also fails, I'll go away for good, and Italy will not see me ever again. It's lucky that I have so little time to live. But let's not speak of melancholy thoughts. I will not be the defeated one; if anything, theater in Italy will be defeated. I'll be always, and everywhere, a victor.

. . . Always think of me, and feel secure in my never-ending love,

Your Maestro

{ 330304 }

Paris, 4. III. 1933
54, Rue Pierre Charron
Le Chateau Frontenac[1]

My Marta,

. . . I marked on my copy of the *Gazzetta del popolo* the sequence of your performances in Turin after my departure, and in the issue of the *Gazzetta* that just arrived today I read about the happy success of *Ruota* and I was very pleased with it. *Marta Abba is today without any doubt our greatest actress*, the newspaper said. They say that now—they should have been saying that since your first appearance on the stage! Here everybody remembers your Parisian triumph. I've never found Paris so depressed in all her manifestations of life as she is at present. Everywhere it looks like a funeral. The crisis of the theaters, including the movie theaters, is perhaps worse than at home—which is really something. It's a general discouragement, like a gasping in emptiness. Giraudoux invited me to his box to attend a dress rehearsal of his *Intermezzo*: an exquisite first act, but the remaining two acts, zero. I also was at the premiere of *Le Téméraire* by Decoin, at the Théâtre des Capucines: two acts were like rapid

---

[1] Pirandello uses the letterhead of the Reale Accademia d'Italia, but writes by hand the address of the Chateau Frontenac in Paris, where he had traveled to discharge his agent Saul Colin and to reestablish a number of important contacts for future productions of his plays in that capital. The envelope with Marta's address was lost, but from the letter itself it seems safe to conclude that it was sent, like the preceding one (here not translated), to the home of Lucio Ridenti, Corso Galileo Ferraris 77, Torino.

sketches, the third like a comedy, but there it showed how bad it was. No doubt we'll soon see it performed in Italy by Ricci, because D'Arborio must have picked it up immediately for Giordani. Who cares what they do! By now. . . .

Here in Paris I saw Dino Alfieri, who had come with Fedele for I don't know what meeting of presidents and directors of authors' societies of various countries. I had lunch with him, and he promised that as soon as he is back in Rome, he'll have a long talk with me; but, as far as I could understand, no favorable wind is blowing in the Palazzo Venezia[2] for any attempt at salvaging the Italian theater. After all, I was suspecting that. Enough, my Marta, I am waiting for your news with trepidation. Best greetings for everybody, and my endless love to you,

Your Maestro

[2] Mussolini's headquarters in Rome.

{ 330316 }

To Marta Abba
Hôtel Bristol
Genoa   Rome, 16. III. 1933
                                                          Via Piemonte 117

My Marta,

I've received your letter of the 14th and I'm happy that your health has improved; I heard the same also from Prof. Capocaccia,[1] who wrote to me and, referring to you, assures me that you are "well," although he would have preferred that your rest had lasted longer. He talks, evidently, about the rest he imposed upon you when you wanted to leave for London. He wrote because he would like to be invited by the Academy for a scientific conference, but unfortunately I cannot do a thing for him, because the directors of the section for the sciences meet separately from us for their deliberations and right on the days when those of the section for the arts and letters do not meet; as a result we never see each other, except for the very rare general assembly, once or twice a year. The last time, for the Mussolini prizes, I was not present, and probably I will not go to the next, which will take place at the beginning of April, on the 9th or the 10th, for

[1] Marta's physician.

the nominations of the new Academicians. My presence is completely useless because of the servility of the Academy's president, who first goes to find out which names the first minister[2] would like to see nominated by the Academicians. The Academy votes for the names the first minister wants; if this is supposed to be the Academy's function, it might as well be suppressed and the first minister can directly nominate (as he actually does) whomever he wants. I don't say that he is wrong; he might be perfectly right. But there are already so many obedient people to do what he wants, that it is absolutely useless for me to expose myself and play the solitary act of expressing, according to my conscience, a contrary opinion. The majority decides, and I do not believe that history is shaped the way we want it. Later perhaps I'll write one myself, my way. But for the time being history goes this way, and there is little I can say, and even less I can do about it. I do not feel like being obedient to that extent—although I recognize as correct as always, my Marta, your reproaches about the many defects and mistakes in my behavior. I'm afraid I am really a "bad character"[3] and—at least in the desired meaning—completely incorrigible. So much the worse for me! But, instead of "improving" in that sense, I'd prefer to die a thousand times, as my life would become unbearable for me. At least I can say and make those who love me also say that if things go badly for me, it is my own fault.

Nobody talks anymore about the nomination of Giordani to be chief of Cines; on the contrary, it looks as though Töplitz will be confirmed, according to the latest gossip. But anyhow, in a few days the second installment for my film will be paid to me, and then they can do whatever they want. I would prefer that you do not bind yourself too early and without firm guarantees for that film in Rapallo, because there is a good probability of filming *Vestire gli ignudi* in Paris with Marais at the end of May. Anyhow, keep me informed. As far as the play by Bontempelli is concerned,[4] it seems that Suvini-Zerboni has given the exclusive rights to the Cimara-Tòfano Company, and therefore there is nothing we can

[2] Mussolini. Pirandello is getting more and more weary of being forced to participate in the parade of acquiescence to the dictatorial rule of Mussolini, especially because he sees that nothing is happening about the only thing he really cares about; that is, the creation of at least one state-supported artistic theater in Italy under his control.

[3] Pirandello refers to Mussolini's remark during Marta's audience that "Pirandello has a bad character."

[4] Pirandello had hinted, in letter 330313 (here not translated), at a play by Massimo Bontempelli, *Bassano, padre geloso,* as a possible choice for Marta's repertory.

do. Bontempelli himself will write to you about it. I'm leaving for Milan, as I told you, a few days before you do, and we'll meet there soon, my Marta. Cele and everybody here send you greetings. I'd love to get at least one more letter from you. Meanwhile have all my endless love,

Your Maestro

{ 330517 }

To Marta Abba
Savoja Excelsior Palace Hôtel
Trieste

Rome, 17. v. 1933
Via Piemonte 117

My Marta,

I've just come back from Bologna, where I attended the Writers' Congress, as you perhaps found out from the newspapers. I presented three motions, which were unanimously approved; I was chosen to be part of a committee that will visit the Duce and present to him the motions and the greetings of the whole congress, and I hope that we'll get something done; that is, first, a separate syndicate for theater writers that can confront that of the theater owners and managers, and then some ruling that can break the excessive power of the commercial theater monopoly. This latter motion was suggested to me by a certain Dr. Bizzarri from the General Federation of Professional Artists, who represented that federation at the congress. The suggestion seemed to me very timely. There is no doubt that *at the highest level* they are looking for a weapon to crush the monopoly. An additional proof of the above is a memo from the secretary of the Syndicate of Authors and Writers, signed by Corrado Govoni, in which I am invited to denounce everything that I think should be charged against the same monopoly. It is therefore evident that an inquiry is being made, after which appropriate measures will be taken. The congress was a triumph for me. Everybody went home with the certainty that we are on the eve of a solution of the theater problem in Italy. On the other hand, all the journalists are furious because of what was said about the drama reviews and the drama critics. I did not want to take part in that quibble, which became—at a certain point—excessive. I only said that a newspaper editor should be called to a higher sense of responsibility about the damage that a spiteful criticism can make to theater economics; that is, to the dramatic companies that are carrying the financial burden of the productions. A reviewer can easily demolish a play and drive away the audience from a theater—as if it were just a literary arena, while on the contrary the interests of a financial enterprise are at stake. I limited myself to saying just that, so that it might not look as if I had personal resentments against one critic or another. All the others threw themselves into personal attacks, with hatred and grudges, which certainly will cause lamentable aftereffects in the press—something that, at this moment, should have been avoided.

I wanted to inform you of everything, my Marta, but I am very tired. At the station in Florence, on my way to Bologna, I met Dr. Marigonda, who was going back to Venice and who spoke to me, in the few minutes during which the train stopped at the station, about your season at the Teatro Goldoni. I don't know whether he told you about it. Now you have been in Trieste for three days, and I don't know how things are going. It seems to me as if I had neither seen you nor talked to you for years, and therefore everything appears to me vain and inconclusive. I am picking up this letter again that I could not finish last night. This morning, the 18th, Marinetti called me to let me know that at 12 noon we members of that committee are going to meet at the General Federation of Professional Artists to decide with Bodrero when we'll visit the Duce. This evening, after that, I'll have supper with Bottai, and after supper Fedele, D'Amico, de Pirro, Bontempelli, Labroca, and others will come to my home—a small congress to talk about the big congress and about the problems of the dramatic theater. In the meantime I found out that Giordani ran immediately to Rome to defend himself and was seen last night with Forzano, who is the true enemy of any initiative for the rebirth of the Italian theater. Giordani cannot be eliminated without at the same time eliminating Forzano; all the problems are in this alliance, because it is well known that Forzano is protected by the Duce. Unless, at the last moment, Forzano, afraid for his own skin, abandons Giordani. But then the danger will be Forzano; although Forzano alone, without Giordani's backing, will not be able to do all the damage that they can do together. . . .

But enough with those theater imbroglios. I heard at Cines that Solza, the new director, is very interested in making a film with you. Cecchi told me that. It is evident that Solza was instructed from higher up.[1] Of course, I did not even hint at that. "It was high time!" I remarked to

---

[1] See in Alberti, *Il teatro nel tempo del Fascismo*, p. 341, the correspondence in which Mario Solza, the new director of Cines who had taken the place of Lodovico Töplitz, is informed of Mussolini's explicit wish that Marta Abba be engaged as an actress in film productions of Cines.

Cecchi. "Now that Solza says it, it will be done; when I told you, you allowed Mr. Ruttmann to have the last word.[2] But that's how things are done in Italy. . . ." Enough. What is certain is that this time you'll make a film. And it will not be the only one. I don't know whether that's the reason you wrote that you'll come to Rome as soon as your duties with the company are over. You can imagine how I am waiting for you, my Marta! With your presence I'll have air and light again.

Give me your news immediately, please. I hope that your father has recovered and that, with some rest, he will soon get his health back. Meanwhile give him my best wishes and my warm regards, together with regards from all my family. They all send their cordial greetings to you too. With all my endless love,

Your Maestro

[2] Walter Ruttmann, the German director of the film *Acciaio*, had made heavy changes in the scenario written by Pirandello, and eventually was backed by Cines in his decision not to engage Marta for the role of Chiara Diana that Pirandello had written expressly for her. See letters 30811, 320905, and 320915.

{ 330713 }

Castiglioncello (Livorno),
Villino Conti
13. VII. 1933 - XI[1]

My Marta,

You can imagine with what joy I read all you wrote about the results of your first film tests—in spite of those reservations of yours which did not make me laugh, but rather made me admire all the more your noble artistic conscience that if on one hand gives you continuous torment, on the other, through your fastidiousness, promotes your continued progress. I have always been certain about the results, and now that you too believe in them, I would not want them to encourage something bad

[1] Around this time Pirandello begins to use the year of the Fascist era (1933 = XI until October 28; then = XII). From now on but without consistency he often adds it to the Christian era and sometimes uses it instead. The envelope is not preserved, but it is clear from the text of the letter that it was addressed to Marta in Rome, where the actress was filming *Il caso Heller* (a movie produced by Cines, directed by A. Blasetti, and released in the same year, 1933). Pirandello is vacationing in nearby Castiglioncello in the Villino Conti with Stefano's family. The letters of this period are very few, because Pirandello frequently was in Rome with Marta.

rather than something good. I don't see anything wrong if they make it possible for you to combine your great expressive power, your intelligence, your beauty, your youth, in one word, the whole of you, to the profit of noble and beautiful things also in the field of the movies. Unfortunately, however, I am afraid that—following your sudden revelation and great success in this field—any scoundrel with a hundred one-thousand-lire bills in his hand might come along trying to seduce you into stupid, false, and vulgar things for the current film trade.

I was informed by Salvini—who passed by here by car with the actor Renzo Ricci, both heading for Florence—that you received a new proposal from the ill-famed Bonnard for a film to be made in two versions; that is, in Italian and French. I know Bonnard's bad taste and the horrors he has always perpetrated. I don't know how he still succeeds in finding a way to "work"! He is one of the three or four major persons responsible for the failure of Italian filmmaking. And he still persists, with Righelli, with Palermi and all that crew! I'm horrified by just thinking about the possibility that Marta Abba could fall into such hands and put her art and her intelligence at the service of such people and of their unworthy endeavors. Luckily there is your intelligence, my Marta, which will serve as your shield, and your awareness of your personality and of the dignity of your art; and so the scoundrels will not succeed. There are many, many more of that type in the field of the movies than in that of the theater; if you so far happened to meet good people, don't have many illusions for the future, my Marta!

I am terribly worried about the tiredness you are noticing, after working so hard all year long, and I tremble at thinking about all that is still left to be done; I tremble, I say, for your health. You need absolute rest, now, to restore your strength and prepare yourself for the work of extraordinary responsibility that is waiting for you! As far as the theater is concerned, you already reached the best you could desire, and that must remain in the field of your great successes, as it has always been. There will be, and there must be, also the cinema, yes, but only as a complement. If only we were in America! But we are in Italy, unfortunately, where the cinema is destined to remain confined within very modest limits. And you'll make all the earnings that are there to be made, do not doubt, when the right time comes, without overtiring yourself now at the risk of ruining your health and of depriving yourself of timely and necessary rest.

Perhaps I'll come in a few days by car, to sign the contract with the House of Ricordi for *La favola del figlio cambiato*, and on that occasion I'll take Fausto with his family in my car from here to Castiglioncello.

I'll come at once to Cines to see the film, which will be almost finished, I'm sure, and perhaps we'll be able to leave together, my Marta; you will hopefully remain here for one or two days, and then continue to Viareggio. By the way, you did not tell me whether your parents are already back there.

. . . I am very worried about my enforced absence during the period of the formation of your company for next year. The contract from America has arrived, and there is no doubt that I will leave on August 17. I'd like to finish the play, but I must also prepare two lectures, and during the time that you will spend in Viareggio I will devote myself to helping you to fulfill the very serious task that you accepted in San Remo.[2] I don't know how I'll manage. I am working, and I feel that the work is coming very well, with inspiration! I am working with the sea in front of me, and the sun has already burned my face, like last year. But if I think that you are there, under the lights of the reflectors, doing very tiring work, I feel guilty.

Enough, my Marta. It is late, and I want to mail the letter. Until soon. I'm waiting for the telegram from Fausto. Tell him, if you see him. At least I'll be able to see you for one or two days. Best greetings to dearest Cele, who, I see, has accepted the role. Congratulations! With all the endless love of

Your Maestro

[2] Pirandello is referring to the formation of the Compagnia Stabile San Remo Marta Abba; that is, the new company that Marta had succeeded in putting together with great effort and with the financial backing of Commendatore De Santis, owner-manager of the Casino di San Remo. A few days after this letter, which is the last one in 1933, Pirandello went to Rome, picked up Marta, and drove her to her peaceful refuge in Lido di Camaiore. During the month that preceded the departure of Pirandello for South America the Maestro and Marta were often together—one staying in Castiglioncello and the other in Lido di Camaiore. After his return from Argentina, Pirandello and Marta again were together in San Remo to prepare the Italian premiere of *Quando si è qualcuno*, which took place on November 7. The lack of letters until February 1934 might be explained by the frequent encounters that probably continued during the tour of Marta's company, between November and February.

Letters of 1934 from
Rome, Milan, London, and Paris

T|HE LETTERS OF 1934 begin in February. Pirandello has just left Marta in Milan, where she has opened her new season at the Odeon with the promise of continued success. The Maestro is now in Rome, extremely busy with the preparations for the production of Gabriele D'Annunzio's *Figlia di Iorio*, which is scheduled to open in October at the Argentina on the occasion of the Fourth Conference of the Volta Foundation. His health is failing. Increasingly serious financial worries have taken the place of earlier dreams of enormous riches; his income is shrinking, both from a Europe in the midst of political and economic crisis and from the United States, where Lee Shubert cannot fulfill the commitments already made. Moreover, the expenses of the ménage at Via Bosio are increasing, and he is reduced to setting all his hopes on winning the Nobel Prize to meet the expenses of this financially worrisome year. The boycott against the composer Malipiero and against Pirandello's *Favola del figlio cambiato* deeply wounds the playwright. Unfortunately Mussolini does not like the work, finds it offensive to religion and especially to the monarchy, and forbids further performances. Pirandello cannot take defeat. Expressions of great tiredness, despair, and desire for death surface again in the letters, signaling a fallback into the worst depression. In May the playwright and Marta are close again, but at the beginning of June the renewed separation for the preparation of the Volta Conference aggravates his painful depression, which makes him see "no reason for anything anymore."

During the summer, Pirandello is again in Castiglioncello at the Villino Conti, where the nearness of Marta and of his family and the beauty of the landscape help him to regain his inspiration. The play *Non si sa come* is written almost effortlessly. Creative work exhilarates the Maestro, who describes at length the content and originality of the play as the story of "two legitimate loves, between which the reality of a dream thrusts itself as a terrible antagonist. You don't know how!"

Pirandello discusses with Marta the project—ahead of his time—of a resident theater, possibly in Milan, and gives the criteria necessary for the success of such an enterprise.

In November at last the great longed-for news of the award of the Nobel Prize arrives, thus opening a new phase in Pirandello's life. After the lull of activity and the acute financial problems, a deluge of offers and invitations from all over the world now overcomes the Maestro, with endless feasts in Paris and in London, and, in December, the ceremonies in Stockholm for the awarding of the high recognition from the hands of the king of Sweden. The impatient expectation of having Marta as guest of honor at his side on this occasion is frustrated by a serious car accident in which Marta's father is injured. However, the hope of finding Marta in Paris on his return from Sweden gives the last letters of 1934 an optimistic surge.

{ 340224 }

To Marta Abba
26, Via Aurelio Saffi
Milan   Rome, 24. II. 1934 - XII
                                                          Via Antonio Bosio 15

My Marta,

... There is something more than my health that at this moment is seriously worrying me; that is, the particularly difficult moment I'm going through now. For the last two years I have not concluded any contracts, and what is left in my account is reduced to a minimum. All my expenses are going up; my taxes are also increasing (I pay five thousand lire every two months); my income is diminishing; all my revenue sources are shrinking, and I have no idea what I can do about it. I've even thought about giving up my car, although it is necessary for me, since I live so far away[1]—now that I don't have enough strength to walk. The day before yesterday Antonelli called me to let me know that Capitani was considering making a film drawn from his play *Il Maestro*; he said that he had talked to you about it in Milan and he wanted to know from me what I thought about it; *just from me.* "Dear Antonelli," I answered, "what do you expect me to think about it? Why do you address just me? If you spoke with Marta, probably Marta told you that she had proposed to Capitani my novel *L'Esclusa*; but if now—because I asked for a price that

---

[1] Pirandello is now living in Via Bosio, in the *quartiere* Nomentano, a good distance from the center of Rome.

Capitani does not feel like paying—Marta agrees to make the film from your play, I have nothing else to say, because Marta is perfectly free to do whatever she wants." But doesn't it seem strange to you, my Marta, that Mister Antonelli would address just me on that matter? I smell a rat, and I suspect that it is not true at all that he talked with you in Milan, because otherwise you would have told me. Given my present financial problems, I would not mind coming to an agreement on a payment that I could lower to fifty thousand lire (Capitani offered me forty) plus a percentage—to be negotiated—on the profits; of course, only in case you have nothing against such a deal and if you still like the idea of doing *L'Esclusa*; we could say that I gave in on the price to please you, since you like the subject—or something else, if you don't like that. What do you say? Fifty thousand lire at this moment, until the award of the Nobel Prize (if I get it!), would certainly be a godsend for me!

. . . Don't worry too much about me, my Marta, and about all that I told you; I have always more or less managed, and this kind of difficulty disturbs me only for a short while. After all, I have so little time to live, and when something can't be done anymore, it just can't. Nothing wrong with that.

Write; give me more good news; be happy and healthy; best greetings to your family; affectionate greetings from Stefano . . . and all the endless love from

Your Maestro

{ 340324 }

To Marta Abba
Hôtel Royal Danieli
Venice
                                        Rome, 24. III. XII
                                        Via Antonio Bosio 15

My Marta,

I've received your dear letter of the 22nd. I gave the interview you advised me to do about the *Favola del figlio cambiato*; but the animosity against Malipiero[1] (perhaps more than against me) is so strong, and the determination to boycott this very beautiful work is so obvious, that I don't think the rescue sworn by all our intelligent friends will be success-

---

[1] Gian Francesco Malipiero, born in Venice in 1882, was the leading opera composer in Italy at that time.

ful. Tonight there will no doubt be a big battle, and let's hope that the presence of the Duce will help in somehow containing it. Last night, at the dress rehearsal, everybody liked both the libretto and the music, especially the first two acts; the execution of the third appeared to be deficient, both as far as the orchestra, conducted by Marinuzzi, and the singers are concerned. In Germany this third act was the best—I was assured of this by some German critics coming from Berlin. Other orchestration and quite different singers! Enough. Let's hope for the best. You'll find out about tonight's reception of the opera in Rome from tomorrow's morning papers, before you receive this letter.

. . . As far as Stefano's play is concerned, Stefano doesn't want to give you any trouble at all, my Marta, and if you decide, as best for you, to put off its production until October, that is, until the next season, do just that, which will be all right with him too. I too believe it's better so, not only for you, but also for him.[2]

I'll follow your advice not to take over the responsibility for *La figlia di Jorio*, because the situation of the Compagnia Stabile San Remo for next October is still uncertain.[3]

Without any doubt I'll come to Turin, as soon as you call me. Here in Rome there is nothing new. Bontempelli's play lasted only two days. I saw the *Conte Aquila* by Alessi;[4] half theater, the rest just padding; the play is in the style of Forzano but without the latter's vulgar dramatic guts; the last act ended with the audience booing and hissing, but the press did not report that because it is known that Alessi enjoys high favors, and the play looks like a self-promotion for taking Forzano's place. Enough! My Marta, receive all my endless love,

Your Maestro

---

[2] The play by Pirandello's son (pen name: Stefano Landi), *Un Padre ci vuole*, had to wait until January 21, 1936, before seeing its premiere at the Teatro Alfieri in Turin, presented by the Compagnia Tòfano-Maltagliati-Cervi.

[3] According to a number of letters not translated here, Marta had several problems with the financial administration of her company, which was in the hands of lawyers at the service of Commendatore De Santis, the owner-manager of the Casino San Remo. Marta had advised Pirandello not to take any final responsibility with De Santis for the production of Gabriele D'Annunzio's play *La figlia di Iorio* until that murky situation was cleared up (Pirandello spells it *Jorio*).

[4] Rino Alessi, a journalist and playwright in the pompous style of Forzano, born in 1885.

{ **340329** }

To Marta Abba
"Compagnia Stabile S. Remo Marta Abba"
Politeama Chiarella
Turin   Rome, 29. III. 1934 - XII
                                              Via Antonio Bosio, 15

My Marta,

I wanted to wait for your arrival in Turin to let you find, as soon as you arrived, my answer to your last letter from Venice, with my most affectionate best wishes for Easter and for the season that you are now beginning.

Yes, my Marta, preconceived hostility, ignorance, bad faith, and deliberate malice won out against a beautiful work, created in purity of spirit and perfect nobility of art. No audience had ever before treated me to a spectacle of incivility like the one on the night of the 24th, which has pained and offended me all the more because—through their malignant interpretation of my allegory—they wanted to attack the musician against whom the animosity, better, the hatred, was directed. And it is not known why; or, better, it is very well known—because he is the best among all the modern composers in Italy. The flop was purposely exaggerated, so much so that by orders from on high further performances of the opera were forbidden. This way the insinuations spitefully disseminated in advance by newspapers, that in the fable there were indecent situations and offenses against religion and the monarchy, found credit. Now the fact is that Malipiero, about twenty days before the opening, wrote a letter to the Duce and asked him whether he thought that it would be *politically opportune* for him—that is, Malipiero—to withdraw the opera and never permit it to be produced, since people wanted to give it such an arbitrary and evil interpretation. Well, after fourteen days (that is, with plenty of time to see and consider whether there really was in the opera any reason for those malignant interpretations), an answer came from the head of the press office to Malipiero, saying that his worries were excessive and assuring him that the performance of the opera would take place in an atmosphere of perfect serenity. You can imagine, after that, how the word about the prohibition of the performances, by order of the Duce, has pained and surprised us. Both I and Malipiero immediately wrote a letter to him to express our grief and our surprise. Not satisfied with that, we also sent a letter to Bottai. The latter sent an answer to Bontempelli, who was with us, in the following letter: "Dear Massimo, last evening I succeeded in seeing the Chief; too late to try to get in touch with you or with the other friends. I'll tell you personally on my return about the long colloquy, from which I drew the persuasion that we are facing a *personal* unfavorable judgment, *not of the persons*, for whom he had high expressions of esteem, but about this particular work of theirs. I succeeded in getting from him the promise that he will receive both our friends, to express to them his admiration and talk about what he expects from their collaboration. If Pirandello and Malipiero will request an audience, perhaps through Marpicati, they'll find the ground ready for it. I add, for Pirandello, that every political consideration of the type he was afraid of is out of the question. And for Malipiero, that he should not worry about the conservatory of Venice.[1] I'll be away from Rome until after Easter, and I hope that, at my return, we'll meet immediately. Greetings to our two dear friends, to whom I'd like to be able to give much greater proofs of my affection."

Malipiero left for Florence, but Stefano informed him about this letter from Bottai. I am waiting for his answer to decide together what to do. In the meantime the opera has been enjoying a triumphal success in Germany.

. . . Again Happy Easter, my Marta, also in the name of Stefano and Olinda.[2] With all the endless love of

Your Maestro

[1] Malipiero was aspiring to become director of the Benedetto Marcello Conservatory of Music in Venice, which he did in 1939.

[2] Olinda was his daughter-in-law, Stefano's wife.

{ 340405 }

To Marta Abba
Turin[1]   Milan, 5. IV. 1934 - XII

My Marta,

. . . I already sent to Mondadori volume 14 of my *Novelle per un anno*, new short stories that will be published, I hope, before the end of May, during the new Book Fair. Meanwhile in England a new volume of my short stories translated into English has been published, which is having a great success. In great confidence I tell you (but we must keep it a tight

[1] This letter was addressed to Marta Abba in Turin, but the address to which it was sent is not preserved.

secret) that Gabetti has confided to me that for the Nobel Prize out of *ten* voters on the first scrutiny I had *nine* in my favor; that is, almost unanimous. I also received a letter from Universal in California, in which the director himself, Carl Laemmle, requests a script for a film. Do you understand? They request directly from America, while nobody asks me for it here in Italy. . . . The nomination of Giordani has caused great alarm and havoc in the whole field of the Italian cinema,[2] with all the independent producers, whose contracts he tore up, committing unheard-of abuses and overbearing actions of an unthinkable arrogance. Can you imagine that he denied payment of nine hundred thousand lire (almost one million) to Capitani—money received from sales of films by Capitani himself, among them *Il caso del giudice Haller*—telling him, without further remarks: "I won't give them to you; sue me." Do you understand? Capitani, Besozzi was telling me, is therefore grounded, because without that money he does not know what he can do. Legal action means losing two or three years, and in the meantime you stay put with your hands tied, without doing anything at all, waiting for the verdict. The scoundrel is profiting from that to oblige him—compelled by need—to agree to a compromise, subtracting two or three hundred thousand lire from his money. And in a civilized country we must allow a rascal of that kind to commit such overbearing actions that could not be committed even in the wilderness! . . . Marchesano supposes that Giordani will not last long because a flood of protests has reached the Banca Commerciale from all sides, which will make Giordani's position indefensible. If only that would happen, and soon! He already has a horrible reputation in the business world, and although he still has big shots who are protecting him, they won't be able to protect him much longer outside of his own field, which so far has been the theater. In the world of theater he has already caused bankruptcies, and people won't allow him to cause more bankruptcies in other fields.

Enough, my Marta! The world is truly not a cheerful place, and I assure you that I can't wait to remove myself from it as soon as possible. I did hope to enjoy a little peace, after so many struggles, at least during my last years, and hope, as everything else, has turned empty. I cannot take it anymore.

Best greetings from my family, especially from Stefano, and all the endless love of

Your Maestro

[2] Giordani had been named head of Cines, the state organization for the production of films.

{ 340429 }

To Marta Abba
Teatro Verdi
Trieste   Milan, 29. IV. 1934 - XII

My Marta,

I've been in Milan for two days, called by my lawyer, Granturco, for the Nulli lawsuit, which should be settled before long; that is, when the reason for the fight is obviated by the expiration of the contract. Ah, what a trap civil law is! In order to obtain nothing, with all the right on my side, I'll have to pay several ten-thousand-lire bills—which I do not own—in expenses and lawyers' fees, and this if an intelligent judge will decide the case in my favor, because the contrary is also possible! I'm here in Milan trying to patch things up, and doing my best. The case looks good, but who can trust anything? The person who is right always loses, especially when the guilty party has nothing to lose. May God help me!

. . . If you only knew, my Marta, in what a state of deep sadness I am living, and in the midst of what anguishing exile my soul is little by little fading away. Only one last light was left to me; but it too. . . .[1]

Enough. Why do I upset you so?

Your mother has just called me on the phone. She received your letter from Trieste and gave me the news that you wrote about the trip, about the telegram from Reinhardt,[2] and about Capitani. I am happy. Write back to me. To you all the endless love of

Your Maestro

[1] Pirandello appears to be lingering in his depression, less violent than in the previous years, but not less profound and constant. Moreover the Maestro is involved in an endless quagmire of lawsuits and financial troubles. He does not fail to repeat from time to time his more or less veiled reproaches and his appeals to Marta, his only "light." The actress, always very busy with a million other things, seems to have found a modus vivendi, which certainly does not satisfy Pirandello but permits an important artistic and practical collaboration with him.

[2] The director Max Reinhardt was inviting Pirandello to be present on May 2 in Milan at a performance of *Six Characters* at the Teatro Manzoni.

{ 340604 }

To Marta Abba
Compagnia Stabile S. Remo Marta Abba
Politeama
Como

Rome, 4. VI. 1934 - XII
Via Antonio Bosio 15

My Marta,

. . . I find myself here like a fly without a head, which happens every time after you leave—when I have spent some time near you.[1] I feel as if I were far away from life itself and I don't see any reason for anything. I'll get back to work today or tomorrow. I'll write some short stories. But Mondadori told me that, in the volume that was ready for publication, the prefecture of Milan marked a passage about which it hesitated to assume responsibility, and therefore they sent the whole set of proofs here to Rome to get the imprimatur from the Central Censorship. Now the fact is that the problem was about an old short story, which has been around—many times printed and reprinted—*for twenty years*, and that passage, as can be seen from the context, is perfectly innocent, without a minimal offense to anyone. All that is ridiculous, and it makes people lose the wish to write. If we must continue that way, any writer worthy of respect will throw away the pen with indignation. To whom will all that be of any use? I wrote to Ciano at the suggestion of Mondadori, and just now Ciano's secretary phoned me not to worry because the permit has already been sent to Milan and therefore the volume will be published without delay. Thank God! But in the meantime this disturbance, caused by the prefecture, did happen, and the true nuisance is exactly that the alarmed subordinates, fearful of assuming responsibility, will create a mountain of such hindrances, spreading bad feeling among the writers.

Enough. In three days you'll be back in Milan to start your new work in the movie.[2] I hope everything will go well, without any unpleasant-

---

[1] During the month since letter 340504, Pirandello had spent most of his time near Marta, who was performing in Milan. The Maestro is now involved in the organization of the Convegno Volta, a convention of which he is the president. He is therefore obliged to stay in Rome at least for the month of June. This new separation has the usual effect of leaving Pirandello in a state of depression.

[2] Marta was going to star in the film *Teresa Confalonieri*, directed by A. Brignone. The script had been taken from *Il conte Aquila*, a play by Rino Alessi that Pirandello did not esteem worthy of Marta's talent. In letter 340504 (not translated in this volume) Pirandello had tried to dissuade Marta from accepting the role.

ness for you. I am waiting here for the committee to decide whether it will be possible, or not, to realize the celebrations for the Convegno Volta. The committee should meet before the end of this week. I'm waiting to hear their decision. In Rome one can hardly breathe because of the heat, but I'll have to stay here at least for the whole month of June. Nothing new for the time being. Write soon, my Marta, and let's hope for the best! Say hello to the Lake of Como for me, and receive the endless love of

Your Maestro

{ 340726 }

Castiglioncello (Livorno),
Villino Conti, 26. VII. 1934

My Marta,

By the time this letter reaches you, you'll have already wound up— with tonight's final performance—your hard work, of which you should be proud and happy, as I know you are.[1] From far away, every evening, I have seen you again in my imagination, as in a dream, so harmoniously composed, all radiant and intellectually brilliant, noble and totally pure, in the splendor of your beauty and of your art. And I thought, my Marta, more about the incomparable nobility of your beautiful soul than about that of your physical person, if that's possible! You cannot imagine what a joy it was for me, on the eve of my departure, to be together with you for a little while and see you happy—at least about the results of your year of intense work—happy like a little girl, clapping your hands, with smiling eyes. In the whole world there is no purer and nobler creature than you, my Marta!

Now you'll get some rest on that enchanting beach of the Lido; probably you already went for a swim; you'll find, I hope, a moment of time to write and keep me informed about what you intend to do. You'll find my address at the top of this letter. I went immediately to work as soon as I arrived. I've almost finished the first act of *Non si sa come*, which is coming along very well: quickly conceived, straight as an arrow. Only five roles; precise, totally immersed in a dense atmosphere of mystery, which

---

[1] Marta has finally completed her hard work on the film *Teresa Confalonieri*. No envelope was preserved, but from the context of the letter and of the following letters 340805 and 340812, it is probable that the present one was addressed to the Hotel Excelsior, Lido di Venezia.

from the very beginning awakens an interest that grows more and more acute very quickly, to a peak. *Non si sa come* reveals the part of our life we live and conceal to ourselves, in the shadowy zone of our conscience— acts without thought; sins without remorse; involuntary, even *innocent* crimes. You'll see, my Marta: it will be, I hope, a masterpiece; a new, unexpected breath of humanity. Fleeting but profound. Almost as inconsistent as a dream, and very dramatic. Airy and at the same time tight and compact. How many things happen in life inside ourselves! And then, later on, no trace is left . . . the whirlpool closes, and everything goes back to the routine.

I hope to finish it very soon, by the middle of August or a little later. But I don't want you to be worried about that. No worry! I'm writing it for the pleasure of writing, in full and absolute freedom. I let it be born as it wants to be born. It is actually born very easily, ready to go straight onto the stage, agile and swift, with its five characters, all alive. I see them running away in their secret fury, and I run after them, adjusting their clothes, so that they may present themselves with a certain order and decency. The female protagonist's name is Ginevra, a sea captain's wife. The male protagonist's name is Romeo Daddi. The name of Ginevra's husband is Giorgio Vanzi—the sea captain. The wife of Count Daddi's name is Donna Bice. The fifth character, negligible, is a certain Marquis Nicola Respi, hopelessly in love with Donna Bice. The originality of the play consists in the fact that it is a love drama—exactly because Ginevra is in love with her husband, and Romeo Daddi with his wife. It seems strange, but it is very natural: the drama is exactly there, in those two legitimate loves, in the middle of which the reality of a dream has entered as a terrible antagonist. *Non si sa come* [*No one knows how*].

The title seems to me appropriate and beautiful. I allow myself to go on talking endlessly about my work, my Marta, and I do apologize. But if I don't talk about it with you, with whom do you want me to talk? I hope there is no need for me to tell you that all this talking on my part is without the slightest intention of an ulterior motive. You are right in waiting, after so much work, for somebody else to form the company.[2] Do accept the proposal of the Bontempelli tour—with adequate compensation—if it is advantageous for you. After the success of *Teresa Confalonieri*, some more film offers will be forthcoming; perhaps more than one; and then, without more overexertion, you'll be all set. It will be a real pity for the theater. But it is good that the theater needs you and feels your

[2] Marta is expecting the people responsible for the finances of the company also to do the hard work of recruiting the members of the company for the following season.

absence—and what a disgrace it would be for it to lose its most lively force, the newest and the most powerful one. For me, God will somehow provide;[3] I hope soon, because I am starting to feel pressured by my finances. But I am not worried. You know that I never worried. Without hurrying, the money that I had never looked for has always come. Perhaps because I never looked for it.

Enough. Be cheerful and have fun, my Marta! Greetings to Cele from me. Please write. Think sometimes, as before, about your poor old Maestro, and feel all his endless love.

[*unsigned*]

[3] This is one of the very rare passages where Pirandello seems to profess an attitude of trust in Divine Providence, evidently in opposition to his usual feeling of resentment against a blind and ferocious "hostile destiny"—a feeling that pervades a great part of his work. Is that a conventional sentence, written to please Marta (who was religious), or the manifestation of sincere trust in a superior benign power?

{ 340805 }

Castiglioncello (Livorno),
Villino Conti, 5. VIII. 1934[1]

My Marta,

How I can feel the sea in this letter of yours! How I can feel, while reading it, that you were writing it on the beach and in several successive stages, distracted by so many things and people and happenings! Invitations, feasts, meetings, all that a beach like the Lido can offer at the peak of the season! And I am happy to know that you are in the midst of so many people, very much in request and welcomed, admired, made the target and the center of attention by everyone.

Here there is absolute quiet, recollection, and, luckily for me, the only solace still left to me—my work! At this moment it would certainly have been convenient for me also to be in Venice, right there in the Lido, if for nothing else to meet Carl Laemmle, the director and owner of Universal, who, as you know, wrote to me from California to get from me some scripts for films; I know that he is in the Lido for the International Film Festival, together with other American producers. I take comfort thinking that at least you will meet them, my Marta—or you already met them, as

[1] The envelope of this letter is not preserved in the Princeton Collection. From the address of letter 340812 we can safely conclude that this letter too was addressed to the Hotel Excelsior, Lido di Venezia.

you wrote, introduced by Fontana—and I hope with all my heart that something great will develop for you out of that situation. I did not get either from Laemmle or from Metro-Goldwyn any answer, and God knows how I need to make a good business deal right now! But I resign myself to wait, and I am happier if my Marta makes one instead, while I concentrate all my hopes for prompt relief on this work of mine due next October. I have no other saint to whom to pray, if they don't award the Nobel Prize to me this year either. . . . Let's hope that you'll have more luck, my Marta, after the great success that cannot fail, of *Teresa Confalonieri*—a great *personal* success that cannot fail for you, although I don't know whether the same can be said about the film. This is the rumor that is all over Rome and was reported by the *Tribuna* of the day before yesterday, which reproduced a cartoon of the film with you and Nerio Bernardi, where you appeared very beautiful and Nerio Bernardi very insignificant. I'm sure that if the Americans see you in this film in Venice, something will certainly come of it for you. You can imagine with what eagerness I can wish it for you, my Marta—although I know that I would feel like dying at seeing you taken so far away by Glory and Fortune. But what would I care about my death, if my Marta had such good fortune![2]

. . . As far as your dream of a *teatro stabile* is concerned,[3] my Marta, you know well how that is also my strongest and most lively aspiration; that's all I am aiming at and dreaming about! But what can Biagi do about that? With only individual forces, as powerful as they might be, I don't believe that it's possible to succeed, given the conditions of Italy; a *permanent institution* must be created. A city like Milan would be able to create it, or like Rome—but it would be much more difficult there. If Naples would do it, it wouldn't amount to anything of importance; it would remain just local and cut off from the vital stream of the country, without any impact, if not very mediocre, elsewhere. Let's wait for the Convegno Volta;[4] perhaps we'll be onto something. But if it will be the state theater, I'm afraid that the pressures, the limitations, the interferences, would be so many that, when I think of them, as far as Art is

[2] This theme will continue to the end of the correspondence, when Marta was playing on Broadway at the peak of that wave of "luck" while Pirandello was dying in Rome, happy to know that his beloved had been "taken so far away by Glory and Fortune."

[3] The dream of a permanent theater, in Milan, with a permanent company chosen from among the best actors of the time and dedicated to art theater, had to wait many years before becoming a reality with the Piccolo Teatro di Milano—a long time after Pirandello had died and Marta had left the stage.

[4] An international convention presided over by Pirandello that would take place in Rome at the beginning of October (see letter 340224).

concerned, I feel like giving up. The best perhaps—for you and for me—would be that the mayor of Milan would really want to establish a *teatro stabile* there.

.. . With all the endless, *never-changing* love of

Your Maestro

{ 340821 }

Castiglioncello, Villino Conti
21. VIII. 1934[1]

My Marta,

My work, having reached the culminating scenes of the third act, really forces me to give up the joy of being present at your triumph on the evening of the 23rd. I feel that it would be a terrible shame to interrupt the completion of the play right at this moment. With your heart and your understanding you will forgive me, my Marta. I send you again my best wishes! Francesco is leaving tonight for Camaiore to pick up your parents and will be in Venice with them by the early afternoon.[2] So I hope to have you as my guest in Castiglioncello very soon, and we'll work together and talk about so many things! In the most perfect peace.

With all the endless love of your Maestro, and good-bye till very, very soon!

[*unsigned*]

---

[1] This short note was certainly sent to the Hotel Excelsior in Lido di Venezia.

[2] Pirandello is sending his car and the chauffeur Francesco to pick up Marta's parents at Marta's villino in Camaiore and take them to Venice. The letters will resume in November, after the announcement of the award of the Nobel Prize, which will bring Pirandello a whirlwind of congratulations from the whole world, plus invitations and trips to London, Paris, and Prague, crowned by the solemn ceremony in Stockholm.

{ 341115 }

To Marta Abba
Hôtel Termale Valentini
Salsomaggiore

Rome, 15. XI. 1934
Via Antonio Bosio, 15

My Marta,

So many days have gone by, and I have received from you only a signature among many other signatures on a postcard, I believe from Biella. I have not found literally one minute to write to you, oppressed—it's the correct word—by the feasts I was the object of, by the journalists of every country who have been besieging me, by interviews and telegrams, telegrams, telegrams. I must have received about five hundred of them, to be conservative, from people ranging from His Highness the prince Adalberto di Savoja-Genova to your ex-maid Lina! They are still coming from all over the world, and I don't know how to cope with answering them.[1]

I've never felt so alone and so sad. The sweetness of glory cannot compensate for the bitterness of the price I had to pay for it. And then, when it arrives, what if you don't know to whom to give it, and what to do with it?

Enough. . . . There is nobody worthy of your trust, my Marta, in that dirty world of the movies—a world of idiotic and brutal rascals, where the dregs and scum of society and its rot have camped out; that is, dishonest lawyers without cases, newly rich salami dealers, businessmen without capital, people of every possible kind and quality. If the cinema is like that, the theater world is no better. I've been meeting with Moissi and Campa[2] for several days about my new play, and I'll see them again tonight at nine in my home. My play is in demand in every country in Europe and in America, but in Italy it's not possible to find four actors who, with Moissi, can interpret the work properly. Above all, we cannot find two actresses. It seems impossible, but it is so. To such a condition has the Italian theater been reduced! All the available actresses are inferior to Wanda Capodaglio! Whom can we cast? And meanwhile we have to reach a decision before my departure. I have already put off this departure of mine too long, and I must absolutely leave on the day after tomorrow; that is, on the 17th. On the 18th I'll certainly be in Milan, and I'll

---

[1] The announcement of the award of the Nobel Prize had caused the deluge of congratulatory telegrams and invitations to dinners in his honor.

[2] The Austrian actor Alexander Moissi and Pio Campa, actor and company manager.

stay there until the evening of the 19th. I would have loved so much to see you and speak with you a little while, my Marta! But on the 20th, I have to be in Paris where they are waiting for me and where I must remain for at least one week. On the 27th I'll leave for London where I'll stay until December 4. From London I'll go back to Paris for two days and then, on the morning of the 9th, I'll be in Stockholm for the Royal Audience, which will be on the 10th; I'll stay in the Swedish capital for all the celebrations, which will last through the 14th, and then, on the 15th, I'll leave for Prague where I'll be present at the premiere of *Non si sa come*, and I'll give my lecture. I'll be back in Italy, I believe, around the 20th, more or less. And I'll go by way of Milan in the hope of seeing you again. As you see, I'll be away for little more than a month. But who knows how many things might mature during this month! And when I come back, if I do come back, how many things we'll have to think about and take care of! I feel that I cannot go on the way I am now.

Is there any hope, my Marta, that I can see you now in Milan, either on the 18th or the 19th? I do hope so! In Milan I'll have to settle many things with Mauri and with Mondadori,[3] for my books, for my trip and all the requests from abroad, and perhaps two days will be hardly sufficient; but I won't be able to stay any longer than that.

I feel that whatever is more alive in me still and always belongs to you, as it did before and even more than before, and I want to believe that you are the same for me. Feel always secure, anyhow, of the endless love of

Your Maestro

---

[3] Dr. Mauri was a lawyer in Milan, and Mondadori, the publisher of an important part of Pirandello's work.

{ 341129 }

To Marta Abba
26, Via Aurelio Saffi
Milan   29. XI. 1934[1]

My Marta,

You cannot imagine the expressions of welcome that Paris has been giving me since my arrival. I am deeply moved by it, even more when I compare them with those Italy gave me! At the reception at the *Figaro*, there were more than 1,500 people, including all the major personalities of politics and letters, all the most famous ladies of Paris, ministers, ambassadors, Academicians, all the major representatives of the French theater, playwrights, directors, actors, and actresses. Crémieux told me that nothing like that had ever been seen before. On the following morning I was honored by the *Paris-Soir*, the newspaper with the widest circulation in France; the director gave a speech in my honor and then all the editors and co-workers attended a luncheon that the newspaper was giving for me. Yesterday the newspaper *L'Intransigent* did the same. And this morning I was honored at the Société des Auteurs, which wanted me to preside over the meeting of all the authors. The president gave a beautiful speech, to which I answered, I believe, also well, and then a luncheon. So many people were talking to me about you, and you can imagine with what pleasure I was listening. Monday night I'll have another reception, at the Société des Gens de Lettres. It is certain that the Comédie-Française will present one of my plays, either *Così è (se vi pare)* or *Enrico IV* or *Vestire gli ignudi.* Fabre[2] would also like to consider *Non si sa come* and is waiting for a translation from Crémieux, who is enthusiastic about the play. In the meantime, around the 20th of next month, Pitoëff will present *Ce soir on improvise* at the Théâtre des Mathurins with a magnificent cast and marvelous staging. Rehearsals have already begun. I'm breathing an atmosphere that is enthusiastic about me. This is something only Paris can do, when she loves someone. I am sure they would have not done so much if the Nobel Prize had been awarded to a Frenchman; Pierre Benoit[3] openly told me so.

---

[1] This letter was written from Paris, on the letterhead of the Hôtel George V, Avenue George V, Paris.

[2] Émile Fabre, director of the Comédie-Française.

[3] French novelist, member of the Académie Française.

Offers are arriving at this moment from everywhere and above all from North America. Five producing companies have requested subjects for films from Curtis-Brown[4] in New York. It would be enough to conclude two or three big deals, in order to realize at least one-and-a-half-million lire. Also Korda[5] in London, with whom I spoke, wants a script of mine for London Film and I hope to sign a contract at once; that is, before my departure for Stockholm, which will happen on the 5th or the 6th. Ah, how I wish that you were here with me and that the plan of Amelia Valdameri could be realized![6] I'd be so happy! Without you, as it is now, my glory is lifeless. You are my true glory. Glory must be young and beautiful, or it doesn't make much sense. You have glory of your own, and you have youth and beauty.

Here everybody is inviting me to stay in Paris. I should be back here before Christmas to attend the performance of *Ce soir on improvise*, which will open around the 22nd; that is, after attending the premiere of *Non si sa come* in Prague. I'll be very tired, and I'll need some rest for a while. Perhaps by Christmas I'll be in Rome. But will you be there? Couldn't you come now to Paris to see a few plays? Last night they opened one that had a great success, but Crémieux told me that it is very Pirandellian, with a woman as protagonist. I'll see it tonight or tomorrow night. Come, my Marta! Mauri is now in London to conclude with Korda; on his way back he will travel through Paris, and you could travel with him on your return, if Amelia Valdameri doesn't want to come and continue the trip to Stockholm with you. Think about it! It would be important that you make yourself visible here in Paris after two years of absence.

Perhaps I'm dreaming. Anyhow, my Marta, feel always surrounded by the endless love of your

Maestro

[4] Curtis-Brown was a leading literary agency in New York City.
[5] The film director and producer Alexander Korda (1893–1956).
[6] Marta's friend, Amelia Valdameri, was trying to organize a trip to Stockholm and make it possible for Marta to be present at the ceremony of the awarding of the Nobel Prize.

{ 341206 }

To Marta Abba
26, Via Aurelio Saffi
Milan 6. XII. 1934[1]

My Marta,

I'm leading a really impossible life! Yesterday morning I wanted to answer your last letter of Sunday evening (don't worry, I received all your letters, the one sent to London and this one sent to Paris); interviews after interview; and then, at one o'clock, lunch at Pierre Brisson's[2] with Émile Fabre, director of the Comédie-Française, to decide which one of my plays will be presented at the House of Molière; as I hoped, *Così è (se vi pare)*, that is, in French, *Chacun sa vérité*, was chosen. I owe that to Brisson, who proved to be a true friend—of such an affectionate kindness as you can find only in France. But I don't want to talk to you any longer about myself and my things, which are, at this moment, in the greatest ferment of high expectation and, we hope, of prompt realization. I want to talk to you about the happiness that the news of your probable trip to Stockholm with Amelia has given me, although she has not yet, until today, written anything to me. It will be impossible, my Marta, to obtain hospitality at the Italian Legation where, as a guest, I cannot bring other guests with me. But that doesn't mean that you cannot be my guests in the best hotel of Stockholm for the time I will spend in the Swedish capital; that is, from December 9 to the 14th, taking part in all the festivities that will honor me. This is a matter of course, and you do not have to worry about anything. I gave up the plan of stopping over in Berlin— thus avoiding exhaustion because of additional visits and interviews over there. I'll leave Paris tomorrow evening at six directly for Hamburg and from there, after a brief stop at the station, I'll continue to Stockholm, where I'll arrive on the morning of the 9th. On the 10th there will be the solemn assembly at the Swedish Academy with the prize-awarding ceremony by the hand of the king. The program for the celebrations is not yet known to me; I know that there is a royal dinner, a performance in my honor of *Il piacere dell'onestà* at the National Theater and other beautiful things of that kind. On the 15th, departure for Prague with endless celebrations also there, enough to die of tiredness; a lecture at the Casa di

---

[1] Letter sent from Paris, on the letterhead of the Hôtel George V.

[2] Pierre Brisson was a writer and dramatic critic and the editor of the *Figaro* and *Figaro littéraire*.

Cultura degli Italiani, banquets, speeches, and, on the 19th, world premiere of *Non si sa come* in the Czech language, in the translation of good
old Jirina, at the National Theater. On the morning of the 21st, departure
from Prague for Paris, where on the evening of the 22nd at the Théâtre
des Mathurins the Pitoëff Company will perform *Ce soir on improvise*;
that is, *Questa sera si recita a soggetto*, which we hope will be well received.
Too bad the theater is too small! In Paris we'll be able to stay as long as
we wish and enjoy here all the Christmas and New Year's festivities, and
also enjoy a little rest, after so much excitement. Let's hope that in the
meantime some big business deal will be concluded in America, where
negotiations are now going on, and in England; after that, going back to
Italy, we'll think about finding some kind of a solution to the problem of
what to do with the four or five days of life left for me to live. Two
American newspapers made me an offer—the first of one thousand dollars
(that means twelve thousand lire) for each of twelve articles (one each
month), and the second one of five thousand dollars for a short novel or
a long short story of about fifty thousand words, like *Il turno*. I'll send
them exactly that, still unpublished in America. Only with these two
small things I'll have enough to live comfortably for two years, almost
without doing anything. I want to set myself up to write novels—without
neglecting the short stories—in a quiet, isolated place. But my own company, after the work to which I'll dedicate myself completely, is unbearable to me. Therefore, after work I need to see somebody or something.
The place I'll choose will have to be near a city. Enough. We'll see. Mauri
returns today in the afternoon to Rome and will call you immediately. I
won't move a finger in Italy to do anything. I don't even know whether
I'll stay in Italy. But we'll talk about that later. Meanwhile, my Marta, I
am expecting you in Stockholm with Amelia or in Paris at my return on
the 22nd, as you prefer. Nothing else is alive in me. Always feel the endless love of

Your Maestro

{ 341212 }

To Marta Abba
26, Via Aurelio Saffi
Milan   Stockholm, 12. XII. 1934

My Marta,

I've received your letter of the 9th. Before leaving Paris I also got the previous one, where you gave me the news of the serious car accident in which your father almost lost his life. You can imagine how sorry I was and the impression I received from your vivid description of what happened. Thank God he escaped the worst, and my hatred of the Balilla has been reinforced.[1]

I am literally crushed by all these festivities. But by now, thank God, the worst is over. I received the prize from the hands of the king during the solemn assembly, which does present a very impressive grandiosity, with the whole court and the crowd of the guests in all the splendor of their decorations—academicians, ministers, generals, and, on the podium, the candidates with their sponsors. I'll talk to you personally and I'll show you the splendid diploma and the big golden medal. After that ceremony we went to the banquet in the magnificent City Hall—a banquet with at least five hundred people, presided over by the royal princes. There I had to deliver a speech, and I had to do it in French, since it was not admissible that an interpreter would translate my Italian. I managed pretty well. The whole day yesterday was spent in visits of thanks and you can imagine how much they tired me. Last evening, dinner at court, with the king and all the royal princes. The king was extremely kind with me; and one of the princes, Prince William, the second born of the king, entertained me the whole evening. Tonight dinner at the Legation in my honor; tomorrow a gala performance of *Il piacere dell'onestà* at the National Theater. The most important Swedish actress, Tora Tje, will interpret *Trovarsi* in a tour through all the Scandinavian countries; on the radio they gave *Vestire gli ignudi*. On the first evening after my arrival, there was also a dinner given in my honor by the federation of the foreign press in Stockholm. It gives me the shivers when I think that as soon as these festivities are over, those in Prague will start. I can't wait, my Marta, to go back to Rome and rest at least until January 10.

. . . When will you leave for Rome? I'd love to spend the Christmas and New Year holidays with you. According to what you had planned, you

---

[1] Balilla was the model name of a compact Fiat car, at the time very popular in Italy.

should be in Rome. I wish you'd let me know promptly, writing to Prague, c/o Légation d'Italie. I'll leave from here on the evening of the 17th; on the 20th, I'll leave from Prague, either for Rome or for Paris; but I assume without delay for Rome, unless you are still in Milan, in which case I'll stop over in Milan.

Enough. Good-bye until soon, my Marta, in Milan or in Rome, wherever you'll be. I am waiting for your news in Prague. Best wishes to your father for having escaped danger and for a prompt recovery, and best wishes to your mother too. With the endless love of

Your Maestro

Letters of 1935 from
Paris, Rome, Milan, and New York

THE FESTIVITIES in Paris, London, and Stockholm on the occasion of the awarding of the Nobel Prize and the trip to Prague for the world premiere of *Non si sa come* (December 19, 1934) fatigued Pirandello and at the same time gave him new confidence that the longed-for financial security was finally at hand. This year's letters often mention a certain Mr. Reece, responsible for trying to set up the Pirandello Company, a corporation to be based in London and financed by English investors with the purpose of marketing Pirandello's entire body of literary works all over the world. This company was to pay in advance to Pirandello every year a large sum of money (more than sufficient for a very comfortable life-style for the rest of his days) in exchange for the worldwide rights to his literary work in translation. Although Pirandello had a high income for many years, most of his life he labored under serious financial strain. The letter of February 17 is of great interest because it explicitly summarizes the sums of money Pirandello earned during the last ten years of his life. It also implicitly shows how poorly those large sums of money were administered. Had Pirandello managed his money wisely, or had he left its management in the hands of a capable and honest administrator, he would never have had to go through so many financial worries.

Once more "adverse fate" prevented the final conclusion of a "sure" business deal. The reason that the Pirandello Company never materialized seems to have been the international political situation, especially the hostility between Mussolini's Italy—involved in the conquest of Ethiopia—and an England that at the time was the very soul of the economic sanctions imposed by the League of Nations against Italy. Pirandello, always responsive to the call of nationalism, openly took a position in defense of Fascist colonialism, and dramatically supported it in several interviews that were widely publicized by the national and international press, especially during his long visit to New York, thus also damaging his chances of concluding important business deals in the United States.

The letters begin at the end of January. After spending Christmas in Italy, Pirandello goes back to Paris with Marta and her mother. Marta is on her way to London, where she plans to study English—finally giving in to the many importunities of the Maestro, who wants to make her a truly international star capable of acting in good English. Although new doors are now open in Italy after the Nobel Prize, new promises are made by Mussolini for a national theater, and although the apparent elimination of Giordani seems to put a definitive end to the hated theater monopoly in Italy, Pirandello is still more than ever convinced that his dream can become true only after a great triumph of Marta as an actress in the United States, combined with many lucrative sales of his film scenarios to Hollywood tycoons. Full of the greatest expectations, he goes to New York, where the official welcome is triumphal. When it comes to business, however, Pirandello finds himself up against a completely unexpected, insuperable wall of courteous but frustrating delays, reflecting the increasingly tense international situation. In addition, many Hollywood producers are now convinced that Pirandello's scenarios do not appeal to the popular taste so essential for commercial success. Moreover, the legal controversy with the Shuberts about the U.S. rights to some of the most desirable works of the Maestro projects a long shadow on any conclusion of deals that might involve the buyer in serious legal complications with those magnates of the American theater industry (see letter 350907 about the damages Pirandello suffered because of the temporary financial problems of the Shuberts during the Depression, and letter 360516 about the background of the controversy as seen by Pirandello). No wonder that in spite of the many inquiries and manifestations of genuine interest, not a single contract was signed. Another important obstacle to the conclusion of business deals is Pirandello's psychological attitude toward his American partners. As it appears in the letters, Pirandello has no doubt whatsoever about the following points (and he talks accordingly with everybody, without any restraint): that the Shuberts are a gang of thieves laying nonexistent claims to some of his works; that Mussolini is right in occupying Ethiopia; that his theater is not only the most important and most alive of his time, but also excellent at generating scenarios for films with the greatest popular appeal for the masses. The American world of show business, however, thinks in a very different way. Everybody in the United States knows that the Shuberts are famous for formulating their contracts in extremely shrewd terms and for defending them with the best lawyers in the country. In 1934–1935 not only do the major political parties present a solid, united front against any form of fascism, but all the leftist groups in America have joined the United Front (at the time extremely influential in the noncommercial theater world) and have just changed their plans of action declaring unity in a definitely anti-Fascist movement, fighting nazism, fascism, and Falangism and particularly condemning the conquest of Ethiopia. Moreover, among the Shuberts themselves (who in 1930 had acquired the U.S. rights to five Pirandello works without succeeding, because of the Depression, in fulfilling their obligation to use them) there is division. Lee favors the production of drama with intellectual content, while Jacob J. fights him, convinced that at the present moment it is not possible to produce such works without incurring great losses (the success of *As You Desire Me* is considered an exception to the rule). In general, Americans feel free to express their differences of opinion, according to their democratic tradition. This is not well understood by Pirandello, accustomed as he is to the intolerance of the Fascist world. The Americans show great deference and admiration for the artistic genius of the Maestro. They also show great interest and respect for Pirandello's opinions, even when expressed in the arrogant tone typical of the presumptuous Fascist rhetoric of the time. The Americans use as an answer a very concrete and obvious language: they do not buy the product.

This means the end, for Pirandello, of the myth of America as Eldorado. The Maestro becomes despondent and totally confused at his failure to close any deals. Not understanding why things seem so different now, he allows himself to become overly irritated by certain aspects of American life and to be tempted by easy generalizations; for example, about American women, thus betraying his superficial knowledge of the complexity of American society. Nauseated by the useless, interminable negotiations, Pirandello returns to Europe with an empty bag. At his arrival in Naples on October 14 he suffers a serious heart attack. The letters now present more frequent reflections on his approaching death and expressions of deep longing for peace, as well as a great repugnance toward any public appearance and especially the theater. He promises to himself not to have anything to do with the stage and to dedicate himself only to writing short stories and essays. The letters also show frequent expressions of aloofness toward life and lack of interest for the planet Earth, with thoughts and a tone that will find an echo in his *Informazioni sul mio involontario soggiorno sulla terra*—fragments of a planned autobiography which were published after his death but written at this time.

Pirandello's letter of December 15 reveals the playwright's great disillusion with the way his work *Non si sa come* is produced at the Teatro

Argentina in Rome for the Italian premiere. The success, however, is enormous. The event is transformed into a tribute of glory by the whole world of the Italian theater and politics to the sixty-eight-year-old Maestro, whose health everybody knows to be frail.

The last letters of the year are busy with suggestions to his beloved, including criteria to follow in deciding about the publication of Marta's *Notes* on her experiences as an actress. The Maestro adds affectionate words of encouragement for a depressed and tired Marta, so that she might pick up again with new courage her career as a great actress, "for the joy and the exultation of all the noble souls who thirst after beauty."

{ 350203 }

Miss Marta Abba
c/o Miss Letitia Emanuel
34, Campden Hill Gardens
Kensington W.8
(England) London   3. II. 1935[1]
    My Marta,
    I've received your telegram and your letter; I'm informing you of their arrival before I leave Paris, so that you won't need to worry about that. Your letter was without a greeting and even without your signature; perhaps you were in a hurry to put it in an envelope and mail it so that it could arrive before my departure. I'm full of joy for the cheerful news you sent me about your first days in London. Yes, my Marta, all you do is very intelligent.
    Here in Paris I had three days of meetings with Reece[2] and as a result we put together a project that he will present to Sir Edmond Davis in London. This project is for a Pirandello Company—a company in the commercial and English meaning of the word; that is, a company for the

---

[1] Pirandello writes from Paris, on the letterhead of the Hôtel George V. After the festivities for the Nobel Prize in Stockholm and Prague, and after spending Christmas and New Year in Italy near Marta, Pirandello—accompanied by Marta and her mother—went back to Paris for the premiere of *Questa sera si recita a soggetto* at the Théâtre des Mathurins. At the end of January, Marta left Paris for London. The actress is now there, studying the English language in preparation for her future as a rising star in the international movie and theater world.

[2] Holroyd Reece was the mastermind in setting up the project (never realized) explained in this letter. Sir Edmond Davis was an English banker who was interested in financing the projected Pirandello Company, Inc.

exploitation of Pirandello's past, present, and future work, with a capital of four million lire, of which three will go to me at the signing of the contract and one will be used for operating expenses. I transfer to the company all income from books, theater, and cinema, until the total advance of three million is recouped; after that I'll have 60 percent of the income and that will leave 40 percent for the company. But the organization of the company, which will be presided over and managed by the same Reece, will be complex, because it will have several branches both in Europe and in America. We worked at it during the last three days for eight hours a day and I hope that everything was taken care of in the project; of course, before signing the contract I'll consult a first-class lawyer, such as Marchesano. Reece has already requested from here a meeting with Davis, but at least one week will be necessary to put together all the members of his group of financiers; when all of them can meet, Reece will be notified in Grasse and will go to London to discuss the deal, but Reece is already sure of it, because Davis has already been informed and seems ready to go for it. You understand, my Marta, that this would be a real stroke of luck, capable of giving me financial security for these last years left for me to live (if they will be "years") without any more worries, and allowing me to work on whatever I like the most! I wanted to write to you before leaving so that you would not think that the deal did not go through. Not at all! However, it cannot be concluded in a hurry. It has to be done within a span of time that cannot be too long—it will take fifteen or twenty days, I don't know.

. . . Meanwhile, my Marta, be cheerful and healthy. I'm feeling happy for you and for me—things are getting better and better for us. With all the endless love of

Your Maestro

{ 350214 }

Rome, 14. II. 1935 - XIII
Via Antonio Bosio, 15[1]

My Marta,

. . . You ask me for news from Italy. The first I can give you is that I have ready in my hands the plan for the institution of a national dramatic theater in Rome, and that I have requested an audience with the Duce to present it to him. The Duce has fixed the audience for the 18th, at 17:30,

---

[1] The London address to which this letter was sent is not preserved.

in the Palazzo Venezia; that is, in four days. The fact that Bottai is now in the position of governor of Rome is very much in our favor. I'll inform you immediateley of the results of the conversation. And may God grant that I'll be able to inform you personally, by coming right after it to London! The two things could happen at the same time; that is, the audience on the one hand, and the invitation of Reece on the other.[2]

 . . . Yesterday I had lunch at Silvio D'Amico's and I heard that the rumor of Paolino Giordani's impending arrest is circulating around Rome. It might be just gossip without any foundation, but it is certain that his position has become very shaky. He is in Rome—he was seen around town perhaps trying to patch things up. During a year of his management, it seems that he milked Cines dry, reducing to twenty-five thousand lire the last twenty-five million of its capital. Your father gave me one of the articles by Aniante in the *Merlo*. You know that, in my opinion, both Aniante and Giannini, the editor of the *Merlo*—the former *Becco giallo*—are two dirty persons. The attack on Giordani, however, is so well documented that I doubt they wrote it. I wish that those who furnished the documentation had used a less compromised signature than that of Aniante and a less rotten newspaper than that of Giannini. The fact, however, that the *Merlo* is permitted to be distributed in Italy with such an open and courageous attack is symptomatic. It might be really true that the so-long-waited-for crash is near, and it would be high time! With Giordani all the destroyers of the Italian theater should also crash! But perhaps it will happen that the very ruin of this miserable theater, reduced by now to the pits of degradation, will bury them all under its debris.

 . . . With all the endless love of

Your Maestro

[2] Pirandello is hoping that the audience with the Duce (decisive for setting up the state theaters) and the call by Reece to go to London for setting up the Pirandello Company, Inc. (decisive for his financial security) will happen very soon, "at the same time."

{ <u>350217</u> }

Miss Marta Abba
c/o Coventry
25 Old Court Mansions
Kensington W.8
(England) London

Rome, 17. II. 1935 - XIII
Via Antonio Bosio, 15

My Marta,

. . . Tomorrow at 17:30 I'll go to Palazzo Venezia for the audience[1] and I'll bring with me the project, worked out to the last detail. I had to reduce the number of members of the company, in order to limit the expense that, by multiplying by three the list of employees, would have reached astronomical figures; I only doubled them. And within that figure we won't be able to do very much. The company would consist of thirty-eight actors; for the whole year it would cost less than three thousand lire per day. Of course, all the salaries would be proportionally scaled; that is, the two first actresses, each at eighty thousand lire; the two first actors, each at sixty-six thousand; and proportionally down the line. But it must be taken into account that the engagement is for the whole year; that the work is divided up; that people can live in their own homes rather than in hotels, and many other advantages.

Let's hope that the project is well received and that this time a conclusion might be reached!

I'm still impatiently waiting for a letter or a telegram from Reece inviting me to London. I know that he is working on the project to be presented to Davis, who has already accepted the general idea of the proposition. The signing of the contract can only be a few days away. Mauri has furnished, with my help, all the details of my income of the last ten years, and it comes to the very respectable amount of several millions, so that it should not be such a big deal to invest three million in order to have forever the rights to all my work—especially after the Nobel Prize. I showed the draft of the contract to the lawyer Casadei, who found it most acceptable for both sides; as a matter of fact, more for the contracting partner than for me; but for me, he said, the major advantage would be that I would no longer be obliged to get involved in business matters; I must, however, put a reliable person in control, both moral and financial,

---

[1] With Mussolini. Pirandello has in his hands detailed plans for the national dramatic theater.

of all commercial activities, and that person will be good old Mauri—so attentive and scrupulous and most competent on the subject. As soon as the invitation to leave for London arrives I'll send you a telegram.

Last evening I was with Bontempelli for dinner at Notari's home. Notari is very grateful to you for accompanying the body of his wife to the burial—he was really moved by your compassionate action. He was saying: "I'll never forget it!" It seems that it was raining, and that there was a lot of mud on the road, and that you followed the carriage to the cemetery on foot. He seems to be still very shaken by the loss.

. . . Enough. Once more, let's hope we'll see each other again soon in London, my Marta! I can't wait! Keep cheerful and healthy, and feel always the endless love of

Your Maestro

{ 350219 }

Miss Marta Abba
c/o Miss Letitia Emanuel
34, Campden Hill Gardens
Kensington W.8
(England) London   Rome, 19. ii. 1935 - xiii
                                                            Via Antonio Bosio, 15

My Marta,
. . . Let's talk about the great news. Well, yesterday, at 17:30, I went to the Palazzo Venezia, carrying under my arm my project for the institution of a national dramatic theater in Rome. I was immediately admitted, and at once the Duce, with his usual admirable promptness and without wasting time in useless preliminaries, got interested in the introductory "premise," with the title "The Theater to the People." He began immediately to nod approvingly at what he was reading, page after page; he went through the whole project, interposing here and there a few words of comment; for example, whether it would be a good idea to name the institution Teatro Reale di Prosa instead of Teatro Nazionale di Prosa; he then remarked, "But perhaps Reale di Prosa sounds ugly," and cutting it short, "Enough, we'll think about it later"; he said at a certain point that it was good that at present Bottai—who will certainly be a very suitable collaborator for the project—was in the position of governor of Rome; in conclusion, I had the precise impression that *it's already a fait accompli.* Can you imagine, he told me at the end: "It would be beautiful if we

could start this very year, in October!" Now, this is in perfect accord with his style, when he wants to get something done. Today he is scheduled to see Bottai, and I'm sure he will talk with him and study with him whether it's really possible to start in October, in spite of the remodeling work that must be done at the Teatro Argentina. He liked a lot the idea of beginning the theater season on October 28, the anniversary of the March on Rome, with the winning play of an international competition, in order to make Rome again a world center for the arts and culture.

As soon as I was back home, full of happiness, I got to the phone to communicate the news to Bottai, who manifested great enthusiasm about it: "I'm happy for the theater," he said "as much as I am for you." In conclusion, my Marta, it seems that we finally got our dream! Last night everybody was in my home feasting: D'Amico and all the editorial staff of *Scenario*, Bontempelli, Alvaro; and they were all talking about you and they were saying that it was not possible to put together a company without you. The problem still to be solved is that of finding another actress who can keep up with you! But we'll talk about that on the occasion of my coming to London, which was put off until about March 9 or 10. Reece wrote to me that the conference of the financiers will not take place before March 4 or 5; that after the first conference he will send a telegram from London at the latest on the 8th, and that meanwhile I should be ready to leave either on the 9th or on the 10th. Perhaps, *around the end of March*, with the final contract and the prospect of great work for the soon-to-come state theater, for the formation of the company, for the formation of the repertory, my Marta, we'll be able to go back together to Italy.[1]

Somebody read my hand, and told me that I'll have everything I desire for the rest of the time that remains for me to live. And I desire only one thing!

Good-bye, my Marta! With all my endless love,

Your Maestro

---

[1] This is probably the moment in which Pirandello felt closest—with a moral certitude of prompt realization—to the great dream of directing a company dedicated to artistic theater, financed by the state, and formed with the best artists of his time, first among whom was Marta, who therefore would always be near him. The sentence "we'll be able to go back together to Italy"—after the conclusion of the deal with Reece that would have ensured his financial independence (three million lire in cash on the spot!)—sounds like an exclamation of victory, implying the hope that going back together would become the beginning of "being together" for the rest of the time left for him to live.

{ 350301 }

Miss Marta Abba
c/o Coventry
25, Old Court Mansions
Kensington W.8
(England) London   Rome, I. III. 1935 - XIII
                                                         Via Antonio Bosio, 15

My Marta,

Without an answer to my last letter, I am writing again to let you know that I had my first talk with Bottai, governor of Rome, from whom I got the precise impression that the state theater is a firm intention of the Chief[1] and that therefore *it will be done*, notwithstanding all obstacles. The Chief must have spoken to Bottai in such a way about this project that the latter has already shown himself all set and ready to go, making a point of declaring to me that he is fully in favor of it, and also that personally he will help in bringing it to completion—in a brotherly way and with all his enthusiasm. But he said that we still had to consult His Excellency Galeazzo Ciano,[2] who will hold a meeting with the president of the Corporation of Performing Arts, the president of the Society of Authors, and also the vice-president of the Academy of Italy, to take counsel together about the establishment of the funds; that is, about the one million two hundred thousand lire of the annual endowment of the theater. They do not have to give the money; it comes from the expenditures made in the public domain and from a percentage of the income from the subscriptions to the EIAR,[3] which is presently entrusted to the Corporation of Performing Arts. Perhaps both the Academy and the corporation will object; but, of course, all it takes is for the Chief to overrule them and impose his approval of the project, pointing out—as it is easy for him to do—that the money received from both sources is more usefully spent on endowing the state theater than wasting it on piddling little handouts of subsidies and encouragement prizes, as the Academy

---

[1] Mussolini.

[2] Count Galeazzo Ciano, the son-in-law of Mussolini (he had married Mussolini's daughter Edda in 1930), was at the time undersecretary—and later in 1935 minister—for Press and Propaganda. He was soon to become the person charged by Mussolini with the task of carrying out the project of the state theaters (see letter 350425).

[3] EIAR (Ente Italiano Audizioni Radiofoniche) was the state organization that monopolized radio broadcasting in Italy, charging each radio user a yearly fee.

and the Corporation of Performing Arts are now doing. Bottai himself has pledged to decide with Ciano on the date of the meeting, between March 4 and 6; that is, in a few days. I established the deadline myself, because on the 8th I expect the telegram from Reece about leaving for London.

Ah, my Marta, if I could only really come and bring you the announcement that, with the conclusion of my negotiations, the state theater is a firm and established thing! I'll see immediately, from the way Ciano receives me, what are the instructions that he got from the Chief. I have every reason to hope that those instructions are favorable. I already had a proof of it, I repeat, in the attitude of Bottai. We'll see in a few days. This week will be decisive, for everything and for everybody.

Here in Rome the weather is horrible, as it is reported in all the newspapers also about Europe and America, with rain, wind, hurricanes, floods, storms, earthquakes—the end of the world. Ships begging for help everywhere are countless. It's becoming a very hard task to cope with so many disasters. The wind, at night, is frightening. I hear about many people swept away like autumn leaves.

I don't know whether you in London are aware of the anguish of this inclement weather. My thoughts are fixed on you, my Marta, in every hour of the day, and I can't wait to see you again! I also am studying English, because it seems to me as if I am in your company—like being a little close to you. I spoke again yesterday with Cele, who is working and is doing well. Yesterday I went for supper at D'Amico's. He and his family are always very cordial.

Fausto is having a good success, also as far as sales are concerned, at the Second Quadrennial Exhibition.[4] I went to see *L'urlo* at the Teatro Valle, and Benassi seemed to me to be terrible. Good, on the contrary, in a secondary role, was Giachetti.[5] It seems to me that he is the only possible leading actor of tomorrow; he should be given a leading role to show his potential.

[4] Until recently Pirandello had been reluctant to inform Marta about good news of his children, but now he reports with pride the success of Fausto, who has established himself as a recognized artist of value. The times when Fausto's modernistic paintings seemed "scrawls" are past. Now an evident admiration for his son's work can be noticed, together with a sense of fatherly joy in seeing him grow in the path of art he himself had traced. In general, the tone and attitude of Pirandello toward his family appear to have mellowed and to have reached a plateau of quasi-normality.

[5] Fosco Giachetti, at the time just about thirty years old, was on the brink of becoming one of the best and most recognized actors of the Italian cinema.

Enough, my Marta! This is just gossip, and you have no time to spend in listening to it. Keep your fingers crossed that everything goes well! Be cheerful and healthy and always feel all the endless love of

Your Maestro

{ 350318 }

Miss Marta Abba
c/o Coventry
25, Old Court Mansions
Kensington W.8
(England) London   18. IV. 1935 - XIII[1]

My Marta,

. . . I am recalled to Italy for the foundation, by now firmly decided, of the state theater, of which project at present Governor Bottai has been put in charge by the Chief. Stefano, as I already wrote to you, was called by Bottai so that I might be informed of everything. A few engineers in the technical office of the governor are preparing the plans for the renovation of the Teatro Argentina: eliminating the boxes, constructing two large balconies with a sloping floor so that the theater may seat two thousand people, as the Chief wishes. You know by now, from your father, about the miserable crash of the whole setup of the Suvini-Zerboni, Sitedramma, etc. Giordani is finished (and, it seems, without a penny of his own), together with Riboldi, Sacerdoti, and company. The Credito Marittimo has bought all the stock of the Suvini-Zerboni with the obligation of depositing the whole repertory of the Sitedramma into the Società degli Autori, for its administration and that of the theaters belonging to the trust. So did, at last, the day of judgment arrive for the whole gang.[2]

Now it's a question of restarting the Italian theater from its very foundations. We shall not fail, my Marta! It is our chance!

Enough, until soon, my Marta! I am full of trepidation and hope. With the endless love of

Your Maestro

[1] Letter written from Paris on the letterhead of the Hôtel George V. By mistake, Pirandello writes "IV" to correspond to April, while in reality the letter was written and mailed in March.

[2] This is the great moment, longed for by Pirandello for many, many years: the fall of the gang of the monopoly—by whom Pirandello had felt constantly and wickedly persecuted.

{ 350408 }

Miss Marta Abba
c/o Coventry
25, Old Court Mansions
Kensington W.8
(England) London

Rome, 8. IV. 1935
Via Antonio Bosio, 15

My Marta,

. . . I arrived in Rome last night at 8:10. I found several novelties. Most important of all, the creation of an Inspectorate of the Theater, parallel to that of the Cinema, in the office of the undersecretary for Press and Propaganda. De Pirro was made head of it, *as a person devoted to me.* In fact, just last night De Pirro, accompanied by two other officials of the inspectorate, Cesare Ludovici and Mario Labroca (the former for the dramatic theater, and the latter for the lyric theater), came to see me at home and stayed until midnight. De Pirro is in charge of the practical carrying out of my project of the state theater, and he came to place himself completely at my disposal. First of all, in order to establish mutual understanding, he has requested for me a meeting with Ciano. I wanted to take my time before answering. I said that I was very tired and that I would not be able even to think of anything before five or six days. You know De Pirro. He made the most open declaration of fidelity and devotion; he said that each word of mine is going to be law for him; those were his instructions from the government, which wanted to satisfy me in all particulars; and the orders were to solve the problem of the theater in Italy; also Milan had expressed an interest in solving the problems of the theater, and therefore the field of action will be broadened. This is what he said. In four or five days I'll talk with Ciano and I'll see what all that really means, in order to finally make my decisions. Naturally, I'll keep you informed of everything.

Today, Sunday, His Excellency Dino Alfieri came to see me at home. As president of the Società degli Autori, he wants to render to me all the honors that so far had not been given to me in Italy. Although I did my best to dissuade him, he was unshakable. On the 23rd there will be that Babel at the Palazzo Ruspoli. I took advantage of the occasion to talk about your father, so that he might name him inspector of the Società degli Autori, or give him some other employment. He promised that he will do so without fail.

... But how are you, my Marta? I cannot erase you from my eyes, looking the way I saw you the last evening in London before our separation. I never felt so much tenderness, so much admiration, and so much love for you, my Marta! You are really a superb creature, such as people think exist only in dreams, so pure and perfect! You'll see, my Marta, that you'll be able to overcome all difficulties sooner than you think; if you only stand fast and do not get discouraged![1] ... Write to me! I'll write to you again very soon. Meanwhile, receive all the endless love of

Your Maestro

[1] The love of a sickly, sixty-eight-year-old Pirandello for his Marta, now thirty-five, is here expressed in a serene, idealized, and fatherly tone.

{ 350425 }

Miss Marta Abba
c/o Coventry
25, Old Court Mansion
Kensington W.8
(England) London   Rome, 25. IV. 1935 - XIII
                                                        Via Antonio Bosio, 15

My Marta,

I'm just leaving for Florence, where tomorrow, at Palazzo Vecchio, I'll give the keynote of the international lectures on high culture with my talk entitled "Introduction to the Italian Theater." I've chosen this theme on purpose so that the conference may serve as a foundation for the state theater at the moment of its birth, and it seems to me that it is of prime importance.

Yesterday I was the honoree at great festivities at the Palazzo Ruspoli; Dino Alfieri spoke; then I gave a brief talk to those present, and, lastly, on an improvised stage in the great hall, *L'Uomo dal fiore in bocca* was performed.

In the evening, at the Hotel Ambasciatori, a banquet was given in my honor, which was attended by His Excellency Galeazzo Ciano, to whom the Chief gave the charge of taking care of the state theater, and with whom I had long conversations before and after the banquet. It seems that they want to do things on a large scale—not one, but three state theaters, one in Rome, one in Milan, and one in Turin. The latter two, however, would be under the control of the cities, while only the one in Rome would belong to the state with the cooperation of the governor's administration. In order to discuss all that without undue haste, since it concerns after all my project approved by the Duce, we made an appointment for the first half of the month of May, so as to give me time to formalize my contract.[1] All the gossip that is going around, spread intentionally by the usual enemies, does not have the slightest foundation, and you can therefore be reassured.

Actually I am the one who will resign and have nothing more to do with the project if things are not done in the way I consider proper for the good of the Italian theater; so far the accord between me and Ciano and between me and the Inspectorate of the Theater is perfect, and everything will be done on the basis of that agreement.

. . . .

Your Maestro

[1] Pirandello is still expecting to be called to London for the signing of the contract with Reece—which is repeatedly put off because of several reasons that are mentioned in the letters, and probably more so because of the one reason here rarely mentioned; that is, the international situation, which is rapidly deteriorating and will explode in a few months with Mussolini's invasion of Ethiopia and the consequent economic sanctions by the League of Nations—of which London was the principal sponsor.

{ 350721 }

To Marta Abba
Hotel Danieli
(Italy) Venice   21. VII. 1935 - XIII[1]
   My Marta,
   I arrived yesterday at dawn after a splendid voyage. I found a crowd of newspapermen and photographers at the pier waiting for me. It was a regular assault. Luckily Colin and Dr. Bonaschi—placed by the mayor of New York in charge of receiving me—defended me. I found all the press here hostile to our African enterprise, in the name of the notorious democratic principles.[2] But I made headway against them all. Today all the

[1] Letter sent from New York and written on the letterhead of the Waldorf-Astoria Hotel. After Marta's return to Italy, announced in letter 350514, Pirandello probably spent most of his time near Marta, preparing for the trip to the United States, from which he was expecting great things for himself and for the international future of Marta. The Maestro will remain in America for a little more than two and a half months and will return on board the *Conte di Savoia* to reach Naples probably on October 13.

[2] The invasion of Ethiopia by Italian troops had just begun in July and occupied the headlines of the newspapers of the whole world.

newspapers are full of my valiant defense of the Italian rationale and quote as headlines of their articles the happy sentence that I threw in the face of the journalists: "America also was once inhabited by the Indians and you occupied it." I don't know how much all this might be helpful for my business deals, but it does not matter![3]

Here I found a suffocating heat, with thunderstorms that explode suddenly, leaving an even more suffocating heat than before; the rain falls boiling hot and also lightning strikes; yesterday it killed four people on the shore of the Hudson. I am staying here on the forty-first floor of the skyscraper tower of the Waldorf-Astoria, almost as tall as a mountain. I have a beautiful suite, and Colin has a room close to mine. I'll stay in New York for perhaps ten more days, and then I'll leave for Hollywood. Today it's Sunday, and the city is dead; everybody is out in the country or at the beach. I can't get in touch with anyone. Tomorrow I'll start seeing everybody, and it seems to me almost sure that I'll conclude some kind of a business deal, perhaps more than one. But for the time being I cannot tell you anything. Only that I was received, as usual, regally, with the Italian flag waving from this big hotel, the car of the mayor of New York at my disposal, concerts in my honor, banquets, receptions, etc.

But all those things, you know, are enormous burdens that put me in a bad mood.

My Marta, where are you? I suppose that today you left for Venice, but I do not know whether you'll stay at the Excelsior; that is, in the Lido; I am sending this letter to the Hotel Danieli in Venice with a request to forward it. I'm mailing immediately so that it will travel on the *Conte di Savoja*, which sails for Italy on Tuesday morning, the 23rd. The letter will be in Naples at the end of the month; that is, on the 30th; and you will have it at the beginning of August. If immediately, as soon as you receive it, you'll send me a telegram, here to the Waldorf-Astoria Hotel (it will be sufficient to write Pirandello—Waldorf-Astoria—New York) with your address and your itinerary, I'll be really happy.

Again, my best wishes, my Marta, for your name day, which falls on the 29th, and I am unfortunately far away, but you'll feel me more than ever near. With the endless love of

Your Maestro

[3] For a documentation of the American press during Pirandello's visit to New York, see Daniela Fink Sani, "Pirandello a New York nei documenti della stampa americana," *Quaderni di Teatro* (November 1980).

{ 350813 }

To Marta Abba
26, Via Aurelio Saffi
Milan
(Italy) Tuesday 13. VIII. 1935 - XIII[1]

My Marta,

If my letter took ten days to reach you, yours took thirteen to reach me! It went first very quickly to Cherbourg, France, and there it stopped, waiting for a ship heading for North America. The German ship *Bremen* called, and the letter left with the *Bremen*. In order to get a letter to move with some speed (I mean, relatively speaking) it is necessary to know the timetable of the ships from Genoa, and mail a few days before.

But let's skip that kind of chattering, and get to us, or better, to you. As soon as I arrived I saw Cutti, who talked to me about *Teresa Confalonieri* with the greatest admiration. She said she was present at the private screening that Capitani set up for the representatives of the major film companies and the press. The film got a mediocre reception, but every-body was impressed by you and asked who and where was "that great artist"; the representative of Paramount was especially impressed. Cutti got immediately into negotiations with him and others, but you must know that this is the country of eternal negotiations that never lead to a conclusion. A deal is closed all of a sudden—you never know when and why, surprisingly, and because of reasons you least expect—of course, when it does happen! The negotiations do not do anything but wear out and annoy the people involved. Annoyance is the strongest impression that one gets from American life. Cutti assures me that you would make big money if you came to America. There are no actresses to match you, either in theater or in film. All the movie companies are looking for a great actress like you, but they don't do anything to find you, and if you did something worth finding, then they would play the haughty role and they would annoy you and wear you out with the usual eternal negotia-tions. Bergner,[2] who had so much success in London, was a big failure here. On the contrary, the little Rainer,[3] who played the role of the Step-

---

[1] Letter written from New York City, on the letterhead of the Waldorf-Astoria Hotel.

[2] At the time that Pirandello writes, the German actress Elisabeth Bergner had not yet achieved her American successes, for instance, in *The Two Mrs. Carrols* by M. Vale (1943) and in *The Duchess of Malfi* by Webster (1946).

[3] Luise Rainer, born in Vienna in 1910, became a successful film star in America and

daughter in Reinhardt's last tour with the *Six Characters*, was a success. It all depends on finding the right "in" at the right moment, when you are needed. It's a matter of luck. It's not a question of either merit or ability. Cutti got under way again as soon as I called her back to the hotel, after receiving your letter, and I told her that you probably would come to America, if serious preparations could be made, with a lot of input, first stirring up a great interest as for a first-class artistic event. But also before your letter arrived, I had talked with our general consul Spinelli, who, together with the representatives of the Italian colony here, would welcome your coming. The financial support of the Inspectorate for the Theater would be necessary, and perhaps some pressure could be applied from there. But I don't trust the Italian colony here because, like everywhere else, it never participates in Italian enterprises. Everything that is presented here in America—the performances by Sterni or those by the ill-famed Guglielmo Emanuel Gatti, and the movies by Musco in a third-rate movie theater, and now the film *Porto* with Gramatica and Pilotto—is really pretty bad, and only reinforces the idea that Italian people are miserable tatterdemalions. The Ministry of Propaganda should forbid such exports, which cause incalculable damage to our good name, and on the contrary it should support a noble, truly artistic enterprise, endowing it generously and helping it out in every possible way. This need is felt deeply, and it is now more urgent than ever. And you are the only one who can perform this service for Italy! As soon as Cutti comes and tells me something about her new projects, I'll write to you again and, if necessary, I'll send a telegram. As you see I am still in New York, in the midst of negotiations that—Colin assures me—are very serious, with Metro, Paramount, R.K.O., Fox, Universal, and then with the theaters, with Anderson, Pemberton, the Guild, Shumlin,[4] and others; there is also in the making a three-week contract with N.B.C. Radio. But still nothing final. Perhaps something will be worked out. It seems that Rubin, a businessman representative of Metro, went to Europe to conclude a deal with me and he did not find me. The fact is that during the trip on the *Conte di Savoja*, I received a marconigram from Irving Marx from London saying: "Rubin here can arrange contract Metro stop cable address Newyork stop regards - Irving Marx." Now we are waiting for Rubin to return to

---

won two Academy Awards in a row for *The Great Ziegfeld* (1937) and *The Good Earth* (1937).

[4] Herman Shumlin, producer and director of theater and film.

New York, which seems to be imminent. The representative of Metro here in New York was sure that Rubin had already got the contract with me signed in Europe. Of all the negotiations this one seems to me—I don't say the surest—but the least uncertain. Colin, on the contrary, is more than sure that we'll close not only this one, but a lot of other deals. We'll see. Meanwhile my trip has certainly been useful to me for something. I see that there is a lively interest in me here; my every step is followed by the press; everybody wants to meet me—theater managers, directors, actors, actresses—not to mention the reporters and photographers. From Hollywood Marlene Dietrich has telegraphed that she was interested in *Trovarsi*. Sylvia Sydney came to see me at my hotel for a script. Also Anderson would like to perform *Trovarsi*, but in a theater. Langner from the Guild is interested in *Il piacere dell'onestà*. But it is useless to keep talking about this mountain of "interests." Perhaps it will come to something. Meanwhile I succeeded in establishing through a lawyer, the best specialist in theatrical contracts, that the contract with the Shuberts is not valid and that all the threats those gangsters are making of getting back at me are just vain attempts at blackmail, and nothing else. The contract does not exist anymore.[5]

I'll let you know by telegram, my Marta, about my leaving for Hollywood, which should be in a few days, perhaps at the beginning of next week. Everybody says that there is a great anticipation out there for my arrival. Yesterday Mamoulian, who has just arrived from Hollywood and will have lunch with me tomorrow, repeated exactly the same thing.

. . . With the endless love of

Your Maestro

[5] See a discussion of the controversy with the Shuberts in the introduction to the letters of 1935 in this volume.

{ 350830 }

30. VIII. 1935 - XIII[1]

My Marta,

. . . Many negotiations continue, but nothing has been concluded so far! And the month of August is gone. Now Thalberg is here. He is staying in this same hotel, but I've not yet seen him. Perhaps I'll see him one of these days, but by now I have stopped hoping for anything, so far is it from the minds of these film producers that I can give them subjects suitable for their productions. They admire me too much, do you understand? They admire the height of my art and they are afraid it cannot be lowered to the mediocre comprehension of the "masses." They do despise what they say they are forced to do, and therefore you cannot argue with them. In conclusion, the situation here is as it is everywhere else, and now maybe worse. If you only saw what the plays are that had the greatest success! And the films you see around! I'm thoroughly disgusted! But now I am in it, and I'll stay to the end of the time I had proposed to stay, so that no one can say that I failed because of my own fault, because I could not overcome my impatience and my nausea. Mamoulian would like to do both *Six Characters* and *L'esclusa*; he suggested that I should get in touch with a big agent in Hollywood, who is also his agent; I did so, giving him an exclusive for three weeks; that is, until September 24. Now let's see whether something happens; but, I repeat, I am not optimistic.

The same is true for you, my Marta. Cutti is struggling uselessly, knocking at this, that, or the other door. She wants you to come over, but to do what, without any assurance? To do another film test? I know that *Teresa Confalonieri* will run here during the fall, but do you know where? In a third-rate movie theater, between Sixth and Seventh Avenue, where also the films by Musco were shown, for an audience of the lowest end of the Italian colony. Neither you from Italy nor I from here, unfortunately, can prevent it, but I strongly doubt that such an exhibition can produce anything good.

I am happy, my Marta, about what you write and about how you were able to describe your admiration and your joy in reading *Saint Joan* by Shaw. I approve your decision to accept a tour of four months in Italy,

---

[1] This letter was sent from New York City, on the letterhead of the Waldorf-Astoria Hotel. It was addressed, most probably, to Milan, Via Aurelio Saffi 26. The envelope was not preserved.

but I wish you would not quit studying English, as I do not wish you to give up your prestige as a great actress both in Italy and in the whole world. It is necessary that people keep seeing you on the stage. It's no good to stay away from it for a long time. Better if you limit yourself only to great interpretations, as you are proposing to do.

. . . I heard about the prize that Stefano won and I am very happy about it.[2] I thank you for your joy. My best greetings, my Marta, and all my endless love,

Your Maestro

[2] Pirandello's son Stefano had just won, a few days before, the 1935 Viareggio Prize for his novel *Il muro di casa*. Pirandello, who in previous years had talked about his children very little, and mostly in a negative way, now shows no hesitation in expressing his great joy and satisfaction with the fact that Stefano has taken his place in the literary field as a recognized author.

{ 350907 }

To Marta Abba
26, Via Aurelio Saffi
Milan (Italy)   7. IX. 1935[1]
My Marta,
. . . When this letter arrives with the *Conte di Savoia* (which leaves from here on the 10th and arrives in Italy on the 17th), my departure will be very near, unless in these last few remaining days of my stay in America some news will come up that could delay my return. Colin continues to hope that it will, but I continue to be sure that it will not. There are here in New York two serious producers, Selznick[2] and Thalberg. The latter came with his wife, who, as you know, is Norma Shearer; the other night at a premiere, as soon as she saw me, she rushed over to greet me, getting away—to the great surprise of everybody—from a group of people who were surrounding her. Both Selznick and Thalberg promised that they will get in touch with me. But is anything going to come out of it? Given the wind that is blowing, I do not believe so. All the films I see are stupid and vulgar, and the producers are more than ever bogged down in sticking to stupidity and vulgarity—unshakable as they are in the belief that

[1] Letter written from New York, on the letterhead of the Waldorf-Astoria Hotel.
[2] Pirandello writes "Siagnitz," but from the context it seems rather safe to assume that he meant the producer David Selznick, who at the time was vice-president of Metro-Goldwyn-Mayer.

the public does not want anything else. Therefore there is no salvation. Perhaps, if *Il piacere dell'onestà* is successful in the theaters, they would take it, because they are very sensitive to the theatrical successes, even moderate ones—and that explains why they took *As You Desire Me.* Those pigs of Shuberts, with their bankruptcy, have inflicted incalculable damage on me. They were contractually bound to produce four plays of mine, including *The New Colony*, from which certainly a magnificent film could have been drawn, but all these are now useless recriminations. I have resigned myself to going back to Italy without having concluded a single deal, and let's not talk about that anymore. I made the experiment that, in conscience, I had to make. I cannot wait to get back to work quietly and make up the time and the large amount of money that I lost.

. . . All we needed was just this unfortunate tension of relations between England and Italy! England is truly showing herself not only greedy, but also stupid and crazy. But she will not prevail. Here too, unfortunately, everybody is against us, although they declared their neutrality. As much as it is impossible for you to go back to England, so it is for me very difficult to do business in America at this time. But it does not matter. What matters most is that Italy should overcome all difficulties and win! I know, my Marta, that you share these feelings and you'll not regret that your plans have vanished.[3]

. . . I am not feeling very well, but it's nothing serious. The weather has become chilly. We had heavy rains and storms on the ocean. Enough, my Marta. I renew all my fondest wishes, with my endless love,

Your Maestro

[3] At this time, the conflict in Ethiopia had been filling world headlines for four months, and the war there was still raging. The alliance between Hitler and Mussolini was rapidly splitting Europe between dictatorial and democratic countries. Pirandello and Marta were evidently enthusiastic about the Fascist "glories," exposing themselves to the consequences of their choice in an America that was getting increasingly strong in her anti-Fascist attitude.

{ 351014 }

To Marta Abba
Albergo Termale Porro
Salsomaggiore   Rome, 14. X. 1935 - XIII

My Marta,

I am writing in bed, where I have been lying since I arrived.[1] Right on the morning of my arrival, when we were already docked in the harbor of Naples after a magnificent voyage—and I could see from the deck of the *Conte di Savoia*, standing on the pier, Stefano, Fausto, and Francesco,[2] who had come to welcome me with a group of reporters—suddenly I felt sick: a burning pain in the chest, which took away my breath and made my legs feel weak. Everybody saw me get as pale as death, and I felt as if I were really dying; I had on my forehead that icy perspiration that precedes death. Instead of giving up, I made myself strong to resist the sudden assault of the illness. Friends and my children, dismayed, at once took me to the Hotel Excelsior. There the prompt treatments, especially some hot compresses on my chest, brought me back to consciousness. I remained in the hotel, well taken care of, until 3:30 in the afternoon; then I got myself into the car, still not completely recovered, and was driven back to Rome. During the trip I was not feeling all that bad, but as soon as I arrived in Rome, at about 8 o'clock, I had to be carried to my bed, where I am still lying—very downcast, very weak, but I believe I am now on the way to recovery. I don't know to what I should attribute this sudden serious illness. I had been very well in New York and also during the voyage that, I repeat, was excellent, with a calm and delightful sea. I did not have, in truth, much appetite, and I ate, perhaps, too little on the ship. The attack was probably triggered by a teaspoon of bicarbonate taken on an empty stomach on the morning of the arrival—because of some acidity that was bothering me. It caused such a fermentation of gases inside my stomach that the diaphragm must have been pushed up so as to seriously disturb the heart, which at a certain point threatened to stop. Enough, now I'm feeling better and I hope that in a few days I'll be completely recovered.

[1] On October 5, after a number of delays, always in the hope of concluding at least one deal, Pirandello finally decided to leave New York empty-handed. He sailed on the *Conte di Savoia*, scheduled to arrive in Naples on the twelfth—as it would seem from the last letter from New York (350923), here not translated.

[2] Pirandello's two sons, Stefano and Fausto, accompanied by the chauffeur Francesco.

I thank you, my Marta, for the telegram I found at my arrival and for the letter you wrote to me from Salsomaggiore. Also Cele sent a telegram from Florence—it was so nice of her. You did the right thing, my Marta, in not coming to Naples—who knows what a scare you would have had if you had seen me arrive in such a condition. But now I have an immense desire to see you again. If I were not in this condition, I would fly to Salsomaggiore, but I cannot. I must wait until I feel better. You were naughty in taking back your picture that I had in a frame in Rome; I was very attached to that portrait, which is one of the most beautiful ever taken of you, so noble and proud and yet simple at the same time. I want it back, my Marta, I need it back. That portrait means, for me, you in my home—like the protective deity of my life and of my work. How could you even think of taking it away from me without considering the pain you were inflicting on me?

I must stop writing, because I am too weak. I will write as soon as I can to tell you the many things that I have to communicate to you. But now I really can't.

Affectionate greetings to your dear mother, who is undoubtedly with you, and also to your father. And you, my Marta, always feel, completely, to the last, surrounded by the endless love of

Your Maestro

{ 351027 }

To Marta Abba
26, Via Aurelio Saffi
Milan   Rome, 27. X. 1935 - XIII

My Marta,

Your dear letter of yesterday has put all the sweetness of your affection back into my heart. Let's not speak anymore about all the troubles of the theater from which, following your advice, I want to keep myself distant. I was forgetting to tell you that the evening before last, at the invitation of Dino Alfieri, I went to the Ministry for Press and Propaganda, where I found all together the so-called Reading Commission of the Società degli Autori, in which many drama critics take part, such as Corrado Marchi, Lorenzo Ruggi, and Sabatino Lopez; they all wanted to stay a moment and give me, together with Alfieri, their welcome back from America. When they left, Alfieri invited me to say a few words on the stage for the opening of the drama season on the evening of the 29th at the Teatro

Argentina / at this point the letter was interrupted by your phone call from Milan /[1] I told you over the phone that I did not want to accept, citing my need of rest after so much overexertion because of traveling. But eventually I accepted, since it is only a question of saying a couple of words. In order not to make an effort to extemporize, I'll write something out and read it.

I am really happy that in four or five days I'll see you again, at last, my Marta! Just seeing you will cure me. Already the sound of your voice, when I was listening to it over the phone, is doing me a great deal of good, as if a balsam were flowing into all my veins. But do not believe, my Marta, that I am very sick. I know that my life can come to an end any moment; but *I don't feel* sick; *I feel alive*, and woe be it for me if it is not so! I could not adapt myself to keep on living; that is, vegetating badly, not doing anything. I would feel anger and disgust. I want death to catch me while I am in full action. Standing upright. What would it otherwise mean to keep on living? Why bother to rest? Why bother to take care of oneself? Living for me means to work, to create; when I'm not able to do so any longer, it's a hundred times better for me to die. Abstaining from work, resting, are possible for me only for a short time, and only if the hope—or better, the confidence—lasts that after that necessary rest I'll get back to my earlier strength and I'll be back on my feet, working.

According to what they told me, it seems that there is no determination, for the time being, of any organic defect or of any lesion on the heart; and that it's only a question of warnings, and that I'll have to be careful not to overexert myself too much with traveling, as I did all this year; not to smoke so much, and to take certain drugs that regulate the blood circulation and slightly lower the blood pressure, which is a bit too high. But, good God, it's clear that at sixty-eight the arteries cannot be as elastic as at twenty-eight. Death can lie in wait as much as it wishes: I ask it to attack me suddenly and finish me, without throwing me into a bed or an armchair with a medicine dropper in one hand, and in the other hand a trembling glass.[2]

But let's not speak about that, let's talk about the joy that your imminent coming to Rome will bring me. I'll be very pleased also to see dear Cele. Yesterday I went to the Excelsior, where they were celebrating the founding of the new film company Columbus Film, with German capital and Gallone as manager. They will start with *Ma non è una cosa seria*.

[1] The slashes are by Pirandello.

[2] A year later Death accepted his request, attacked him, and finished him in a few days.

Marchesano prepared the contract; it is for sixty-five thousand lire, with thirty-five thousand for each foreign version: the most that has ever been paid in Italy. They gave a big dinner; the whole cinema world was there— what a collection! I stayed there only five minutes, to meet the German producers: it seems that they are the representatives of Rabinovich from UFA. Enough, we'll talk again at your approaching arrival, which I'm hoping will be as quick as possible. Best greetings to your parents, and to you all the endless love of

Your Maestro

{ 351030 }

To Marta Abba
26, Via Aurelio Saffi
Milan   Rome, 30. X. 1935 - XIV

My Marta,

I had from Stefano your dearest letter with the prescriptions dictated by Giaconìa and the recommendations dictated by your affection.

The medicines prescribed by my doctor are more or less the same as those indicated by Giaconìa, except the iodide, which does not apply in my case. Rest in bed is not necessary, since I have no lesion in my heart and I have no angina pectoris as Giaconìa does. The type of rest I need is something else—in my whole way of life. I must build up my resistance. In conclusion, I must work a little less, not travel so much, and stop smoking too much. And that's all. In fact, I haven't had any symptom of the illness lately.

Last night I gave my speech in the theater without any bad consequences. The Duce was present, as you might have heard from the newspapers; he invited me to his box after the speech, and was very nice to me. He liked my speech very much and he ordered that it be published all over Italy through "Stefani."[1]

The theater was packed. But unfortunately the two works chosen for the opening of the season were very boring. The *Mese mariano*, performed by Palmer, was pitiful: everybody was out of tune, worst of all that little ugly thing of a Palmer who wanted to play the Neapolitan, can you imagine! And that Betrone, what a dog! Less terrible than the others was Scalzo, in a small character role. I won't say anything about the silliness of *Tela di Penelope* by Calzini, unbearable. Three acts without structure

---

[1] Stefani was the official news agency in Italy.

and without action: a text that is bad as literature and lacking sincerity, tirades à la Benelli,[2] mannerisms by Maltagliati, who performed the role of a cheap hetaera; only the scenery and the costumes were designed, in good taste, by Tòfano himself. On the whole, the company seemed to me a bit, or rather very, boisterous. Cervi, in the role of Ulysses, was a dog that could match Betrone, the only difference being that Betrone is always a dog, while Cervi can be occasionally believable, because of the role. I don't see how they can do *Ma non è una cosa seria* well, which they have on their schedule. Certainly Tòfano with De Sica and Rissone could do a better job. It seems that they were successful in Bologna. We'll see.

. . . Affectionate greetings to your parents; a big hug to you, with all my heart,

Your Maestro

[2] Sem Benelli (1877–1949), Italian playwright and poet.

{ 351209 }

To Marta Abba
26, Via Aurelio Saffi
Milan

Rome, December 9, 1935 - XIV
Via Antonio Bosio, 15

My Marta,

Four days have gone by since you departed,[1] and the passing time seems to have gone *deaf*—the deafness of death, because only the sound of your voice is alive for me, and if it no longer rings in my ear and in my whole soul, the voices of other people, the sounds of life do not reach me and do not mean anything to me. I was following you with my thoughts during your whole trip, and experiencing its whole length, especially when the evening shadows began to fall. I couldn't wait for 11:30 to come, to finally see you getting off at the Milan train station—who knows how depressed and fatigued from the trip. By now you should have rested and begun the study of your roles. I see you now around your bedroom, your little study, and the living room. I know how you learn your lines; how many times you say them over and over again to find the right tone and the most effective expression. I gaze at you, I follow you and hang on your

[1] Marta had stayed in Rome from the end of October to the beginning of December. As was the case at every separation, Pirandello remains "dazed." Mentally he follows every moment of the journey that takes his beloved far away, "seeing" her in every detail.

lips and forget my body—abandoned almost lifeless in an armchair, the usual one, where I always sit in my studio. What life is there left for me? I don't care anymore about anything. Only about you do I care, and all that concerns you, my Marta; if you suffer, suffering with you and for you; if you get angry, getting angry with you; if you hope, hoping with you and for you. And remaining—for as long as I stay alive, for as long as my eyes stay open, for as long as my heart keeps beating, for as long as the soul burns in me—with my eyes, my heart, my soul, enchanted by your beauty, by the charms of your person, by the divine nobility of your feelings and of your spirit. In adoration.

I have not seen anybody. I once more read over your notes and I can't find anything you should change or tone down.[2] On the contrary, all you say about yourself seems to me to be too little! Friday when you left, and Saturday, I was at rehearsal. I cannot tell you how much I suffered! By the end, I was a regular rag! I don't know whether I should wait until Alfieri tells you something about your manuscript, concerning its publication.[3] Today, or rather tonight, after rehearsal, I would like to drop in at the Tevere to talk with Interlandi about the publication of "My Life as an Actress" in *Quadrivio*, without putting it off any longer. That means that you will have enough time to contact me, in case you get an unfavorable report from Alfieri.

I am waiting to hear from you anyhow. I wouldn't want to have you waste time in writing to me at length. I'd be happy even with a few lines on a card telling me how you are, how you feel, whether you are working—that would be enough to keep me going. I won't say anymore, because anything you do will be fine with me, and I am aware that you know what you mean to me.

I most fervently hope, my dear Marta, that I have little time left to live: I truly do not wish to prolong it. I feel every desire vanishing from me, and everything, my very body, is a burden to me.

I just noticed that I wrote on two sheets that were stuck together, and I beg you to forgive me. I am attaching them with glue so that you can easily glance over the letter. Give my affectionate regards to your parents, and you, my dear Marta, always feel completely surrounded by the love without end of

Your Maestro

[2] Pirandello is referring to Marta's manuscript, "My Life as an Actress."
[3] Marta was worried about the possible political consequences of her writing and had asked for the opinion of Vittorio Alfieri on the subject.

{ 351218 }

To Marta Abba
26, Via Aurelio Saffi
Milan   Rome, 18. XII. 1935 - XIV
                                                       Via Antonio Bosio, 15

My Marta,

I've received your letter of the evening of the 16th. I confirm the exceptional success of *Non si sa come*. It might be enough for you to know that
in only three days, Friday, Saturday and Sunday, the box office has taken
in over forty-four thousand lire, twenty thousand of which in the Sunday
performance; also yesterday, at the fifth performance, there was a good-
sized audience, and everything has been going well, after the premiere
with the usual four hundred habitués of each opening night in Rome.[1]
Let's not talk about it anymore. You are right, my Marta, in reminding
me that—in the present condition of the Italian theater—I could not
have found anyone to get my play performed better than that, but I was
mad above all at myself, for allowing it to be performed at all. Since such
is the condition of the theater in Italy, I should have not allowed it to be
performed. I needed an actor like Moissi; he was no longer there,[2] and
that should have been enough to call it off. I needed two actresses. I
needed to create an atmosphere around the work that Ruggeri was the
least apt to create. If all that was not there, I was responsible; I could
neither expect nor obtain what I wanted; I got already too much with the
success, and therefore I should not complain. Only Art had to weep, but
the royalties were saved. The success was there and big; only the Italian
theater has given a further proof of its frightening poverty: *it could not
find five actors to put together to perform a play as it should be performed.* If
we do not get to have a state theater, it is crazy to continue to work in
these conditions. I am not talking just about myself, of course! For me it
is over. I repeat, my Marta, your bitter words: "We fall always into the
same furrow, a furrow that is by now dug into our own hearts."

Let's come now to what you write to me about the publication of your
notes.[3]

---

[1] *Non si sa come* had opened on December 13, at the Teatro Argentina.

[2] The actor Alexander Moissi had died a few months before, on March 23 of that same
year.

[3] Pirandello is talking about Marta's short autobiography, *La mia vita d'attrice*, an outline of her memories as an actress, which Marta was in doubt as to whether she should
publish. In several letters she wavers, gives permission, then retracts it in great anxiety

You know, my Marta, that for me the only rule of behavior is to obey the personal feeling that each one of us has, of what is good and what is bad, for everything we are going to do. If you have a feeling that you call, in a sublime way, "your sense of privacy"—which is therefore the most intimate, the noblest, and the purest—you must respect it, my Marta, and follow it. I cannot and I should not put myself in your place, nor substitute any feeling of mine about good or evil for your own. As far as I am concerned, I do not see anything bad in publishing it, but the case is different if you feel uneasy about it—as if the publication were a violation of what you call, with so much purity of spirit and exquisite feminine sensibility, your "sense of privacy." I can only tell you that the impression, not only mine, but of all those who read your notes—D'Amico, Antonelli, Sergio, Trigona, I believe also Graziadei—was excellent. Your notes are all marked by great nobility; if there is some anger, if there is any bitterness, this anger and bitterness are equally noble and nobly expressed, without any trace of self-interest. You speak with veneration of your teachers, with veneration of Duse; you speak about the good things you did in your country and abroad; of all the love you always, all the time, had for the Italian theater, in the face of so many struggles and so many sacrifices; you speak with so much reverence about the Duce; you do not exalt yourself because of your victories except in the name of Art, without any personal vanity; I don't see where and how anybody can attack any point of what you say, or blame or "demolish" you, as you say. Quite the contrary! It does not seem to me that you expose yourself to the professional denigrators, to the slanderers, to the enemies that you do not name, either by arrogant airs or by attitudes that might provoke easy ridicule. But all these are my personal ideas, which are not meant to nor should count at all against your *intimate feeling*. If you *perceive inside yourself* that, for the time being, you should not publish your notes, do not publish them! There will always be time. It might suffice for you that you did write them as a need of your spirit. For me every decision of yours is sacred—as an expression of what in you is noble, pure, just, superior to the human, truly angelical in its nature—and it will be respected.

I am waiting for a word from you on this point.

. . . Thank you, my Marta, for your loving concern for me and for my health; I'd really like to have someone here who, at this difficult mo-

---

about the possible consequences of the publication. See that title in the *Indice dei Nomi* of the Italian edition for further references on this theme. These notes are published in the journal *Il Dramma*, in three installments (issues of July 1 and 15 and August 1, 1936).

ment of my life, would do just that. I am a little better, but certainly not well; it seems to me that they do everything possible to prevent me from eating and from nourishing myself. Enough. Whatever will be will be! Be sure to stay healthy and serene, my Marta, protect yourself from this terrible winter we are going through, and receive always the endless love of

Your Maestro

Letters of
1936 from Rome

·⟨∽⟩⟨∽⟩·

THE FIRST LETTERS of this year find Marta in Milan, where she is
still recovering from a lingering illness but seems ready to begin
rehearsals for the upcoming theater season. Notwithstanding the
recent Fascist reforms, supposedly intended to break the monopoly of the
theater managers, Pirandello continues to lament the critical situation
of the Italian theater, still fragmented into a plethora of worthless companies, in which the talent of a few good actors is submerged in the mediocrity of the majority. Pirandello insists on attributing the responsibility
to the managers, who continue to multiply the number of companies
without any consideration for quality in order to squeeze profits from the
many places they control; moreover, they are imposing an almost exclusively foreign repertory, thus aggravating the snobbish xenomania of Italian audiences and critics. According to Pirandello, all the good actors in
Italy would be hardly enough to put together one, or at most two, high-
level companies. The only way to heal Italian drama still remains, for
him, a total realization of his plan of a resident national theater, managed
with rigorous artistic criteria and dedicated primarily to an Italian repertory—as he had personally explained to Mussolini. The Fascist government, however, is now making the situation worse than before the reform
with a rainfall of new subsidies that are indiscriminately distributed to
a few capable artists, to many incapable hacks, and . . . to the usual dishonest profiteers! Scandalized, the Maestro bursts into an exclamation:
"Everybody is wallowing in the trough . . . it's disgusting!"

Starting in April, an offer to Marta by the American theater impresario
Gilbert Miller for a season of performances on Broadway becomes the
central theme of almost every letter. Pirandello, although well aware of
his precarious health and of his swiftly approaching end, appears completely dominated by the emotions stirred by the preparation and the
realization of the great adventure awaiting his beloved. He elevates the
American contract to a symbolic level as the final success of his long
efforts for the worldwide recognition of Marta's art. The Maestro is
prodigal with suggestions; he looks for the best possible legal counsel to

determine the most advantageous terms in every detail of the contract; he encourages her in every possible way to face the many difficulties involved. Marta had been longing for an occasion to conquer American audiences. As soon as she is finished with her Italian engagements, at the beginning of June, she goes to England to improve her English, rehearses with the actor who will play with her one of the leading roles on Broadway, and for the first time faces an English-speaking audience, performing in their language in the suburbs of London. She has a point in her favor: the comedy *Tovarich* is ideal for a foreign actress because the protagonist, a Russian noble emigrée in Paris who is working as a maid, must speak with an exotic accent, and errors in the pronunciation, and even in the grammar, must make the situation still more authentic and amusing. After this fatiguing trial period, in mid-August Marta comes back to Italy, rests for a little while, and then leaves for the land of so many promises. On September 17, she lands in New York, tries out on the stages of Baltimore and Philadelphia, and eventually, on October 15, has her debut on Broadway, with a promising reception from both audience and critics.

Until the very last moment before Marta's departure Pirandello refuses to let his attention rest even for a short time on the impending separation—which will be definitive. However, when the reality of the distance hits him, he feels that he has fallen into an "abyss without end." Depression attacks him with new violence, giving him the feeling of "sinking . . . without a holding point" and making it impossible for him to work, giving him a sense of nausea for the theater and the desire of dedicating himself fully to narrative. He is despondent and restless, even wants to leave his Roman dwelling that now oppresses him as a prison. His mind is all with Marta; the rest is for him foreign and a matter of indifference. He does not care about the honor conferred on him by Nazi Germany, where Goebbels officially announces to him, during a visit to Berlin, the preparation of a new translation and publication in German of his complete works. He does not care about the proposal for a plush production of his *I giganti della montagna* for the coming May Festival in Florence. His only real joy is the news of Marta's successes in Baltimore, Philadelphia, and finally in the very heart of the American theater world, on Broadway.

At this point the Maestro tries to convince himself that Marta does not need him any longer. He can now slip away in silence, on tiptoe, and vanish almost without her noticing it. One month before the end, he declares that he never felt "so alone and without life," and a few days before his death he writes once more that he is wandering around "like a fly without a head."

In the last letter, which reaches Marta after his death, he sends to his beloved an extreme lament: "If I think about the distance, I feel I am sliding into a horrible loneliness, like into an abyss of despair." A few evenings after this adieu without hope, from the stage of the Plymouth Theatre in New York a deeply moved Marta announced to her audience that on December 10 Luigi Pirandello had died of pneumonia in Rome.

{ 360114 }

To Marta Abba
26, Via Aurelio Saffi
Milan   Rome, 14. I. 1936 - XIV
                                                              Via Antonio Bosio, 15

My Marta,

Unexpectedly this morning I received one more letter from you, written on Sunday afternoon, and just the thought that you think of me makes me happy. I'd love to spend all my time writing to you; I'd love to share with you all that goes through my mind, all that weighs on my heart, all that gives air to my soul; phantoms of art, dreams that would be so beautiful if they could come true.[1] It is really true, completely true, my Marta, that my spirit is still twenty years old, and when I consider that, on the contrary, I am in the age bracket in which people die, full as I still am of so many things to do, I think that the time assigned to man is truly short and that death would be really unjust for me. But let's not think such melancholy thoughts. Moreover, at the moment, I'm feeling fine.

. . . I have been purposely staying away from the workings of the Corporation of Performing Arts, which is an institution different from and much more complex than the Inspectorate for the Theater. It seems that the preparatory work is not yet finished, and I do not know what conclusions they've reached. I heard rumors that the section for the cinema has taken the upper hand. It seems that all expenditures and thought will go for the cinema, which will get nothing less than a brand-new city built from scratch.[2] As far as the theater is concerned, there was talk about

---

[1] Pirandello expresses his deep longing for a continuous communication and perfect communion of spirit with the beloved—a never-realized dream he craved all life long.

[2] This is the time when the construction of Cinecittà was decided.

municipal theaters, which you, my Marta, have always fought for; also about freeing the "condominium" boxes and remodeling the interior of the theaters, and the stages. But it seems that they are not yet talking about setting up a genuine state theater. Not a word about my project— my projects that triggered all those talks now going on about the theater. Nobody has even thought to ask me. As if I did not exist, or as if I were nobody. Let them go ahead! It means that they can do without me, or do not like the idea, or do not believe it is convenient for them that I get involved. Therefore can you imagine if I want to get involved! Let's hope that they will pick up the good points of my plans; and if then they do not want to give me any credit, let them go right ahead, I'll be happy either way.[3] But will they get anything done?[4] That's all. But let them once and for all do something seriously and honestly!

Enough. Give me your news as soon as you can. Take care. Be serene. With all the endless love of

Your Maestro

[3] Pirandello by now seems to have forgotten that "his" plan was actually taken in great part from others—to whom he never gives credit either! See the Subject Index of the Italian edition of these letters, entry Teatro di Stato, for the history of the project.

[4] Pirandello is deeply offended and pessimistic. Fascist populism is getting the upper hand, thus giving precedence to the project of building Cinecittà on the outskirts of Rome in order to produce pretentious propaganda movies for the masses, while the idea of an art theater, considered an elite luxury, is set aside together with Pirandello, who was its champion.

{ 360116 }

To Marta Abba
26, Via Aurelio Saffi
Milan
         Rome, 16. 1. 1936 - XIV
         Via Antonio Bosio, 15

My Marta,

. . . After so many months of suffocating in Rome, I feel an extreme need to move out and change my surroundings. After that I don't know whether I'll come to Rome or end up making other arrangements for where I stay. We'll talk about that during my visit in Milan. I absolutely must make a decision. As I am now, I feel as if I were dying among petty and confining routines. It is true that there is the project of a new trip of mine to South America for next April, which is not too distant. I am supposed to leave on April 1 and arrive in Buenos Aires on the 15th, the day of the start of the festivities celebrating the foundation of that city. I wouldn't stay there more than about twenty days; so I could be back in the second half of May. The decision about providing a different direction for my life should be better put off until my return from America, but I'd like to set something up starting right now. Your sound judgment, always so correct, your advice, so wise and just, will help me. I have already plans to do so many things.

. . . I heard that the funds for the state theater have been allocated, and that it will be built on the same place where the Teatro Argentina now stands. No date for its dedication has been set. All projects are in a phase of study. There is nothing definitely decided as yet, only that there will be a state theater. And that is already a lot! Afterward we'll see how it will be done. Let's hope for the best.

.   .   .   .   .   .

Your Maestro

{ 360117 }

To Marta Abba
26, Via Aurelio Saffi
Milan
                                        Rome, 17. I. 1936 - XIV
                                          Via Antonio Bosio, 15

My Marta,
. . . You'll see that in the end we'll get what is most important for us, even though we won't get any recognition for what we did. They want to take all the credit for themselves, taking advantage of our work, even at the cost of realizing it poorly, as long as it doesn't appear that the state theater is due to our efforts. They want to be the ones who bring it to realization—even if badly. What do you want to do? I say, after all, let them do it! Later, once complete in whichever form, it will fix itself by itself, if the mistakes made at the beginning are not irreparable. They act like petulant and pompous children who set themselves up to construct, without the help of the grown-ups, a building without the necessary foundation, even at the cost of being crushed under it. They don't want to listen to the advice of those who know more than they do and have already foreseen everything. The most serious danger they face is that the building will not stand, because the harmony of all the component parts is predictably not there; and those parts are many, all to be prepared beforehand, so that they develop all together, like a living body that from

the beginning develops in all its parts at the same time; otherwise, a monster will be born, deformed in all its parts, here too developed and there lame and deficient. It is useless just to place the stones of the building one on top of the other if all the other things are not prepared at the same time—programs, company, technicians, and, above all, the vital spirit coordinating the great enterprise.

Do they have such a spirit? Are they capable of such a complex and coordinated preparation?

. . . . . .

Your Maestro

{ 360306 }

To Marta Abba
"Compagnia dei Grandi Spettacoli d'Arte"
Teatro Corso
Bologna   Rome, 6. III. 1936 - XIV
                                             Via Antonio Bosio, 15

My Marta,

Yes, I did notice myself that my handwriting is getting more and more illegible, irregular, uncertain, and wavering—but not because of carelessness, nor because I write in a hurry, or I am nervous, or feel sick.

Perhaps my body, without my being aware of it, is feeling neglected and run-down. I abuse it, and it takes it and says nothing. For a long time my eyes have been in need of help, and nobody has helped them, and they are forced to read and write, as if they could see as well as they used to before. "Oh, look, Pirandello, you still read without glasses? Lucky you!" My vanity is such that I read without glasses, and I read with difficulty, straining my eyesight more and more to decipher the letters, because I do not wear glasses. It bothers me to go to an oculist, get my eyesight tested—it's different in each eye but weak by now in both—and get a pair of glasses made. Perhaps that's one of the reasons why I write so poorly. You've made me start to think about it now, my Marta. However, I always write the name Marta well. Even blind, I will always write it well.

Moreover, I've almost lost the habit of writing in longhand—since I've started to use the typewriter. I write by hand only to you, my Marta. But it's true that I write often, and I wish I'd gotten into that habit again, since I write so much to you. It must be the eyesight, or certain uncontrolled and uncontrollable motions of the nerves that betray, for those who can trace the symptoms, secret imbalances of the organism. Those people should be aware, for example, that I am writing this letter with special care to make clear, as much as possible, every single letter. You must have perceived that too, which means that I must take better care of the way I write, so that your dear eyes do not have to strain to decipher what I write. The fact that I see poorly and I need eyeglasses—that's a completely different matter.

.   .   .   .   .   .

Your Maestro

{ 360311 }

To Marta Abba
Hôtel Excelsior
Florence   Rome, 11. III. 1936 - XIV
                                                                Via Antonio Bosio, 15

My Marta,

I received your letter of Monday 9, which has worried me a lot because of the news you give me about your tiredness and the condition of your spirit. I don't know how independent one is of the other—although you say that the state of affairs of your company and the unpleasantnesses that you take so much to heart have an influence on both.

I can't wait for your arrival in Rome, my Marta! I don't know why, but I do trust that you will immediately feel better here. Cele is here; I am here; your company will do better here than elsewhere. You'll see; I am not deceiving myself. We'll cheer you up; we'll have fun; we'll go out for excursions; the weather hints at getting better, and my car will be at your disposal; everybody is ready to gladly receive and welcome you. Come as a victor, come with serenity. I want so much to put the color of the sky into this black mood of yours—but, before all, I want to give you back the strength you have not yet well recovered, the fullness of your health. We'll talk about so many things, including those blessed box-office receipts of your company, which for a long time have left both you and me perplexed. If you remember, I called them to your attention also in Milan. I don't know whether it is a matter of stupidity, dishonesty, or carelessness. Perhaps all three together. But when the money belongs to other people, and even worse, to the government, unfortunately in Italy, maybe more than elsewhere, it has always been like that. Conscience is the rarest thing in the world.

... I thank you, my Marta, for the advice you gave me and for the interest you show in my eyesight. I cannot do it now. But I promise that I'll have glasses, at least for reading, by the time you'll be in Rome. I also called Doctor Trenti for a general checkup.

. . . . . .

Your Maestro

{ 360313 }

To Marta Abba
Hôtel Excelsior
Florence   Rome, 13. III. 1936 - XIV
                                                    Via Antonio Bosio, 15

My Marta,

I've received your letter of yesterday, written in a different handwriting, so much so that at the beginning I thought it was a letter from Cele, who writes exactly like that. If I can tell you the truth, it seems to me that this way your handwriting loses its character and becomes uniform with that of many other women. You must have your own; the one that is your own and natural and cannot be mistaken for any other—Marta's handwriting. Let it be as it will, but let it be your own. This way, on the contrary, it can belong to anyone, and therefore it's no good.

This morning I had to go to the Academy for the awarding of the Mussolini Prizes. I am happy because I succeeded in performing a good deed this year, getting it to be awarded, for literature, to Emilio Cecchi, who finds himself in a dire financial situation. You know, Marta, that I cannot keep a grudge against anybody. There are many ways of winning, and perhaps the best, or at least the most Christian, is that of winning by doing good to someone who did you harm, especially when somebody else has already avenged the evil done to you. Performing a good action in such circumstances is not easy, and doing so is a meritorious deed. Therefore I am happy. Today a wife and three poor children in need will bless me.

... I'll see you in three days, my Marta! Be cheerful, don't worry about anything, we'll have fun![1] With all the endless love of

Your Maestro

[1] Pirandello appears happy, pleased with himself because of the "Christian" deed, and—at least for the moment—relaxed, because Marta will be in Rome soon and it will be possible to have fun, without worrying. The tone of the letters will change completely

starting with the next one—sent three weeks later—and will be inspired by feverish preparations and important decisions. After endless negotiations that Pirandello had started
during his visit in New York with the purpose of opening for Marta "the path of Glory
and Fortune" in America, at last the longed-for proposal arrives. A powerful American
impresario now wants to launch the Italian actress as a new star on Broadway, cast in a
leading role that does not require a perfect command of the English language—just the
way Pirandello had been dreaming all along for Marta. Gilbert Miller offers Marta the lead
in the comedy *Tovarich*, now being prepared for Broadway. This event, which will change
Marta's life, dominates the correspondence with the beloved until the end of the Maestro's life.

{ 360406 }

Rome, 6. IV. 1936 - XIV
Via Antonio Bosio, 15[1]

My Marta,

I've received your letter of yesterday from Livorno. It's exasperating, at
times like this, to follow your continually interruped itinerary when, in
order not to lose time, it would be necessary for you to stay put in one
place and wait for news about such important negotiations.[2] But patience!

I enclose here (1) Colin's letter sent before his telegrams, important
because it reflects the intentions of Miller about you, better defined in
successive telegrams; (2) Colin's telegram in answer to yours from Naples,
in which the departure of Miller for London and his arrival in Rome at
the end of the current month are announced, and then the conditions are
clarified, not in the form of a legal contract, but rather as an understanding with Miller in New York regarding you. You'll sign the contract with
Miller here in Rome. . . . After calmly reading the telegram again, it seems
to me that the following is to be understood: in New York, Miller has
agreed to sign a contract with you in Rome for performing *Tovarich* in
October in New York;[3] after ninety days (that is, after three months) he

---

[1] The envelope of this letter is not preserved, and from the content it is not possible to
establish whether Marta was still in Leghorn or already in La Spezia, where the following
letter 360408 is addressed.

[2] The dream of becoming a star in America appears to be close to its realization. The
negotiations with the theater producer Gilbert Miller for the launching of Marta in New
York are entering a conclusive phase.

[3] *Tovarich*, the adaptation by Robert E. Sherwood of the comedy by Jacques Deval, is
about a couple of Russian aristocrat émigrés in Paris after the revolution, who, although
they are the custodians of an enormous fortune belonging to the Romanovs and deposited
in a French bank, work as servants in the home of a French Communist deputy in order

will decide two things (of course, after the success you'll have had with *Tovarich*): first, to exercise or not the option for a second play, paying you a minimum of 750 dollars per week; or, second, to sign a contract for five years, theater and cinema, with 40,000 dollars guaranteed per year. Everything, in conclusion, will depend on your success in *Tovarich*. If it is fairly well received, he will try again with a second play. If on the contrary the success is excellent in *Tovarich* (as I am sure it will be), then he will sign without delay the contract for five years, with 40,000 dollars guaranteed per year. Since Miller knows you only by reputation and has never seen you on the stage, his proposal seems to me now more reasonable. . . . It is advantageous for you, anyhow, to accept, even though the contract is not, as Colin considers it, "magnificent." What is certain is that you'll be launched by a great impresario like Miller (who is today the most important of all) as a "great star." All the rest will come by itself.

Be cheerful, or, at least, calm, my Marta; everything will certainly happen as you desire and deserve. With the endless love of

Your Maestro

---

not to have to touch the money belonging to the deposed czars. Marta was to play the role of the grand duchess Tatiana Petrovna, with actor John Halliday in the role of Prince Mikail Alexandrovic Ouratiev, her husband. *Tovarich* is a typical Broadway comedy, with broad commercial appeal. The characters are stereotypical, the situations are paradoxical, and the odd English of the Russian émigrés is cleverly exploited. The comedy opened in London on April 24, and in New York, with Marta, on October 15, 1936.

{ 360413 }

To Marta Abba
Grand Hôtel Colombia
Genoa   Rome, 13. IV. 1936 - XIV
                                                    Via Antonio Bosio, 15

My Marta,

. . . At last a first contract coming from America![1] I'll send it back with
my signature right away tomorrow, after getting my signature notarized
by the American consul.

But the letter is especially interesting for you, my Marta. Interesting,
because it shows that Miller foresees that *Tovarich* can last on the stage
for more than one year with your interpretation, so much so that they
are thinking that *Trovarsi* might be performed by another actress, Helen
Hayes. You can imagine how happy I would be if Donata Genzi[2] is you
also in America, but thinking of you, of the great stroke of luck it would
be for you if you could last a whole year in the comedy by Deval, I wish
that Hayes, not you, would be Donata Genzi. Someone else certainly
cannot be Donata Genzi, because you are Donata Genzi by birth, and
there will never be another one like you. But what do I care, if with
Tovarich you'll succeed in making your fortune over there?

. . . I don't need to recommend to you again that you make yourself
more beautiful than ever, my Marta, in these days; it should not be
difficult, because you are already beautiful, but make yourself also super-
elegant, and quiet and serene! It will help if you could completely stop
worrying about whatever can happen in this final breakup of your company! Get rid of it as soon as you can, so that you can be in Rome in time
for Miller's arrival, and in the best condition to receive him, without
haste and free from worries. Let him find you in bloom, with your soul
full of the refreshing smile of spring.

I am talking as if, after your departure for America, I am not going to
feel like dying. The thought of your happiness and the anxiety with
which I will be waiting for your success over there will sustain me, my
Marta. And when I know that you are victorious and happy, I'll be able to
close my eyes forever, not having anything more to expect down here.[3]

---

[1] Pirandello is referring to a contract from Gilbert Miller acquiring the rights for
Trovarsi, as reported in a letter from his New York agent Saul Colin.

[2] The leading role in Pirandello's *Trovarsi*.

[3] Pirandello died a few months later, just as Marta was reaching the goal of succeeding
on an international level in New York.

But no melancholy thoughts, at least for the time being! Have fun, relax! With all the endless love of

Your Maestro

{ 360427 }

To Marta Abba
Grand Hôtel de la Ville
Trieste   Rome, 27. IV. 1936 - XIV
Via Antonio Bosio, 15

My Marta,

. . . I am still being pressured from all sides to go to South America. All the newspapers of Argentina, Brazil, and Chile, from which Giacompol sent me numberless clippings, are full of my imminent trip to those countries. In the presence of the Italian ambassador and of the official representatives of the Argentinian government, the fiftieth performance of *Questa sera si recita a soggetto* in Spanish was solemnly celebrated; it was an evening in my honor, with a speech by de Védia, who announced my forthcoming visit; and everybody is talking about the many welcoming celebrations on the occasion of the premiere of *Non si sa come*, translated by Guibourg for the Quiroga Company. But I cannot go. Last evening Prof. Trenti came back to see me; he took my blood pressure again. He told me that I would have to be insane to go. Well, if it were the case of another kind of insanity—I mean a more pleasant and gratifying one— I would gladly do it. But, my Marta, I have no desire whatsoever of risking my skin in South America for honors of which I am already sick and that I couldn't care less about. I don't really know to whom I can give that glory, or what I can do with it. I have never felt so alone! Alone, now, with death hanging over my head. There is nothing to be sad about, because it doesn't hurt at all.

Away! Away! Away! Let's blow away all those melancholy thoughts! Prof. Trenti would like to scare me, but he cannot succeed. I am waiting for your triumph in America. After that, yes, I can die. In the meantime, my Marta, always feel surrounded by the endless love of

Your Maestro

{ 360430 }

                                  Rome, 30. IV. 1936 - XIV
                                    Via Antonio Bosio, 15

My Marta,

. . . You did not tell me how *Questa Sera* was received in Venice and Trieste, where it was new, and you were right, because by now I do not put any more importance on those things. I do not know how good that is, because by dint of not giving any more importance to the things of life, life loses its consistency, becomes empty, and finishes. But perhaps it is not a bad thing that—at a certain point—life ends. If I count the things that interest me, besides you, I find nothing, and then does it not seem right to you that—after your triumph in America, on which you must now concentrate all your efforts—the best wish you can have for your Maestro is this: that he may close his eyes forever, with the vision of you over there, far away, victorious and happy? With that I'll have had my happiness, and I won't have anything else to hope and to wait for.

I did not call Prof. Trenti, because of the pressure from South America; he came by himself to see the result of the treatment prescribed for my blood pressure. The pressure is still identical, 200 over 90. And that was enough to make him say that I would have to be out of my mind to go on such a long trip and be subjected to so much overexertion and emotional strain. But I do not feel either better or worse than before. I am still strong and able to work. I do not complain about my body, which is losing its will to live and does not want to fuss in any way to help itself and fill up not so much the void, but the abandonment of everything, into which deliberately, little by little, it sinks and drowns. It would be necessary that a hand catches it again. But it is too late, and death starts getting impatient.

Let's end it here! You should not concern yourself with these things, my Marta, until you've won, until you've reached in life the happiness you deserve, and as long as I am still alive and on my two feet, with all my strength and my whole soul—which are still great and ready, I assure you. If still one more occasion should arise, I would suddenly wake up, because it is still in my power to live. It would be enough if I want to do so.

Until soon, my Marta! Regards to your parents. For you all the endless love of

                                                Your Maestro

{ 360516 }

To Marta Abba
26, Via Aurelio Saffi
Milan

Rome, 16. v. 1936 - xiv[1]
Via Antonio Bosio, 15

My Marta,

I've being putting off writing to you from one day to the next because of so many incidents that happened, among which the most serious one is a telegram by Mr. Miller to Colin regarding that damned contract of mine with the brothers Shubert in New York. One of those gangsters is now in London; he called on Miller and told him that he has previous rights to *Trovarsi*; based on this claim he will take legal action against the contract that Miller signed with me for the acquisition of that play of mine. Miller immediately asked Colin for an explanation. Thank God, Colin had already informed him in New York about all the threats that those rascals—well known as such in the whole of North America—had made against me. But the answer that, among the plays sold in 1928 to the Shuberts, *Trovarsi* was not included at all was not enough for Miller. The Shuberts got back to him and said that the contract was for five plays, of which I had submitted only three, and that—although it was true that *Trovarsi* was not included in the remaining two—according to the contract they had the rights just the same, because of the down payments they had already given. All that is false, and they know it very well. There was the bankruptcy; there was the fact that, without continuing the payments as stipulated, they tried to retain the rights to my works beyond every term of maximum-permitted delay, so that they are debtors to me and not I to them. But they believe they can ignore all that and blackmail me, thus preventing me from doing any business in America. I was forced to go several times from home to the Excelsior and from the Excelsior to Graziadei's studio in order to calm Miller down with telegrams, letters, and documents. Fortunately Miller knows the Shuberts very well, but he wants to be sure that they don't give him trouble and therefore wants to make sure that this business is in the clear. Colin will leave tomorrow for London to face Shubert and put Miller's mind at rest, although he is not

---

[1] Marta arrived in Rome on May 7. A couple of days later she met with Miller and signed the contract that was going to bring her to Broadway for the production of *Tovarich*. On that occasion, the almost immediate departure of the actress for England was decided, so that she could start her preparation with the study of the language and the rehearsals of the play as soon as possible.

at all surprised. I am wrong; Colin will leave first for Paris, because Miller is now there, and then for London. In Paris he will stay probably until your arrival, and then from Calais you'll go with him to London. It seems that Miller himself will suggest to the Shuberts that they settle things with me. They believe they have the rights to two more works of mine: well, they shall have them. Colin will give them *Quando si è qualcuno* (written in the contract) and *Non si sa come*, instead of *I giganti della montagna* (not yet finished), and that will be it. In the case that they want to produce one of the two works, or both of them, Miller declared himself ready to co-produce them, which will be a good enough guarantee for me.[2]

But let's drop all this talking about intolerable business!

My Marta, I know that you are still in Italy; I know that in a few days, on the evening of Tuesday of next week, I'll see you again in Milan; that still keeps me going. But what will happen to me on the evening of May 23, when you leave for London? And what will happen to me in August, when you leave even Europe and depart for America? I feel as if I am slowly sinking, as if the ground is becoming soft under my feet; I do not know what to hold on to; I have no more support. But you should not worry about me, my Marta. Allow me to sink. Fly alone toward your fortune and your happiness, and you'll make me happy too when you reach both. We must think about that. You must be happy.

Until soon, my Marta! Regards to your parents. I'll send you a telegram before leaving, on Tuesday 19. With all the endless love of

Your Maestro

[2] Important archival materials on the contract between the Shuberts and Pirandello and on the controversy about the rights to produce some of Pirandello's works in America (which had a follow-up later, when Marta Abba took legal action against the Shuberts, claiming her rights inherited from Pirandello) are preserved in the Shubert Archives of New York. Unfortunately there is no definitive study about this controversy. On Pirandello and the United States—including his deals with American film producers, his visit to New York, and a stage history of his plays in the United States—see Mario Mignone, ed., *Pirandello in America* (Rome: Bulzoni, 1988), and Daniela Sani Fink, "Pirandello a New York nei documenti della stampa americana," *Quaderni di Teatro* (November 1980).

{ 360530 }

Miss Marta Abba
The Dorchester Hotel
Park Lane
London W.1 (England)   Rome, 30. v. 1936 - xiv
                                        Via Antonio Bosio, 15

My Marta,

At last I've received your first letter from London, with the news of your trip and your arrival.[1] But I already knew from your telegram that everything had gone well. And everything will go well, you'll see, and from well to better, as soon as this first feeling of loss subsides—a feeling probably attributable to the motionless solitude of your hotel room. These are the first sensations, almost suspended in the uncertainty of this new life far away from anything familiar: apprehension, bewilderment, emptiness, all things that will pass, my Marta, as soon as you start feeling your way solid and secure under your brave little feet. Perhaps I'm talking about things that you have already overcome. You probably already had the first lessons from your new teacher; you have probably already set up a timetable for your work and other occupations, to fill up your whole day; soon you'll find no more time to feel lonely and to cast about uncertainly in your mind. Remember that the path you have chosen is bound to please you—even though it is rough and full of difficulties at first— because it is a path leading you to great fortune and to complete happiness. Don't try to avoid the difficulties; on the contrary, look for them and face them; only that way can you become strong enough to surmount them. But I don't have to tell you these things that you know well by yourself; in the past you've become strong and you've always come out on top, and now you are on the way to a victory gained with so much effort and so many sacrifices. You have every right to continue on that path, my Marta, without asking anyone for anything.

You know I am happy for you, although I have fallen into a bottomless abyss of sadness since you left. But I don't want to talk to you about that. I want to talk only about you who, in leaving, took away with yourself whatever was left of my life. I cannot talk about the rest of life I have in

---

[1] Within a few days Marta had arrived in London via Paris. Pirandello courageously tries to conceal the bewilderment and depression that follow every separation from his beloved, but he cannot keep himself from writing brief hints at the "bottomless abyss of sadness" into which he has fallen.

you, which will enjoy whatever you will enjoy, and will receive light and breath from the life that you will live. Enough.

. . . Your mother has written from Milan and invited me to join her in Camaiore, during June, when Cele will be there. I answered at once thanking her and promising that I will go.[2] It is the only thing that can do me any good—to sleep in your little study. I'll take some work with me. But I don't have any desire to do anything. And yet I still have so many things to do! Bah! I am still too young, and already too old. Perhaps you understand what I mean.

Without taking into account my movements, please continue, my Marta, to write to me in Rome. Francesco will take care of forwarding my mail, wherever I'll be, if I ever move around. I cannot set up a program for myself, because I cannot bear to make any decision, sure as I am that I won't be able to feel at home anywhere. The only good I can have and I can expect is from your letters, my Marta. With all the endless love of

Your Maestro

[2] The letter to Giuseppina Abba, dated May 28 and addressed to 26, Via Aurelio Saffi, Milan, is preserved in the collection of Princeton University. Pirandello writes in it, among other things: "It seems to me that Marta, with her departure, has taken away with her whatever had remained in me of life, and that I am left here, empty and lifeless."

{ 360629 }

Miss Marta Abba
c/o Miss Doddy Glyka
22, Jermyn Street
London S.W.1 (England)   Rome, 29. VI. 1936 - XIV
                                                    Via Antonio Bosio, 15

My Marta,

. . . I suggest that you pay the most attention to the mise-en-scène, the interpretation of your role, and artistic creativity, according to the various situations, attitudes, and expressive movements—without concentrating all your attention and concern on language and pronunciation. The more the play is alive and yours—that is, belonging to the character that will come to life through you and through the inimitable expression of your art—the less people will notice your pronunciation. On the other hand, if you do make some mistakes, they will be seen as part of your characterization, and will not discourage you, but give you more courage. The spirit uses also material difficulties to confirm its victory, by not letting itself be overcome, but on the contrary, by taking advantage of them.

. . . Well, yesterday I was sixty-nine years old. I am at the threshold of the seventies. I don't feel the years, my Marta; it seems to me I was born yesterday, and if I consider that I am already in the age bracket in which people usually die, it seems to me that life is frightfully short and absolutely unjust. What a sad thing it is to see so many around fall, already finished. My time will come soon, and addio, but it will not arrive before I see my Marta triumphant and happy, and then I wish also to live some time of her happiness, and God will not make me disappear before I see her again and give her a hearty kiss to greet her for the last time.

But let us not talk about melancholy thoughts at this moment. My Marta must work, be strong, think only about her work and about her most certain triumph. Addio, my Marta, be cheerful and serene and confident, and receive all my endless love,

Your Maestro

{ 360712 }

Miss Marta Abba
Eyrie Mansion
22, Jermyn Street
London S.W.1 (England)   Anticoli Corrado,
                                                    S. Filippo, 12. VII. 1936 - XIV

My Marta,

I've received your letter of Tuesday 7, and I am happy about the news you send me after your first rehearsal in the theater. I was more than sure that that would be the case, but seeing my inward certainty so splendidly confirmed has filled me with such an exultant joy that my eyes are filled with tears. Had you been present, I would have given you a big hug with endless tenderness. It could not have happened otherwise—that the miracle would not happen again this time—given the vigor of your spirit, which succeeds in making it happen every time, and *in a natural way*, as the saints used to do and as geniuses always do. The miracle happens when the soul, at the cost of so many palpitations of the heart, so much trepidation, so many anxieties, so many worries, predisposes itself and slowly matures in such a way as to make it happen almost by itself, as if merely being present would be enough to make it happen. You appear, you get into the play, you move with the others and speak: the tone is right, the gesture is right, your eyes brighten up the words, and your whole person expresses the life of the character. I imagine that Miller was enthusiastic about the prodigy he was experiencing right in front of his eyes! It's not that I am right; it's you who are a divine creature; I am right because I've always believed in you, in the divinity of your spirit that can do everything, because there are no difficulties, as hard and terrible as they can be, that your spirit does not know how to overcome. And now you'll see the triumph, my Marta! You are far away, but you found a way—even from far away—to make me happy!

. . . I don't know how I fill up my time, how the days go by, one after another. Today I do not know what I'll do tomorrow; it does not matter to me at all whether I do one thing or something else, whether I stay where I am or I move along. Fausto and Pompilia, who return your affectionate greetings, are taking the greatest care of me, and I do not know how to repay them. Perhaps I'll go back to their home, after Venice. . . . I won't be living with Stefano and Olinda anymore when they come back from the Alto Adige. They will go to live somewhere else, and on the floor downstairs, starting in October, my daughter Lietta will be living—she is returning to Italy with her children, separated from her husband. I did not want to give you this news before, which I'm sure will cause you to worry about me. I am falling out of the frying pan into the fire; my expenses will double. My only hope is that it will be just for a short time, and so my children will have caused me to fall to my doom.[1] I am planning to stay in Rome as little as possible and hopefully destiny will call me somewhere else, if it is written that I must still live.

But do not worry about these things, my Marta. As long as I have your affection, I have everything—I have a shelter to protect me from all adversities. And I'll always have your affection, as long as I live—I am sure of that, and it will grow more, the greater the adversities grow. Because of that my heart is full of gratitude for you. A big, strong hug, with all my soul,

Your Maestro

[1] Pirandello could not accept the thought of Lietta's separation from her husband. As already noticed, he seems more inclined to communicate the unpleasantnesses received from his children—writing in moments of anger—than giving recognition to the many signs of affection from his family. In the last two years of his life, however, along with passages full of pride for the artistic successes of his sons, a couple of instances of such recognition do appear, as in the case of his praise for the care given by Stefano and Olinda

on the occasion of the recent cardiac attack (351016: "I have near me the love of Stefano") and, a few lines above in the present letter, for the fact that Fausto and Pompilia take the greatest care of him.

{ 360721 }

Miss Marta Abba
Eyrie Mansion
22, Jermyn Street
St. James
London S.W.1 (England)   Milan, 21. VII. 1936 - XIV
                                                    Hotel Corso

My Marta,

. . . I'm happy you are satisfied with the actor Halliday. There is nothing worse than working with a fellow artist who is unpleasant or too inferior. And I think above all about the run of your play in New York, which I wish for you to be very long.

. . . Tomorrow I'll go back to Rome, where I'll probably stay to concentrate a little on my work, from which I've been away for a long time. I hope the heat will not bother me too much. If it is so, I'll go back to Anticoli to Fausto's.

Così è (se vi pare) has been already scheduled at the Comédie-Française for the end of October, and perhaps I'll take that occasion to go back to Paris, after the arrival of my daughter in Rome. I don't know where to flee to, my Marta! The only place would be to flee from life.[1] Truly, I cannot take it anymore!

They are all starting to understand by now what a loss they suffered with your departure. In Venice that's all they were talking about. But De Pirro answered that the completion of the state theater is three years away, according to the calculations of the project; and that, in three years, when the theater will be built, you will certainly be back and will take your place after the triumphs in America. Do you understand? They look at those triumphs in America as an advantage for them. Of course, I let them talk. They were all in a group, the Roman critics, and also D'Amico was there, and, among the critics from Milan, Lori was there. The construction of the state theater will begin soon, near Villa Borghese, at the Villa Strohl-Fern. A sum of thirty-five million was allocated. Remember,

---

[1] See footnote 1, letter 300227, about Pirandello's fleeing from hopeless situations.

my Marta, what I always told you? That in Italy nothing is done unless a lot of graft is made available? Thirty-five millions allocated—now the theater will certainly be completed. With my project, I wanted to do it with no money involved.

.   .   .   .   .   .

Your Maestro

<hr>

{ 360801 }

Miss Marta Abba
Eyrie Mansion
22, Jermyn Street
St. James
London S.W.1 (England)   Rome, 1. VIII. 1936 - XIV
                                                      Via Antonio Bosio, 15

My Marta,

. . . You can imagine, my Marta, all my joy on receiving the telegram from Miller.[1] I was sure of your success, but to see it reported and confirmed by the impresario was for me a tangible proof of its extent, and truly, that telegram made me cry with joy. I beheld you like one assumed in glory, after so much heroism—a creature worthy of the good fortune deserved at the cost of so much courage and so much hard work!

. . . Last evening I came back from Anticoli. I wanted to compose myself in the solitude of the deserted house, but I did not succeed. I wish I could flee, but I do not know where anymore. Flee from myself. I don't find myself comfortable in any place. The truth is, that I should die. And yet I still have so much life inside! But it does not seem to me that it is worthwhile to live it, to invest it in something. Writing makes me nauseous. The work is there waiting, but it does not invite me anymore, neither can I get close to it. Let's hope that this horrible moment passes. For the time being I live only for your news, which gives me so much joy and fills me with all your happiness.

Until soon, therefore, my Marta! With all the endless love of

Your Maestro

[1] Telegram announcing Marta's success in her first public performance in London's outskirts. Pirandello misunderstands the content and believes that Marta had a successful debut in a theater in the capital.

{ 360919 }

Miss Marta Abba
c/o Henry Miller Theatre
124 West 43rd Street
New York City (U.S.A.)[1]   Castiglioncello (Livorno),
                                                              19. IX. 1936

My Marta,

I've received your letter of the 11th from Gibraltar, which brought me so much joy. I hope that the whole voyage continued in the excellent weather conditions of the first days. You certainly received my marconi-gram sent on the third day of your trip. For the whole time you were traveling, that is, until the 17th, I followed you in my thoughts, almost moment by moment, taking account of your daily change of one hour, and imagining you, either inside the ship that I know so well or on the deck lying on your deck chair.

I'm dying to have news of your arrival. Just a hint was published on the sly in the *Corriere della sera*, in which there was word of the disappoint-ment of the reporters who came on board to interview the ex-queen of Spain, and who instead had to settle for taking pictures of Marta Abba being festively welcomed by many American artists. The reportage, of course, was done for the arrival in America of the deposed ex-queen, as if it were more important than the arrival of an authentic queen, triumph-antly reigning on the throne of art. But such is the mental narrowness of our journalists.

By now you have been in New York for two days, and I imagine the first impressions you got of that colossal and phantasmagorical city—if not always beautiful, certainly always very impressive. But I always think that colossal never equals majestic. The spectacular skyscrapers will never be the grandiose monuments of our civilization. They impress you, but you do not admire them. And your spirit, which is so great, should not let itself be overwhelmed by the breathless, adventurous restlessness of American life. Remember that the courage you had, facing, with such a

---

[1] The letter was forwarded to Baltimore, Auditorium Theatre, c/o Tovarich Co. After finishing the shakedown performances in the London suburbs, Marta visited Italy for a short rest before leaving on the *Conte di Savoia* for New York, where she arrived on September 17. In the present letter, Pirandello appears consumed with enthusiasm for Marta's American enterprise and with the desire of morally sustaining his beloved—so much so that he succeeds in omitting the usual complaints about his loneliness!

persevering will, difficulties that no American would succeed in overcoming, makes you superior to everybody; and that you, therefore, should
not be in awe of what the others over there did and are doing, but the
others should be stunned by what you did and will do.

. . . I imagine how busy you must be in these first days of your arrival,
my Marta—in the confusion, better, in the assault of the new impressions
of another life, the rehearsals in the theater, the searching, more of yourself than of the place where you'll establish yourself. You'll find yourself,
little by little; for a while, however, you'll feel a little disoriented. But I
hope you'll find a moment to write at least a couple of words in a great
hurry to your poor faraway Maestro who doesn't really live except for you,
my Marta, doesn't think, feel, dream, except of you, always near you with
all his soul, with all his heart. You too, my Marta, feel always my endless love,

Your Maestro

{ 361007 }

Miss Marta Abba
Hôtel Pierre
New York (City)
(U.S.A.)   Rome, 7. x. 1936 - XIV
                                                        Via Antonio Bosio, 15

My Marta,
I've heard about your triumphant success in Baltimore.

. . . Now that the trial run has turned out magnificently also in America, and the tumult of first impressions has probably subsided, you'll see
that you will experience again the full and relaxed joy of your great heroic
conquest. You'll savor all its advantages. You'll feel happily victorious and
certain of the brightest future.

You have probably received by now my first two letters, one from
Rome, addressed to the Miller Theatre, and the other from Berlin, addressed to the Hôtel Pierre. Two letters almost without content because
I did not know anything yet about you. Even now I do not know much,
because your letters cover only your first five days in New York, but at
least now I know that you find yourself at ease at the Hôtel Pierre, that
you hired a magnificent black maid, and that the theater where you'll
start the performances in New York is big, central, and, I believe, close to
your hotel. You can imagine how many good wishes I send you, my

Marta, for a happy outcome of your work in New York. I am sure about you, I mean, about the success that you will have, but also the play must be very well received in order to keep running for at least one year of performances; so that, after so much labor, you may eventually rest, gain a lot of money, and have leisure and a way of finally enjoying your life. I want you to be happy, my Marta, without worries and serene, because that is what you deserve, for what you are, for what you are worth, for the heart you have, for the mind you have, for your beauty, for your goodness—my adored creature.

I won't tell you how I was left feeling. You can figure it out. With you I lost my light. I cannot see anything anymore. I do not know why I keep on living. There is nothing that interests me or attracts me. They took me to Berlin; I went there; they gave me a lot of welcoming parties; Goebbels[1] gave orders that my complete works for the theater, translated by Jews,[2] be retranslated and performed again in the theaters of Germany. A new publisher offered me a very advantageous contract, and the revival will begin pretty soon at the State Theater of Berlin with special ceremonies. In other times all that would have made me proud and happy; now, without you, it doesn't have any effect on me. And so it goes with everything. I don't know how to relax; nothing gives me any zest for life, and my tiredness is increasing day by day, so much so that I don't feel like dragging myself through life any longer.

I tell you all that only in order to make you understand that one thing alone remains alive inside me and still can give me an aim and a reason for surviving, and that's you, my Marta—the fact that I know you are happy; that you keep me in your mind and still have some affection for me; that you will give me air to breathe with the news you'll give me about yourself and a bit of warmth that will restore and comfort me, talking about you, about your happiness, about the things of your life, by which I'll keep on living here, far away, until my last breath.

Addio, my Marta. Do feel always, completely, in the endless love of
Your Maestro

---

[1] Paul Josef Goebbels was at the time the Nazi minister for education and propaganda.

[2] Pirandello shared common prejudices against the Jews, which were reinforced by the fact that some of the people who worked for him and gave him a lot of trouble were Jewish (Colin, Torre, Feist). In the correspondence there are a few places in which he makes short anti-Semitic remarks, e.g., letters 291001, 300424, 310407, and 310409, which are not translated in this volume but are published in the Italian edition.

{ 361025 }

Miss Marta Abba
Hôtel Pierre
New York (City)
(U.S.A.)   Rome, 25. X. 1936 - XIV
                                                       Via Antonio Bosio, 15

My Marta,

I've received your letter of the 16th, the one you started in Philadelphia and finished in New York following your triumphant success;[1] you were able to express all your trepidation and eventually your exultance, which in you always has the tendency to become religious, because it ends up in giving thanks to God. While I was reading your letter I had tears in my eyes and, when I finished, I kissed it I don't know how many times. My Marta, what you did is really miraculous, and therefore it should be recognized that you are right when you thank God with divine humility. That makes your glory worthy of the greatest respect and of a consecration that is almost supernatural, even though afterward the woman in you might suffer a bit because of it. I said those things—I believe in the best possible way—in *Trovarsi* and, as you know, I said them just for you, my Marta! But no joy on earth is worth the joy one's spirit alone can give, when, as yours did, it succeeds in overcoming all difficulties, in a formidable challenge you faced alone, without any help, and overcame so victoriously in just a few months.

. . . What is happening about your contract with Miller seems strange

---

[1] The opening of *Tovarich* on October 15, at the Plymouth Theatre on Broadway, was greeted by the critics of the major New York newspapers as "the first smash of the season" of "a really good light comedy," which was applauded as "the most beguiling comedy of the season," "a real joy," "a real theatrical treat." Marta Abba was described as an "enchanting new-comer" who interpreted "to perfection" the leading role of the grand duchess in her "auspicious American debut." The major reviews and the articles in newspapers and journals reflecting both the publicity before and the comments after the opening—as well as remarks on the type of acting Marta chose for the interpretation of her role of the grand duchess Tatiana Petrovna—are preserved in the archive of the Lincoln Center for the Performing Arts in New York City. In general the critics praised the vivaciousness, spontaneity, and vitality of the actress and did not spare their compliments, at most indicating some reserve for her overcharged exuberance of gestures; in the following summer, however, there was a note by D. S. Fairchild in *Knott Knotes* regretting the change now noticeable in Marta's acting, which had acquired—little by little, through the wearying long run—"an excessive amount of gesture and grimace," defects that, according to the same critic, did not exist at the beginning of the run.

to me, but not anything to worry about. I say, not anything worrisome, because by now, after your success, it is in the interest of Miller not to let an actress like you get away. However, keep your contract intact, if everybody assures you that it is good for you. It is evident that Miller despises Colin and cannot stand him. But it seems to me that you answered very well. Colin is always that incorrigible, inept, and frivolous person who will never get anywhere. But, if I am right in saying so from my point of view, you cannot say the same about your contract. He won't be an agent worthy of you in the future, as Miller tells you, but you must keep your eyes wide open before putting yourself in somebody else's hands. What Miller told you is only interesting as far as the movies are concerned, but be careful that the help he is offering in that field does not require you to give up something that is to your advantage as far as the theater is concerned. Anyhow, I repeat, don't worry before the time comes and wait with trust for Miller's return from England. You now have the upper hand, and you don't have to be afraid of anything.

. . . My expenses have increased enormously with my daughter, who has crashed on me once more with her two daughters. I am in urgent need of earning money in order not to exhaust the few dollars I have saved up, but I also need to escape from here so that I won't die of a broken heart.[2] I am crushed, oppressed. Under such conditions it is not even possible for me to work. I should finish the third act of *I giganti della montagna*, which without my final consent was included in the program of the coming "Maggio Fiorentino" in agreement—can you believe it?—with the Company of the City of Milan that will be augmented for the occasion, and that later will tour all the cities of Italy with that play. I canceled my rental contract for my apartment for the end of this year and I plan to go to a hotel, so that I don't have to stay with any of my three children. But this cannot be a final solution for me. I understand that, but I don't see any other solution. It is very hard for me to live again with a piece of luggage in my hand, at my age. But what can I do? If at least I could work!

I do not want to trouble you, my Marta, by always talking to you about myself. I would rather disappear as soon as possible—if I have to keep on giving you such news about me. You must be happy, as I want you to be, exultant in your victory and cheerful, serene, healthy, in order to recover

---

[2] A few weeks before dying, a desperate Pirandello is once again thinking of fleeing, as a last resort—as usual without a clear plan about where to go and without any real hope that escaping might solve his problems. See the entry Flight in the Subject Index for other related passages and commentary on this subject.

your strength, after the terrible abuse you inflicted on it. Please, my Marta, take all possible care, eat well, rest and relax as much as you can. Now the good weather starts, after the storm. Enjoy it, my Marta, and send some to me with your dear letters, which are the only good thing I have. An embrace with all my heart,

Your Maestro

{ 361121 }

Miss Marta Abba
6, West 53 St.
New York (City)
(U.S.A.)   Rome, November 21, 1936 - xv
    My Marta,
    I have in my hand your letter of November 10, sent via the *Normandie*. It took eleven days to reach me, but it first had to cross France, too. You have perhaps by now received my letter addressed to the Plymouth Theatre and the one from Graziadei addressed to the Hotel Pierre, sent before you informed me about the street and the number of your little apartment. New York is like a chessboard,[1] and, being familiar with it, I can have a very good idea of where you live. I know 53rd Street, where it intersects with 6th Avenue (West). The only thing I don't recall is whether the odd numbers are on the right or on the left side of the street. What floor are you on? I can ask the doorman. I am already there. I go up in the elevator. I ring the doorbell. I am face to face with a "magnificent" black maid.
    –Miss Marta Abba?
    And I hear your scream from the other room:
    –Maestro! Maestro!
    My Marta, what a dream! Merely having it makes me feel like a new man. First of all, I would give you a big loving scolding because you neglected your health. You don't want me to talk about it. You assure me that now you are well, that you will take care of yourself, now that you are settled in this little apartment. But at the same time the first thing I noticed—when Graziadei came to show me your photo in *Time* magazine

---

[1] At this point Pirandello begins to dream of a brief surprise visit to his beloved in New York. It is a last moving and poetic cry of hope before dying—at the beginning of one of the saddest, most desperate letters of the entire correspondence.

where together with Halliday you are pictured smiling while drying a dish—the first thing I noticed was that you certainly are always so beautiful, so full of grace with that mischievous, knowing smile that peers over the shoulder of your prince consort, yet so worn out, so very worn out, showing clear signs of a physical tiredness that doesn't want to give up. I know, I really know that you had so much to do, and that what you did was miraculous, and we must thank God that you were able to withstand such immense strain and overcome it. But now everything depends on keeping up your resistance so that it may not suddenly collapse because of your abusing your energies! I beg you, my Marta! Otherwise you will risk losing all the fruits of such a big victory. You need to eat, not much, but nutritious food, and regularly; you want some relaxation but at the same time you need some rest, and above all you must get rid of the poison that excessive stress produces in your muscles and in your nerves. The pains in your legs, the cramps in your stomach are caused only by this muscular poisoning—step by step and with great care you must get rid of it. I would like to put my faith in your assurance that you are now very well and that "this is the truth." Of course, if you say so, I will trust you, but only up to a certain point. The concern for your health never leaves me; and it shouldn't abandon you either; nor should you put too much trust in your strong and healthy constitution. Remember, winter is coming, which is rigorous and treacherous over there, with sudden and violent changes, heavy storms, cyclones, whirling snowfalls, freezing air that cuts the face. You now want to save money, but I think it would be a good idea for you to get a car as soon as possible—after all over there you could have it inexpensively.

. . . Let us talk about something else. Well, you are also a lecturer, a lecturer in two languages! Well done, my Marta! The words you said at the "Dante Alighieri"[2] are truly beautiful, and I can imagine the applause you received.

. . . You ask me about myself, Marta; you complain that I don't tell you about myself, and what I do. I do not do anything anymore, my Marta, I spend the whole day thinking, alone like a dog, about everything I still should be doing, so much—yet it doesn't seem to me worthwhile to add anything anymore to all that I've already done; people do not deserve it, pigheaded as they are becoming more and more—stupid, beastly, and quarrelsome. Our times are against us: people are ill disposed. Medita-

[2] Pirandello is referring to a lecture Marta gave at the Dante Alighieri Society in New York.

tion is impossible amidst so much turmoil and such fierce longing for slaughter.[3] But then, in the secret depths of my heart, there is a more real and profound reason for my self-annihilation into silence and emptiness. There was once a voice, close to me, that is no longer there; a light that is no longer there. . . . I don't feel like working anymore, and yet I should; I will need to in a short while, to work as if I were condemned—such an atrocity at my age, after having worked so much. What little money I had put aside is diminishing, and my expenses and the new burdens weighing me down have grown, they always keep increasing; I do not know how it will end.[4] That is why, my Marta, I forbid myself to speak to you about myself. Why worry you? The only thing I care about is the knowledge that you have won, that you are triumphant, that you are happy, and you have every right to be so, because all you have accomplished is not some gift from fortune, but you well deserved it, and much more you still deserve, my Marta, for what you are, for the great, pure light of your soul, for the no less great nobility of your heart, for the beauty and grace of your body, my adorable, chosen one.

Do you remember that critic, D'Amico's friend in Milan? He read all the American newspapers that spoke and continue to speak of you, and he was astonished that the Italian press published nothing about your great triumph, that not one of the Italian correspondents in New York reported the extraordinary event.

Misery! Misery! Misery! Carnera has lost?[5] Three columns in the *Corriere*. Marta Abba triumphs? Not even one line.

Enough, don't be distressed, my Marta. Stay happy and take care of yourself! And always remember you are surrounded by the love without end of

Your Maestro

[3] Pirandello is referring to the civil war already raging in Spain and to the menacing clouds of war that were gathering in the skies of Europe.

[4] This passage, written only a couple of weeks before he died, gives a sense of enormous sadness because it sums up Pirandello's tragedy as read in the correspondence. The writer is definitely "old," "alone like a dog," without Marta's love—the way he would have wanted it to be—while the actress is also physically very far away (she is the voice and the "light that is no longer there"). Pirandello is psychologically tired to the point of feeling aversion for the cherished refuge of creative work, physically prostrated from the years of deep depression and poor health, and facing the renewed specter of financial collapse, which worries him to the point of having to work as if condemned—"such an atrocity" at his age, after having earned so much money in his lifetime.

[5] Primo Carnera, the Italian boxing champion, had lost the world heavyweight title to Max Baer in 1934.

{ 361204 }

Miss Marta Abba
6, West 33 Street
New York (City)
(U.S.A.)   Rome, 4. XII. 1936 - XV
                                              Via Antonio Bosio, 15

My Marta,

... This letter is already long,[1] and it is time that I send it to the post office. But when will it reach you? If I think about the distance, I at once feel I am sliding into a horrible loneliness, like into an abyss of despair. But you should not think about that! I embrace you tightly, tightly, with all, all my heart,

Your Maestro

[1] Pirandello wrote this letter just before falling ill with the pneumonia that was going to finish his life six days later, on December 10, in his home at Via Antonio Bosio 15. The envelope of this last letter was postmarked at the New York post office on December 14 and therefore reached Marta after the Maestro's death. The long letter deals with Marta's contract with Miller and shows Pirandello to be concerned with persuading Marta that her contract was excellent and that she should not change it. Only the ending is translated here, the sad ending indeed—into an abyss of despair—of a sad, unfulfilled love story. After Pirandello's death, Marta received a prize by the American Dramatic League in 1937 and, after fulfilling her contractual obligations with Gilbert Miller, married the wealthy socialite Severance A. Millikin on January 28, 1938, announcing at the same time her withdrawal from the stage. In 1953, after her divorce, she had a short theatrical comeback in Italy with a company she formed with the actor Cornabuci. She died in Milan on June 24, 1988, the day before her eighty-eighth birthday.

BIBLIOGRAPHY

Abba, Marta. "Dieci anni di teatro con Luigi Pirandello." *Il Dramma*, November–December 1936.

———. *La mia vita di attrice*. Rome: Stab. Tip. Europa (no date but 1934 or 1935).

———. "Prefazione." In Vittore Nardelli. *Pirandello, l'uomo segreto*. Milan: Bompiani, 1987, vii–xiii.

Aguirre D'Amico, Maria Luisa. *Album di famiglia di Luigi Pirandello*. Palermo: Sellerio, 1979.

———. *Album Pirandello*. Milan: Mondadori, 1992.

———. *Paesi lontani*. Palermo: Sellerio, 1983.

———. *Vivere con Pirandello*. Milan: Mondadori, 1989.

Alberti, Alberto Cesare. *Il teatro nel tempo del Fascismo: Pirandello e Bragaglia*. Rome: Bulzoni, 1974.

Alonge, Roberto. *Pirandello tra realismo e mistificazione*. Naples: Guida, 1972.

Alvaro, Corrado. "Pirandello in Germania." *L'Italia letteraria*, April 14, 1929.

———. "Prefazione." In Luigi Pirandello. *Novelle per un Anno*. I Classici contemporanei italiani. Milan: Mondadori, 1956.

———. *Quasi una vita*. Milan: Bompiani, 1950.

Angelini, Franca. *Il teatro del novecento da Pirandello a Fo*. Rome and Bari: Laterza, 1992.

———, ed. *Il punto su Pirandello*. Rome and Bari: Laterza, 1992.

Antonelli, Luigi. *Maschera nuda di Pirandello*. Rome: Vittorini (no date, but 1937).

Artioli, U. *L'officina segreta di Pirandello*. Rome and Bari: Laterza, 1992.

Barbina, Alfredo. *Bibliografia della critica pirandelliana, 1889–1961*. Istituto di Studi Pirandelliani, 3. Florence: Le Monnier, 1967.

———. *La biblioteca di Luigi Pirandello*. Rome: Bulzoni, 1980.

Barilli, Renato. *Pirandello. Una rivoluzione culturale*. Milan: Mursia, 1986.

Bassnett-McGuire, Susan. *Luigi Pirandello*. London: Macmillan, 1983.

Battistini, Fabio, Maria Grazia Gregori, and Mario Sculatti. *Pirandello l'uomo lo scrittore il teatrante*. Milan: Mazzotta, 1987.

Bentley, Eric. *The Pirandello Commentaries*. Evanston, Ill.: Northwestern University Press, 1986.

Bloom, Harold, ed. *Luigi Pirandello*. New York: Chelsea House, 1989.

Bontempelli, Massimo. "Luigi Pirandello." Commemorazione alla Reale Accademia d'Italia (17 gennaio 1937), *Annuario della Reale Accademia d'Italia*, vol. 8, 1937.

———. "Il Teatro degli undici o dodici." *Scenario*, February 1933.

Borsellino, Nino. *Ritratto di Pirandello*. Bari: Laterza, 1983.

Borsellino, Nino, and Alberto Spaini. "Pirandello, Luigi." *Enciclopedia dello Spettacolo*, vol. 8, 1961.

Bouissy, André. "Réflections sur l'histoire et la préhistoire du personnage 'alter ego.'" *Lectures pirandelliennes*. Paris: Université de Paris VIII, 1978.

Büdel, Oskar. "Pirandellos Wirkung in Deutschland." In F. N. Mennemeier, ed. *Der Dramatiker Pirandello*. Cologne: Kiepenheuer & Witsch, 1965, 209–39.

Cacho Millet, Gabriel. *Pirandello in Argentina*. Palermo: Edizioni Novecento, 1987.

Callari, Francesco. *Pirandello e il cinema*. Venice: Marsilio, 1991.

———. "Pirandello soggettista e sceneggiatore di cinema." In Stefano Miloto and Enzo Scrivano, eds. *Pirandello e la cultura del suo tempo*. Milan: Mursia, 1983, 177–246.

Cambon, Glauco, ed. *Pirandello: A Collection of Critical Essays*. Englewood Cliffs, N.J.: Prentice-Hall, 1967.

Cannistraro, Philip V., and Brian R. Sullivan. *Il Duce's Other Woman*. New York: William Morrow, 1993.

Caputi, A. F. *Pirandello and the Crisis of Modern Consciousness*. Urbana: University of Illinois Press, 1988.

Castri, Massimo. *Pirandello ottanta*. Milan: Ubulibri, 1981.

Cometa, Michele. *Il teatro di Pirandello in Germania*. Palermo: Edizioni Novecento, 1986.

D'Amico, Alessandro. "Cronologia." In Pirandello's *Maschere nude*. I Meridiani. Vol. 1. Milan: Mondadori, 1986.

D'Amico, Alessandro, and Alessandro Tinterri. *Pirandello capocomico*. Palermo: Sellerio, 1987.

De Castris, Arcangelo Leone. *Storia di Pirandello*. Bari: Universale Laterza, 1971.

Di Gaetani, John L., ed. *A Companion to Pirandello Studies*. New York: Greenwood, 1991.

Di Pietro, Antonio. *Pirandello*. Milan: Vita e Pensiero, 1950.

Donati, Corrado. *Bibliografia della critica pirandelliana, 1962–1981*. Florence: La Ginestra, 1986.

Faustini, Giuseppe. "Ancora su Pirandello a Bonn e il suo rapporto col mondo culturale." *Scena illustrata*, July 7, 1988.

Ferrante, Luigi. *Pirandello*. Florence: Parenti, 1958.

Fiocco, Achille. "Abba, Marta." In *Enciclopedia dello Spettacolo*, vol. 1, 1954.

Frassica, Pietro. *A Marta Abba per non morire: Sull'epistolario inedito tra Pirandello e la sua attrice*. Milan: Mursia, 1991.

Gardair, J. N. *Pirandello, fantasmes et logique du double*. Paris: Larousse, 1977.

Gioanola, Elio. *Pirandello la follia*. Genoa: Il Melangolo, 1983.

Giovannelli, Paola Daniela. *La società teatrale in Italia fra ottocento e novecento.* Rome: Bulzoni, 1986.

Giudice, Gaspare. *Pirandello.* Turin: UTET, 1963.

Jordan, James. "Audience Disruption in the Theatre of the Weimar Republic," *New Theatre Quarterly,* August 1935, 283–91.

Landi, Stefano. "La vita ardente di Luigi Pirandello." *Quadrivio,* December 13, 1936.

Laurenzi, Carlo. "La preferita di Pirandello." *Il Giornale,* March 4, 1990.

Lauretta, Enzo, ed. *Pirandello e il cinema.* Agrigento: Centro Nazionale di Studi Pirandelliani, 1978.

———. *Pirandello e il teatro.* Palermo: Palumbo, 1985.

Lelièvre, Renée. *Le théâtre dramatique italien en France, 1885–1940.* Paris: A. Calin, 1959.

Lugnani, Lucio. *Pirandello, letteratura e teatro.* Florence: La nuova Italia, 1970.

Macchia, Giovanni. "Luigi Pirandello." In *Storia della letteratura italiana.* Vol. 9, *Il Novecento.* Milan: Garzanti, 1969.

———. *Pirandello o la stanza della tortura.* Milan: Mondadori, 1981.

Mignone, Mario B., ed. *Pirandello in America.* Rome: Bulzoni, 1988.

Milioto, Stefano, and Enzo Scrivano, eds. *Tutto Pirandello in dieci convegni.* Agrigento: Centro di Studi Pirandelliani, 1983.

Ojetti, Ugo. *Cose viste, 1921–1923.* Milan: Treves, 1923.

O'Keefe Bazzoni, Jana, and Nina daVinci Nichols. *Pirandello as Filmmaker.* Lincoln: University of Nebraska Press, forthcoming.

Paolucci, Anne, ed. "Pirandello." Special Pirandello Issue. *Review of National Literatures* 14:1987.

Pirandello, Fausto. *Piccole impertinenze.* Palermo: Sellerio, 1987.

Pirandello, Luigi. Ed. Sarah Zappulla Muscarà. *Carteggi inediti* (con Ojetti, Albertini, Orvieto, Novaro, De Gubernatis, De Filippo). Rome: Bulzoni, 1980.

———. *Epistolario familiare giovanile (1886–1898).* Ed. Elio Providenti. Florence: Le Monnier, 1986.

———. "Lettere ai famigliari." Ed. Sandro D'Amico. *Terzo Programma,* n° 3, 1961.

———. "Lettera a Fausto da Pordenone." *Quaderni d'italianistica* 2 (Fall 1981).

———. *Lettere da Bonn.* Ed. Elio Providenti. Rome: Bulzoni, 1984.

———. *Pirandello-Martoglio: Carteggio inedito.* Ed. Sarah Zappulla. Milan: Pan Editrice, 1979.

Providenti, Elio. "Marta Abba: Una vita per il teatro." *Scena illustrata,* March 1987.

———. *Mnemosine: Archeologie pirandelliane.* Catania: Guiseppe Maimone, 1990.

Puppa, Paolo. *Dalle parti di Pirandello.* Rome: Bulzoni, 1987.

———. *Fantasmi contro giganti. Scena e immaginario in Pirandello.* Bologna: Patron, 1978.

Ragusa, Olga. *Pirandello: An Approach to His Theatre.* Edinburgh: Edinburgh University Press, 1980.

Romano Rochira, Giuseppina. *Pirandello capocomico e regista nelle testimonianze e nella critica.* Bari: Adriatica, 1987.

Sani Fink, Daniela. "Pirandello a New York nei documenti della stampa americana." *Quaderni di teatro*, November 1980.

Sciascia, Leonardo. *La corda pazza.* Turin: Einaudi, 1970.

―――. *Omaggio a Pirandello.* Almanacco Letterario Bompiani 1987. Milan: Bompiani, 1986.

―――. *Pirandello dall'A alla Z.* Rome: L'Espresso, 1986.

―――. *Pirandello e la Sicilia.* Palermo: S. Sciascia, 1961.

Scrivano, Riccardo. *La vocazione contesa. Note su Pirandello e il teatro.* Rome: Bulzoni, 1987.

Serri, Mirella. "L'immagine dell'attrice in Pirandello." *Rivista di studi pirandelliani*, October 1984, 7–33.

Sipala, Paolo Maria. *Capuana e Pirandello.* Catania: Bonanno, 1974.

Sogliuzzo, A. Richard. *Luigi Pirandello, Director: The Playwright in the Theatre.* London and Metuchen, N.J.: Scarecrow, 1982.

Squarzina, Luigi, "Pirandello e il fascismo." *Prospettive settanta*, April–June 1976.

Tamberlani, Carlo. *Pirandello nel "teatro che c'era. . . ."* Rome: Bulzoni, 1982.

―――. "La riforma dell'interpretazione pirandelliana." *Atti del congresso internazionale di studi pirandelliani.* Florence: Le Monnier, 1967.

Tinterri, Alessandro, "Pirandello regista del suo teatro: 1925–1928." *Quaderni di teatro* 34:1986.

Vene, Gian Franco. *Pirandello fascista.* Milan: Sugar, 1971.

Vergani, Orio. *Misure del tempo.* Milan: Leonardo, 1990.

Vicentini, Claudio. *L'estetica di Pirandello.* Milan: Mursia, 1985.

―――. *Pirandello e il disagio del teatro.* Milan: Marsilio, 1993.

Zappulla Muscarà, Sarah. *Pirandello e il teatro siciliano.* Catania: Maimone, 1986.

The letters written by Marta Abba to Pirandello, edited by Pietro Frassica, are in preparation for publication by Mursia in Milan. Many unpublished letters by Pirandello are preserved in the archives of the heirs of Stefano Pirandello, Lietta Pirandello, and Lina De Castro Pirandello.

SUBJECT INDEX

Subjects relating to Marta Abba and Luigi Pirandello are also indexed under **Marta** and **Pirandello**. See also the Name Index for locations, play titles, and names of people mentioned in the letters. The names Pirandello and Marta are indicated with the initials P and M.

NAME INDEX

Cochran, Sir Charles Blake (*cont.*)
in 1926 organized the performances of *Sei personaggi* of P's Teatro d'Arte at the New Oxford Theatre in London. 290416; 300727

Colin, Saul (1909–1967). An employee of the Osso Film Company in charge of choosing Pirandello's scenarios for possible production, was also a scenarist for Paramount in Paris before becoming an agent for Pirandello's theater business outside Italy. 301215; 310401; 310515; 310718; 310722; 310726; 320118; 320126; 320206; 320211; 320214; 320216; 320310; 320318; 320427; 320504; 320804; 320822; 330209; 330304; 350721; 350813; 350830; 350907; 360406; 360413; 360427; 360430; 360516; 360530; 360721; 361007; 361025; 361121; 361204

Columbus. Film-producing company. 351027; 351030

Comédie-Française. 290628; 310109; 310208; 310718; 341129; 341206; 360721

Come prima, meglio di prima. Play by P, performed for the first time on October 27, 1926, at the Teatro Garibaldi in Padoa; became thereafter part of P's company repertory in Italy and abroad, with M in the leading role of Fulvia Gelli. 290505; 310216; 310401; 310427; 320214

Come tu mi vuoi. Play by P, performed for the first time on February 18, 1939, at the Teatro dei Filodrammatici in Milan by the Compagnia Marta Abba. 290720; 290722; 291110; 300228; 300301; 300303; 300324; 300417; 300430; 300505; 300514; 300517; 300518; 300727; 301226; 301231; 310101; 310103; 310109; 310112; 310220; 310225; 310330; 310427; 320211; 320504; 320804; 320908; 321108; 321125

Comitato Francia-Italia. 320310

Como. 260820 (horrible night in); 300527; 300603; 310208; 340604

Comoedia. Theater journal. 310722

Compagnia dei Grandi Spettacoli. 360311; 360313

Compagnia Stabile San Remo Marta Abba. 340324

Congresso Volta. See Convegno Volta

Conte Aquila. Play by Rino Alessi. 340324

Conte di Savoia. Italian transatlantic liner. 350721; 350813; 350907; 351014; 360427; 360430; 360919

Convegno Volta. 340224; 340329; 340429; 340604; 340805; 341115; 361025

Coquette, La. Play by Ann Preston Bridges and George Abbott, performed for the first time on November 8, 1927, in New York at the Maxine Elliot Theatre on Broadway. Pirandello rewrote its Italian translation for Compagnia Marta Abba's repertory. 290722; 300227; 300303; 300324; 300402; 310108; 310109; 310512

Corda, Alessandro. Hungarian film director. See Korda, Alexander

Corporazione dello spettacolo. 320122; 350301; 360114

Corradini, Enrico (1865–1931). Journalist and playwright influenced by Gabriele D'Annunzio. Was senator and minister of state during Fascist rule. As director of the newspaper *Giornale d'Italia* he took a hostile attitude toward P and is therefore considered by P as an "enemy." 290317; 300514; 300518; 300519; 320326

Corriere della sera, Il. Milan's most influential daily newspaper, often abbreviated as *Il Corriere* in the letters. 260805 (intr.); 290315; 290320; 290401; 290408; 290422; 290722; 300228; 300504; 300518; 301217; 310515; 310531; 320214; 320909; 330304; 350907; 360919; 361121

Cosi é (se vi pare) (1916). Play by P drawn from his short story "La signora Frola e il Signor Ponza, suo genero." 290416; 310127; 310427; 360721

Cotrone. Character in P's play *I giganti della montagna.* 300425

290428; 290505; 290628; 290629;
290716; 290720; 290913; 300601 (orga-
nizes the boycott of the premiere of
Questa sera); 300603; 300606

Ferreira. Owner of a film agency in Paris
that dealt with P about the project of
filming *Six Characters.* 280708; 280925

Ferro, Antonio. President of the Lisbon
Convention. 320118

Fiamma (*Die Flamme*, 1922). Play by
Hans Müller, which P considered for
M's repertory. 300324; 300412 (review
of the Berlin production); 300602

Figaro. Paris newspaper. 341129

Figlia di Iorio, La. Play by Gabriele
D'Annunzio. 340224; 340324; 341125;
360117; 360306

Figliastra. Character in P's *Sei personaggi
in cerca d'autore.* 291212; 300418

Figlio cambiato. See *Favola del figlio cambiato, La.*

"Filo," o Filodrammatici. Teatro dei Filodrammatici in Milan, was demolished
in 1958. 300301; 300303

Fisco. Italian internal revenue system.
310531

Fontana, Eugenio (born in 1889). Film director and producer. 300415; 340805∗

Forges-Davanzati, Roberto. Editor of the
Roman newspaper *Tribuna* and president of SIAE. 310524; 310527; 320318

Formichi, Carlo (1871–1943). Specialist in
Indian studies and author of studies on
English language and literature, was
vice-president of the Accademia d'Italia.
290323; 320206; 340329; 340405

Forster, Rudolf (1889–1969). German
actor. 300412

Forzano, Giovacchino (born in 1883). Playwright, author of librettos, and director.
Was protected by Mussolini, who loved
his Fascist propaganda and grandiose rethoric, and hated by P, who despised
his superficiality. 320427; 330517;
340324; 350214

Fox of America (Twentieth Century-Fox).
290627; 290629; 320214

Francesco. P's driver. 351014; 360406;
360530

Frankenstein. Lawyer in Berlin. Took care
of P's lawsuit with Feist. 290716; 290913

Frola, Signora. Character in P's play *Così
è, se vi pare.* 291212

Fulvia Gelli. Leading character in P's play
Come prima, meglio di prima, performed by M at the opening in Padoa,
at the Teatro Garibaldi on October 27,
1926. 260817; 291212

Gallian, Marcello. Writer. 341115

Galli-Gandusio. Theater company.
310206; 340405

Gallo, Fortunato. Theater impresario.
290628; 290629; 290716

Gallone, Carmine. Film director born in
1886. 351027; 351030

Gandusio, Antonio (1873–1951). Italian
film and theater actor. 350907; 360313

Gantillon, Simon. French playwright and
scenarist, born in 1887. 320211; 321108

Garbo, Greta. Film actress. 300522

Gatti. Manager of the Teatro di Torino.
290927; 300415

Gazzetta del popolo. Daily newspaper in
Turin. 300417; 301226; 310101; 310112;
310422; 310524; 320214; 330304

George, Heinrich. German actor. 300412

Giacompol, Romiglio. Representative of
the Società degli Autori in Buenos
Aires. 360427

Giaconìa. Lawyer. 340604

Gianturco. Lawyer. 320214; 320222;
321125; 330304; 340429

Giganti della montagna, I. P's unfinished
last play. 290408 (creative process);
290422; 290720; 300415; 300417 (something great!); 300425; 300430; 300727;
310127; 310210; 310225; 310401; 361025

Ginevra. Character in P's play *Non si sa
come.* 340726

Giordani, Paolo (often called Paolino).
Lawyer, theater impresario, covered im-
portant positions as an executive of the
Società Suvini-Zerboni, of la Gestione